Psychoanalytic Theory
and Cultural Competence
in Psychotherapy

Pratyusha Tummala-Narra

Psychoanalytic Theory and Cultural Competence in Psychotherapy

American Psychological Association

Washington, DC

Published by
American Psychological Association
750 First Street, NE
Washington, DC 20002
www.apa.org

To order
APA Order Department
P.O. Box 92984
Washington, DC 20090-2984
Tel: (800) 374-2721; Direct: (202) 336-5510
Fax: (202) 336-5502; TDD/TTY: (202) 336-6123
Online: www.apa.org/pubs/books
E-mail: order@apa.org

In the U.K., Europe, Africa, and the Middle East, copies may be ordered from
American Psychological Association
3 Henrietta Street
Covent Garden, London
WC2E 8LU England

Typeset in Goudy by Circle Graphics, Inc., Columbia, MD

Printer: Sheridan Books, Ann Arbor, MI
Cover Designer: Beth Schleneff Design, Bethesda, MD

The opinions and statements published are the responsibility of the authors, and such opinions and statements do not necessarily represent the policies of the American Psychological Association.

Library of Congress Cataloging-in-Publication Data

Tummala-Narra, Pratyusha, author.
  Psychoanalytic theory and cultural competence in psychotherapy / Pratyusha Tummala-Narra. — First edition.
    pages cm
  Includes bibliographical references and index.
  ISBN 978-1-4338-2154-7 — ISBN 1-4338-2154-0 1. Psychoanalysis. 2. Psychotherapy. I. Title.
  RC504.T86 2016
  616.89'17   de23

                    2015027679

British Library Cataloguing-in-Publication Data

A CIP record is available from the British Library.

Printed in the United States of America
First Edition

http://dx.doi.org/10.1037/14800-000

For my husband,
Vinod Narra,
and
my children,
Keshav and Ishan

CONTENTS

vii

ACKNOWLEDGMENTS

Numerous mentors, colleagues, and friends have influenced my understanding of psychoanalytic psychotherapy and of sociocultural identity, some since my training years. They include Salman Akhtar, Anne Bogat, Lillian Comas-Díaz, Jaine Darwin, Beverly Greene, Mary Harvey, Judith Herman, Bertram Karon, Kenneth Reich, and Janna Smith. I thank these brilliant mentors and friends for their generosity and inspiration. I am grateful to Paul Erickson and Jack Burke for helping me early in my career, when it would have been easier for them to look the other way, to embark on a journey of working with communities that are socially marginalized.

Several colleagues also have made it possible for me to move forward with writing this book. In particular, I thank Nancy McWilliams; Frank Summers; and the American Psychological Association, Division of Psychoanalysis (Division 39), Johanna K. Tabin Book Proposal Prize Committee for their support and encouragement. I am deeply thankful to Patricia Harney and Pamela Hays who provided important and valuable comments in the process of preparing this book. I am fortunate to work with the American Psychological Association (APA), and I thank Susan Reynolds and Andrew Gifford in APA Books for their excellent guidance throughout the writing process.

My former colleagues and students at the Cambridge Health Alliance and my colleagues and students at Boston College have provided me with enriching dialogues and interactions that have helped me to develop as a researcher, educator, and clinician. With regard to my clients, I am truly honored to witness their healing and am indebted to them for transforming me in ways that are at times difficult to articulate.

Finally, I thank my family and friends, without whose encouragement I could not have written this book. I am especially grateful to my husband, Vinod, and my sons, Keshav and Ishan, to whom this book is dedicated, for their love and generosity and supporting my dedication to my work. Their patience and sense of humor have been a life line.

Psychoanalytic Theory and Cultural Competence in Psychotherapy

INTRODUCTION

It is important to situate this book in its particular social, historical, and political context. I have written this book during a time of war, terrorist attacks, intense national debate concerning immigration policy and same-sex marriage, ongoing racial profiling and violence and gender-based physical and sexual violence, and a growing income gap between the wealthy and the poor. This is also a time in the United States when children and adolescents are exposed either directly or indirectly to alarming rates of school and community violence and when many young women and men assume that the word "feminist" refers to women who "hate" men. The president of the United States is a biracial, African American and White man, and yet we continue to witness injustice around racial lines. On a global scale, we are witnessing an unprecedented rate of internal and external displacement (due to war, poverty, and ethnic and religious conflicts), human trafficking, and violence against women and girls. There is tremendous innovation in information technology, which

http://dx.doi.org/10.1037/14800-001
Psychoanalytic Theory and Cultural Competence in Psychotherapy, by P. Tummala-Narra

simultaneously has provided needed access to information to an extraordinary number of people globally and has become a space for voicing hatred and prejudice toward other human beings. With an increasing demand for delivering more services in a briefer amount of time, the mental health professions have been losing ground on the ability to adequately address the needs of individuals who face serious challenges, many of which are rooted in social injustice. We are sorely in need of theory that reflects the lived realities of individuals and communities who are typically not heard in the mainstream and that explicitly recognizes the impact of social oppression and the complexity of identity and relationships in the contemporary world.

The influence of psychoanalytic concepts in the United States and elsewhere is pervasive. Across many parts of the world, we witness this influence in our day-to-day lives when we hear people talk about the unconscious, Freudian slips, or defense mechanisms. Yet, everyday use of psychoanalytic language is typically not associated with issues such as race, gender, culture, sexual identity, social class, and dis/ability. Even within the mental health professions, sociocultural issues are associated with feminism and multiculturalism, not psychoanalysis. However, over the past two decades, there have been significant developments in the conceptualization of sociocultural issues within psychoanalysis, many of which are largely unfamiliar to the public. When we conduct clinical practice or research or when we teach, we are faced with realities of individuals and communities that are far more complex than what is described in existing psychological frameworks. While recognizing the historical neglect of social context within psychoanalysis, this book draws on the contributions of psychoanalytic scholars, particularly relational and intersubjective theorists, to present a culturally informed psychoanalytic perspective that addresses the complex realities of people in the contemporary world.

Drawing on different perspectives within and outside of psychoanalysis (multicultural, feminist), this book presents a culturally informed psychoanalytic perspective. I come to this perspective as an Indian American woman who immigrated to the United States as a child; a multicultural, feminist, psychoanalytic psychologist and practitioner; a researcher in the areas of immigration, race, and trauma; and a professor in a counseling psychology graduate program. As a practitioner, I have worked in a variety of clinical settings (e.g., community-based outpatient clinics and inpatient units in hospitals, day treatment, independent practice) and community-based interventions (e.g., schools, outreach). These experiences have informed my conceptualization of cultural competence in practice, research, and teaching, which integrates multiple perspectives within psychoanalysis and psychology to examine the inextricable connection between the individual and his/her sociocultural context.

The book is composed of nine chapters. The first two chapters situate psychoanalytic approaches to sociocultural issues in historical context.

Chapter 1, drawing from historians (e.g., Nathan Hale, John Demos) and psychologists (e.g., Philip Cushman, Lewis Aron, and Karen Starr), provides an overview of the history and migration of psychoanalytic conceptualizations of social context in the United States. The chapter explores the movement of a revolutionary psychoanalytic discipline in Europe to a more socially conservative and medicalized discipline in the United States. It also presents the views of psychoanalysts of the Cultural School, such as Harry Stack Sullivan, Eric Fromm, and Karen Horney. Chapter 2 involves an exploration of the psychoanalytic perspectives of Sandor Ferenczi, Donald Winnicott, and Heinz Kohut, particularly their influence on relational and intersubjective theories. This chapter focuses on contemporary approaches to various aspects of sociocultural context and identity, including gender, race, immigration, social class, sexual orientation, and religion/spirituality, and emerging areas of study (e.g., dis/ability).

The next six chapters present a psychoanalytic framework of cultural competence, drawing from the contributions of contemporary psychoanalysis to the study of diversity. Chapter 3 examines the overlaps between psychoanalytic and multicultural perspectives and introduces a framework for culturally informed psychoanalytic psychotherapy, which contains five areas of focus. Chapters 4 through 8 provide detailed descriptions of these five areas of emphasis in culturally informed psychoanalytic psychotherapy: (a) attending to indigenous narrative; (b) considering the role of language and affect; (c) addressing social oppression and traumatic stress; (d) recognizing the complexity of cultural identifications; and (e) expanding self-examination. Collectively, these chapters emphasize the experiences of people on the margins, the role of social injustice and privilege in identity development, relational life and psychological health, the dynamic and hybrid nature of culture, and the client's and the therapist's self-inquiry. Chapter 9 explores the implications of a culturally informed psychoanalytic perspective for practice, training, and research in psychology. The final chapter focuses on some contemporary challenges within psychoanalysis and the disconnection between psychoanalytic theory and academic psychology. Looking toward the future, I offer some ideas for new directions in addressing these problems and highlight some important applications of psychoanalytic theory in nonclinical domains.

This book is intended for mental health professionals across disciplines (e.g., psychology, social work, psychiatry), educators, and graduate students interested in clinical practice. This book also would be of interest to researchers who are interested in examining culturally informed practices in psychotherapy, the therapeutic process, and psychotherapy outcome. Throughout the book, I present illustrations from my clinical practice and from my interactions with colleagues and students to demonstrate the direct relevance of theoretical concepts and of dilemmas that we all may struggle with in our work. All of the case examples in the book have been anonymized. The clinical illustrations are not meant to be comprehensive accounts of my work with my clients, but rather highlight certain aspects of the therapeutic process that are connected with particular aspects of theory.

Attending to cultural competence in psychotherapy encompasses the experiences and worldviews of all communities. In this book, I aim to describe the experiences of multiple communities, but these communities by no means compose an exhaustive list. It is important to recognize that although I focus primarily on issues of race, culture, gender, sexual identity, social class, religion, and dis/ability, I do so with varying degrees in each chapter. It is important to realize that what defines the term "minority" is contextual, and, as such, I want to be clear that I am using the United States as a reference point in this book. My intent is not to present an exhaustive review of experiences of each U.S. minority community but rather to engage the reader in thinking, witnessing, and struggling with me about the complexity that is inherent to the interaction among the intrapsychic, relational, and sociocultural and its implications for conflict, identity, and well-being.

In his essay *Criteria of Negro Art*, published in 1926, W. E. B. Du Bois wrote the following:

> What do we want? . . . We want to be Americans, full-fledged Americans, with all the rights of other American citizens. But is that all? Do we want simply to be Americans? Once in a while through all of us there flashes some clairvoyance, some clear idea, of what America really is. We who are dark can see America in a way that white Americans can not. And seeing our country thus, are we satisfied with its present goals and ideals? (as cited in Napier, 2000, p. 17)

Du Bois's words still resonate today, as minority groups in the United States continue to struggle with the marginalization of their voices, and an entire society is marked by a painful legacy of social injustice and by the challenge of having honest dialogues across the lines of gender, race, ethnicity, religion, sexual orientation, social class, and dis/ability. This book is an attempt, within the mental health professions, to move beyond dominant narratives that disenfranchise some communities while privileging others and toward an engagement with multiple narratives. Such a movement is essential for understanding the lived realities of people who are socially marginalized. At the same time, this book is not intended only for majority status (e.g., White, heterosexual, middle-class, able-bodied) mental health professionals who provide psychotherapy to minority status clients or for therapeutic dyads in which the therapist and client differ on one or more sociocultural dimensions. Rather, the book speaks to the experiences of professionals of all sociocultural backgrounds and calls attention to the importance of examining their practice with all of their clients.

1

A HISTORICAL OVERVIEW AND CRITIQUE OF THE PSYCHOANALYTIC APPROACH TO CULTURE AND CONTEXT

When I was a psychology intern, I wanted the help of a therapist to gain a better understanding of myself. I am a visible woman of color, a 1.5-generation, Indian American woman, born in India, and raised primarily in the United States. As an intern, I had been working with clients who were coping with mental illness, traumatic stress, and severe life conditions, such as poverty and homelessness. I wanted to learn more about how my own personal life and history influenced my thoughts, affects, and relationships, and how working with my clients affected me and how I affected them. I was referred to a White, European American psychoanalytically oriented therapist who was able to provide me with therapy sessions at a reduced fee. We met only twice. During our first meeting, we talked primarily about my relationships with my parents. In our second meeting, to my surprise, he held a brown paper bag from which he took out a samosa (a spicy Indian snack) and began to eat it while talking to me. The therapist directed our conversation toward my

http://dx.doi.org/10.1037/14800-002
Psychoanalytic Theory and Cultural Competence in Psychotherapy, by P. Tummala-Narra

mother and my relationship with her as he ate his samosa. He never asked me anything about my immigration to the United States from India or about my parents' immigration. I was stunned that a therapist would engage with me in this way. I wondered why he had not explicitly asked me anything about my experience of my cultural background and instead chose to eat Indian food as he sat with me. In certain moments, I imagined that this was his way of demonstrating his interest in my culture, and in other moments, I experienced him as uninterested in my real, lived experience. I was also aware that as a client, I did not want to bear the responsibility and burden of trying to understand his choices. We never talked about the samosa. I never returned to work with him again.

There are questions, of course, that remain today about what the therapist was communicating through his behavior toward me. I chose to stop working with him because I simultaneously felt invisible and exoticized. His behavior spoke to his own personal needs more so than mine. In retrospect, I wonder how many other ways he may have caused harm to clients and if eating a samosa was his way, albeit offensive, of expressing his interest in me and my culture. This enactment involving the therapist's acting out his attitudes toward Indians and my reaction to him caused a rupture that, at the time, I believed could not be addressed. Unfortunately, his dismissive approach to my sociocultural background is not uncommon or unique to therapists of any particular theoretical orientation. This book is an effort to move away from insensitive and harmful interactions such as the one in my example. It is a concern of many minority individuals who experience themselves as outside of "mainstream" culture in the United States that they will not be understood or that their social and cultural contexts will not be considered as relevant to their psychological life if they were to see a psychotherapist. But a changing demography and social and political changes in the United States support an urgent need for a deeper understanding of cultural context in mental health interventions. A movement toward a culturally competent psychoanalytic approach to psychotherapy requires an honest examination of the social and historical context of psychoanalysis and its progression into present day applications.

Psychoanalytic practitioners have developed a reputation among minorities (e.g., racial, sexual, religious) that reflects a minimizing of contextual issues that are critically important to development and mental health. In fact, issues of culture and context have largely been ignored throughout the history of psychoanalysis. Theoretical developments in psychoanalysis in the 20th century were especially devoid of attention to cultural competence and issues of gender, age, race, culture, language, social class, sexual orientation, and physical disability. However, there were exceptions to the broad dismissal of diversity among psychoanalysts in the United States.

In this chapter, I review some highlights in psychoanalytic history to demonstrate, in brief, a complicated journey into the sociocultural realm. I provide an overview of the migration of psychoanalysis to the United States; the sociopolitical factors that contributed to a new, reductionistic form of psychoanalytic theory and practice in the country; and early psychoanalytic approaches to diversity. I briefly describe the challenges that some theorists from the "cultural school" of psychoanalysis posed to Sigmund Freud's theories and to American ego psychology. I draw primarily from accounts of psychoanalytic history by psychologists such as Philip Cushman, Lewis Aron, and Karen Starr, and by historians, such as Nathan G. Hale, Jr. These accounts are among the most comprehensive to date. Having a sense of how psychoanalytic ideas have developed in the United States during the past century can be helpful in better understanding the contributions to the neglect of sociocultural issues in the past and the attention to sociocultural issues in contemporary psychoanalytic psychotherapy.

PSYCHOANALYSIS AS IMMIGRANT AND REFUGEE

By 1900, Sigmund Freud (1856–1939) had developed a new discipline, psychoanalysis, which centered on unconscious drives and conflicts as the source of mental distress, countering existing somatic explanations for mental disorders. Salman Akhtar (2006) noted that Freud, although an immigrant and refugee himself (from Freiberg to Vienna early in his life and from Vienna to London late in his life), never attended to these experiences in his theory. Some of Freud's (1915) major theoretical developments included the suggestion that a primary function of the mind is to rid itself of excessive stimulation from sexual and aggressive instinctual wishes and impulses that could lead to pathological symptoms (i.e., hysteria), that repression of instinctual wishes and drives contributes to unresolved internal conflict (e.g., the Oedipus complex) and neurotic symptomology, that the individual seeks gratification of drives (i.e., the pleasure principle) despite their removal from conscious awareness, and that mental life is located primarily in the unconscious (e.g., dreams, symbolism; Eagle, 2011). Freud's ideas, particularly those concerning sexual and aggressive drives, were on the margins of Viennese society and remained controversial in Europe well beyond his death in 1939. In the United States, within a decade of Freud's visit to Clark University in 1909, psychoanalysis had caught the attention of physicians, psychologists, and the press. Hale (1995) described Freud's ambivalence about the reception of his theories in the United States. He noted that Freud had wanted psychoanalysis to become a discipline independent of medicine and psychiatry and feared that the American emphasis on material wealth and pragmatism would lead to a misguided application of psychoanalysis. Yet Freud's ideas have been deeply influential to the psyche of American society, among others around the world.

The Early Context of Reception of Freud's Ideas in the United States and the "Americanization" of Psychoanalysis

At the turn of the 20th century, American psychologists, such as William James and G. Stanley Hall, and American psychiatrists, such as Adolf Meyer, embraced Freud's ideas. Psychiatry in the United States had developed a new dynamic phase that involved a movement away from relying solely on biological explanations of mental disorders and toward an exploration of psychological theories (Aron & Starr, 2013; Cushman, 1995). Although distinct from psychoanalysis, dynamic psychiatry emphasized the role of the individual's life history in mental distress. Adolf Meyer, a key figure in dynamic psychiatry in the early 20th century, conceptualized mental distress as resulting from the interaction of the individual and his or her environment. Although biological approaches to treatment (e.g., shock therapy, psychosurgery) persisted, Meyer's approach, known as "psychobiology," along with the work of other influential figures in dynamic psychiatry, such as William Alanson White, influenced a growing receptivity to Freud's ideas (Aron & Starr, 2013).

The social, economic, and political climate of the early 20th century played an important role in whether psychoanalysis would come to be accepted in the United States and how psychoanalysts would assimilate Freud's ideas into a uniquely North American sociocultural context. Specifically, the industrial revolution, the World Wars, and related changes in the economic and social lives of Americans have been thought to contribute to a readiness for Freud's ideas. According to Hale's (1995) analysis, the introduction of Freud's theories to the United States paralleled a developing mental hygiene movement that aimed to secure humane treatment for psychiatric patients. Before to the Great Depression, a behavioral approach dominated psychiatry and the mental hygiene movement. However, the movement gave way to a growing interest in psychoanalytic ideas, and by the end of the 1920s, psychiatrists criticized behavioral techniques for failing to address "underlying" factors (Hale, 1995). A poignant example of this shift toward psychoanalytic perspectives is evident in the work of the National Committee for Mental Hygiene, which was established by Clifford Beers, a former psychiatric patient, before World War I. The Committee became a guiding force in addressing cases of shell shock among soldiers during and after the war. The Committee's medical director, Thomas W. Salmon, opposed punitive approaches to the treatment of soldiers with shell shock, such as being told that symptoms indicated a weakness of character and will, solitary confinement, and electric shock. Although not a

Freudian, Salmon was influenced by British psychiatrists who had increasingly attended to psychical conflicts as lying at the heart of shell shock. In psychiatry and in the popular press, there was growing recognition of Freud's theoretical constructs, such as repression, dreams, defense mechanisms, the role of trauma and environmental stress and conflict in symptom formation, catharsis as a method of releasing repressed memories, and defense mechanisms. Freud's theories helped to transform earlier somatic explanations and treatment of shell shock and other psychiatric ailments and laid the groundwork for a more hopeful psychotherapy (Aron & Starr, 2013; Hale, 1995).

An expanding interest in the psychical aspects of traumatic stress is further exemplified in the work of Abram Kardiner, an American psychiatrist who was analyzed by Freud in Vienna. Kardiner eventually developed a theory of war trauma from a psychoanalytic perspective. In 1941, Kardiner's *The Traumatic Neuroses of War* outlined symptoms of traumatic neurosis in ways that closely resemble the present-day description of posttraumatic stress disorder in the *Diagnostic and Statistical Manual of Mental Disorders* (DSM). Along with Herbert Spiegel, Kardiner proposed that the best way to address overwhelming feelings of terror in combat was to attend to soldiers' relationships with their units and their leaders (Herman, 1992). Thus, treatment approaches during World War II focused on maintaining interaction and connection between a patient with combat neurosis and his fellow soldiers. Although Kardiner and Spiegel used hypnosis to help patients access traumatic memories, they recognized that it was necessary for such memories to be integrated into conscious awareness through "talking" for treatment to be effective (Herman, 1992).

The notion of talking as a mechanism for healing extended to other facets of human experience. Specifically, although psychoanalysis for many today does not appear to be a progressive therapeutic perspective, in the early part of the 20th century, psychoanalysis provided a framework for a growing number of Americans, mostly from educated, middle- and upper-middle–class backgrounds, to challenge existing traditional "Puritan" beliefs and values concerning sexuality. Freud's concept of repression as lying at the root of neurosis contributed to changing sexual mores, along with new, progressive approaches to education and psychotherapy. Writers and psychoanalysts joined in creating a newer, "liberal" American ideology, and many young intellectuals not only promoted psychoanalysis as a path to fulfilling personal needs but also sought psychoanalysis as treatment for their personal benefit (Hale, 1995, p. 58). During the next several decades, the influence of psychoanalysis spanned various areas, such as attitudes toward sexuality, and settings, such as schools and child guidance clinics.

Other changes more directly related to the culture of the American family have contributed to the appeal of psychoanalytic theory in American society. The early 20th century witnessed massive shifts in demography and pluralism of the United States, with increasing numbers of immigrants primarily from Western and Eastern Europe and migration from rural to urban areas. The historian John Demos (1997, p. 66) described a "critical period in the history of the American family" that took place at the end of the 19th century and the beginning of the 20th century. While parents exercised more control over reproduction and had fewer children, Americans came to see the family and the world outside of the family as distinct spheres, whereas in previous decades, family and community were thought to be complementary in preparing children for the transition to functioning in broader society. Life outside of the home in an increasingly industrialized, technological society was characterized by unpredictability, agitation, and a sense of disorder. In contrast, life within the family home was thought to be a characterized by love, kindness, and order. The changes in the conceptions of the family unit further entrenched sex-role typing of men and women and fostered a focus on the child as having her or his own psychological needs. Demos (1997) further noted that these structural changes resulted in a "hothouse family" or an "oedipal family," a type of family structure that helped to bring Freud's ideas to fruition in the United States. In fact, popular literature concerning child-rearing proliferated in the United States, as did parenting experts who emphasized more careful parenting, with primary responsibility resting with the mother. There was also an emphasis on parents' simultaneous encouragement of independence and self-control, the internalization of values through parental example, and an intensified relationship between the parent and the child.

Throughout the history of psychoanalysis in the United States, Freud's ideas have been embraced, revised, and refuted to both suit and shape the social, cultural, and economic needs of Americans. According to Philip Cushman (1995), Americans in the early to mid-20th century, which was a time of geographic expansion and increasing scientific inquiry, became interested in exploring the unconscious as a new territory, namely, the interior of the self. Various forces shaped the "Americanization" of the more pessimistic elements of Freud's ideas. Interestingly, Freud, in an effort to promote psychoanalysis in his only talk in the United States, admitted that he had emphasized the pragmatic aspects of psychoanalysis and de-emphasized the more pessimistic aspects of his theories (Cushman, 1995). The mental hygiene movement, in conjunction with the introduction of Freud's ideas in the United States, further shaped the medicalization of emotional problems. Psychoanalysis, along with other branches of psychotherapy, such as behaviorism, contributed to a view of mental health as residing inside an individual by function of feelings, thoughts, and intrapsychic processes (Cushman, 1995). Psychiatry and psychology emphasized the value of individualism at the cost of explanations of mental health and illness that considered social and environmental causes. The therapist became the expert in helping people to achieve self-exploration and liberation, independent of social and cultural context.

War, Trauma, and Exile

Psychoanalysis in the early part of the 20th century reflected an exchange of ideas between a culturally and politically shifting American society and European, specifically Viennese, society. Several American psychiatrists traveled to Europe to train under Freud and other psychoanalysts. Hale (1995) noted that by 1938, almost half of the candidates in psychoanalytic training in Vienna were from the United States, many of whom returned home and became actively involved in developing psychoanalytic institutes. While the migration of psychoanalytic ideas to the United States occurred under nontraumatic circumstances initially, the traumatic aftermath of World War II set the stage for significant changes in theoretical developments and in the practice of psychoanalysis. The Nazi regime in Europe altered the course of psychoanalytic history such that many psychoanalysts, including Freud and his daughter, Anna Freud, were forced to flee their homes to other parts of the world.

Before the war, psychoanalytic practice had been changing in the face of the Great Depression, during which greater numbers of patients, most of whom were college-educated professionals, were being seen by psychoanalysts for lower fees, leaving fewer hours for scientific research, which had been thought to be an important venture of psychoanalysts (Hale, 1995). Clinical psychologists, many of whom were trained by psychiatrists/psychoanalysts, played a prominent role in meeting the military's need to treat an increasing number of soldiers with traumatic stress (Aron & Starr, 2013). The demand for psychoanalytic treatment continued to rise throughout the Great Depression and World War II, and psychoanalysis offered optimism in the face of new challenges during these difficult economic and social periods for many Americans. In particular, American psychoanalysts such as Karl Menninger (1930) reconceptualized Freud's ideas with "an optimistic American twist" (Hale, 1995, p. 84). In doing so, psychoanalysis offered promising solutions to various ailments, such as sexual problems and mental illness, all within a context of the North American tradition of individualism.

During the war and its aftermath, psychoanalysis became increasingly connected with psychiatry, and a long-standing negative sentiment among American psychoanalysts regarding lay analysis led to further medicalization. In the 1930s, there were struggles between analysts who advocated the restriction of the practice and training of psychoanalysis to physicians and analysts who advocated for broader applications of psychoanalysis in the mental health disciplines. The American Psychoanalytic Association in 1938 established a policy, which would last until the 1980s, that excluded the involvement of lay or nonphysician analysts from practice and training. The American Psychological Association's Division of Psychoanalysis (Division 39), formed in 1979, provided a community for psychologists and allied professionals during a time of exclusion from the medically directed psychoanalytic training institutes and organizations. The attitude toward lay analysis in the United States stood in contrast with that in Europe, including that of Freud, where psychoanalysis was practiced more broadly with respect to both the analyst's discipline and outside of the medical profession. Psychoanalysis in the United States developed a reputation as an expensive form of treatment available to fewer and fewer patients that rested in the hands of a few medical experts.

Between 1938 and 1943, the Emergency Committee on Immigration of the American Psychoanalytic Association helped approximately 149 refugees, many of whom (e.g., Heinz Hartmann, David Rapaport) became important figures in modifications to psychoanalytic theory in the United States. Many of the European analysts who became exiles in the United States were supported by a younger generation of American analysts they had trained in Europe and by other professional and social networks (Hale, 1995). These émigrés, although idealized for their closeness to Freud, had experienced horrible losses in the face of the Nazi Holocaust and faced anti-Semitism in Europe and the United States. Displaced from their homes, they fostered a more orthodox form of psychoanalysis compared with that in Europe in the hopes of securing the future of psychoanalysis. In fact, psychoanalysis in recent years has been conceptualized as a survivor of the Holocaust (Aron & Starr, 2013). With rising anti-Semitism in the United States from the 1920s through the 1940s, racial categorization of Jews in the United States had fluctuated from White to Black. Efforts to secure "Whiteness" (Altman, 2010), which can be equated with physical and economic survival, power, and privilege, contributed to a silence concerning the traumatic experiences of the émigrés. The émigrés experienced severe, sometimes brutal, loss of family, friends, communities, homes, languages, and traditions. The association with White, male privilege and the medical establishment and a connection with fellow émigrés, who settled primarily in the Northeastern part of the United States, all became important means of survival among Jewish émigré analysts. Yet there was little dialogue about the effects of the Holocaust on the émigrés themselves or on the lives of patients who were survivors. The émigrés did not write about their experiences as "foreign" analysts (Akhtar, 2006).

Many émigrés of the post–World War II era supported a medical discipline with a changing theoretical emphasis on the centrality of the ego, possibly in response to their witnessing of the tragedies of wartime and genocide. Interestingly, this focus on the ego's adaptation to external sources of stress and trauma became exclusively a function of the interior, without attending to the realities of social oppression. Furthermore, psychoanalytic developments in the United States increasingly ignored social and cultural influences on intrapsychic life, including persecution of women, racial and ethnic minorities (e.g., Native Americans, African Americans, non-White immigrants), sexual minorities, and the poor. Instead, the new American psychoanalysis reified the expanding American ideal of the melting pot; the assimilation of "foreign" ideas and customs into White, North American norms; and the idealization of self-reliance and individual autonomy. Aron and Starr (2013) astutely pointed out that although psychoanalysis in Europe had revolutionary roots, the émigré analyst in the United States was no longer valued as a social activist and instead became "depoliticized and conservative" (p. 118) so that there was no cause to believe that he or she was subversive in anyway. This new American stance was different from that of analysts in Europe before World War II. The European analysts, including Freud, had aimed for psychoanalysis to be accessible to the public at large, as evident in the establishment of free clinics. Free clinics in Vienna and other parts of Europe made psychoanalysis accessible to farmers, laborers, students, factory workers, domestic servants, and others who were unable to pay for their treatment (Danto, 2005).

It is worth considering that social, cultural, and political factors shaped the dynamics of immigration and assimilation of psychoanalysis in countries other than the United States. For example, in both the United States and Argentina in the early to mid-1900s, there was a preoccupation with understanding criminality and preserving the "purity" of the White race (in the United States) or the Latin (e.g., European) race (in Argentina) that was guided by a somatic paradigm. Although physicians and psychologists in the United States and Argentina were exposed to psychoanalytic literature and conferences during this time period, a predominant interest in the somatic paradigm in psychiatry precluded the receptivity to Freud's ideas until the middle of the 20th century in Argentina, and psychoanalysis developed independently of the medical profession (Taiana, 2006). In India, the psychiatrist Girindrasekhar Bose, by 1914, developed psychoanalytic ideas that reflected Hindu spirituality and culture and, in 1921, published the book *Concept of Repression* (Akhtar & Tummala-Narra, 2005). In fact, Bose maintained a correspondence with Freud that lasted more than 16 years, through which Freud expressed his difficulty with Bose's culturally specific developments in theory. The development of psychoanalysis in India occurred in the context of British colonial rule, through which the Indian psyche was thought to be a repertoire of racist notions of inferiority and submissiveness. For example,

Owen Berkeley-Hill, a British member of the Indian Psychoanalytic Society, suggested that Indians have undesirable character traits in contrast to the higher order character traits of the British (Hartnack, 1987; Mehta, 1997). Despite the influence of colonialism, under the guidance and influence of Bose psychoanalysis further expanded in India with the work of several Indian psychoanalysts, such as Tarun Sinha, Bhupen Desai, and Sudhir Kakar (Mehta, 1997).

Between 1929 and 1933 Freud's writings were translated into Japanese by a group led by scholars Yaekichi Yabe and Kenji Ohtsuki. Although Freud's ideas were largely dismissed in Japan initially, psychoanalysis was introduced in psychiatry in Japan by Kiyoyasu Marui, who had traveled to the United States in 1919 to study with the psychoanalyst Adolf Meyer. Heisaku Kosawa introduced his theory of the Ajase complex to Freud when he met with him in Vienna, where Kosawa studied psychoanalysis from 1932 to 1933. Kosawa's Ajase complex, rooted in a Buddhist legend, contrasts with Freud's Oedipus complex, which is rooted in Greek mythology. According to a version of the Buddhist legend, Ajase (or Ajatasatru) was an Indian prince whose birth was the product of his mother's conflict. Ajase's mother, Queen Idaike, wished to have a child in the hope of securing her husband's affection. She consulted with an oracle, who revealed that a hermit in a nearby forest would be reborn as her son in 3 years. Ajase's mother then killed the hermit to hasten the birth of her son, but the hermit warned her before his death that, once reborn, he would kill her husband. Although the queen attempted to kill her baby to protect her husband, the hermit, reborn as Ajase, survived. After Ajase learned about the circumstances of his birth, he imprisoned his father and attempted to kill his mother; he later developed intense feelings of guilt and a painful skin disease. Despite his mother's care and nurturance, Ajase did not recover until Queen Idaike sought the help of the Buddha. Through her interaction with the Buddha, she came to realize her misdeeds. Ajase recovered from his illness after he and his mother had forgiven each other, moving them toward mutual harmony and a sense of oneness. The Ajase complex encompasses the importance of forgiveness and sense of oneness or unity between the mother and her child (Kosawa, 2009; Ozawa-de Silva, 2007). This is in contrast to the story of Oedipus, in which conflict is resolved through separation and independence of the child, rather than a sense of oneness with the mother.

Kosawa introduced the Ajase complex to Freud in his paper *Two Kinds of Guilt Feelings: The Ajase Complex*. Freud apparently took little interest in Kosawa's ideas. Kosawa later introduced the practice of psychoanalytic psychotherapy in Japan that more closely resembled psychoanalytic practice in Europe and the United States than did that practiced by Marui, who emphasized the theoretical aspects of psychoanalysis, rather than technique, in explaining psychopathology (Okinogi, 2009). These are among numerous examples of the ways in which migration, assimilation, and oppression facilitated the pluralism in psychoanalytic theory across cultures. Indeed, the migration of psychoanalysis across different countries throughout the 20th century and into the 21st century has been an enterprise of integrating the ideas of Freud and European analysts, local political and economic forces, and cultural and social mores and sensibilities. However, until recent decades, psychoanalysis in the United States steered away from recognizing the cultural nuances of theory and practice.

EARLY PSYCHOANALYTIC APPROACHES TO SOCIAL CONTEXT

Although his theories were rooted in the belief that civilization and the individual coexist in tension, Freud emphasized the centrality of biological structure and functions in what he viewed as the individual's need for freedom from civilization's demands. In *Civilization and Its Discontents* (1930), Freud noted that "severe suffering" is caused by the demands of the external world, which "refuses to sate our needs" (p. 731). He described ways in which people ward off suffering by "shifting the instinctual aims in such a way that they cannot come up against frustration from the external world" (p. 731). He viewed colonialism as an enactment of intrapsychic fantasies of mastery over the world (Lane, 1998). Yet Freud's attention, as that of many of his successors, to the external world and its variations was superseded by a focus on biological instincts and sexual aggressive drives and a quest to describe the human psyche in universal terms. This is evident in Freud's rejection of sociocultural explanations of psychological distress and symptomology.

Freud, on the basis of his work with many of his female patients, in 1896 proposed his seduction theory, according to which obsessional and hysterical symptoms were thought to be rooted in experiences of sexual abuse, often by the patient's father. Although this idea rested on the critical role of actual trauma on intrapsychic life, Freud later abandoned his seduction theory and formulated his patients' neuroses along a more inward theory of sexuality that focused on internal conflict and fantasy. In a letter to Wilhelm Fleiss in 1897, Freud wrote that he was unable to achieve complete success in his treatment of these patients and that the unconscious cannot differentiate fact from fiction (Schimek, 1987). The repercussions of the abandonment of the seduction theory were, of course, profound because patients' reports of being sexually abused in childhood were dismissed by many therapists.

Freud's approach to social realities and cultural beliefs tended to recede to the preeminence of intrapsychic conflict. With respect to his conceptualization of religion and spirituality, in *The Future of an Illusion* (1927), he stated:

> Thus we are perfectly willing to acknowledge that the 'oceanic' feeling exists in many people, and we are inclined to trace it back to an early phase of ego-feeling. The further question then arises, what claim this feeling has to be regarded as the source of religious needs. To me the claim does not seem compelling. (p. 727)

He later stated that religious needs are derived from a sense of helplessness and later in development "sustained by fear of the superior power of Fate" (p. 727). Freud's views of religion and spirituality as neurosis, immature, and infantile reflect a Eurocentric and imperialistic sensibility and Freud's reluctance to consider ideas that challenged the positivism of psychoanalysis (Rubin, 2003; Tummala-Narra, 2009b). These views would later be challenged by Carl Jung (1938), who emphasized the spiritual dimension of the human psyche, even though Jung's ideas also reflected an exoticization of Eastern spiritual traditions (Parsons, 2001).

Freud's conceptualization of the psychological experiences of women and girls is among the most contentious theorizing concerning social and cultural dimensions. Constructions of gender were intertwined with biological determinism, and mothers were closely observed because their interactions with their children became the predictors of children's character and behavior. Women were guided by their physicians to be passive with regard to their sexual interests and to believe that being married and having children was a cure to their lack of satisfaction. The domination of women's sexuality and the diminution of their sexual desires are obvious in such an approach. The 19th century emphasis on biological functions as responsible for development of personality laid the foundation for early psychoanalytic theory (Hale, 1995). Although psychoanalysis explicitly recognized the importance of women's sexual feelings, women's psychological health and character were conceptualized by Freud and the early analysts in Europe as being determined by repressed sexual wishes, castration anxiety, and penis envy. Further, psychoanalytic theory concerning character development was deeply influenced by the view of women as inferior and that women's health involved renouncing their desire to be men (i.e., penis envy) and accepting a passive position in a world that is male dominated (Aron & Starr, 2013). Considering this perspective, one can imagine the degree to which female patients were guided by their analysts to suppress their sexuality and, more broadly, their desires for the sake of maintaining male authority within the consulting room, home, workplace, and broader society. Freud's views on women and women's mental health would come into question by several psychoanalytic theorists, such as Karen Horney, and feminist scholars in the mid- to late 20th century.

Early psychoanalytic theory was further influenced by Charles Darwin's theory of evolution. In the mid- to late 19th century through the early part of the 20th century, Darwin's *On the Origin of Species by Means of Natural Selection* (1859) provided a framework for psychological inquiry concerning various aspects of human development and the nature of the mind. In this framework, human beings came to be viewed as part of a natural order, although they were distinguishable from animal species with regard to complexity. Human behavior was increasingly subject to scientific investigation, and a paradigm of Social Darwinism sparked the eugenics movement, founded by Francis Galton. This movement aimed to "avert the decline of the quality of the human, and especially British 'stock'" (G. Richards, 2012, p. 20) and promoted racialized science and policy in Europe and the United States. Although some psychologists, such as Thomas Russell Garth, challenged the belief that there are innate differences in intelligence, among other psychological constructs, and advocated for the place of social conditions in scientific observations of "racial differences," many psychologists in the United States and Europe promoted the notion of superiority of the "White" race and the inferiority of other "races" (G. Richards, 2012; Tummala-Narra, 2014b). Darwin's evolutionary biology would further shape views regarding the position of men and women, with men being viewed as intellectually and socially superior to women. These notions of sociocultural evolutionism influenced early psychoanalytic conceptualizations of what and who composed the primitive/civilized, the masculine/feminine, and the dependent/autonomous (Aron & Starr, 2013).

It is important to recognize the ways in which Freud's model of the unconscious was influenced by the 19th-century preoccupation with the "primitive." In his essay "The Unconscious" (1915), Freud compared the nature of the unconscious to an "aboriginal population of the mind" (p. 195). Although Freud's theory of the "primitive" or "savage" unconscious emphasized the universal aspects of intrapsychic conflict, psychoanalysts such as Carl Jung developed theories that conceptualized the Western psyche as qualitatively different from the non-Western psyche, which was thought to be less evolved (Lane, 1998; Richards, 2012). Richards (2012, p. 192), in fact, noted that Jung, in his travels to India, Africa, and the Southwestern United States, was fascinated with his discoveries but haunted by "a fear of 'going native'" or being overwhelmed by primitive states of consciousness. Unfortunately, some early psychoanalytic work reified the belief in actual differences in mental life between "primitive" and "civilized" people, and the assumption of a static or fixed, inferior position of the "primitive." The focus on the "primitive" in psychoanalysis in conjunction with race psychology was later used to spur and justify genocide (e.g., genocide of Native Americans, Nazi Holocaust) and various other types of oppression, including colonialism, slavery, and segregation, and more broadly that directed against non-Whites. After World War II, as the paradigm of race in psychological research shifted, so too did theorizing about the implications of the "primitive" in psychoanalysis. Psychoanalytic theory has since moved toward a reflexive approach to race and racism and its effects on the therapeutic process and a view of racism as a form of social injustice that has important implications for intrapsychic, interpersonal, and intergroup conflict.

In Europe, homosexuality was another issue that was debated in the late 18th century and early 19th century. There was debate concerning whether homosexuality was "normal" and whether homosexuals composed a third sex (Drescher, 2008). Freud (1905) argued against the idea of homosexuality as a type of degeneracy and instead suggested that it was an "inversion" that was unrelated to mental health problems and that all people are capable unconsciously of "making a homosexual object-choice" (p. 145). Freud further supported the decriminalization of homosexuality. However, he did characterize homosexuality as immature, albeit not an illness (Drescher, 2008). Later, some psychoanalysts, such as Sandor Rado (1940), would come to challenge Freud's conceptualization of bisexuality and the "normality" of homosexuality, and align homosexuality with deviance and degeneracy. In this framework, a task of the analyst was to cure patients of their homosexual thoughts and behaviors. Drescher (2008) suggested that these post-Freudian views contributed to the inclusion of homosexuality as a diagnosis in the *DSM* and to the exclusion of openly gay applicants to psychoanalytic-oriented training institutes. The post-Freudian and medical perspectives on homosexuality would later be challenged by the psychoanalysts Judd Marmor (1965) and Thomas Szasz (1960), who challenged psychiatry to reflect on its own presumptions about morality and the role of its own power and influence in the pathologizing of homosexuality. Post-Freudian views were also challenged by emerging research concerning sexual behavior in the mid-20th century, such as that conducted by Alfred Kinsey and Evelyn Hooker in the 1940s and 1950s, which noted that homosexuality was in fact not rare and not pathological (Drescher, 2008).

The psychoanalytic theories concerning the primitive mind, gender, character, and homosexuality put forth in the early part of the 20th century by Freud and the European analysts were adopted by American analysts. This included theories of sex, gender, religion, and homosexuality and conceptions of different mentalities across races, all of which influenced conceptualizations of character or personality and mental health. Although psychoanalysis became a cornerstone of American psychiatry gradually through the mid-20th century, it carried important messages about social and cultural context into the mental hygiene movement in the United States. The relationship between unconscious conflict and psychopathology was examined primarily in the context of the interior self. This was especially problematic in a nation that largely silenced the perspectives of women, racial minorities, sexual minorities, and the poor, among others. Whiteness and maleness, in classical psychoanalysis, were largely seen as "neutral" categories against which normality and pathology were evaluated (Seshadri-Crooks, 2000). Yet the assumptions concerning social context and the interior were later reconsidered by psychoanalysts in the United States, contributing to both progressive developments in theory and practice and to dissent within organized psychoanalysis.

EVOLVING PERSPECTIVES IN PSYCHOANALYSIS

Criticisms and Schisms

Freud was himself an outsider in Viennese society. His surround was characterized by scrutiny of his Jewish background and the perception of psychoanalysis as a Jewish science. According to Aron and Starr (2013), Freud masked his own and his patients' Jewish identities in his case studies, and he both identified with his Jewish identity and internalized anti-Semitic stereotypes from Viennese culture. Ironically, while he aimed to create a discipline that would not be identified as Jewish, some psychoanalytic concepts may well have been rooted in Jewish tradition. For example, Freud's conceptualization of interpretation may have been influenced by the Jewish principle of interpretation, in which each letter of the Torah is thought to contain meaning and multiple interpretations (Aron, 2004). It is also worth noting that anti-Semitism involved not only hostility concerning religious differences but also perceived racial differences between Christians and Jews. In this sense, Freud was on the margins, as was psychoanalysis. His concerns about protecting psychoanalysis from being dismissed as a Jewish discipline would be carried forth to future generations of psychoanalysts in Europe and the United States. The trauma of war and the Nazi Holocaust intensified these concerns and transformed the future of psychoanalysis.

In the United States, psychoanalysis became increasingly connected with psychiatry, used a greater sense of optimism compared with Freud's theories in the face of war and the Great Depression, and disconnected from the margins where it lay in its early stages in Europe. Adolf Meyer, Franz Alexander, and Karl Menninger were among the psychoanalysts who helped to consolidate the place of psychoanalysis in psychiatry and supported the scientific observation of psychoanalytic concepts. In the post-World War II era, American and European émigré psychoanalysts developed the American ego psychology movement in an effort to build a scientific basis for psychoanalysis, expand theory concerning normal development in keeping with the aims of academic psychology, and revisit the nature of drives, especially aggression. Hale (1995) pointed out that the creation of ego psychology in the United States was instigated in part by psychoanalysts' experiences with World War I and World War II. The ego psychologists (e.g., Heinz Hartmann, David Rapaport) emphasized the adaptive functions of defenses. For example, Heinz Hartmann, a refugee analyst and a founder of ego psychology, believed that aggressive drives serve to preserve the self rather than having only destructive consequences for the individual (Hale, 1995). Charles Brenner, a psychoanalyst in New York, further emphasized the centrality of drives, affect, and conflict and led perhaps a more reductionistic version of psychoanalysis, assuming that psychopathology is fully determined by one's childhood.

In American ego psychology, the influence of the environment on the child remained in the confines of the family, leaving the world outside of the family largely external to theory. The notions of ego autonomy and ego strength reflected North American and Western European value of individual autonomy. Ego psychology promoted an approach that required interpretation as the analyst's primary function and undermined the potential influence of the analyst in the therapeutic relationship because a patient may develop dependency on the analyst. According to this perspective, a patient was "analyzable" if he or she could bear the analyst who does little to intervene, tolerates frustration and delayed gratification, and relies on his or her own autonomous self to develop structural intrapsychic change. The promise of structural change in ego psychology has been viewed as a reaction formation, a manic defense, in the face of tremendous anxiety associated with the post–World War II and Cold War eras and a fear of the "primitive" (e.g., women, homosexuals, racial minorities, Jews; Aron & Starr, 2013).

What was at one point considered a revolutionary, progressive discipline in Europe became a socially conservative and mainstream form of therapy in the United States. Pluralism in psychoanalysis largely remained in the realm of theoretical differences, rather than in the sociocultural experiences of patients. Since the 1950s, psychoanalysis in the United States faced a division with psychodynamic psychotherapy in an attempt to maintain a sense of "purity," justifying high costs for services and training (Aron & Starr, 2013). This was a departure from its roots because the early psychoanalysts "were not mainstream, high income professionals" and instead were intellectuals on the margin who "barely eked out a living" (Aron & Starr, pp. 28–29). Although Freud emphasized the individual as distinct and bounded separate from his or her cultural context, psychoanalysis in the United States further separated itself from attending to social and cultural context, concerning itself primarily with individual instincts and drives, with notions of health directed through a European-American, White, male, middle-class lens. In fact, even published accounts of the history of psychoanalysis rarely mention the interaction of psychoanalysis with individuals from marginalized communities, particularly racial minorities.

This trend has continued to the present. In my review of psychoanalytic writing (Luborsky & Barrett, 2006; Shedler, 2010) concerning major theoretical areas of emphasis, I found no articles that mention that attending to the client's and the therapist's social and cultural contexts is a core value of psychoanalysis or psychoanalytic psychotherapy (Tummala-Narra, 2015). Research reviews of the efficacy of psychoanalytic psychotherapy also do not include information concerning race, ethnicity, sexual orientation, or other social identity variables. In a meta-analysis of psychodynamic therapy (a total of 104 studies with more than 9,000 participants) over the past decade, Watkins (2012) found that approximately 75% of the studies provided no information about race or ethnicity, and when such information was provided, 75%, 21%, and 4% of the participants, respectively, reported being White, Black, or other (i.e., Asian, Hispanic, American Indian, and unspecified). In a more recent follow-up examining 13 studies of psychoanalysis conducted between 1960 and 2010, including more than 1,100 analysands in total (Leichsenring & Rabung, 2008), Watkins (2013) found that only half of the studies included any information about gender, almost all of the studies did not include any information about race or ethnicity, and a majority of studies either did not include any information or provided incomplete information about education and socioeconomic status. The exclusion of race and ethnicity is further evident in case studies and case material, when the social identity of the client and that of the therapist are either not mentioned or discussed in a way that is not connected with therapeutic work. Psychoanalytic testing instruments, as with some other nonpsychoanalytically oriented testing instruments, also exclude social identity. Although the purpose of these instruments is to assess inner capacities and healthy functioning, they do not contain any items corresponding to sociocultural context, identity, or adjustment.

Psychoanalysis has been criticized for the lack of empirical validity of its concepts, its lack of attention to social and cultural realities of clients and therapists, and the insular nature of its practice and training. Throughout the history of psychoanalysis, theoretical and political schisms developed among theorists concerning the role of social and cultural context, plaguing the potential application of psychoanalytic ideas to a deeper understanding of the interaction between the individual and sociocultural context.

Although psychoanalysis has been criticized for an overemphasis on subjectivity and the lack of testability in academic psychology, developments in the cultural school of psychoanalysis would come to be critical to contemporary psychoanalysis, which places subjectivity and intersubjectivity at the core of interaction between the individual and the social. In the 1930s, classical psychoanalysis in the United States was challenged by numerous interpersonally oriented psychoanalysts, such as Harry Stack Sullivan, Erich Fromm, and Karen Horney. These theorists argued for the role of social and cultural factors, rather than biological instincts and drives, in the development of psychopathology. They focused on the interpersonal and social causes of neurosis, influenced by their interdisciplinary knowledge and interests (e.g., politics, culture, religion) and their personal histories. For example, Harry Stack Sullivan grew up in poverty and experienced challenges throughout his education; was influenced by Adolf Meyer, who shared an interest in ethnic and racial prejudice; and studied history and anthropology, attempting to integrate these disciplines in the practice of psychotherapy (Cushman, 1995). The ideas of the interpersonal, cultural psychoanalysts would spur divisions within organized psychoanalysis and lead to the formation of alternate training institutions in the United States. Although Freud's ideas were challenged by these analysts, ego psychology's focus on the interior of the individual seemed better suited to the values of mainstream, White middle-class society and to the political and social needs of those who held most power and privilege in psychiatry. Although their theories were not "mainstreamed" into American psychoanalysis because of the domination of ego psychology, the interpersonal, cultural psychoanalysts would come to have significant influence on contemporary psychoanalytic perspectives.

The Cultural School: Sullivan, Fromm, and Horney

In the post–World War II era, schisms developed between classical or Freudian analysts and revisionists, often involving political conflicts among psychoanalysts. Although ego psychology departed from Freud's emphasis on drives, it emphasized the role of social institutions in helping people achieve adaptation (Aron & Starr, 2013). Anna Freud, daughter of Sigmund Freud and a leader in ego psychology, examined normal or typical processes in development from a model that would continue to emphasize drives and defenses. Anna Freud and analysts such as Franz Alexander, Heinz Hartmann, Erik Erikson, and Margaret Mahler supported the idea of a "conflict-free zone," where functions of the ego, such as separation-individuation and reality testing, developed independent of the social world (Cushman, 1995).

Challenges to the reductionism of classical psychoanalysis and ego psychology were initiated by analysts such as Erich Fromm, Karen Horney, Clara Thompson, and Harry Stack Sullivan. Although they had distinct perspectives, these theorists, whose intellectual background drew from interdisciplinary knowledge, are known to have formed the cultural school, which focused on an interpersonal framework of psychoanalysis. Erich Fromm (1900–1980) studied with Freud and eventually criticized Freud for his dualistic thinking and lack of attention to the effects of patriarchy on his theories. He also criticized ego psychology as a "conformist dilution of European psychoanalysis" (Aron & Starr, 2013, p. 17), arguing that the new orthodoxy that developed in the United States actually had lost the essential spirit of Freud's ideas. He advocated for a revision of Freud's ideas to suit the needs of modern day problems, such as the preoccupation with material wealth over happiness, spiritual values, concern with social injustice, and relationships with others. He developed a theoretical perspective influenced by Marxist and existential concepts. Fromm (1956) emphasized the interpersonal aspects of emotion, such as love, and the importance of an individual's experience of freedom in emotional well-being. Along with D. T. Suzuki, a Zen master, Fromm developed a synthesis of Buddhist philosophy and psychoanalysis that centered on concepts such as self-realization (Fromm & Suzuki, 1960; Miovic, 2004). Unlike most psychoanalysts of his time, Fromm wrote about the importance of his Jewish identity on his theoretical ideas.

Karen Horney (1885–1952) was also a European analyst and émigré to the United States who studied with Freud. Horney's differences with Freud concerned the latter's lack of understanding of female development and sexuality. Horney argued that Freud's model of female development was conceptualized along male sexuality in a male-dominated society. She instead suggested that the ability to bear children gave women a place of superiority that men unconsciously envied. Horney (1937) emphasized the power of suggestions from society of the inferiority of women and explored women's feelings of resentment toward men. While agreeing with Freud that there is conflict between individual desires and the external world, she viewed psychic distress as being caused by social conditions and proposed that destructive drives are not innate but acquired through external demands in the family and society. The idea that women's biological drives are frustrated by social demands is elaborated by another interpersonally oriented psychoanalyst, Clara Thompson (1893–1958). Clara Thompson (1950), in collaboration with Patrick Mullahy, pointed out that biological sex was found to have meaning because of cultural ascriptions made to women and men. The authors further elaborated on the actual interactions between the analyst and the patient, not only the relationship in terms of the unconscious or the transference.

Harry Stack Sullivan (1892–1949) was an American-born psychoanalyst and a consulting psychiatrist to the United States military during World War II. He established a reputation for treatment of schizophrenia at Sheppard and Enoch Pratt Hospital in the 1920s. In recent years, it has been noted that Sullivan was a gay man and that his psychiatric ward provided treatment to gay men, many of whom likely did not have schizophrenia but rather faced challenges of being gay men in a homophobic society (Wake, 2007). Sullivan's milieu therapy involved talking with patients about the destructive aspects of their homophobic surround as the cause of their distress, rather than homosexuality itself. He chose male staff who were more accepting of homosexuality to decrease the patient's anxiety; the ward has been reported to have had an 86% cure rate for schizophrenia, which is especially remarkable because this was in an era preceding the use of neuroleptic medication (Aron & Starr, 2013). Sullivan characterized Freud's individualism as an "illusion," suggesting that people are not isolated but instead continually influence each other. He developed the notion of the self as situated in interpersonal interactions. In contrast to Freud's intrapsychic self, Sullivan's self is one that contains a drive toward health and is motivated by security needs, making attempts to reduce anxiety in interactions with others (Cushman, 1995). He believed that the therapist is a participant-observer who should be more actively involved than a classical analyst. Specifically, he viewed the therapist as an expert in interpersonal relations who, with the patient, forms and tests working hypotheses about the patient's past and present (Aron & Starr, 2013). For Sullivan (1953), the classical approach of the analyst interpreting the patient's unconscious life actually worked to increase the patient's anxiety in potentially harmful ways.

In the 1940s and 1950s, Sullivan (1953) increasingly turned his attention to social inequities, such as poverty, racism, and international conflict. Unfortunately, his involvement with social and political issues contributed to his isolation within psychiatry. Aron and Starr (2013) noted that although Sullivan disagreed with screening homosexuals from the military, he was concerned about their susceptibility to psychological distress in the military and ironically supported the exclusion of homosexuals in an attempt to support the military and the war effort. Nevertheless, Sullivan's social constructionist framework would come to influence contemporary hermeneutic and relational psychoanalytic perspectives. His position was especially threatening to existing conceptualizations of psychotherapy because it challenged the idea of a universal or objective clinical practice and existing political structures (Cushman, 1995).

As the work of the cultural school continued to influence psychoanalytic theory, "mainstream" psychoanalysis in the United States would be dominated by ego psychology and later British object relations theories and self-psychology. Object relations theory initially was developed by Melanie Klein, who viewed the self as containing innate psychic structures or "objects" that are produced innately and through partial, distorted experiences of the caregiver (e.g., mother). Social and cultural experiences did not play a role in the development of objects. The objects were driven by the life and death instinct (Cushman, 1995). Klein's theory brought psychoanalytic theorizing back to placing social interaction inside the individual psyche, in line with classic Freudian theory. Later, theorists such as Ronald Fairbairn, Harry Guntrip, John Bowlby, and Donald Winnicott made important contributions to object relations theory. Whereas Freud viewed the satisfaction of drives to be the primary motive in human development, object relations theorists conceptualized the gratification of drives as secondary to an individual's need for connecting with a primary object or caregiver. In particular, Donald Winnicott (1971) emphasized the relating within the mother–caregiver dyad and the importance of the caregiver providing a "holding environment" for the infant such that the caregiver attunes to the infant's needs. Through this interaction, the infant or toddler develops a sense of safety, trust, creativity, and autonomy. Winnicott's theory became highly influential in contemporary psychoanalytic practice and is discussed in more depth in a subsequent chapter.

Heinz Kohut, in the United States, developed a theory that also challenged classic psychoanalysis. Kohut's self-psychology focused on the ways in which people develop and maintain cohesion, esteem, and autonomy of the self (Cushman, 1995). In Kohut's (1971) view, the self develops through interactions between the child and the caregiver, and a healthy narcissism forms when parents empathically attune to the needs of the child. One of Kohut's greatest contributions to contemporary psychoanalysis is his attention to the subjective experience of the self and the role of empathic attunement in psychotherapy (Greenberg & Mitchell, 1983). Both object relations and self-psychology expanded the scope of internal life to more closely examining the relationships between the individual and his or her caregiver, and emphasized subjective experience, anticipating the development of relational psychoanalysis (S. A. Mitchell, 1988). However, neither the British school of object relations nor Heinz Kohut developed a theory that challenged psychoanalytic conceptualizations of sociocultural context.

CONCLUDING THOUGHTS

Contemporary psychoanalytic understandings of sociocultural context on the development and psychopathology have been influenced by ego psychology, the cultural school, object relations theory, self-psychology, and relational psychoanalysis. The essence of Freud's ideas remains alive in all of these theoretical approaches, and yet each framework proposes a unique understanding of how social context shapes the psyche. Although there are classical psychoanalysts who continue to argue for the universality of mental life and express concern over the dilution of psychoanalysis by extending into the inquiry of social context, contemporary psychoanalytic practitioners are increasingly concerned with adequately addressing the influence of social conditions on intrapsychic conflict, interpersonal processes, and symptomology. Returning for a moment to my experience with which I began this chapter, I want to point out that I was fortunate to have other, more positive and productive experiences with psychoanalytic psychotherapy in which my social identity was more fully considered. Psychoanalytic practitioners and therapists, in general, should be reflective of the history upon which their theoretical perspectives rest. This is essential to moving forward in developing theory that is rooted in contributions of the past and the context of today. The recognition of traumatic loss, backdrop of social change, political struggles, and privilege is further important for theorizing that is authentic and not presumptive of universal truths, but rather is one that seeks a more complex truth concerning mental life in a pluralistic society. This is perhaps more important than ever before in a highly technological American society, as we continue to struggle with social and political issues such as racism, immigration policy, and same-sex marriage that have an important impact on both a collective psyche and individual psychological well-being. These issues are alive in the therapeutic relationship, as can be seen in my interaction with my therapist, in which race, culture, and gender were palatable but unspoken.

Psychoanalysis as a profession in the United States entered a crisis in the late 1960s, when training institutes had financial troubles and decreasing numbers of training candidates of students. Women and nonmedical professionals have increasingly entered psychoanalytic training and now outnumber men and medical professionals, respectively. Over the past several decades, there has been a disentangling of psychoanalysis from medicine. A resurgence of somatic therapies (e.g., medications) and psychotherapies conceptualized from other frameworks (e.g., cognitive–behavioral, humanistic, family systems) contributed to the decline of psychoanalysis as a practice and to a rise of psychodynamically oriented psychotherapy (Hale, 1995).

Psychoanalytically oriented practitioners face several challenges today. Changing conceptions of scientific standards in psychiatry and psychology and questions concerning the cost of psychoanalysis have contributed to the uncertainty of psychoanalytic practice. Training in graduate programs in psychology has veered away significantly from psychoanalysis as the neglect of social and cultural factors in classical psychoanalysis and ego psychology has been challenged. Indeed, most graduate students in psychology are not exposed to the writings of Freud or other psychoanalysts or to the pluralism among psychoanalytic theories. However, the influence of psychoanalytic concepts on psychological practice and broader North American culture is pervasive; even as neuroscience research supports the importance of unconscious processes, empirical evidence for the efficacy of psychodynamic psychotherapy grows, psychoanalytic concepts are applied to community interventions, and film and social media reflect Freud's fundamental assertion that unconscious life is central to basic conflict between the individual and society.

A psychoanalytic perspective is uniquely suited to an understanding of complex issues such as gender, race, culture, sexual orientation and identity, social class, and dis/ability. Present-day realities such as information technology and the global economy offer new social and material possibilities, and yet emotional disconnection at the very least remains and perhaps is heightened as people struggle with interpersonal relationships (Tummala-Narra, 2008). A deep understanding of these issues and their relevance to psychotherapy practice requires attention to the interplay of unconscious and conscious processes, the intrapsychic and the interpersonal, and the individual and the social. It is, in fact, an urgent time to consider the contributions of psychoanalytic perspectives in developing complex conceptualizations of culturally competent psychotherapy practice. These contributions have not yet been integrated into mainstream academic psychology, and psychoanalytic scholars have not yet systematically included cultural competence as a core emphasis of psychoanalytic psychotherapy practice. The next chapter describes some major contributions of scholars from different psychoanalytic frameworks (e.g., object relations, relational psychoanalysis) to approaching issues of social and cultural diversity in contemporary psychotherapy. The work of these scholars helps inform a conceptual framework of cultural competence in psychotherapy from a psychoanalytic perspective.

2

PSYCHOANALYTIC CONTRIBUTIONS TO THE UNDERSTANDING OF DIVERSITY

At a professional conference in the mid-2000s, I sat next to an ethnic minority colleague I had met a year earlier. In the course of our conversation, I told her I was affiliated with a psychoanalytic professional organization. She looked at me with a surprised expression, and stated, "They let you in?" I responded, "Yes, things are not quite the same anymore." We continued to discuss what she had assumed about psychoanalysis and what I had learned from psychoanalysis. It became clear that my colleague had not been aware of more recent developments in psychoanalytic theory and was understandably apprehensive about the ways in which psychoanalysis had approached issues of social context and identity in the past.

I could relate to my colleague's apprehension because I, too, had completed my graduate training during a time when psychoanalytic perspectives and the lived experiences of ethnic minorities seemed incompatible. The 1980s were also a period of time when the early literature in multicultural

http://dx.doi.org/10.1037/14800-003
Psychoanalytic Theory and Cultural Competence in Psychotherapy, by P. Tummala-Narra

psychology promoted the use of cognitive–behavioral therapy (CBT) for ethnic minorities, based on the notion that ethnic minorities prefer solution-focused and problem-solving approaches and a directive style of psychotherapy. In the conversation with my colleague, I remembered how significant the multicultural literature has been to psychology as it brought to the foreground the centrality of race and culture. At the same time, something felt amiss because the literature provided broad-based descriptions of individuals and communities, rather than attending to the highly complex internal experiences of ethnic minority persons. I would often wonder about the place of the unconscious in the lives of ethnic minorities and, more broadly, the individuals who were not represented in any of the mainstream models in psychology (e.g., CBT, psychodynamic, humanistic, family systems). The overemphasis on problem-solving approaches applied indiscriminately to ethnic minorities since the 1980s marked a resistance to psychoanalytic models that previously had pathologized those not fitting mainstream "analyzable" patients. It also inadvertently dismissed any possible role of the unconscious in psychological development. When I read some of the early multicultural psychology literature during my training years, I found myself relieved to see that culture and race were actually being discussed and, at the same time, wondering, "Are these perspectives assuming that people like me don't have an unconscious, or that if we did, would the unconscious matter less for us than it would for a White, middle-class person in psychotherapy?"

Returning to the conversation with my colleague, I reassured her that psychoanalysis, much like other theories of the mind, was a work in progress. She responded by telling me that she was glad to hear that psychoanalytic theory had "moved beyond Freud" and that an ethnic minority psychologist who is connected with her Indian identity was trying to contribute to this shift. It was in such moments that I have been reminded that relatively few psychologists (clinicians and academicians) are exposed to psychoanalytic contributions to diversity and that many racial and ethnic minority psychologists remain unsure about whether psychoanalytic theorists have really addressed the marginalization of various communities (e.g., women, racial and ethnic minorities, sexual minorities, people from lower income backgrounds). It has become clear to me that developments concerning social context and psychoanalytic theory need to be brought into the dialogue on diversity in psychology because they provide critical insights into the unique, lived experiences of people from all sociocultural backgrounds.

There have been significant strides in addressing social and contextual issues in psychoanalytic theory. My aim in this chapter is not to provide a comprehensive review of the psychoanalytic literature and social context and identity, but rather to describe some major ideas concerning diversity that have been influential in transforming earlier psychoanalytic approaches that dismissed the importance of sociocultural context to more culturally informed conceptualizations and practices. Scholars, particularly during the past two decades, have explored the applications of psychoanalytic concepts, such as transference, countertransference, enactments, and therapeutic neutrality, to issues of diversity (e.g., gender, race, ethnicity, social class, sexual identity, dis/ability) in the therapeutic relationship.

It is also important to note that psychoanalytic scholars, primarily through their practice with clients of diverse sociocultural backgrounds, have developed new language (e.g., "racial melancholia," "Whiteness"); presented new formulations regarding health and pathology, including culturally embedded notions of development; and challenged psychoanalytic clinicians to reconfigure the therapeutic relationship based on an understanding of sociocultural context. Paul Wachtel (2002), in fact, noted that many psychoanalytic clinicians work in public hospitals, clinics, and agencies with poor clients, where they modify psychoanalytic concepts and techniques, including setting the frame. Scholars have further revisited John Demos's claim that American psychoanalysis attended to White, middle-class, heterosexual people, extricating people of their social contexts (Aron & Starr, 2013; Layton, 2004), and instead have moved toward a psychoanalysis that explores the layered realities of people on the margins of the "mainstream" population. There has also been a call for a reexamination of theory and intervention based on observations of and interactions between clients and therapists from various sociocultural backgrounds, and the place of social injustice and oppression within the therapeutic relationship, rather than only in the inner world of the client (Greene, 2007; Tummala-Narra, 2007; Wachtel, 2002).

Although the progression toward cultural specificity in psychoanalytic theory is a culmination of contributions by scholars from various countries (Akhtar, 2011; Doi, 1989; Kakar, 1995; Kogan, 2010), I primarily review the contributions of scholars within the United States because my focus on issues such as race, sexual orientation, and immigration is shaped by unique social and political forces within a specific national context. However, I recognize that this review of work being conducted in the United States is relevant to the ways in which practitioners elsewhere in the world may conceptualize aspects of sociocultural identity. I begin the review by describing the influence of object relations theory, self-psychology, and interpersonal and relational psychoanalysis on the conceptualization of the interplay between the individual and social context and the ways in which psychoanalytic scholars have transformed crucial concepts related to diversity. I review some major psychoanalytic developments in the areas of gender, race, immigration, social class, sexual orientation, and religion and spirituality, and address some new directions of inquiry.

OBJECT RELATIONS, SELF-PSYCHOLOGY, INTERPERSONAL, AND RELATIONAL PERSPECTIVES

Object relations theory emphasizes the role of social interaction in shaping the psyche, with a particular emphasis on the mother–infant relationship. Donald Winnicott, a British pediatrician and psychoanalyst, was most influential in American psychoanalysis in the post-world War II era. Cushman (1995) wrote that Winnicott was "devoted to children, respectful of the innate capacities of mothers, and intensely focused on the micro-interchanges between the two" (p. 253). Winnicott proposed that the mother provides a holding environment for her infant and plays a critical role in creating a sense of safety and trust for her child by interpreting and providing for her child's needs. Further, the mother provides a mirroring function through which she reflects to her infant an image or vision of the infant, which gradually facilitates the development of the infant's sense of self. The infant (and later the child) is able to develop an ability to be spontaneous, creative, safe, and true to his/her own impulses and feelings and to be alone and with others (Cushman, 1995; Winnicott, 1971).

Winnicott's perspective did not assume that the mother would be perfectly attuned to the needs of her child, but rather that a "good enough mother" makes mistakes and works toward finding more attuned ways of attending to her child's needs. When the mother does not or is unable to attend to the child's needs, the child's development is negatively affected in numerous possible ways, such as the fear of being abandoned or difficulty in expressing one's needs to others. A critical aspect of Winnicott's theory (1971) involved the function of play, as evidenced in the use of transitional objects. A transitional object, such as a child's teddy bear, contains qualities that are both real and fantasied and allows the child to experience a space that lies between his or her imagination and the real, external world. The child's experience with transitional space, without impingement by the parent or others, becomes necessary for the child's ability to develop a separate sense of self and transition to developing genuine relationships with others. These conditions (safe holding environment, positive mirroring, transitional space) were thought to be critical to the development of a "true self," whereas the experience of abandonment or overinvolvement of the mother was the basis for the development of a "false self," in which the child defensively attempts to please his or her mother such that a connection with the mother can be maintained (Cushman, 1995; Winnicott, 1971).

Winnicott's emphasis on the interaction between the mother–infant dyad became a basis for parenting among middle-class White families in the post–World War II era in the United States and moved psychoanalysis in the direction of attending to social interaction as it shapes the psyche and psychopathology. More recently, psychologists within and outside of psycho-analysis have drawn on Winnicott's ideas to better understand how broader social contexts have mirroring functions for individuals' psychological adjustment. For example, Carola Suárez-Orozco (2000), an expert researcher on the psychological experience of immigrant children and families, coined the term "social mirror," referring to the social and cultural forces that shape a child's identity. Suárez-Orozco has argued that although Winnicott provided important insight into the mirroring function within the mother–infant dyad, he neglected the role of systemic factors in shaping interpersonal relationships. Her extension of Winnicott's ideas to social mirroring is evident in responses of immigrant children across numerous studies. For example, in one such study (Suárez-Orozco, 2000), in which immigrant children from various cultural backgrounds (e.g., Haitian, Latino) were asked to complete the sentence "Most Americans think (people from my country) are . . . ," Haitian and Latino children most typically stated, "Most Americans think that we are bad." The experience of a negative social mirror or the negative perceptions from mainstream society and their profound effects on identity formation and psychological well-being have been documented in a vast number of studies with minority children and adults (Alegría et al., 2008; García Coll & Marks, 2012; Helms & Cook, 1999). Winnicott's ideas continue to be expanded in various contexts as they inform the internal experience of the self that is inextricable from social influences.

As mentioned earlier, Heinz Kohut (1971) developed a theory of the self in which the individual's sense of cohesion, esteem, and autonomy of the self is regarded as essential to psychological life (Cushman, 1995). Like Winnicott, Kohut's notion of the self developed in the context of the infant's interactions with her/his parents. Parents' empathic attunement to the infant/child is critical for the development of "healthy narcissism." The infant's merged experience of the parent–infant relationship is known as the *selfobject*, stemming from the parent's ability to manage tension, self-esteem, and self-cohesion (Cushman, 1995). Kohut's attention to the nuances of the self, particularly to the examination of the subjective experience of the self, laid the groundwork for deeper analysis of subjectivity in psychoanalytic approaches.

Relational psychoanalysis, drawing from the growing emphasis on social interaction and relatedness in interpersonal psychoanalysis and object relations theory and the attention to subjective experience in self-psychology, set the stage for exploring the influence of social interactions within the family and broader society on identity and development. Relational psychoanalysis has also been influenced by the work of psychoanalysts such as Harry Stack Sullivan and Sándor Ferenczi, who emphasized the role of subjectivity in the therapeutic relationship. Ferenczi, a Hungarian psychoanalyst and associate of Sigmund Freud, refuted Freud's theory of infantile sexuality. Freud had abandoned his conclusion that patients with symptoms of hysteria previously suffered sexual violation in childhood by a parent or another adult in favor of a theory in which unconscious fantasy related to sexual conflicts, rather than the reality of sexual abuse, was responsible for symptoms. Ferenczi's assertion that patients were in fact truthful in their accounts of sexual abuse eventually contributed to a split in his relationship with Freud (A. E. Harris, 2011). He also advocated for an active role of the analyst, including self-disclosure, and spoke of mutuality in the relationship between the analyst and the patient, all of which were radical departures from previously held notions of the analyst as a diagnostician and the patient as the recipient of a suitable treatment determined by the analyst (Rachman, 2007).

Relational psychoanalysts have been heavily influenced by Ferenczi's emphasis on the subjective experience of the patient and by the conceptualization of the patient as a collaborator, as described by Ferenczi and Sullivan. Adrienne Harris (2011), a leading relational psychoanalyst, noted that different psychoanalytic traditions (e.g., object relations, self-psychology, Kleinian, relational) in contemporary practice overlap with and influence each other, in contrast to the sharp distinctions that existed among these traditions in the past. Relational psychoanalysis was a theoretical turn in the 1980s that was initiated by Stephen Mitchell (1988) and developed by several of his contemporaries, including Lewis Aron, Neil Altman, Adrienne Harris, Jessica Benjamin, Irwin Hoffman, Emmanuel Ghent, Philip Bromberg, Muriel Dimen, Thomas Ogden, Donnel Stern, Owen Renik, Robert Stolorow, and Jody Davies (A. E. Harris, 2011). Whereas object relations theory and self-psychology shifted the one-person or drive perspective of classical psychoanalysis, relational psychoanalysis extended the dyadic or two-person psychology of object relations theory and self-psychology to a three-person psychology.

S. A. Mitchell (1988), while noting that Freud's most important contribution was the discovery of a method of explaining unconscious phenomenon and the making of meaning itself, challenged the source of authority in the analytic relationship. S. A. Mitchell (1988) pointed out that Freud had developed a method of inquiry that relied on an asymmetrical relationship between the analyst and the patient but that the treatment itself was thought to be successful as the patient came to "gradually assume authentic self-authorization" (p. 12). Some analysts (Kernberg, 1996) continued to espouse the therapist's position as involving technical neutrality, but Mitchell proposed that it is impossible for the analyst to assume a purely neutral and value-free position. In fact, S. A. Mitchell (1988) raised questions about whose subjectivity was privileged in the therapist–patient dyad and suggested that the patient's internal life can be understood through a process of "interpretive construction"

(p. 16), with the patient and the analyst together cocreating the meaning of the patient's experience. Further, Mitchell placed at the center of relational psychoanalysis the idea that the analyst's understanding of the patient's psyche is rooted in the analyst's own life experiences and in the dynamics of transference and countertransference.

Relational analysts have since extended S. A. Mitchell's revolutionary ideas to inquiry concerning the specific subjective experience of the patient and the analyst and the reframing of asymmetry and mutuality in the analytic relationship. Increasingly, relational scholars (Bromberg, 2006; J. M. Davies, 1998) have recognized the importance of multiple self-states and the fluidity of identity, both of which mark an increasingly complex model of the human mind and of the interaction among the psychic, interpersonal, social, and political. A major task of relational psychoanalytic psychotherapeutic work involves attention to self-states of the client and the therapist, fostering greater awareness of how one feels, thinks, and reacts in different contexts such that the client can better tolerate painful affect and gain insight into how he or she may influence others in his/her interpersonal relationships (Aron & Putnam, 2007). J. M. Davies (1998) described the self as "multiply organized, associationally linked network of parallel, coexistent, at times conflictual, systems of meaning attribution and understanding" (p. 195). In the relational view, the mind consists of multiple selves or self-states that coexist in states of tension and function to form psychic meaning. J. M. Davies (1998) further suggested that psychotherapy, particularly in the case of traumatic stress, necessarily involves the therapist and the client's attempts to experience a discontinuity within the self (e.g., self-states), which is associated with heightened anxiety such that defenses that preclude the expression of these aspects of the self can be addressed and a "cooperative compromise" (p. 196) among the different self-states can be achieved.

Intersubjective theories draw attention to how emotional experiences are shaped within an intersubjective field and view the analytic relationship as involving an interplay between two subjective experiences, those of the therapist and client (D. N. Stern, 1995; Stolorow, 1988). Relational psychoanalysis recognizes an interdependence of the therapist's and the client's perceptions and responses to each other (Ghent, 1995). Relatedly, psychotherapy attends to enactments, in which dissociated self-states of the client and therapist facilitate the repetition of unconscious patterns of behavior in their interactions with each other (Aron & Putnam, 2007; Bromberg, 1996). Enactments in psychotherapy are viewed as inevitable and potentially harmful because they can interfere with the goal of breaking through old, destructive patterns of relating. The therapist's ability to attune to the client while simultaneously holding the tension that can arise from contrasting subjective experiences of the therapist and client is critical for working through enactments. Further, the ability of the therapeutic dyad to engage with multiple subjectivities in a transitional space where they can spontaneously relate to each other, a stance known as the "analytic third" (Ogden, 1994, 2009), is thought to be critical in working through enactments and promoting change that is beneficial to the client (Aron & Putnam, 2007). Numerous relational psychoanalysts have further attended to the meanings of self-disclosure. For example, J. M. Davies (2001), in reference to the deeply intimate relational experience that characterizes relational psychoanalytic work, has written about the potential use of the therapist's self-disclosure in helping the client to access and recognize dissociated and disowned aspects of his/her experience, such as that related to sexuality.

Relational (S. A. Mitchell, 1988), intersubjective (Atwood, Orange, & Stolorow, 2002), and hermeneutic perspectives (Cushman, 1995) have further contributed to the understanding of subjective experience within the context of a social, cultural, and political landscape. Recognizing the significance of sociohistorical context, the hermeneutic perspective (Cushman, 1995) calls for attention to the sociopolitical role of theory itself in the healing process, the exercise of power, and social justice. In the subsequent sections of this chapter, I describe some of the ways in which various psychoanalytic traditions, especially relational perspectives, have conceptualized different aspects of sociocultural identity in psychotherapy. Although I have organized the following discussion by using sections that elaborate on psychoanalytic conceptualizations of distinct aspects of identity (e.g., gender, race, immigration, social class, sexual orientation, religion, spirituality), it is important to recognize that identity is not singular. Rather, every aspect of identity coexists and interacts with all other aspects of identity and potentially poses dilemmas and conflicts concerning privilege and marginalization with considerable variation. The sections that follow facilitate an exploration of psychoanalytic scholarship concerning specific aspects of sociocultural identity with the purpose of highlighting the significance of each aspect of identity and of laying the groundwork for addressing the complex and layered nature of identity.

GENDER

Psychoanalytic perspectives concerning gender have moved significantly away from Freud's conceptualizations of women and femininity as inferior to men and masculinity, respectively; from patients' reports of sexual violation as reflective of intrapsychic conflict related to sexuality (Herman, 1992); and from the dichotomous division of gender (Butler, 2000; Goldner, 1991; J. Mitchell, 2000). Perhaps most significantly, Freud's conceptions of sexual violation of women, as representative of internal fantasy rather than as real events, have been repudiated by feminist, psychoanalytic scholars. Judith Herman (1992) noted that the most common posttraumatic disorders are those related to the oppression of women. Herman has been a key thinker and activist in revealing the problem of sexual and physical violence against women in the consulting room, where "women had dared to speak of rape, but the learned men of science had not believed them" (p. 29). Herman's seminal work, informed by feminism and psychoanalytic concepts, elucidated the psychological experience of traumatic stress as inextricably tied to broader social structures and hierarchies that excluded and silenced women's voices. Her conceptualization of complex posttraumatic stress disorder encompasses the profound intrapsychic, interpersonal, and social costs of severe trauma on survivors. She emphasized the importance of recognizing physical and psychological captivity experienced by women and child survivors, a problem that often remains unseen today, and described the processes involved in psychological domination and control. For example, in describing the experience of captivity, Herman extended Winnicott's transitional objects, such as securing a photograph or an image of loved ones, as a way to understand how victims make attempts to preserve connection to others and to the self under prolonged isolation. Herman's contributions have had a significant impact on the conceptualization of traumatic stress among survivors and among subsequent scholars from a wide array of theoretical backgrounds, including feminist and psychoanalytic perspectives (Boulanger, 2007; Bryant-Davis, Chung, & Tillman, 2009; Courtois & Ford, 2014; J. M. Davies & Frawley, 1994; Fonagy & Bateman, 2008; Tummala-Narra, 2011).

Contemporary psychoanalytic perspectives concerning gender, influenced by feminism, feminist psychology, object relations theory, relational psychoanalysis, and postmodernism, place context at the center of theory concerning psychological trauma, gender socialization, development, and identity. Similar to feminist psychologists (Brown, 2010), psychoanalytic feminist scholars (Benjamin, 1988, 2002a; Chodorow, 1989; Dimen & Goldner, 2002; A. Harris, 2005; Kristeva & Moi, 1986) have underscored the significance of social and political systems, inequities, and oppression as backdrop to the devaluation and/or pathologizing of girls and women. However, feminist psychoanalysts carry an additional focus on the connection between sociopolitical context and psychic life. Specifically, unconscious processes and interpersonal dynamics are thought to be essential to individual meaning-making and interpretations accompanying gender. Jessica Benjamin, in her highly influential book *The Bonds of Love* (1988), explored how the relationship between love and domination among women and men develops in the context of a society that idealizes masculinity. Benjamin's view does not place women or men in an idealized position but rather proposes that domination and control, situated in social norms and structures, are related to a denial of dependency (Atlas, 2013). She suggested that boys and girls have separate differentiation processes. Masculine identity rests on separation from the mother, and boys separate from identifying with their mothers by denying dependency on them. Further, it is acceptable and even desirable for girls and women to be dependent and for boys to deny their dependency. Benjamin (1998) observed that the issue of agency is implicit in the idea of subjectivity and that authorship and ownership are implicit in the definition of activity. As such, she challenged Freud's associations of agency and activity with masculinity. Having a subject self implies that one has an internal experience and recognizes that others have their own unique experiences. In Benjamin's perspective, an intersubjective perspective involves the recognition of women and men having agency, authorship, and ownership over their own subjective experiences, reshaping previously held asymmetrical notions of masculinity and femininity.

According to A. Harris (2005), "Gender is personal and social, personal and political, private and public" (p. 175). As such, gender identity reflects inextricable individual and cultural meanings. Nancy Chodorow (1989, 1999) suggested that individuals form meanings of gender through drawing from existing cultural or linguistic categories and their own unique life histories in a way that moves beyond and even contradicts cultural and linguistic categories. In her view, people's conscious and unconscious emotions and fantasies recreate cultural meanings attached to gender. Muriel Dimen (2002) noted that although gender typically refers to the psychological and social aspects of biological sex, the implications of gender meanings are far more complex. In particular, gender is rooted in cultural representations, which inform how one comes to view the self and others. Dimen has written about an incident in which she asked a friend who lost a tennis match how he felt, after which he replied, "Like a girl" (p. 44). She used this as an illustration of how one can feel as though they are "out of gender," indicating a lack of compatibility with either masculinity or femininity. In Dimen's view, gender is constructed through the contrast between conceptions of "male" and "female" as determined by culture, interpersonal dynamics, and intrapsychic experience. Therefore, masculinity and femininity consist of different "moments of the self," (p. 57) rather than fixed features of gender. Thus, social constructions of masculinity and femininity create subjective experience, stereotypes, and the objectification of women and men (Dimen, 2002; Kaftal, 1991).

Dimen illustrated how the social, interpersonal, and intrapsychic dimensions of gender become enacted among women in the therapeutic dyad (e.g., female client and female therapist). She suggested that the female client and the female therapist contend with coexisting feelings of aggression, envy, competition, and intimacy as a longing for nurturance from a maternal figure.

These feelings are juxtaposed against the devaluation of women's authority and subjective experience. Relatedly, Emmanuel Kaftal (1991) pointed out that boys and men need a strong emotional connection with their fathers or father figures, in contrast to Freud's notion that men cannot resolve their ambivalence toward their fathers and therefore the relationship between a father and a son is composed primarily of opposition rather than intimacy. Kaftal highlighted the problems inherent to stereotypes of masculinity that can steer the relationship between a male patient and a male therapist toward denial or avoidance of emotional intimacy. Robert Grossmark (2009), among others, also recognized that feminist scholars have overlooked the multiplicity of men's subjective experiences and have made broad generalizations concerning men's lack of empathy toward women.

The exploration of gender in contemporary psychoanalysis has further involved the reconsideration of female desire, particularly the reality that women want both a sense of agency and a sexual subjectivity in contrast to objectification within a male-dominated social and cultural context (Elise, 2000). Dimen (1991), for example, wrote about how sexual desire tends to be dystonic for women, whereas sexual desire tends to be syntonic for men. Feminist psychoanalysts have explored the role of the interaction between socialization and intrapsychic conflict in women's desire. Benjamin (1988), underscoring the importance of societal expectations of women and men, challenged Freud's conclusion that the acceptance of passivity is an inherent part of girls' development. She proposed that passivity is connected with a lack of desire, a product of a girl's identification with her mother who is typically desexualized and thought to surrender her own will to care for others, as a function of structural power inequities across men and women. The representation of the mother as lacking subjectivity and desire is juxtaposed against the representation of the father as an idealized figure with agency who provides a bridge into the external world. Benjamin further noted that even in the case of a woman who is viewed as sexy, her stance remains as an object, and not as a subject, where her power lies in her ability to attract others rather than within her own desire. She elaborated, "If woman has no desire of her own, she must rely on that of a man, with potentially disastrous consequences for her psychic life" (Benjamin, 1988; p. 89). Relatedly, Diane Elise (2000) suggested that girls, similar to boys, want and long for their mothers, but unlike for boys, girls' desire tends to be repudiated in a family unit that is characterized by male dominance, inhibiting the expression of desire among girls and women. Women then become objects, rather than subjects, of their desire, maintaining the power imbalance in patriarchal structures. In psychotherapy, the lack of subjectivity among some female clients is evident when they report not knowing their needs. Marilyn Charles (2011) suggested that patriarchy is detrimental to women, who are "desubjectified," and to men, who are told that they are "feminine." She observed that a paradoxical ideology concerning gender pervades Western societies, in which equality is seemingly embraced and yet hierarchical dichotomies between men and women persist.

Gender, from a contemporary psychoanalytic perspective, is described as a process, fluid, and at times a core part of the self and at other times, tenuous and fragile (Goldner, 2011; A. E. Harris, 2002). A. Harris (2005) suggested that gender is a "soft assembly," involving multiple and layered drafts of experience. In her view, the complexity of intersex and transgender experiences draws attention to the fact that gender can be both "fluid and rigid" (p. 210). Unconscious processes, as evidenced in dreams, are not constricted by gender binaries. Benjamin (1988), in particular, suggested that self-representations of a specific sex can exist alongside a self-representation that is without a specific sex or one that is of an opposite sex. Contemporary psychoanalytic scholars value a gender-affirmative approach (Ehrensaft, 2014, p. 572), which assumes that all variations of gender indicate health rather than pathology, and that the goals of psychotherapy are to explore an "authentic gender self," develop resilience to cope with social marginalization, and challenge society to become more inclusive of all genders. Recent scholarship exploring transgender experiences has emphasized that, contrary to Freud's notion that gender is rooted in genital awareness, one's sense of gender actually shapes an awareness of one's genitals and meanings regarding sexual differences (Goldner, 2011). Avgi Saketopoulou (2014) described *massive gender trauma* as culminating from the experience of being misgendered or misrecognized as belonging to one's birth sex even after a child has expressed a different gender identity, and gender-inflicted body dysphoria, or the misalignment of the physical body with gender and the subsequent wish for coherence between the body and gender. From this perspective, both social and cultural intolerance for the trans experience and the internal anguish of misalignment of the body and gender identity should be considered together in psychotherapy. The therapist is in the position to help the client mourn multiple aspects of gendered experience, and to do so must examine his/her own anxiety concerning the discontinuity between the body and the psyche (Saketopoulou, 2014; Salamon & Corbett, 2011; Suchet, 2011).

Psychotherapy offers a transitional space that can hold the tensions arising from seemingly contradictory self-representations. A number of feminist psychoanalysts (Benjamin, 2002a; Chodorow, 1989; Dimen, 2002; Goldner, 1991) have elaborated on the importance of transitional space in deconstructing gender in psychotherapy and facilitating a therapeutic space in which both external realities of gender categories and fantasies concerning gender experience, and the contradictory feelings associated with these experiences, can be safely explored. Psychoanalytic scholars emphasize the importance of tolerating and respecting ambiguity and the variability of gender categories and gendered experiences (Goldner, 1991). It has been noted that gender is an interaction among various, shifting influences and that gender dichotomies themselves are influenced by cultural and psychological context, suggesting a mutual influence of the internal and external (Chodorow, 1999; Goldner, 1991; A. Harris, 2005; Layton, 2004). For example, several different developmental experiences may contribute to an individual's sense of rigidity regarding the self and others, which then exacerbates and perpetuates one's tendency to adhere to gender dichotomies. Conversely, the ways in which an individual translates social norms concerning gender can rely heavily on interpersonal dynamics, such as those within a family unit (Chodorow, 1999; A. Harris, 2005).

RACE AND RACISM

Psychoanalytic perspectives (e.g., relational, intersubjective, object relations, ego psychology) have conceptualized race as having profound effects on intrapsychic and interpersonal life (Ainslie, Tummala-Narra, Harlem, Barbanel, & Ruth, 2013). Race and racism as socially constructed phenomenon have been explored by a number of psychoanalytic scholars who identify with various racial and ethnic backgrounds (e.g., White, Euro-American, Black, African American, Asian American, and Latino/a American). Farhad Dalal (1993) noted that race remains a powerful force, despite being a socially constructed phenomenon. Race, according to Dalal (1993), is "stereotype disguised" (p. 282) because a stereotype is a means of categorizing and seeing others and the self. Race makes sense only in the context of racism, whereby physical features are used to signify the other. Race is not a fixed entity but rather determined by dynamic, shifting context. This is evident in American perceptions of which groups of individuals are categorized as "Black" or "people of color." Racist attitudes and discrimination have also been viewed as a function of existing internal objects characterized by intolerance and a sense of superiority, dominance, and cruelty (Hinshelwood, 2007). Hinshelwood (2007) proposed that attitudes concerning race are absorbed through interacting with a racist society and that possessing an intolerant internal object facilitates a "receptive hook" (p. 16) upon which racist attitudes rest. In his view, social explanations of racism, which locate the source of racism in economic and political factors, are necessary but not sufficient to explain how and why racism is absorbed and perpetuated by individuals.

Psychoanalytic perspectives offer an understanding of internal representations and conflict as they intersect with social constructions of race. Psychoanalysts, such as Dorothy Holmes (2006), have focused on how a society's attitudes and responses concerning race and social class have significant detrimental effects on the self for both racial minority and majority status individuals and communities. Holmes (2006) stated, "All transactions in our culture regarding race and social class are premised on the views that non-dominant races and the poor are inferior, and that Euro-Americans are the rich superior" (p. 215). Similar to scholars such as Elisabeth Young-Bruehl (1996), who suggested that racism, sexism, anti-Semitism, and homophobia are rooted in particular forms of character disturbance (e.g., obsessional, hysterical), Holmes related hatred, as it presents itself in misogyny, homophobia, and racism, to distorted ego functions. Hatred becomes a defense for the perpetrator of racism, misogyny, and classism. Whereas some people victimized by hatred may reject the hateful messages directed toward them, others who experience "success neurosis" are affected by these messages in a "primary way" (Holmes, 2006, p. 216), causing damage to the self and doubt in one's abilities, even when success has been achieved. Relatedly, Cleonie White (2004) wrote about some of her African American patients who expressed envy of White Americans' privilege in choosing to "forget" the history and impact of slavery in the United States, whereas the traumatic stress of slavery and ongoing racism carries into the daily lives of her African American patients.

Neil Altman (2010) extended the psychoanalytic concepts of projection and introjection to explain the intrapsychic construction of race and racism. Projection involves a disidentification, in which an individual attempts to disavow unacceptable impulses by attributing them to someone else and at the same time entails a connection to the other such that some type of affect, such as hatred, can be sustained (Altman, 2010). Altman's use of Harry Stack Sullivan's (1953) conceptualization of the self is particularly important in considering a psychoanalytic perspective on the construction of race. Sullivan's formulation of the self involves three components: the "good me," the "bad me," and the "not me." The good me involves the part of the self that one likes and shares with others, producing the least anxiety, whereas the bad me is the part of the self that contains negative features one tries to hide from others and oneself to avoid feeling anxious. The not me is felt to be the most anxiety provoking, with the individual repressing any qualities he/she cannot consider as a viable part of the self. Altman (2010) argued that for Whites in the United States, African Americans represent the not me. Intrapsychic experiences of painful and unacceptable aspects of the self, such as violence, greed, exploitation, passivity, and dependence, are projected onto others, and although these experiences are disavowed from the self, they remain in the unconscious mind, evoking anxiety and attempts to contain the anxiety. Further, in this case, African Americans may introject messages rooted in White images of African Americans. The consequential feelings of rage among African Americans are then pathologized by Whites and others, denying the subjective experience of African Americans and the reality of racism and oppression (Altman, 2010;

Wachtel, 2007). Wachtel (2007) suggested that although African Americans may be physically visible to Whites and other ethnic minorities, their psychological experiences often are invisible, and the physical othering of African Americans reflects the perceiver's stereotypes and fantasies of the other.

The role of fantasy in the construction of race and experiences of racism is further related to mourning processes within a society hinged on racial hierarchy, inclusion, and exclusion. David Eng and Shinhee Han (2000), extending Freud's conception of melancholia, described the experience of Asian Americans. They argued that Asian Americans cannot fully blend into mainstream American society (e.g., the melting pot) because they are faced with racial othering, and because of this immigration and assimilation become conflicted and unresolved. For Eng and Han, racism complicates Asian Americans' fantasies about becoming "American" or meeting an ideal of Whiteness, which remains at an "unattainable distance" (p. 668). The model minority stereotype refers to the notion that all Asian Americans are economically and academically successful and that they experience little or no personal distress. This stereotype is applied broadly and indiscriminately to Asians in the United States. The stereotype, through projection and introjection, is internalized by Asian Americans and facilitates individuals' and communities' loss of cultural and historical knowledge and heritage and of unique identities. Eng and Han (2000) coined the term "racial melancholia" to describe the psychic splitting that characterizes the Asian American psyche, in which one "knows and does not know, at once, that she or he is part of the larger group" (p. 670) (e.g., American), and one experiences both success and failure in the attempt to assimilate to the norms of Whiteness. Eng and Han further explained that Asian Americans internalize and enact the model minority stereotype as a way to be seen and recognized by mainstream society and in a sense simply to exist in the minds of Whites. Ambivalence is a defining feature of racial melancholia, in which the individual claims and disclaims these racial projections, impeding the process of mourning for identifications with the heritage Asian culture and ideals of Whiteness in mainstream society. The concept of racial melancholia is especially significant to a psychoanalytic understanding of race because it aptly describes the profound intrapsychic and interpersonal consequences of racism and exclusion.

Psychoanalytic scholars (Altman, 2010; Eng & Han, 2006; Leary, 2012; Tummala-Narra, 2007) have noted that racial representations facilitate images of the self and other as characterized along the lines of goodness and badness, intellectual and social competence and intellectual and social inferiority, and hypersexualization and desexualization. Specifically, the racial other becomes a container of unacceptable, disavowed aspects of the self and is oppressed such that the majority status individual can maintain his/her sense of power and superiority (Altman, 2010; Holmes, 1992; Leary, 2012).

Kimberlyn Leary (2007) suggested that the experience of being "raced" interferes with genuine engagement in interpersonal relationships. In previous work (Tummala-Narra, 2007), I have written about the impact of skin color on multiple layers of meaning within the psyche and interpersonal dynamics for Whites and racial and ethnic minorities. Skin color can be an indicator of one's sense of belonging within a racial and/or ethnic group and of one's sense of goodness and badness. Skin color also plays a role in acculturation and racial identity development as individuals negotiate negative conceptions of darker or lighter skin color in the heritage culture and in mainstream society. The negative associations to dark skin color and oppression both within the United States and elsewhere in the world lie at the heart of racial trauma. Traumatic stress rooted in racial and political oppression has important implications for intrapsychic and interpersonal processes, including anxiety about being attacked, identification with aggressive aspects of the oppression, collective memories of traumatic stress, and changes in cultural and racial identity (Tummala-Narra, 2005).

Taken together, contemporary psychoanalytic perspectives attend to how distinct psychological experiences of race and racism influence intrapsychic conflicts, identity formation, and interpersonal dynamics. Scholars (Altman, 2010; Holmes, 2006; Leary, 2012) have pointed out that the effects of racism, sexism, homophobia, and classism do not necessarily rely on personal experiences but that these forms of hatred have systemic effects that permeate unconscious and conscious interactions, including the therapeutic relationship. According to Michael Moskowitz (1995) and Neil Altman (2006), psychoanalysis became "White" in the United States largely as a function of turning to ego psychology, colluding with the medical establishment, and locating itself primarily in practice for the economically and socially privileged. With this background, psychoanalysis dismissed issues of oppression and the practical issues facing people in their daily lives. Altman suggested that this development within psychoanalysis speaks to the disavowal of psychoanalysts' own racial, cultural, and social class backgrounds. In contemporary practice, his analysis begs the question how may therapists systemically participate in and maintain social inequities along race and class lines, even though they may personally denounce oppression.

The examination of race and stereotypes has been increasingly seen as a critical component of psychoanalytic psychotherapy. Altman (2000) and Leary (2000) have noted the differential impact of racism on the day-to-day lives of White people and people of color and how these differences contribute to distinct psychological experiences of social context and the self. Leary (2012) described race as an "adaptive challenge," characterized by different racial subjectivities of racial majority and minority individuals. Wachtel (2007, 2014) has called for the need for White people to address the invisibility of their contribution to injustice and inequality and the need for Black people and White people to confront stereotypes and fantasies about each other's group that contribute to a highly problematic and sustained interaction across groups. In psychotherapy, "racial enactments" (Leary, 2000) occur when the client and/or the therapist express unconscious thoughts, feelings, and reactions reflective of broader societal relations concerning race, racism, and stereotyping within the context of the therapeutic relationship. Race, in Leary's perspective, involves a negotiation between the therapist and the client such that the goal of psychotherapy would not necessarily be to eliminate racial enactments but to collaboratively deconstruct and examine the enactment. The exploration of enactments entails the therapist and the client to attend to his/her own complicity in oppression.

The role of transference and countertransference and related enactments has been a central focus of the role of race and racism in psychotherapy. Lillian Comas-Díaz and Frederick Jacobsen (1991) used the terms *ethnocultural transference* and *ethnocultural countertransference* to describe the ways in which therapists and clients project to each other qualities that are characteristic of their own ethnic identifications in psychotherapy. Ethnocultural transference can manifest in various forms, such as an ethnic minority client's overcompliance to a White therapist because of power differentials between the therapist and the client or the deidealization of an African American therapist by an African American client because of the client's feelings of envy of the therapist's success (Comas-Díaz & Jacobsen, 1991). Similarly, ethnocultural countertransference is evident when a therapist creates emotional distance from the client to avoid feelings of closeness and/or overidentification with the client. The ability to work through ethnocultural transference and countertransference is seen as necessary to effectively exploring unconscious wishes, needs, and fears in psychotherapy (Comas-Díaz & Jacobsen, 1991; Hamer, 2006; Tummala-Narra, 2007). In addition, from an intersubjective perspective, racial transference is coconstructed by the therapist and the client, wherein the client's and the therapist's subjective experiences of race interplay unconsciously. Kris Yi (1998) observed that racial minority therapists are often more aware of the impact of race on the psychotherapeutic process than are White therapists, calling attention to the racial positionality of the therapist and client and its influence on transference and countertransference.

Contemporary psychoanalytic perspectives suggest that as therapeutic process reflects a microcosm of broader society, it is critical that feelings of ambivalence and vulnerability related to racial dynamics be examined through transference and countertransference (Altman, 2010; Bonovitz, 2005; Morris, 2003). Lynne Layton (2006) described the importance of attending to conflict related to the transmission and internalization of racial categories and stereotypes. Specifically, the transmission of racial constructions through one's family and community has been thought to be characterized by ambivalence, conflict, and splitting defenses (Layton, 2006). In other words, the internalization of race and associated social norms is not met without resistance. According to Layton (2006), "normative unconscious processes" (p. 242) reflect unconscious patterns that maintain the same norms causing distress, which are then unconsciously enacted in the therapeutic relationship. In such an enactment, the client's true feelings and identifications remain unexamined as the client attempts to minimize or avoid conflict with the therapist. Psychoanalytic perspectives continue to examine the ways in which social discourse or lack of discourse on race influences therapeutic interactions.

A salient line of inquiry concerns the experience of Whiteness, described by a few White psychoanalysts. These analysts (Altman, 2006; Cushman, 2000; A. Harris, 2012; Suchet, 2007) have written about the importance of the examination of the assumption of Whiteness as reflecting an accepted standard and their own fantasies concerning their racial identifications as Whites and those of non-Whites in order to engage fully with their clients. They have also examined the problem of White guilt that is produced as a result of past and ongoing complicity with oppression of racial minorities and how, if unaddressed by the therapist, it can have detrimental effects on the therapeutic process (Altman, 2006; Cushman, 2000). Melanie Suchet (2007), a White psychoanalyst born and raised in South Africa who became a U.S. citizen, suggested that Whiteness is "everywhere but absent from discussion . . . a silent norm" (p. 868) and that silence itself sustains power ascribed to Whiteness. Drawing from Eng and Han's (2000) conceptualization of racial melancholia among Asian Americans, Gillian Straker (2004) described melancholia among Whites as values, such as equality and justice, that are lost ideals amidst the realities of racism. An awareness of one's own complicity in oppression can evoke a sense of loss and shame (Suchet, 2004, 2007). These contemporary psychoanalytic perspectives (A. Harris, 2012; Suchet, 2007) are bringing Whiteness to visible ground and are beginning to address White guilt in a meaningful way. The recognition of the complexity of White guilt requires movement toward integrating the disavowed or split off aspects of past and present racial positionality, experiencing remorse rather than defensive guilt, and changing attitudes and responses that perpetuate racism.

IMMIGRATION

Although the issue of immigration had been designated previously as a social circumstance or condition that is less significant to the workings of the psyche within classical psychoanalysis, over the past two decades the psychological experience of immigration has garnered more attention in psychoanalysis. Various aspects of the immigrant experience, such as loss and mourning, language, culture, race, developmental shifts, and traumatic stress, have been explored by psychoanalytic scholars (Ainslie et al., 2013). The process of mourning has been described as a central feature of the immigrant's adjustment to living in a new country (Ainslie, 1998; Grinberg & Grinberg, 1989). For example, Ricardo Ainslie (1998) used the term "cultural mourning" to describe the process in which immigrants mourn aspects of the culture of origin which are deeply embedded within an individual's sense of self through a range of different experiences, such as being consumed by or denying loss. Mourning has been thought to be shaped by a number of different factors, such as the reasons for leaving the country of origin, exposure to traumatic events, and reception within the new country (Ainslie, 1998; Akhtar, 1999; Volkan, 1993). Mourning has been further connected with immigrants' fantasies about home, those involving returning to the country of origin and re-creating a sense of home in the new country (Tummala-Narra, 2009a).

Salman Akhtar (1999), a psychoanalyst who was born and raised in India and immigrated to the United States, has been among the foremost thinkers of the intrapsychic shifts that occur in the context of migrating from one country to another. Akhtar has noted that immigration is characterized by complex structural intrapsychic changes and identity transformation that result from culture shock and mourning of losses. Extending Margaret Mahler's (1970) ideas concerning the developmental tasks inherent to separation and individuation, Akhtar (1999, 2011) termed the psychological experience of immigration as a "third individuation." He delineated various factors that influence the psychological experience of immigration, including whether immigration is temporary or permanent, the degree of choice in leaving one's country of origin, the possibility of revisiting the country of origin, and the age of immigration (e.g., childhood, adolescence, adulthood), reasons for leaving the country of origin, the extent to which one has an intrapsychic capacity to separate before immigration, the reception by the new host culture, the magnitude of cultural differences between the country of origin and the new country, and the extent to which one can maintain one's role (e.g., career, education) from the country of origin within the new cultural context. Akhtar has further identified four major developmental shifts that occur in the process of adjustment to the new culture. Specifically, immigrants cope with idealized and devalued images of the country of origin and the new country because of the splitting of self and object representations as the ego is overwhelmed by the demands of the new external environment. Gradually, it is expected that, through a process of adjustment in the new country, the immigrant synthesizes the two or more contrasting self-representations and develops a hyphenated identity. In addition, the immigrant faces the adjustment of his/her sense of nearness and distance from others in the country of origin and the new country. Akhtar (1999, 2011) emphasized the importance of homo-ethnic relationships, through which immigrants can engage with the heritage culture in the new country. Activities such as listening to one's heritage music and connecting with loved ones via phone and the Internet are thought to be transitional objects that help connect the heritage and adopted cultures. In addition, because mourning is an aspect of separation and individuation processes, immigrants cope with fantasies of returning to the country of origin and nostalgia, which serve defensive functions of protecting the ego from feelings of frustration and inadequacy (Akhtar, 1999; Lijtmaer, 2001). Another major developmental shift, according to Akhtar (1999, 2011), entails a movement from a sense of psychological split between "mine" to "ours" (e.g., my country, my values) to a sense of "we-ness" (e.g., our country, our values), typically occurring when there is access to a transitional space in which the individual begins to engage in the new culture and language (e.g., movies, music, sports, literature). Akhtar's pioneering contribution to the intrapsychic experience of immigration is especially important because it has shifted psychoanalytic theory to a consideration of the depth of structural change that can occur as a function of the separation, mourning, and identity shifts inherent in the process of migration.

Akhtar (1999, 2011) and more recently Andrew Harlem (2010) have further addressed the distinct experiences of mourning among immigrants and refugees. Akhtar, from an ego psychology and object relations perspective, has focused primarily on the ways in which refugees cope with unresolved feelings of aggression and anxiety that complicate the mourning process. He suggested that refugees do not experience nostalgia in the same ways as immigrants because refugees typically experience severe trauma caused by war, violence, and/or natural disaster and an unexpected and traumatic departure from the country of origin. Harlem (2010), extending a relational psychoanalytic approach, noted that the experience of exile involves dissociative processes in which an individual faces challenges with remembering and bridging various aspects of the self or self-states. Harlem aptly observed that the experience of exile is characterized by an unintentional disappearance from and of those left behind that typically would help bridge time and space in the case of immigrants. In this formulation, the exile is without a home, "caught in the space between leaving and arriving, neither near nor far from one's homeland, without apparent love or hate of any place in particular" (p. 466).

Relational psychoanalysts have challenged classical approaches to the psychological experience of immigration. Ghislaine Boulanger (2004) noted that classical (e.g., ego psychology) approaches to immigration, such as that proposed by Akhtar, overemphasize the role of the intrapsychic impact of the mother and early object relations in explaining the consequences of immigration. She observed that, in classical approaches, one's culture and context of origin is seen as an extension of the mother and that assimilation to the new culture requires movement away from the primary objects (e.g., mother, motherland) or a process of individuation (Akhtar, 1999). Alternatively, Boulanger (2004) proposed that immigrants experience a loss of "contextual continuity" (p. 354), resulting in dissociation of aspects of the self that reflect the culture of origin. These dissociated self-states manifest unconsciously in emotional experiences, dreams, and enactments well into one's immigration, accompanied by a sense of despair regarding not being fully known by others in the new context. Similar to Eng and Han (2000), Boulanger suggested that immigrants identify as the other as a way of being seen. In her view, an authentic integration of culture of origin and new culture is complicated and cannot occur without loss.

The exploration of immigrant identity has further encompassed a focus on heritage language. Language has been conceptualized as a transitional space through which one's associations with the heritage culture and the new culture can be processed, with psychotherapy holding a potential for connecting both sets of experiences (Sharabany & Israeli, 2008). Early childhood experiences (e.g., object relations) and heritage language are thought to be intricately linked in psychoanalytic perspectives, and as such, they bear importance in the verbal and nonverbal expression of thoughts and feelings in psychotherapy (Akhtar, 2011; Amati-Mehler, Argentieri, & Canestri, 1990). RoseMarie Perez Foster (1996) wrote eloquently about the connection between primary or heritage language and interpersonal relationships. In particular, Foster (1996) suggested that for bilingual or multilingual individuals, each language contains implicit and explicit rules and can be associated with different cognitive and emotional experiences and ways of being. Rafael Javier (1996) further noted that bilingual people organize memories distinctively in their primary and secondary languages. For example, he observed that recalling an event in the language within which the particular experience occurred yielded more vivid and emotionally attuned recollections than did recalling it in a different language (Javier, 1996; Foster, 1996). Language, in Javier's perspective, gains meaning through its relationship with important figures in one's life and within specific contextual conditions. As such, psychoanalytic scholars have continued to deepen understandings of language and its role in intrapsychic and interpersonal processes.

Psychoanalytic explorations of the immigrant experience have also called attention to cultural values and the Western, White ideals that are inherent to psychotherapy practice in the United States. Layton (2004), drawing on John Demos's (1997) work on the reception of Freud's ideas in the United States, pointed out that American psychoanalysis has adopted White, middle-class, heterosexual norms concerning health and pathology and in doing so has colluded with the ideals of American optimism, in which there is a denial of pain and oppression. The idea of the American Dream is inherent to the fantasy of a self-made, individualistic person who becomes successful in a society that is rooted in meritocracy. The notion of meritocracy assumes that the individual can overcome any oppressive social and political condition as long as he/she works hard (Layton, 2004). A belief in meritocracy further perpetuates the idea that Western, middle-class, heterosexual norms are superior to the ideals of other cultures.

Psychoanalytic scholars (Eng & Han, 2000; Kakar, 1995; Roland, 1996; Tummala-Narra, 2014a) have begun to challenge the values inherent to the practice of psychotherapy across and within cultures. Alan Roland (2006) focused on the practice of psychoanalytic therapy with Asian Americans from the standpoint of a White, Euro American therapist. He suggested that conscious and unconscious cultural assumptions of individualism in psychological theories often contribute to the pathologization of Asian Americans and that it is necessary for the therapist to educate himself or herself regarding the client's worldview concerning what is normal and what is pathological. Roland observed, for example, that for many Asian clients, a hierarchical style of relating with an expert, such as a doctor or healer, based on age and gender, is normative within the culture of origin and influences affective experiences, communication, and transference and countertransference. Roland (2006) elaborated on the immigrant's experience of the bicultural self, which reflects an attempt to sustain the internalization of values from one's family and culture of origin and those from mainstream society. He used the term "bicultural tightrope" to describe the precarious nature of immigrant-origin individuals, particularly the second generation (e.g., those born and raised in the United States who have immigrant parents), as they navigate across different "modes of being and becoming" (Roland, 1996, p. 35). The exploration of the effects of immigration on the family system and the specific trajectories of first and second generation immigrants within the psychoanalytic literature is still in its infancy, although some scholars have written about the significance of divergent cultural beliefs among parents and children and related family conflicts (Ainslie et al., 2013; Akhtar, 2011; Bonovitz, 2005; Mann, 2004; Tummala-Narra, 2004).

The experience of racism in the new country and histories of colonization in the country of origin have been noted to have lasting effects on the immigrant experience. Frantz Fanon (1952), an Afro-French psychiatrist and philosopher born in Martinique, has written about the domination of European countries over people in the "developing" or "Third World" and its damaging effects on sense of self among its victims as colonialism worked to convince the colonized that they needed the colonizer to survive. According to Fanon, psychiatry contributed to colonialism by pathologizing aggression in response to domination (Altman, 2010). Comas-Díaz (2000) extended Fanon's ideas and referred to *post-colonization stress* disorder as encompassing the profound and lasting effects of colonization, such as identity conflicts, self-denial, and alienation, on colonized people and their descendants. The effects of racism and colonization among immigrants and their children in the United States and elsewhere is a problem central to psychoanalytic practitioners as they alter affective and perceptual experiences for both the client and the therapist. As such, scholars continue to expand the effects of multiple sources of oppression (e.g., racism, classism, sexism) and trauma on the psychological experience of immigration (Ainslie, 2009; Tummala-Narra, 2014a).

SOCIAL CLASS

Freud and many of the early analysts provided psychoanalysis to patients who could not afford treatment and in fact had established free clinics (Aron & Starr, 2013; Danto, 2005). A number of psychoanalytic practitioners (Altman, 2010; J. L. Darwin & Reich, 2006; Twemlow, Fonagy, Sacco, Vernberg, & Malcom, 2011) have revived an interest in psychoanalytic applications within community-based settings and have modified traditional notions of the therapeutic frame in their work with clients who cannot afford psychotherapy. A social justice orientation is being integrated with psychoanalytic concepts, such as transference and enactments, to address issues of social class and economic inequalities. Paul Wachtel (2002) and Neil Altman (2010) have argued against a long-held belief in psychotherapy practice (psychoanalytic and nonpsychoanalytic) that clients who are either poor or minorities or both are not suitable for the same type of treatment as White, middle- or upper-middle–class clients. Wachtel has asserted that modifying a therapeutic approach does not dilute the treatment or diminish its therapeutic effects. Further, cultural norms situated in the middle class can affect the therapist's understanding of crucial developmental issues, such as the therapist's evaluation of the client's cultural parameters defining separation and individuation as either healthy or pathological. Wachtel (2002) further raised questions about how a therapist from a middle-class background may evaluate an adult client's decision to live in the same home as his or her parents after getting married. Would the therapist conceptualize the client's decision with a consideration of social class and culture? The client and the therapist may, in fact, have different expectations of each other and ways of communicating with each other because of divergent cultural contexts connected with social class (Whitson, 1996). Altman has suggested that whereas a classical approach would reduce any therapeutic material related to social class as manifest content that is meant to be interpreted to better understand the client's drives and defenses, a relational psychoanalytic lens allows for an examination of the therapeutic relationship as situated in a broader social context in which the therapist and the client are each members of a particular social class group. Importantly, Altman (2010) pointed out that the membership of a particular social class group shapes the therapist's and the client's "assumptions about the self and each other" (p. 86) and provides the ground for projection and introjection by the therapist and by the patient.

In Wachtel's (2002) view, the therapist's position involves exploring both the effects of social disadvantage and marginalization and the actual disadvantage itself. Specifically, psychoanalysis provides a way to understand the psychic determinants and consequences of social and political oppression, such as poverty and classism. Javier and Herron (2002) have further suggested that for most therapists, especially those from middle and upper–middle–class backgrounds, working with poor clients often evokes a range of different feelings for the therapist, such as anxiety, hostility, and disdain. They emphasize the importance of the therapist attending to their countertransference and of recognizing and validating the reality of discrimination against the poor. The therapist must remain open to hearing the client's feelings about the therapist's class position.

Ainslie (2011) wrote about the ways in which class identities are an important aspect of immigrants' experiences in a new country. Class identities, reflecting either higher or lower socioeconomic status after migration, in his view are deeply embedded in individuals' unconscious and play a powerful role in interpersonal relationships. He underscored the psychological shifts that accompany class positions, particularly because there often is an intergenerational transmission of feelings (e.g., anxiety) and expectations concerning social class in that one of the reasons immigrants go to a new country is to seek better educational and economic opportunities. Bearing in mind that class identities operate largely in the unconscious for both the therapist and client, scholars have called for increased attention to the anxiety and related defenses used to avoid the issue of money and social class in the therapeutic process. Several psychoanalysts have noted that most therapists are apprehensive or uneasy when discussing money matters with their clients and managing their own guilt, shame, and anxiety about their class privilege (Dimen, 2006; Layton, 2006). Others (Hollander & Gutwill, 2006) have brought to the foreground questions about how psychotherapy can better engage the place of political conditions that shape class inequalities and the importance of recognizing and bearing witness to the painful realities of injustice.

SEXUAL ORIENTATION

Kenneth Lewes (1988) contended that psychoanalysis must confront its own countertransference to sexual identities and particularly the homophobia that has existed throughout much of its history. Sexual orientation and sexual identity in psychoanalysis have moved significantly away from early notions of homosexuality as either reflecting a regressive state or a pathological condition, particularly with developments in relational perspectives. Jack Drescher (2007) noted that over the course of the 1980s and 1990s, after the American Psychiatric Association rejected the Neo-Freudian perspective on homosexuality, a number of gay and lesbian analysts began to reveal their sexual identities publicly and redirect dialogue about sexual orientation. Richard Isay (1988, 1991) was among the first contemporary gay analysts to describe developmental processes that are unique to gay male children and adolescents. In particular, he described early attachment processes to the father and the mother, the nature of the coming out process, and the impact of homophobia and marginalization by others. S. A. Mitchell (1981) was also among the first analysts to question the application of heterosexual norms as the point of reference for successful treatment with gay, lesbian, and bisexual clients. According to S. A. Mitchell (1981, 2002), analysts should move away from focusing on overt sexual behavior and instead examine the quality of relationships and intrapsychic experience among gay, lesbian, and bisexual clients, just as is done when working with heterosexual clients.

Contemporary relational perspectives have been influenced by queer theory, which challenges the binaries that have been used traditionally to define gender and sexual identity. Drescher (2007), among others, has called for a psychoanalytic theory and practice that is informed by queer theory as it deconstructs traditional categories of gender and sexuality. Queer theory, rooted in lesbian and gay studies and feminist perspectives on heterosexuality and gender norms, suggests that sexuality has been marginalized by heterosexual narratives (Kassoff, 2004). Gender and sexual orientation, from this perspective, are social constructions that are acted out in the context of relating to the self and to others. Social constructions of gender and sexual orientation then determine an individual's sense of healthy adjustment by selecting whom one should love (Butler, 1995; Kassoff, 2004). Judith Butler (1995) suggested that the requirement for and the domination of heterosexuality in society results in loss and melancholia, which is disavowed. This type of melancholia can present itself when an individual rigidly adheres to social norms of masculinity or femininity. Queer theory and relational psychoanalysis call for a reexamination of cultural norms and stereotypes concerning gender and sexual identity. Analysts have elaborated on how gender and sexual identity are interlinked in social constructions, resulting in the marginalization of the individual's subjective experience. For example, the variations that exist among tomboys, who may be heterosexual, bisexual, or lesbian, are often collapsed such that girls who are tomboys are objectified along traditional binaries of masculinity/femininity and heterosexuality/homosexuality (Harris, 2005; Kassoff, 2004).

Relatedly, Ken Corbett (2002) highlighted the ways in which male homosexuality has been constructed along conventional notions of masculinity and femininity. Specifically, gay men are assumed to have "feminine" characteristics, such as passivity, thereby restricting an engagement with masculinity. He aptly stated, "Calling gay men feminine does not go very far toward understanding them; it simply displaces them" (p. 23). Corbett further pointed out that for many gay men, the experience of gender is mixed, neither masculine nor feminine, and does not rely on a model based on a binary of masculinity and femininity. The negation of subjective experience of gender and sexual identity and assumptions of what is "natural" (e.g., masculine/feminine, heterosexual) has profound consequences for one's sense of self and contributes to deep psychic and interpersonal distress (Corbett, 2002; Sand, 2012). This problem is illustrated in cases of regulation of sexual practices among gay men. Specifically, Jeffrey Guss (2010) suggested that when hostility and aggression are normative reactions to men engaging in anal sex with other men without the use of condoms, the potential for alternate narratives, such as those involving a longing for intimacy and connection and the expression of trust, are diminished, and gay men are viewed as objects, "criminals, mental cases, and sociopaths" (p. 129), rather than as subjects with their own narratives.

Relational approaches emphasize the deconstruction of subjective experience. One practical implication of this deconstruction entails a reexamination of what the therapist and the client assume to be "natural" with respect to sexuality and gender (Drescher, 2009). Relational psychoanalysts have noted the importance of engaging in an "open inquiry" (S. A. Mitchell, 2002), including the therapist's exploration of his/her own sexual feelings, beliefs, and attitudes concerning the client's experience of sexual identity and gender (Corbett, 2002). S. A. Mitchell (2002) wrote about the problem of the client's compliance with his or her understanding of the therapist's goals and wishes. Relatedly, scholars have suggested that therapists revisit the issue of neutrality, the use of language that reifies heterosexual normativity, and the use of therapist's self-disclosure as way to bring an authentic dialogue concerning sexual identity into the therapeutic relationship (J. M. Davies & Frawley, 1994; Drescher, 2007; Kassoff, 2004). Increasingly, analysts have written about their own sexual identities, biases, and anxieties concerning sexual identity and gender in their work with clients, a practice that helps to address the problem of consciously and unconsciously assuming heterosexual norms (Drescher, 2009; Kassoff, 2004).

The potential impact of therapists' own experiences with and/or feelings and beliefs concerning sexual identities on the process and outcome of psychotherapy has been an important aspect of contemporary psychoanalytic approaches. Isay (1991) wrote about his countertransference as a gay man working with gay clients and challenged the idea that the transference would be disrupted should the therapist disclose his or her sexual identity to the client. Rather, he found that the therapist's self-disclosure can be helpful when therapeutic work is conducted with a sense of collaboration with the client, placing the client's well-being at the foreground. Further, he underscored the importance of attending to countertransference, particularly that involving internalized homophobia, and the isolation that often is experienced by gay therapists. Relatedly, Bertram Cohler and Robert Galatzer-Levy (2013) recently suggested that the therapist's conscious and unconscious narratives regarding same-sex desire influence whether the client's subjective experience is seen and heard or negated. Indeed, issues of countertransference are particularly important because psychotherapy can recreate broader societal dynamics concerning sexual identity characterized by homophobia and heterosexism.

Several scholars have emphasized that the range of potential experiences as a sexual minority individual, based on individual history and other aspects of social identity, such as age, gender, race, and social class, should be recognized as significant influences on the subjective experience and the external reality of the client and the therapist (Greene, 2007; Pytluk, 2009). Beverly Greene (2007) wrote eloquently about all individuals having multiple identities but individuals belonging to more than one marginalized group often are invisible in psychological models, contributing to the partitioning of identities into hierarchies. She highlighted that various dimensions of identity (e.g., gender, sexual identity, race) for clients and therapists are experienced as more salient than others based on context. In Greene's view, the therapist's or client's defensiveness in examining the meanings associated with each aspect of identity is rooted in discomfort associated with power and privilege accompanying each of these components of identity. In a similar vein, Suchet (2004, p. 432) described how "power/powerlessness, domination/control, affirmation/exclusion, and rejection/acceptance" within and outside of therapy lie at the heart of the dynamics of social identity in the client–therapist relationship. She stated that it can become overwhelming to understand how power is negotiated between the therapist and the client when multiple identities are intertwined. In her writing, Suchet revealed that she is White, South African, Jewish, and lesbian, each aspect of identity holding varying degrees of privileged and marginalized positionality and experience in the United States. Psychoanalytic scholars continue to explore the meanings of sexual orientation and identity both within their own lives and their clients' lives, more and more with eye toward the intersections of multiple identities.

RELIGION AND SPIRITUALITY

Freud's (1927) notions of religious experience as illusion, neurosis, or regression to a symbiotic relationship with one's mother were challenged by several analysts, including Carl Jung, Erich Fromm, and Erik Erikson, and by various humanistic and existential theorists, such as Abraham Maslow, Carl Rogers, Viktor Frankl, and Rollo May. However, ideas opposing Freud's view on religion were largely dismissed in psychoanalytic models until the advent of object relations and relational psychoanalysis. Object relations approaches to religion and spirituality are influenced by the work of Harry Guntrip (1956), who suggested that religion is transmitted by parents to children in ways that can impose a sense of subordination or in ways that protect a sense of true self, distinguishing those who grow up to fear or hate God from those who trust and love God. Ana-Maria Rizzuto (1996), a psychoanalyst from a Catholic background, extended Winnicott's (1971) ideas concerning illusion (e.g., transitional space) and symbolism to support the intrapsychic significance of God representations (Roland, 1996). Winnicott's concept of transitional space, which lies between internal and external realities, supported the possibility of religious subjectivity. Guntrip's and Winnicott's ideas have been extended by object relations analysts who have examined internal God representations in parallel with other early relationships with caregivers, such as in the case of an individual with representations of God as omnipotent and loving reflecting similar representations of a parent (Lijtmaer, 2009; Rizzuto, 1996).

Scholars from various parts of the world have written about the importance of approaching psychoanalysis with an understanding of the cultural and spiritual meanings within different spiritual traditions (Akhtar, 2008; Kakar, 1995; van Waning, 2009). Over the past decade, several analysts from object relations and relational traditions have written about the significance of their religious and spiritual beliefs in their own lives and in their identities as analysts. A number of scholars have connected their psychoanalytic ideals with their spiritual values, such as that on introspection. Rizzuto (2004), for example, drew a parallel between her psychoanalytic sensibility and components of her Catholic upbringing. She pointed out that both perspectives value the need to engage in self-inquiry, a symbolic understanding of life, and the belief that transformation occurs in the context of confessing sins to a respected person. Aron (2004), in reflecting on the influence of his Jewish background on his approach to psychoanalysis, noted the relational nature of Jewish traditions. He connected the value of a reciprocal, intersubjective relationship with God and humanity in Jewish spirituality with his relational approach to psychoanalytic practice. Roland (2005) wrote about his spiritual life, which involves the study of Eastern meditation, and how his engagement in this tradition has helped him to feel more comfortable with the unknown and with becoming attuned to his clients. Other analysts, such as Jeremy Safran (2003), Jeffrey Rubin (2003), and Mark Epstein (2001), have described the importance of integrating the Buddhist faith with their psychoanalytic practice. For each of these analysts, connecting with their own spiritual experiences has expanded their ability to more authentically engage with their clients.

At the same time, these scholars (Aron, 2004; Rizzuto, 2004; Roland, 2005; van Waning, 2009) have revealed, in their writing, the challenges they faced in synthesizing their psychoanalytic ideals and their more private spiritual beliefs. In fact, some analysts have written about the precarious nature of openly discussing religious and spiritual beliefs with their colleagues and clients because conflicts concerning the "secular" nature of psychotherapy and related anxiety impede an in-depth exploration of the client's religious and spiritual life. Jeremy Safran (2003) suggested that classical psychoanalysis does not pose deeper questions inherent to religion, such as those concerning the meaning of life, and the individual's sense of belonging in the broader cosmos. In addition, in classical psychoanalysis, religious life was seen as located outside of the person and in a sense an imposition of the external world on the individual, rather than spirituality being an inextricable part of internal life. Roland (1996) further suggested that psychoanalysis and modern, positivistic science have contributed to the relegation of the "magic-cosmic world" (p. 146) to a devalued position within dominant society. Yet the spiritual world remains essential to many people across the globe. For example, in describing his work with Indian clients, Roland concluded that the self for Hindus is "open to the spirit world, to ancestors, to planetary influences, and to actions and experiences in the present that will impact on future lives" (p. 147). Roland underscored the fact that even when a therapist may experience these conceptions as foreign, he or she may be confronted by a spiritual orientation that is of great importance to the client's internal and external realities. As such, the analysis of transference and countertransference is thought to be critical as the client and the therapist discuss spiritual beliefs and practices and address any potential divergence in belief systems between each other (Lijtmaer, 2009; Tummala-Narra, 2009b). For example, the assumption that spiritual practices, such as astrology, are mere superstitions can be profoundly harmful to a client whose spirituality lies at the core of the self.

Recent conceptions of spirituality have shifted to a social constructivist view in which notions of God and/or spirituality are constructed and revised throughout a person's life (Spezzano & Gargiulo, 1997; Tummala-Narra, 2009b). In previous work, I have suggested that spiritual practices, such as prayer, can compose a transitional space through which a client and therapist are better connected to a real sense of self and that the presence of an "analytic third" (Ogden, 1994) or God in the psychotherapy relationship can facilitate authentic engagement with conflictual religious and spiritual identifications. In particular, as issues of religion and spirituality have continued in some ways to be marked as belonging "outside" of analytic work, it is especially important that the therapist allow for a space in which all aspects of subjective experience enter into the therapeutic space. The exploration of spirituality in psychoanalytic scholarship has further attended to intersections of identity, such as that between spiritual identity and cultural identity. In my own work (Tummala-Narra, 2009b), I have attempted to integrate religious and spiritual experiences as they intersect with my identities as a Hindu, Indian American, cisgender woman who is an immigrant, middle class, heterosexual, and able-bodied. Following the lead of feminist psychologists and psychoanalysts (Espín, 2008; Kristeva & Moi, 1986; Rayburn & Comas-Díaz, 2008), I have come to recognize and address the role of power, privilege, and marginalization accompanying the therapist's and the client's constructions of God images and spiritual practices and gendered interpretations of religion and their intersections with racial, ethnic, and sexual identities.

NEW DIRECTIONS

Various areas of diversity remain largely unexplored within psychoanalytic psychology and, more broadly, within psychology. For example, people with disabilities (physical, cognitive, sensory, psychiatric) compose the largest minority group in the United States and across the world (Olkin, 1999; Watermeyer, 2012). Although they are still in their infancy, developments in the area of disabilities within the psychoanalytic literature are emerging. In particular, Dan Goodley (2011) explored the process of splitting as a key problem in the exclusion of people with disabilities and the importance of a "social psychoanalytic" approach to disability studies. Other scholars have challenged the focus on physical "defects" in previous psychotherapy models, including psychoanalysis, and instead recognize how ableism and stereotyping are influenced by unconscious processes (Marks, 1999; Watermeyer, 2012). Psychoanalytic practitioners have also considered the problem of ableism in traumatic experience and specifically the vulnerability to violence experienced by people with disabilities (Goodley & Runswick-Cole, 2011). There has been a growing emphasis on disability as indicating both a distinct cultural and/or linguistic experience and a minority status, calling attention to the importance of disability communities (Olkin, 1999, 2002; Serani, 2001). Scholars have underscored the role of political and social advantages and disadvantages associated with ability status and related implications for the therapeutic relationship, particularly enactments of broader societal marginalization of people with disabilities (Chalfin, 2014).

There are various types of disabilities, so practitioners must attend to both the commonalities of the disability experience and to the specific, unique experiences of a particular client (Olkin, 2002). Richard Ruth (2012) suggested that therapists need to attend to variations in the ways that clients experience their specific disabilities as they intersect with other aspects of identity, such as cultural identity. Various defenses have been thought to protect the therapist from fears of disability, resulting in the exclusion and silencing of the client's subjectivity (Marks, 1999). These perspectives emphasize clinicians' responses, assumptions, and unconscious fears and wishes about the client with a disability and clinicians' willingness to rethink binaries of the client as either "tragic" or "inspirational" to closely hear the client's narrative (Watermeyer, 2012, p. 412). In addition, questions regarding physical boundaries and the therapeutic frame have been reconsidered. Scholars who have written on the topic of disability, many of whom have a physical or sensory disability, have noted the importance of addressing the ways in which experiencing a disability involves a complex negotiation of physical boundaries, therapeutic frame, language use, and transference and countertransference dynamics (Borg, 2005; Crown, 2008; Orzolek-Kronner & DeSimone, 2012; Serani, 2001; Watermeyer, 2012). For example, Nancy Crown (2008) wrote about how psychotherapy conducted in sign language with culturally deaf clients may reveal aspects of the client's and therapist's intrapsychic life that are not possible to access through spoken language. Brian Watermeyer (2012) pointed out the importance of therapists' attending to their disability-related anxiety rooted in socialization, assumptions, and unconscious fantasies about a client with a disability such that social inequities are not reproduced in psychotherapy. Further, he examined the specific ways in which his countertransference as a therapist with severe visual impairment may affect his interactions with his clients.

Interest concerning multiple identities and the intersections of these identities, such as those between race and gender or between immigration and social class, has been steadily increasing in psychoanalytic theorizing (Ainslie et al., 2013; Greene, 2007; Ruth, 2012; Suchet, 2004; Tummala-Narra, 2007, 2014a). The psychoanalytic conceptualization of identity as complex, multidimensional, fluid, variable, and conflictual is particularly relevant to approaching issues of sociocultural context in psychotherapy. Individuals construct their internal experiences through their perceptions and feelings produced in interactions with others. These internal experiences (e.g., objects) are then thought to organize meanings attached to significant people and events in one's life (Ruth, 2012). From a psychoanalytic perspective, the therapist's ability to create space to engage with various aspects of the client's identity is critical for therapeutic change. Each area of psychoanalytic inquiry (gender, race, immigration, social class, sexual orientation and identity, religion and spirituality, dis/ability) that I have described thus far has advanced theory and applications in its own right and at the same time raises important questions about the intersections of multiple social identities and their implications for psychological development, health, and pathology. All of these areas of scholarship, separately and together, call for the need to attend to culture and context and establish ground for a necessary framework of a culturally informed psychoanalytic approach to psychotherapy.

SUMMARY

There has been notable psychoanalytic scholarship exploring the application of psychoanalytic concepts, such as unconscious processes, transference, countertransference, and enactments, to the study of diversity. Scholars have developed new language, such as racial enactments, third individuation, and normative unconscious processes, to describe the nuances of sociocultural experience and identity. Psychoanalytic contributions to diversity focus on the external realities and subjective experiences of the individual. Although this chapter focuses on distinct aspects of sociocultural identity (gender, race, immigration, social class, sexual orientation and identity, religion and spirituality, dis/ability), drawn primarily from the work of object relations and relational psychoanalytic scholars, multiplicity is a defining feature of identity. Because of this, psychoanalytic psychotherapy emphasizes the interaction of multiple aspects of sociocultural identities. It is worth noting that psychoanalytic theory, as is true of all theories, is a work in progress with regard to issues of diversity. Psychoanalytic scholars continue to broaden and deepen understandings of areas of diversity that have received relatively sparse attention. The next chapter, drawing on psychoanalytic contributions to the study of diversity, outlines a systematic approach to addressing sociocultural context in psychoanalytic psychotherapy.

3

CULTURAL COMPETENCE FROM A PSYCHOANALYTIC PERSPECTIVE

A supervisee told me, in her presentation of a 25-year-old Puerto Rican female client, that she thought her client's frequent contact with her parents was unusual and perhaps that the client was enmeshed in her relationship with her parents. Then, my supervisee, a White Euro American woman, asked me whether I thought that the client's frequent contact with her parents was "a cultural thing." I responded to my supervisee by asking her to engage with me in a discussion about how we can decide whether a client's feelings, thoughts, and behaviors are determined by culture or by something other than culture. When faced with helping a person whose cultural background differs from that of ours in some way, we grapple with how to connect fully with someone who seems to think, feel, and behave in ways that are less familiar to us. In the mental health professions, we often hear the question from students and faculty, "How many of the client's issues are cultural?"

Adapted from "Cultural Competence as a Core Emphasis of Psychoanalytic Psychotherapy," by P. Tummala-Narra, 2015, *Psychoanalytic Psychology*, *32*, pp. 275–292. Copyright 2015 by the American Psychological Association.

http://dx.doi.org/10.1037/14800-004

I, too, have engaged with this question, although as I have come to better understand the lives of individuals identified with various cultural contexts, it has become increasingly clear to me that the individual and the cultural cannot be separated. Rather, we should ask how the individual and the cultural shape each other across time and in relation to others. We tend to draw an artificial dichotomy between the psyche and culture largely as a function of our difficulty with not knowing. Yet even when we are working with a client who appears culturally similar to us in some way, we are apt to dismiss significant differences in perspectives and life histories as a function of assuming familiarity. Further, it is interesting to consider that when the therapist and the client are both of dominant sociocultural backgrounds, it is less likely that an unfamiliar response from the client would be questioned as a "cultural thing."

Contemporary society both within and outside of the United States reflects an increasingly culturally, racially, linguistically, and socioeconomically diverse population. For example, if we consider the category of "race" only, more than one third of the U.S. population identifies as racial minorities (African American or Black, American Indian or Native Alaskan, Asian, Native Hawaiian or Pacific Islander, Hispanic or Latino, Multiracial; U.S. Census Bureau, 2010). Among new immigrants to the United States, more than three fourths have origins in Asia, Latin America, the Caribbean, Africa, and the Middle East (U.S. Census Bureau, 2010).

Racial and ethnic factors intersect with a multitude of other experiences, such as those related to gender, sexual orientation, social class, immigration status, spiritual beliefs, and dis/ability, to shape identity and interpersonal interactions. The complicated ways in which sociocultural context and individual life histories influence each other require mental health professionals and researchers to attend to an increasingly layered intersubjective space (J. E. Davies, 2011). The growing diversity within the United States and the underutilization of mental health services among marginalized populations (e.g., racial and ethnic minorities; American Psychological Association, 2012) call for a conceptualization of mental health practice that recognizes the unique needs and experiences of people adapting to multiple, often culturally divergent, social contexts. Although a number of psychological approaches to sociocultural issues, particularly those rooted in multicultural psychology and feminist psychology, have been and continue to be critical to addressing the needs of diverse populations in psychotherapy, I argue that a culturally informed psychoanalytic framework is necessary for addressing the complexities of sociocultural context.

In this chapter, I extend existing psychoanalytic contributions to the understanding of diversity to a more systematic inclusion and integration of cultural competence as a core, essential component of psychoanalytic theory and practice. In the following sections, I discuss how cultural competence has been defined in academic and professional psychology, existing descriptions of central features of psychoanalytic and psychodynamic psychotherapies, and overlaps between psychoanalytic theory and multicultural psychology. I then propose a culturally informed psychoanalytic framework that expands existing psychoanalytic theory and understandings of cultural competence more broadly in psychology.

CULTURAL COMPETENCE IN PSYCHOLOGY

Multiculturalism, identified as the "fourth force" in psychology (Pedersen, 1991), aims to "encourage inclusion and enhances our ability to recognize ourselves in others" (Comas-Díaz, 2011). The multicultural counseling movement in mental health paralleled the Civil Rights movement of the 1950s and 1960s (Arredondo & Perez, 2003; Hurley & Gerstein, 2013). Psychologists began to challenge the universal applications of psychotherapy approaches rooted in Euro American cultural values and norms. The multicultural movement in psychology, along with feminist psychology, challenged traditional approaches to psychotherapy for ignoring issues of power, privilege, and more broadly social context. From this view, Western based psychotherapies, such as psychoanalytic, cognitive–behavioral, and humanistic therapies have historically decontextualized, ahistoricized, and depoliticized individual development. Scholars such as Abram Kardiner and Georges Devereaux, using a psychoanalytic-anthropological framework, challenged the cross-cultural application of psychoanalytic ideas, and a number of psychoanalysts in the middle of the 20th century, such as Eric Fromm, Karen Horney, Harry Stack Sullivan, and Erik Erikson, argued that development is shaped by contextual issues that vary across cultures and time periods. In the 1970s, 1980s, and 1990s, American psychiatrists and psychologists who took an anthropological perspective, such as Arthur Kleinman (1995), focused on culturally distinct explanatory models of distress. However, as Comas-Díaz (2011) noted, psychiatric and psychological anthropology, and the cultural school of psychoanalysis did not develop specific methods to translate the theoretical understandings of culture and context to clinical practice.

Multicultural psychology, on the other hand, involved a turn toward new models that would explain minority and majority group identities as rooted in the context of particular social (gendered and racialized) interactions. The new frameworks that emerged recognized that psychotherapy that decontextualized, apoliticized, and ahistoricized development may actually contribute to internalized oppression and a compromised sense of agency (Atkinson, Morten, & Sue, 1998; Comas-Díaz, 2011; Helms, Nicolas, & Green, 2010). The American

Psychiatric Association (1994) published the cultural formulation and culture-bound syndromes in response to the increasing awareness of the role of culture in diagnosis. The National Association of Social Workers (1999, 2007) adopted a code of ethics that integrated the importance of respecting individuals' cultural contexts, recognizing strengths in all cultures, and validating individuals' experiences with social oppression. The American Psychological Association (APA) developed guidelines for providers of services to ethnic, linguistic, and culturally diverse clients, and it was not until 2003 that the APA approved its *Guidelines on Multicultural Education, Training, Research, Practice, and Organizational Change*. These guidelines support the place of context in a client's life and call for culturally competent practice, including using culturally appropriate assessment tools and psychological tests, the inclusion of a broad range of psychological interventions, and the inclusion of culture-specific healing interventions (Comas-Díaz, 2011).

Cultural competence developed as a framework in mental health in the 1970s and 1980s to address therapists' neglect of sociocultural context in the client's life and its impact on psychotherapy process (Kirmayer, 2012). Pioneering work by Derald Wing Sue (2001) and Stanley Sue (1998), among others (Arredondo & Toporek, 2004; Pedersen, 1991; Pope-Davis, Liu, Toporek, & Brittan-Powell, 2001), responded to the recognition that psychology had not adequately addressed issues of oppression and discrimination and that psychotherapy itself becomes a mechanism of oppression when it characterizes racial and cultural minorities as deviant. *Cultural competence* refers to a process or an orientation that is not wedded to any specific technique but rather involves "a way of construing the therapeutic encounter" (S. Sue, 2003, p. 968). Stanley Sue (1998) suggested that the essence of cultural competence involves scientific mindedness, which encourages therapists to resist premature conclusions about clients who are from a different sociocultural context than themselves; dynamic sizing, which involves the therapist's ability to appropriately generalize and individualize the client's experiences such that stereotyping is minimized; and culture-specific expertise, which involves the therapist's specific knowledge about his or her own sociocultural context and that of the clients with whom he or she works. Derald Wing Sue (2001) identified several obstacles to cultural competence, such as the difficulty of addressing one's personal biases, the tendency to avoid unpleasant topics such as racism and homophobia and accompanying emotions, and the challenge of accepting responsibility for actions that may directly or indirectly contribute to social injustice.

D. W. Sue's conceptual framework (2001) for organizing the multiple dimensions of cultural competence has been among the most influential paradigms for cultural competence in psychology. This approach involves the need to address universal, group, and individual levels of personal identity, emphasizing that therapists tend not to attend to the influence of individual's connection with groups, such as ethnic or religious groups, on their psychological well-being. In this perspective, cultural competence is linked with social justice, providing access to appropriate, relevant mental health services for all people (D. W. Sue, 2001). Culturally competent therapists aim to engage with several tasks: (a) develop (therapist's) self-awareness; (b) develop general knowledge about multicultural issues and the impact of various cultural group membership on clients; (c) develop a sense of multicultural self-efficacy, or the therapist's sense of confidence in delivering culturally competent care; (d) understand unique cultural factors; (e) develop an effective counseling working alliance in which mutuality and collaboration are emphasized; and (f) develop intervention skills in working with culturally diverse clients (Constantine & Ladany, 2001; D. W. Sue, 2001).

Multicultural psychology has expanded significantly over the past two decades with respect to research, education, and clinical practice. Multicultural issues have been explored by practitioners and scholars who identify with a variety of different theoretical orientations (e.g., cognitive–behavioral, psychodynamic, humanistic, feminist, liberation psychology, integrative, eclectic). One aim of scholars within multicultural psychology has been to create awareness of the unique psychosocial experiences of marginalized groups, such as racial and ethnic minorities; lesbian, gay, bisexual, transgender, and questioning or queer (LGBTQ) individuals; and immigrants, particularly in the United States (Casas & Corral, 2000; Comas-Díaz & Greene, 2013). Scholars have written about the specific knowledge and skills required to work effectively with different ethnic groups in an effort to adapt to the needs of the client and his/her cultural values, beliefs, and traditions in psychotherapy (Comas-Díaz, 2006; Gone & Trimble, 2012; Inman & DeBoer Kreider, 2013; D. W. Sue, Gallardo, & Neville, 2014). Research and clinical scholarship in the area of multicultural psychology has also encompassed attention to the central role of racial identity and ethnic identity in psychological well-being (Helms, 1990; Phinney, 1996). For example, Janet Helms (1990) developed a model of racial identity that aims to address intrapsychic and interpersonal reactions to societal constructions of race and the realities of racism. Helms's people of color racial identity model (1990), extending an earlier framework of racial identity proposed by William Cross (1978), describes specific ego statuses that correspond to individuals' internalization and negotiation of racism:

- *conformity*: reflecting an adaptation to White mainstream definitions of one's group; *dissonance*: involving disorientation and confusion regarding racial experiences and a recognition of a lack of belonging in White mainstream society;

- *immersion*: characterized by an idealization of one's socioracial group and devaluation of the White majority group;
- *emersion*: reflecting a sense of well-being and solidarity from engaging within one's own socioracial group;
- *internalization*: consisting of a positive sense of acceptance of one's own socioracial group and a growing ability to objectively assess and respond to Whites; and
- *integrative awareness*: involving a developing capacity to value one's identities (socioracial and mainstream) and collaborate with people in other marginalized groups.

In a similar vein, Helms (1990) developed a model for White racial identity, which assumes that Whites tend to develop a false sense of superiority and privilege, and as such, racial identity development involves the overcoming of internalized racism and movement toward a realistic and positive collective racial identity.

Attention to particular aspects of racial and ethnic experience for specific marginalized groups has been critical to new conceptualizations of individuals' responses to sociocultural conditions. Over the past decade, multicultural psychologists have proposed frameworks of organizing sociocultural influences on individual development, psychological well-being, and psychotherapy process. Pamela Hays (2007, 2016), for example, proposed an approach organizing sociocultural influences on psychological well-being, known as the ADDRESSING framework. This acronym ADDRESSING refers to various categories that should be considered by the therapist in formulating assessment and psychotherapy: Age (generation), Developmental and acquired Disabilities, Religion, Ethnicity, Socioeconomic status, Sexual orientation, Indigenous heritage, National origin, and Gender. Martin La Roche (2013) provided a framework of culturally competent psychotherapy that examines the interactions among individual, relational, and contextual factors, with the therapeutic relationship as the central point of analysis. Various scholars in multicultural psychology have noted the importance of the therapist's self-examination of values, assumptions, and biases, and contribution to the therapeutic relationship (Comas-Díaz, 2012; Hays, 2007; La Roche, 2013). An integration of multiple approaches to cultural competence (e.g., ADDRESSING framework) is evident in Lillian Comas-Díaz's (2012) "multicultural care" perspective, involving the therapist's reflexive self-examination, cultural empathy, and cultural humility. Multicultural psychology has also increasingly attended to the role of advocacy in psychotherapy practice. Competencies in advocacy, in fact, have focused on the need for practitioners to help clients and communities address systemic barriers to appropriate resources and care (Toporek, Lewis, & Crethar, 2009).

Considering the importance of attending to social, political, and cultural contexts, it has been suggested that practitioners can serve as cultural brokers and advocates, a task that is especially helpful for people who are socially marginalized in connecting with resources (Gallardo, Yeh, Trimble, & Parham, 2012).

Although the multicultural movement has been a major influence in research and practice in psychology and continues to provide important knowledge concerning the experiences of minority individuals and communities, approaches to cultural competence have been criticized by mental health professionals. For example, literature concerning cultural competence has been criticized for reducing culture to ascribed or self-assigned membership to a specific group, contributing to a view of culture as characterized by fixed features that are disconnected from the individual's life history (Fowers & Richardson, 1996; Kirmayer, 2012; La Roche, 2005). Relatedly, James Hansen (2010) observed that psychoanalytic theory has been dismissed in its entirety because many psychologists have little or no exposure to developments in postmodern psychoanalytic perspectives (e.g., relational, hermeneutic). Among Hansen's recommendations for new directions in multicultural psychology is the integration of the contributions of contemporary psychoanalytic perspectives to the understanding of intraindividual diversity or the multiple aspects of being and existing within individuals.

For many practitioners and academicians, the term *cultural competence* often evokes feelings of anger, helplessness, and frustration. Interestingly, similar to the way the word *feminist* is received in contemporary society, this term can even be experienced at times as oppressive and burdensome. The use of the term *competence* has been criticized for implying that the clinician should become a technical expert, achieving certain presumed outcomes, rather than an expert who engages in an evolving process of understanding sociocultural issues with the client. Scholars have cautioned against the institutionalization of cultural competence because of the potential for constricting definitions of successful outcomes in psychotherapy (Kirmayer, 2012). Alternatively, theorists have proposed that the concept of competence be broadened such that culturally responsive and competent treatment be defined to be more inclusive of a variety of different therapeutic approaches. Some mental health professionals have also recently advocated for an expansion of multicultural competencies to include an international focus, drawing attention to increasing economic and cultural interconnectedness in contemporary society (Hurley & Gerstein, 2013). Further, although advances in multicultural psychology have been driven by psychologists who identify with a variety of different theoretical orientations, conceptual frameworks rooted in specific theoretical traditions that are modified as a function of sociocultural understandings are only emerging in psychology. Rather, "traditional" frameworks, such as psychoanalytic theory, have been largely set aside in the multicultural literature, contributing to the neglect of critical aspects of human experience and of the therapeutic process.

On a practical level, clinicians struggle with the application of multicultural guidelines because they typically have little support during and beyond their training years in the translation of these guidelines to their interactions with clients in psychotherapy (Tummala-Narra, Singer, Li, Esposito, & Ash, 2012). Although many programs in counseling psychology and clinical psychology now require a course in cultural diversity, with the hope of implementing these principles of cultural competence, there is a great deal of variation in definitions and implementation of cultural competence in training and beyond, the receptivity to this framework, and the evaluation of cultural competence in practice. Much of the criticism of existing approaches to cultural competence in professional psychology centers on the complexity of navigating across and within individual, interpersonal, and systemic issues relevant to the client, therapist, and therapeutic process, and of addressing the dynamic nature of culture itself. A psychoanalytic perspective can facilitate an understanding of why the implementation of cultural competence requires a deeper examination of social context and identity.

CENTRAL FEATURES OF PSYCHOANALYTIC PSYCHOTHERAPY

The conceptualization of cultural competence from a psychoanalytic perspective requires an understanding of key features of psychoanalytic psychotherapy. A review of these defining features provides background for examining the overlapping areas of interest of psychoanalytic theory and multicultural psychology later in this chapter. Numerous psychoanalytic practitioners and researchers have delineated key features of psychoanalytic psychotherapy, drawing from various traditions (e.g., classical, object relations, self-psychology, relational; Blagys & Hilsenroth, 2000; Luborsky & Barrett, 2006; McWilliams, 2004; Sarnat, 2010; Shedler, 2010). For example, Lester Luborsky and Marna Barrett (2006) described central concepts in psychoanalytic theory that shape practice, including unconscious conflict, drives or instinctual urges, parent–infant and parent–child interactions, the Oedipus complex, and defenses. More recently, Jonathan Shedler (2010) outlined the following distinct seven features describing psychoanalytic process and technique:

1. focus on affect and expression of emotion (e.g., emotional insight),
2. exploration of attempts to avoid distressing thoughts and feelings (e.g., defense and resistance),

3. identification of recurring themes and patterns,
4. discussion of past experience and the relation between past and present,
5. focus on interpersonal relations,
6. focus on the therapy relationship, and
7. exploration of fantasy life (e.g., dreams, fantasies).

Shedler further emphasized that the focus of psychoanalytic therapy includes but also moves beyond the relief of symptoms to address intrapsychic and relational capacities.

Although there is no singular way to conceptualize psychodynamic technique, Nancy McWilliams (2004, 2014) has delineated some principal techniques of psychoanalytic practice. Notably, McWilliams has described the importance of the therapist having a psychoanalytic "sensibility" through which she or he experiences an attitude of curiosity, assumes complexity, is willing to identify with the client, empathically immerses into the client's experiences, relies on a disciplined subjectivity, attunes to affective experiences, appreciates the role of attachment, and has faith in the unfolding process between herself/himself and the client. An ethic of honesty underlies this sensibility, wherein the therapist is honest about what she or he knows or does not know. At its core, psychoanalytic therapy has been described as "inherently subversive" because it sets out to "tell the truth about sexuality, aggression, dependency, narcissism" (McWilliams, 2005, p. 139). McWilliams further included the therapist's self-knowledge, particularly of the therapist's unconscious life, through one's own therapy, and the development of a comfortable working alliance as essential components of psychoanalytic therapy. Additional techniques in psychoanalytic therapy include the therapist's engagement in listening to the client in an active, empathic, and respectful manner, the encouragement of free expression (e.g., free association), search for meaning of the client's experience, attention to what is not talked about and what is not named or owned in the client's experience, attention to resistance and reducing the client's shame concerning the challenges involved with therapeutic change, and the ability to address transference and countertransference (McWilliams, 2004, 2014). Among other conceptualizations of the aims of psychoanalytic therapy, scholars have emphasized the importance of self-realization, the "containment and transcendence of opposing tension states" (Summers, 2000, p. 551), and authorship over one's own life (Benjamin, 1988). As such, psychoanalytic approaches tend to conceptualize diagnosis more so in terms of personality organization (psychotic, borderline, neurotic), defenses, relational patterns, and subjective experiences, rather than *Diagnostic and Statistical Manual of Mental Disorders* (*DSM*) categorization (McWilliams, 2012; PDM Task Force,

2006), and the therapeutic process as involving the therapist's attention to his/her own unconscious processes in addition to those of the client.

Although psychoanalytic scholars have developed new conceptualizations of sociocultural context and identity, knowledge gained from these developments has not been systematically integrated with existing definitions of what constitutes psychoanalytic therapy. The neglect of cultural competence as a core emphasis of psychoanalytic theory stands in contrast to recent efforts of theorists from some other theoretical paradigms. For example, some cognitive–behavioral theorists (Hays, 2009; Newman, 2010) have explicitly stated that cultural competency is a foundational principle of CBT, on par with principles such as respecting and understanding scientific underpinnings of treatment and an emphasis on the therapeutic relationship. Pamela Hays (2009) identified strategies rooted in mainstream cognitive–behavioral concepts and her ADDRESSING framework to help integrate considerations of sociocultural context in cognitive–behavioral therapy. These strategies include the following:

1. assessing the client's and client's family's needs with an emphasis on culturally respectful behavior;
2. identifying culturally related strengths and supports;
3. clarifying which part of the presenting problem is external to the client and which part is cognitive or internal with attention to cultural influences;
4. focusing on helping the client to make changes that minimize stressors and build skills for interacting more effectively with one's social and physical environment;
5. validating client's experiences of oppression;
6. emphasizing collaboration over confrontation, with attention to client–therapist differences;
7. questioning the helpfulness, not the validity, of the thought or belief in cognitive restructuring;
8. refraining from challenging core cultural beliefs;
9. using the client's culturally related strengths and supports to develop helpful cognitions to replace unhelpful cognitions; and
10. developing homework assignments with an emphasis on cultural congruence and client direction.

Hays's framework is a necessary revision to mainstream CBT that is gaining attention among both cognitive–behavioral practitioners and multicultural psychologists. In my view, a parallel process of reconceptualization concerning the inclusion of sociocultural issues is overdue in psychoanalytic theory and practice.

OVERLAPS BETWEEN PSYCHOANALYTIC THEORY AND MULTICULTURAL PSYCHOLOGY

Despite distinct conceptual emphases across multicultural psychology and psychoanalytic theory, there are some notable overlaps worthy of discussion. These overlaps concern the issue of evidence-based practices, conflict with the medical model approach to diagnosis, and an emphasis on social justice. The development of empirically supported treatments, with the use of randomized clinical trials as the gold standard methodology, has become a major force in the reshaping of clinical training and practice. More recently, as a challenge to the growing focus on manualized treatments, the APA redefined *evidence-based practice in psychology* (EBPP) as "the integration of the best available research with clinical expertise in the context of patient characteristics, culture, and preferences" (American Psychological Association Presidential Task Force on Evidence-Based Practice, 2006, p. 271; Hays, 2009). A number of multicultural and feminist psychologists (Bernal & Scharrón-del-Río, 2001; S. Sue, 2003) have noted the relatively small number of studies that have considered gender or the experiences of racial and ethnic minority and LGBTQ clients and clients with physical disabilities in examining empirically supported treatments. Multicultural and feminist psychologists further recognize that empirically supported treatments do not consider the role of therapist's personal factors, the therapeutic relationship, or the nondiagnostic aspects of the client's experience (Brown, 2006; Gallardo, Yeh, Trimble, & Parham, 2012).

Both multicultural psychology and psychoanalytic psychology have responded to narrow definitions of what is considered to be "evidence." Multicultural psychologists, such as Miguel Gallardo, Thomas Parham, Joseph Trimble, and Christine Yeh, have pointed out that EBPP is rooted in the client or community and values multiple sources of "evidence." This bottom-up perspective of EBPP suggests that theory and intervention are derived from clients' experiences (Gallardo et al., 2012). In recent years, research conceptualized from this perspective has been emerging among clinical practices with various communities (e.g., Afro Caribbean, Asian, Latino/a). This perspective is also more aligned with feminist psychology, which emphasizes an egalitarian relationship between the therapist and the client that empowers clients to voice their own narratives in therapy (Brown, 2010).

Similar to multicultural and feminist psychologists, psychoanalytic practitioners and researchers have described the importance of clinical evidence, or the client's narrative, as paramount to the development of theory and intervention. Over the past several decades, there have been unwarranted claims that the efficacy of psychodynamic therapy lacks empirical evidence or that psychoanalytic theory is irrelevant to clients in the modern day (Barlow & Durand, 2005). In fact, there is ample evidence within psychology and neurobiology research for psychoanalytic concepts, such as the unconscious and defenses, and for the role of psychoanalytic concepts in the workings of the mind, such as the mechanisms underlying attachment in the face of traumatic stress (Blatt & Zuroff, 2005; Fonagy & Bateman, 2008; Gabbard, Miller, & Martinez, 2008; Leichsenring & Salzer, 2014; Luborsky & Barrett, 2006; Shedler, 2010). Effect sizes for psychodynamic therapies have been found to be as large as the effect sizes for treatments commonly considered "evidence based" and "empirically supported" (Shedler, 2010). In the case of personality disorders, psychodynamic therapy has been found to be at least as effective if not more so than dialectical behavioral therapy (Clarkin, Levy, Lenzenweger, & Kernberg, 2007). Further, Shedler's (2010) article in the *American Psychologist* noted the considerable amount of empirical support for the effectiveness of psychodynamic therapy, referencing numerous studies, including meta-analyses (Fonagy & Bateman, 2008; Leichsenring & Rabung, 2008) indicating that the "benefits of psychodynamic therapy not only endure but increase with time" (pp. 101–102). Research concerning the efficacy of psychodynamic therapy has recognized that studies must account for the therapist's interpersonal style and variations in the ways that interventions are implemented outside of what is recommended in a treatment manual (McWilliams, 2004; Shedler, 2010). Relatedly, La Roche and Christopher (2009), in an examination of empirically supported treatments and cultural context, observed that the therapist's interpersonal skills, personality style, and capacity to tolerate distress influence the client's response to psychotherapy.

An important overlap between psychoanalytic and multicultural approaches involves the problem of diagnosis from the medical model perspective. Multicultural psychologists have cautioned against the use of diagnostic categories that ignore cultural explanations of psychological distress and impose mainstream notions of health and pathology on clients from diverse sociocultural backgrounds. Culturally informed assessment and diagnostic practices attend to clients' strengths, use culturally appropriate and relevant instruments and interpretations based on an understanding of the client's sociocultural and political contexts (Gallardo et al., 2012). Multicultural psychology supports the use of an emic perspective in the assessment and diagnosis process, in which the individuals of a particular sociocultural background define their own narratives concerning psychological issues. For example, it has been recommended that clinicians use projective tests, such as Tell-Me-A-Story and the Draw-A-Person Test, which are more consonant with storytelling and metaphorical traditions of indigenous people (e.g., American Indians, Native populations; Trimble, Trickett, Fisher, & Goodyear, 2012).

Psychoanalytic psychology, similar to feminist and multicultural psychologies, has moved away from *DSM* classifications of psychological distress and instead has focused on the whole individual in the process of assessment and diagnosis. In fact, feminist psychologist, Laura Brown (2006) challenged traditional *DSM* categorization of distress, stating, "Feminist therapy, along with our old nemesis and strange bedsister psychoanalysis, as well as our narrative and constructivist friends, resists" (p. 19). Nancy McWilliams (2012) pointed out that only a limited number of *DSM* and the *International Classification of Diseases (ICD)* categories are recognized by insurance companies, which exclude personality issues or *DSM* Axis II diagnoses, despite marketing themselves as offering "comprehensive" mental health services. She argued that trait-based assessment tools that describe observable phenomena are unable to capture the client's subjective, inner experiences.

One of the most significant advances in the applications of psychoanalytic theory in diagnosis is the publication of the *Psychodynamic Diagnostic Manual (PDM)* in 2006. The PDM (PDM Task Force, 2006) extended the *DSM* and *ICD* diagnostic systems to include descriptions of both commonalities and individual differences in psychological distress. Psychoanalytic concepts, neuroscience research, and psychotherapy outcomes research provide a foundation for the multidimensional approach of the *PDM* system (McWilliams, 2012). In contrast to the *DSM* and *ICD* systems, the *PDM* considers the complexity of internal subjective experience of the individual, including affective, cognitive, biological, and relational experiences, as critical to a comprehensive understanding of specific diagnoses. The problem of categorization of mental disorders without adequate attention to the context of the individual's life is related to the conceptualization of psychotherapy process and intervention. According to McWilliams (2013a), the idea that the amelioration of overt symptomology is the exclusive goal of psychotherapy reflects a "category mistake." Specifically, she referred to the expectation that psychotherapy be driven by and modeled after a particular type of research (e.g., empirically supported treatments), rather than real-world, complex experiences of clients and therapists, shaping how psychotherapy process and outcome research is conducted. Because of this expectation, the decontextualization of assessment, diagnosis, and psychotherapy has contributed to a shift in the role of the therapist from that of a collaborative healer to one of a technical expert (McWilliams, 2013b).

Multicultural and psychoanalytic practitioners also share a common interest in social justice. The equal access to adequate and relevant mental health care lies at the heart of multicultural psychology. A key feature in the development of multicultural psychology concerns the resistance against historic and ongoing collusion with structures that oppress marginalized people (D. W. Sue, Bingham, Porché-Burke, & Vasquez, 1999; Vasquez, 2012). The issue of whether social justice and multiculturalism are congruous with each other continues to be debated in psychology. Nevertheless, multicultural psychologists espouse the belief that psychologists should address injustice and oppression. Further, similar to feminist psychologists, multicultural psychologists consider the role of political, historical, and cultural factors and the role of power and privilege in the experiences of clients in creating distress and resilience within and outside of the therapeutic relationship (Brown, 2006; Pope-Davis, Liu, Toporek, & Brittan-Powell, 2001).

Within psychoanalysis, there has been a renewed interest in social justice and oppression, extending the mission of a number of early analysts who established free clinics in Europe to provide psychoanalytic treatment to individuals who could not afford to pay for psychotherapy (Danto, 2005; Richards, 2013). Following in the tradition of Ferenczi (1949), who attended to the power differences between the therapist and the client and recognized that social injustice is related to psychological distress, a number of psychoanalytic psychologists have integrated their identities as activists and psychoanalytic practitioners. These scholars and practitioners have applied psychoanalytic concepts, such as transference, countertransference, enactments, and defense mechanisms, to better address the critical interpersonal processes that guide community mental health care, community-based interventions, and political processes (Ainslie & Brabeck, 2003; Borg, 2004; J. L. Darwin & Reich, 2006; Gaztambide, 2012; Hollander, 2013; R. A. King & Shelley, 2008; Tummala-Narra, 2013a; Twemlow & Parens, 2006). The examination of group dynamics, including those related to race, ethnicity, social class, and gender, has been thought to be an important component of psychoanalytic interventions in the community setting. In addition, a psychoanalytic approach to social justice in psychotherapy and community intervention supports the ability to bear witness to the client's story and facilitate an "in-depth understanding of individual and collective meanings of experience" (Tummala-Narra, 2013a, p. 482). In fact, Boulanger (2012), among others (Hollander, 2013; Summers, 2009; Wachtel, 2002), has suggested that therapists have a moral obligation to bear witness to social injustice (e.g., traumatic events) that has profound effects on the client's sense of self.

In considering the overlaps between multicultural psychology and psychoanalysis, it is important to note that many practitioners identify with various aspects of multicultural psychology, feminist psychology, and psychoanalytic psychology. Unfortunately, the political divides across psychoanalytic psychology and multicultural psychology, in particular, have created a conflated sense of "us" versus "them" within the broader discipline of psychology with respect to how divisions within the APA are organized and how each perspective is, at times, pitted against each other within training programs and professional discourse. In fact, many psychologists choose to be members of several divisions within APA in an attempt to expand our knowledge of and interaction with issues of diversity and psychoanalytic psychology. Separate divisions within APA are critical for knowledge building and networking. Yet a view that some divisions are sole bearers of knowledge concerning sociocultural context and identity and that other divisions are the sole bearers of depth psychology makes it increasingly difficult to develop theory and practice strategies that respond to the needs of a pluralistic society.

Scholars and practitioners of the integrative psychotherapy movement have suggested that although a single theoretical orientation can be useful in advancing a particular approach and fostering a sense of confidence in this approach, the reliance on a single theoretical orientation can place clinicians, educators, and researchers at risk for neglecting important knowledge gained from other perspectives and, more broadly, from advances in science (Dimaggio & Lysaker, 2014). In this view, theories should be modified by integrating new, emerging data so that clients can benefit from theoretical models that reflect this information. As psychoanalytic psychology and multicultural psychology share a common goal of working with whole individuals and communities, the interchange of knowledge through professional dialogue and theory building is essential for contemporary practice.

CONCEPTUALIZING CULTURAL COMPETENCE FROM A PSYCHOANALYTIC PERSPECTIVE

There is no doubt that there has been growing attention to the importance of sociocultural context on individual development and psychic life in the psychoanalytic literature. Yet the question of how to engage with cultural competence and related guidelines in professional practice as a psychoanalytic practitioner remains. Bearing in mind psychoanalytic contributions to the understanding of complex issues of social context and identity, I suggest that a more systematic inclusion and integration of cultural competence is needed for advances in psychoanalytic theory and for a more sophisticated understanding and implementation of cultural competence in professional psychology. I use the term *cultural competence* to refer to a process of recognizing, understanding, and engaging with sociocultural context and its influence on intrapsychic and interpersonal processes, including the therapeutic relationship. Further, cultural competence is inextricably linked with professional competence more broadly. In other words, cultural competence should not be located only among those thought to be "experts" in multiculturalism but is an approach that belongs to all practitioners, researchers, and educators. As such, cultural competence is not an endpoint, as the term "competence" can imply, but rather a process that is a lifelong endeavor (S. Sue, 1998). I view cultural competence as a dynamic process that involves a psychoanalytic theoretical frame that integrates the multicultural and feminist perspectives, a firm grounding in empirical and clinical evidence concerning people of diverse sociocultural backgrounds, and a therapeutic approach that is flexible enough to be informed and shaped by the client's unique set of experiences.

As such, I outline a culturally informed psychoanalytic framework that considers several key areas that build on existing contributions, particularly those from relational theorists, and that expand existing conceptualizations of cultural competence. These areas of emphasis and related therapeutic strategies reflect a call for active engagement of psychoanalytic theory with cultural competence and the application of psychoanalytic contributions to culturally competent therapeutic practice. The framework includes the following areas of emphases and strategies:

1. recognize clients' and therapists' indigenous cultural narrative and the conscious and unconscious meanings and motivations accompanying these narratives;
2. recognize the role of context in the use of language and the expression of affect in psychotherapy;
3. attend to how client's experiences of social oppression and stereotyping influence the therapist, the client, the therapeutic process, and the outcome;
4. recognize that culture itself is dynamic and that individuals negotiate complex, intersecting cultural identifications in creative, adaptive ways and in self-damaging ways, as evidenced in the use of defense; and
5. expand self-examination to include the exploration of the effects of historical trauma and neglect of sociocultural issues in psychoanalysis on current and future psychoanalytic theory and practice.

Each aspect of this framework is outlined next and explored in more depth in the remainder of this book.

Recognize Indigenous Narrative

Although some therapeutic approaches based in multicultural psychology have emphasized using therapeutic approaches with racial minorities that tend to overgeneralize the experiences of racial and ethnic groups (Seeley, 2005), psychoanalytic theory has failed to consider how individual narratives are shaped by their respective cultural groups. The clients' psychic material lies at the core of psychoanalytic theory. Listening to the clients' indigenous narrative (Seeley, 2005) goes beyond listening to individual meanings and interpretations of sociocultural context. It entails listening to what lies beneath these meanings, how and in which context they were formed, the intrapsychic and extrapsychic implications these meanings have for the client's day-to-day life, and the anxiety that is produced in the client's articulation of indigenous narrative for both the client and the therapist. Harlem (2009) suggested that this type of listening involves interpreting the client's desires, fears, behaviors, and relationships in the context of a cultural meaning system by "thinking by means of the other" (p. 281). Listening to indigenous narrative necessitates a collaborative relationship in which there is a recognition of the therapist's cultural narrative and the client's cultural narrative and that accompanying motivations interplay unconsciously. As such, it is especially important for the therapist to attend to which narrative (that of the therapist or that of the client) is privileged and under what circumstances within the therapeutic process. Indigenous cultural narrative allows for a better understanding of resilience and strengths, which are defined in distinct ways across cultures (Comas-Díaz, 2011; Tummala-Narra, 2007). An analysis of the interactions among cultural narratives is also essential to a more accurate understanding of development, pathology and health, and the therapeutic process, from the client's perspective.

For example, a female immigrant client with limited financial resources may express her belief that her depressed mood is rooted in her inability to fulfill her duty as a daughter to her aging parents who live in her country of origin. She may feel that she has abandoned her responsibilities as a daughter by not taking care of them in old age and as such feels responsible for bringing shame to her family's reputation in her community. The therapist's upbringing may incline him or her to focus more on the client's conflicted feelings about being a good daughter or perhaps on her limited ability to travel to her country of origin. A psychoanalytic emphasis on indigenous narrative would involve attention to both how the client experiences the loss of access to visits with her parents and the client's conflicted feelings about her role as a daughter in the context of physical distance from her parents and her adjustment to living in a new cultural environment. Specifically, the therapist may inquire about how the client imagines herself as a daughter if she were still living in the country of origin, and her identification with her culture of origin and her changing cultural identifications since living in a new country. The client is also apt to discuss aspects of her cultural narrative if she experiences the therapist as someone who either implicitly or explicitly conveys that her perspective is valued within their interaction. The therapist, in this case, has to bear his or her own feelings of uncertainty and discomfort that are produced in listening to a narrative that either diverges from or challenges his or her own cultural narrative or preconceived notions of the client's cultural narrative.

Understand the Nuances of Language and Affect

Indigenous narrative and culturally based explanations of development, health, and pathology are closely linked with language and affective experience. Psychoanalytic psychotherapy, similar to other types of therapy, relies heavily on language and verbal expression of affective material. Psychoanalytic perspectives emphasize the ways in which psychotherapy can function as a transitional space (Winnicott, 1971), bridging old and new languages and cultural experiences. Scholars have suggested that the use of native or heritage language in psychotherapy can both facilitate the clients' connection with early experiences and reflect defensive functions in psychotherapy (Akhtar, 2011). Psychoanalytic theory concerning the use of language considers individual meanings of language use, and as such, emphasizes the complex use and interpretation of language. Similarly, the expression of affect should be carefully considered. For example, the experience of silence in psychotherapy can hold different meanings based in sociocultural context. The therapist may assume that the client's silence is indicative of resistance, and the client may assume that the therapist's silence reflects indifference and lack of understanding. Psychological distress may also be expressed in physical symptomology, such as headaches and gastrointestinal pain, because the direct expression of negative affect may be experienced as conflictual for the client. The therapist in this case is met with the dilemma of whether or not to interpret the physical symptoms as reflecting emotional distress and must think carefully about how such an interpretation is experienced by a client whose cultural narrative about health and pathology may contrast with that of the therapist. The nuances of verbal and nonverbal communication and the conscious and unconscious meanings attached to these communications are especially well-suited to a psychoanalytic perspective that values the deconstruction of the therapeutic exchange, rather than the imposition of one narrative over the other.

Attend to Experiences of Social Oppression

Strong empirical and clinical evidence demonstrates the negative effects of social oppression, such as sexism, racism, homophobia, classism, ableism, and transphobia, and related microaggressions (Altman, 2010; Comas-Díaz, 2011; Greene, 2007; Jefferson, Neilands, & Sevelius, 2013; Tummala-Narra, 2007). Discrimination and stereotyping contribute to a powerful social mirror (Suárez-Orozco, 2000) and "social unconscious" (Dalal, 2006) that shape self-images and perceptions by others, both of which are recreated both consciously and unconsciously in the therapeutic relationship (Altman, 2010; Holmes, 2006; Leary, 2000). The exploration of oppression in psychoanalytic psychotherapy is not a new idea; however, such exploration has remained circumscribed primarily to experiences of trauma, neglect, and intrapsychic conflict, excluding social and political oppression. The exploration of oppression, social, racial, and political trauma involves an emotional transformation of the client and therapist. The psychoanalytic emphasis on transference, countertransference, and the examination of repetitive patterns is especially relevant to the examination of social oppression.

The therapist must open herself or himself up for scrutiny of her or his own stereotypes and assumptions and that of the client and recognize that she or he may be complicit in the client's experience of oppression (Leary, 2006). In addition, the therapist should be prepared to recognize and validate the client's lived experiences of oppression in daily life. Therapeutic work involves the movement toward speaking truthfully about and accepting painful realities (McWilliams, 2003). In such a case, the therapist and the client privilege what happens outside of the therapeutic relationship and what happens inside of the therapeutic relationship (Wachtel, 2009). Wachtel (2002) suggested that this approach not only conceptualizes the role of the therapist as someone who helps the client cope with disadvantage, but also addresses the disadvantage itself, implicating the place of social justice in psychoanalytic therapy. Furthermore, psychoanalytic theory can be especially helpful in addressing multiple forms of social oppression experienced by individuals and their families. For example, the therapist can explore how a client may experience racism in one context and sexism in a different context, and how she or he may or may not integrate these competing experiences and how the context may contribute to these experiences.

Recognize the Complex Ways That Intersecting Cultural Identifications Are Negotiated

Individual and social identities develop in the context of dynamic cultural change and transformation. Variations in cultural identity are evident in the heterogeneity of experience within cultural groups and communities. Although much of the psychoanalytic literature has focused on cultural experience from a dominant psychoanalytic tradition, such as classical theory or relational psychoanalysis, the complexity of cultural identity formation requires multiple psychoanalytic perspectives and an integration of clinical and research knowledge rooted in other traditions (e.g., feminist psychology, multicultural psychology, social psychology, critical psychology). Hansen (2010) pointed out that the term *identity* assumes a value of unity, rather than diversity, and highlights the role of unconscious conflict in "intraindividual diversity" (p. 16). He suggested that the centrality of internal conflict is shared across different psychoanalytic theories and that postmodern and relational approaches, in particular, emphasize the importance of multiplicity of subjective experience. Layton (2006) and Boulanger (2004) have further highlighted the role of conflict and ambivalence in the formation of cultural identifications.

I argue that theory concerning conflict in cultural identity development has to be situated in the social context and the cultural narrative of the therapist and the client. For example, a client who experiences conflict about coming out as a gay man to his family has to consider what being openly gay in his family may mean for him and his connection with his family, particularly if his family has strong cultural and religious beliefs that homosexuality is a sin. The therapist's and the client's cultural narratives also influence how cultural identity is approached in psychotherapy. One particular supervisory example is relevant to this dilemma. I consulted with a White, European American colleague who had been working with a young, second-generation, Indian American woman who expressed feeling anxious about getting married, particularly after her parents had introduced her to several men with the hope that the client would choose one of these men as her spouse. My colleague expressed her feelings of helplessness in working with this client and felt that her client was being oppressed by her parents. I asked my colleague whether the client was experiencing ambivalence about her parents' involvement or whether she was experiencing negative feelings only about meeting potential partners through her parents. My colleague told me that she could not imagine that her client felt anything except anger and frustration because the idea of arranged marriage was oppressive and outdated. She did, however, in a following session, ask her client if she ever felt ambivalent about arranged marriage. The client stated that there was indeed a part of her that liked meeting someone her parents introduced to her and that she felt embarrassed to share these feelings with a non-Indian person.

The complexity of identity and its variations across and within cultural groups and generations is also relevant to the issue of intersectionality. The meanings attached to some aspects of identity, where and when they become more salient, and their connections with early life and ongoing interpersonal experiences can be uniquely addressed through a psychoanalytic lens. The intersectionality of social identities is also relevant to the therapist, who must ask himself/herself which aspects of identity feel more salient when working with a client of any particular sociocultural background and which social identity issues the therapist is more comfortable addressing with a client (Greene, 2007). The therapist's ability to engage with the client's internal conflicts concerning social identity and bear the anxiety of not knowing or experiencing difference from the client's cultural identification is critical for a therapeutic relationship that is collaborative and productive. From this perspective, the therapist is required to refrain from the tendency to minimize difference and universalize experience. The therapist's ability to bear anxiety helps to facilitate the client's willingness to negotiate the multiplicity and hybridity of his/her identity, explore shared fantasies of sameness and the other, and "face reality together" (Benjamin, 2011, p. 29). As such, the therapist socializes the client to talk about social context, rather than conveying an implicit or explicit message that this issue is irrelevant or peripheral to the clients' internal life.

Expand Self-Examination

Although psychoanalysts have written extensively about the importance of self-reflection and self-examination, the recognition of the historical trauma and cultural context that shape theory and practice today has not been explicit in much of psychoanalytic literature. Yet this lack of recognition contributes to the ongoing separation between the psychic and the social. With respect to technique, the disconnection between historical and cultural influences on the psychotherapy process contributes to the therapist's practices, such as dismissing or not initiating discussions about social context with clients. Therapists have been socialized to think that they may be disrupting the transference, diluting the therapeutic frame, or perceived by the client as a racist or perpetrator if they initiate discussions about context. Indeed, these can be difficult discussions to have, with the potential for experiencing feelings of shame, vulnerability, and incompetence. Therapists who hold a minority status and those who hold majority status with respect to race, ethnicity, immigration, sexual orientation, religion, social class, and dis/ability should consider how their personal experiences of oppression may influence their interactions with clients. Relatedly, Beverly Greene and Dorith Brodbar (2010) edited a special issue of *Women & Therapy* focused on the experiences of Jewish women therapists. These experiences ranged from therapists who identified as Orthodox Jews to a therapist who was raised believing that her family was White, Anglo-Saxon Protestant and in adulthood came to learn about her Jewish ancestry. It is evident in this collection of essays that the Jewish experience has remained invisible despite its influence in Western psychotherapy. It is also clear that many authors struggled with bringing to their conscious attention the relevance and meanings of their social identity and publicly discussing their personal experiences within their professional circles. This type of self-examination in theory and practice is critical for developing a sense of authenticity and listening to culture because the therapist's subjectivity influences his/her attention to the client's experience and what he/she hears in the client's words (Seeley, 2005; Wheeler, 2006).

SUMMARY

Pioneering work by multicultural psychologists culminated in cultural competence as a framework that addresses sociocultural issues in the psychotherapy process. Despite the notable influence of cultural competence in the discipline of psychology and the mental health professions, its existing frameworks have been criticized. In particular, clinicians often struggle with the practical application of multicultural guidelines and the complexity of addressing the interaction among individual, interpersonal, and systemic issues relevant to the therapeutic relationship and process. This chapter presents some distinctive features of psychoanalytic psychotherapy and areas of overlap between psychoanalytic theory and multicultural psychology, such as those concerning evidenced-based practices, approach to diagnosis, and social justice. Although psychoanalytic scholarship concerning issues of diversity has expanded significantly over the past several decades, attention to sociocultural context has not been systemically integrated as a core feature of psychoanalytic psychotherapy. I have drawn on existing contributions of psychoanalytic theory and multicultural and feminist perspectives to develop a framework of culturally informed psychoanalytic psychotherapy. In this framework, cultural competence is viewed as a dynamic process that involves engaging with sociocultural context and its influence on intrapsychic and interpersonal processes.

The framework includes five areas of emphasis: recognizing the client's and therapist's indigenous cultural narrative; recognizing the role of context in the use of language and expression of affect; attending to how the client's experiences of social oppression and stereotyping influence the therapeutic relationship, process, and outcome; recognizing that culture is dynamic and that individuals negotiate complex, intersecting cultural identifications in creative and self-damaging ways; and expanding self-examination to include the exploration of the effects of historical trauma and neglect of sociocultural issues in psychoanalysis on current psychoanalytic theory and practice. The next five chapters (Chapters 4–8) elaborate on each of these components of the framework.

4

ATTENDING TO
INDIGENOUS NARRATIVE

My client, Maricel, brought a gift for me in a session soon before I left for my maternity leave. She held my hand after giving me the gift and said, "You have been taking care of me, and now I want to do something nice for you. I pray for you and the baby." I thanked her for the gift, and upon her request, I opened the bag, which contained an infant feeding bowl and spoon. She asked whether I liked it, and I responded, "I like it very much, and I think that the baby will like it too." We proceeded to talk in the session about what it would be like for her while I was away for maternity leave.

After the session with Maricel, I was left wondering about several aspects of our exchange. Maricel and I had been working together for approximately 1 year before my leave. She had sought help to cope with stress related to chronic headaches, fatigue, and anxiety. Maricel, a 32-year-old woman, was born and raised in Honduras and, as an adult, relocated to the United States to escape ongoing violence in her community. She came to the United States,

http://dx.doi.org/10.1037/14800-005
Psychoanalytic Theory and Cultural Competence in Psychotherapy, by P. Tummala-Narra

joining a few family members who had moved to the country several years earlier. She left her 3-year-old daughter in Honduras in the care of her mother and hoped that her mother and her daughter would be able to immigrate to the United States. However, over the course of time since her immigration, she had begun to lose hope of this possibility. Over the years, she became fluent in English and secured employment and visa status but was unable to find a way to bring her child to the United States.

Maricel's gift held layers of meaning. In fact, we spoke about her gift in subsequent sessions, during which I learned that she had struggled with feeding her daughter as an infant amidst an unpredictable, chaotic environment in which her life and the lives of her family members were in continual threat because of regional political conflict. She remembered feeling terrified about the possibility of losing her daughter. In our conversations, Maricel and I also came to understand the importance of her being a mother despite her separation from her daughter and of creating a relational space in which she and I metaphorically could feed each other. Maricel's narrative of the gift simultaneously contained a story of trauma and a story of intimacy and separation, all of which was shaped by sociopolitical conditions and cultural beliefs and traditions.

I, too, held my own narrative, infused with feelings of sadness and guilt as I reflected on Maricel's separation from her daughter. As a function of my own feelings of guilt and anxiety, as I entered my last trimester of pregnancy I found myself at times emotionally distancing from her pain so that I would not have to imagine losing my baby. My narrative also involved a connection to my Indian cultural heritage, which values the role of mutual caregiving among family members and within professional helping relationships. Maricel's gift reminded me of how important it is for me to stay connected with people who have helped me, a reflection of my immigration experience and my identity as an Indian.

At the same time, I wondered whether there were other meanings of the gift and Maricel's feelings about my pregnancy that we had not explored. Questions came to my mind frequently. Did Maricel worry that my baby wouldn't survive, or did she feel angry about her separation from her daughter as she saw her therapist prepare to hold her baby in her arms? Had she felt my anxiety about childbirth as I anticipated the arrival of my baby, and had I communicated to her in some way that I needed for her to take care of me and my baby? Was her gift a reflection of her intrapsychic wishes and fears, or that of a relational dynamic that transpired between us, or both? Whose lived experience was privileged in our dialogue in psychotherapy? At the heart of my internal dialogue as I thought about Maricel's predicament was my concern that I did not truly understand her. I wondered about my not having experienced the types of traumatic events, daily anguish of separation from her child, and lack of economic resources she had experienced. I was also aware that I had not been fully exposed to her cultural, linguistic, and religious context. Yet as a mother, I shared some aspect of her experience, one of longing for a child.

Therapeutic process involves the interplay of narratives both within the inner life of the client and of the therapist, and within the intersubjective space between the therapist and the client. The meanings attached to the client's attitudes, beliefs, and behaviors are of critical importance to a culturally informed psychoanalytic approach to psychotherapy. In addition, construction of theory itself reflects cultural meanings. Psychoanalytic scholars across various countries have questioned cultural judgments and biases regarding the nature of psychological maturity and development, including concepts such as attachment, separation–individuation, and "positive" resolution of oedipal conflicts (Akhtar, 2011; Kakar, 1995; Kogan, 2010). In this chapter, I describe the importance of Indigenous narrative in psychotherapy. Indigenous narrative refers to an individual's particular subjectivity that is shaped by his or her sociocultural experience. This term encompasses both narratives of an individual's cultural groups and his or her experiences of being associated with and/or identifying with these groups. Karen Seeley (2005), in describing indigenous cultural material in psychotherapy, noted that attending to the client's "particular cultural world" (p. 436) is necessary for the therapist and the client to engage with the client's cultural subjectivity and to explore the client's lived experience more fully. In the following sections, I discuss the issues of cultural embeddedness of theory and the ownership of narrative and then focus on listening to the nuances and variations in indigenous narrative (Seeley, 2005), all of which have important implications for the therapeutic relationship.

CULTURE AND THEORY

Despite the efforts of various theorists to raise awareness of the problematic application of a Euro American diagnostic system to individuals across diverse sociocultural backgrounds, contemporary psychotherapy practice is challenged by decontextualized formulations of clients' psychological distress commonly used in assessment and diagnosis. Emil Kraepelin (1904), in fact, cautioned against the use of his diagnostic classification system among non-Western cultural groups and instead proposed the specialty of comparative psychiatry for gaining an understanding of the psyche within cultures and of psychopathology more broadly (Marsella & Yamada, 2010). In the 1980s, cultural psychiatrists and anthropologists such as Arthur Kleinman, Bryon Good, Juan Mezzich, and Horatio Fabrega drew attention to sociocultural issues in mental disorders, which contributed to the inclusion of the cultural formulation and culture-bound syndromes in the fourth *Diagnostic and Statistical Manual of Mental Disorders* (*DSM–IV*; American Psychiatric Association, 1994). These syndromes, now known as cultural syndromes in the *DSM–5*, refer to "clusters of symptoms and attributions that tend to co-occur among individuals in specific groups, communities, or contexts and that are recognized locally as coherent patterns of experience" (American Psychiatric Association, 2013, p. 758).

The development of the cultural formulation and culture-bound syndromes coincided with significant advances in psychology with the pioneering works of numerous multicultural psychologists (Comas-Díaz, 2006; Leong, 2007; Marsella & Yamada, 2010; S. Sue, 1998) and with the publication of the report *Mental Health: Culture, Race, and Ethnicity* (U.S. Department of Health and Human Services, 2001), which recognized the disparities in mental health services to racial and ethnic minorities. Scholars challenged medical approaches, particularly explanations of psychological symptoms that relied exclusively on biological and/or universalistic perspectives. Anthony Marsella and Ann Marie Yamada (2010) pointed out that Western, Euro American approaches to mental health are a "cultural construction" (p. 106) and have promoted, through their powerful economic and political influence, an acceptance of and imposition of Western conceptualizations of development, health, and pathology across many parts of the world. He also cautioned that power and dominance of a conceptualization do not ensure its accuracy. Indeed, mental health professionals across countries continue to express their concerns with the expansion of diagnostic categories in the *DSM* system (e.g., *DSM–5*) as Western diagnoses are exported to countries without consideration for their validity in different cultural contexts (Nadkarni & Santhouse, 2012).

The importance of cultural constructions of psychological theory cannot be overstated. Cultural context contributes to an understanding of etiology of and experience of psychopathology, types of stressors, coping strategies, personality patterns, language and expression, concepts of normal and abnormal behavior, and the classification of psychological distress and disorders (Marsella & Yamada, 2010). For example, dissociative experiences can occur as a function of a variety of different contexts. These experiences can arise in culturally sanctioned religious or spiritual practices, in response to trauma, or as spontaneous moments in conscience life that may go unnoticed unless they relate to a familiar system of meaning (Seligman & Kirmayer, 2008). Even within a Western, Euro American perspective, two different disciplines may perceive dissociation differently. On one hand, in psychiatry and psychology, dissociation has been viewed as serving a psychological function and involving neurobiological changes. On the other hand, in anthropology, dissociation is thought to be a social phenomenon that creates a particular space or position to articulate self-experience (Seligman & Kirmayer, 2008). These divergent perspectives (e.g., medical, psychological, anthropological) rooted within Euro American cultures contribute to significantly discrepant views of dissociation and more broadly what we in the West classify as psychiatric or psychological symptoms. One can then only imagine the potential for discrepant views regarding health, pathology, and healing across cultural groups and nations.

The individualism of Western, Euro American psychology is evident in developmental concepts, wherein self-reliance and individual autonomy are the hallmark of mental health. Several psychoanalysts have challenged individualistic assumptions of healthy development. For example, Winnicott (1971) proposed the importance of interdependence between an infant/child and mother, and Kohut (1984) suggested that mirroring and idealization in the child's early caregiving relationships are critical to the development of self-cohesion and self-esteem. Although there have been many advances toward a more complex view of the interpersonal field of the child and its impact on development, it is necessary to further reconsider the concepts that underlie what is typically thought in the West to be psychologically healthy. An illustration of this type of reexamination is evident in recent conceptualizations of attachment across cultural contexts. It is generally thought that an infant's/child's secure attachment to his or her mother or maternal figure is essential to positive cognitive, emotional, and social development (Bowlby, 1969). Several factors, such as the amount of time a caregiver spends with the infant/child, the quality of the caregiving relationship, and the emotional investment of the adult in the infant/child, contribute to the nature of the child's attachment style (Fonagy, 2001). The availability of the caregiver is central to the development of internal working models, or a system of representations, which then has implications for the child's relationships not only with the primary caregivers but also with important figures throughout his or her life.

Although it may be that theories of psychology across cultures converge with respect to the importance of the infant's and child's experiences of being loved and cared for and of a positive emotional connection with his or her caregivers, the ways in which secure attachment is achieved are markedly different depending on one's sociocultural background and worldview. For example, my client, Lucy, a 30-year-old Sri Lankan American mother of a 2-year-old girl, stated in a session, "I know I have to take my daughter to the doctor for her yearly visit, but sometimes I don't want to talk with him." She proceeded to tell me that her doctor has advised her that her daughter should feed herself and that adults in the home (e.g., parents, grandparents) should not feed her with their hands because this would make the child more dependent on them. Lucy, in session with me, wondered, "Dependent? Isn't that what children do?"

When I asked Lucy whether she had tried to talk with her daughter's pediatrician about how her and her family's feeding of the child was important for the child's emotional connection with her family, Lucy said, "I tried, and he doesn't get it. You just have to get your baby to be on her own as soon as possible." Lucy's experiences with the pediatrician reflect divergent views on how secure attachment, that is attachment with "just enough" dependence, can vary significantly across cultures, which bears important consequences for the conceptualization of normality.

Over the past two decades, scholars have criticized the indiscriminate application of Western conceptualizations of attachment to non-Western cultural contexts (Cushman, 1995; Roland, 2006; Rothbaum, Weisz, Pott, Miyake, & Morelli, 2001; Wang & Mallinckrodt, 2006). Rothbaum and colleagues (2001), for example, in their studies of attachment patterns in Japan and the United States, found that there are fundamental variations in how attachment is constructed because each cultural context views maternal sensitivity and child security differently. In fact, they called for an indigenous study of attachment that involves "locally generated observations, theories, and measures" (Rothbaum et al., 2001, p. 1102). Research and clinical observations indicate exploration and individuation may not be as valued as emotional closeness and interdependence in cultures outside of Euro American White, middle-class society (Tummala-Narra, 2011). Thus, parenting behaviors specific to cultures may not necessarily indicate the quality of attachment between children and their parents. Yet family relationships that diverge from White, Euro American middle-class norms often are interpreted as pathological, characterized by enmeshment or a lack of appropriate boundaries.

Increasingly, psychoanalytic theorists have extended the concept of attachment from a sole focus of the child's relationship with caregivers to his or her relationship with larger social groups. Hanna Turken (2007), for example, suggested that identity formation involves three distinct tasks: the ability to integrate the mother, the father, and their beliefs and expectations, the world outside of the family, and culture reflecting self-defined goals (e.g., ego-ideal). The individual's ability to form attachments to larger social groups is thought to foster a sense of security and belonging and ethnic and racial identities (Aviram, 2009; Helms, 1990; Tummala-Narra, 2011). Indeed, ample evidence suggests that a positive ethnic identity or a sense of belonging, pride, and connection with one's ethnic group(s) is associated with positive psychological well-being across ethnic groups and particularly among ethnic minorities in the United States (Phinney, 1996; T. B. Smith & Silva, 2011).

Alan Roland (1996, 2006) noted three distinct approaches that have been used to examine the role of culture in development in anthropology (Shweder & LeVine, 1984): (a) evolutionism, which assumes that there are definitive norms, and those based on Northern European and North American individualism are considered to be superior to those characterizing other contexts; (b) universalism, which assumes a universal relevance of developmental concepts such as separation but does not assign a sense of superiority or inferiority to any one particular cultural context; and (c) relativism, which supports the development of a unique conceptualization of development situated within an indigenous culture. Although the first two approaches, evolutionism and universalism, dismiss the relevance of culture-specific patterns that may influence conceptions of healthy and pathological development, relativism poses difficulty with comparing patterns across cultures because of the lack of shared developmental concepts and diagnostic categories.

There are numerous illustrations of how psychoanalytic ideas have been considered from an indigenous perspective. One such example concerning the issue of attachment is evident in the ideas of Takeo Doi (1989), who is among the foremost psychoanalytic scholars in Japan. Doi noted that Western psychoanalysis does not capture critical aspects of the Japanese psyche. Instead, Doi described relational dynamics rooted in Japanese culture while maintaining a "psychoanalytic sensibility of exploring the inner world of Japanese" (Roland, 1996, p. 15). Specifically, Doi (1989) wrote about the concept of *amae*, the Japanese word that refers to a particular style of emotionally connecting with important others in one's life, where an individual expresses a wish to be cared for. Doi argued that *amae* characterizing a child's behavior toward his or her parent to evoke caring and a sense of dependence is discouraged in Western, Euro American cultures because it is thought to diminish the child's sense of self-reliance.

The tensions across different approaches to sociocultural context and the challenges that each approach poses in theory and the practice of psychotherapy underscore the need for a paradigm that can simultaneously attend to the universal and culture specific dimensions of the self (Akhtar, 2011; Roland, 1996). An approach that honors the permeability of theoretical constructs across cultures and within subgroups of any given culture and the specific theoretical constructions of development within cultures shaped by unique sociohistorical histories and circumstances is critical to the understanding of individual narrative as complex and multiply determined. A collective narrative of a cultural group is often necessary for a sense of an individual's sense of continuity amid cultural change and/or social marginalization. Individuals experience various aspects of their sociocultural contexts in unique ways that are shaped by layers of influence. For example, the constructs of individualism and collectivism are often thought to be located in specific cultures. People from collectivistic cultures (non-Western or non–Euro American cultures), in contrast to those from individualistic cultures (Western or Euro American cultures), have been found to prioritize goals of a broader group (e.g., extended family, community), to attend less to internal determinants of behavior, to be more likely to attribute events to situational causes, and to be more self-effacing (Markus & Kitayama, 1991; Triandis, 2001). Since the inception of these constructs, there has been ongoing debate in cross-cultural psychology as to whether individualism and collectivism lie on a continuum or whether they are two independent constructs, and there continue to be challenges in the measurement of these constructs in studies conducted across cultures (Taras et al., 2014). Nevertheless, the constructs of individualism and collectivism and related constructs (e.g., independent vs. interdependent) have guided research in various areas, such as social attitudes, attachment, mental health, and organizational behavior.

Although cultures vary with respect to an emphasis on communal relationships in the lives of individuals, assigning worldviews as traits, rather than as dynamic processes, places us at the risk of assuming that culture is static. In this case, there is a potential for either an idealized or a negative evaluation of behavior, and misdiagnosis. In addition, this approach contributes to a reductionistic understanding of internal experiences and meanings accompanying one's sociocultural context. Isn't it possible, after all, that someone from a collectivistic culture values a sense of self-reliance and that someone from an individualistic culture values communal connections? The problem of reductionism, coupled with a view of inferiority, is evident in language used to describe the experiences of people outside of one's cultural group. For instance, people identified with collectivistic cultures are often described as passive, self-effacing, and fatalistic, all words that contrast with the valued ideals of self-reliance and autonomy in Euro American cultures. Ironically, the intention to deepen understanding of cultural variations in worldviews, in such cases, is met with a superficial understanding of how people view themselves by assuming that one specific aspect of a cultural worldview shapes all of development, regardless of context, circumstances, and people's multiple sociocultural identifications (e.g., age, race, culture, gender, social class, religion, sexual identity, dis/ability).

The attention to individual variations in personal narrative has been a central feature of psychoanalysis since its beginnings. A culturally informed psychoanalytic perspective values the importance of indigenous perspectives and engages a deeper analysis of how psychological experiences of individuals and communities are shaped by sociocultural belief systems, sociohistorical conditions, and individual relational histories. In this view, culture and psyche are not separate but instead influence multiple layers of experience and meaning. Similar to narrative theorists, psychoanalytic therapists conceptualize personal memory as intertwined with collective or historical memory. Psychoanalysts, such as Mark Freeman (2002) and Paul Ricoeur (1986), have emphasized the significance of the narrative and its function of expressing social and historical experiences. Mark Freeman (2002) developed the concept of the *narrative unconscious*, referring to the unconscious aspects of individuals' cultural and historical experiences. Narratives have been thought to offer a way to understand one's life and give voice to one's cultural history and one's own experience, and it has been suggested that the "process of remembering and experiencing is dependent upon the practice of the social and cultural groups to which one belongs" (Frie, 2013, pp. 329–330). As such, one's indigenous narrative, as voiced in one's own words rather than in the words of others, is central to identity and an experience of authenticity. The Western, Euro American middle-class gaze, as evident in some interpretations of development, such as those related to separation, individuation, collectivism, and sexuality, carries the potential of imposing and distancing rather than deepening therapeutic inquiry.

WHO OWNS NARRATIVE?

The therapist's attention to the place of privilege in the therapeutic relationship is essential to an accurate understanding of the client's indigenous narrative concerning development, pathology, and health. The criteria used to determine what is healthy and pathological behavior reflects the context of authorship and ownership of cultural narrative. This is especially important in the therapeutic interaction, in which the client and the therapist engage with each other through the lens of their own life narratives, shaped by sociocultural context. The intersubjective nature of the therapeutic relationship raises questions about whose narrative is privileged at which moments in the course of psychotherapy. From a psychoanalytic perspective, the therapist attunes to both the client's subjective experience (e.g., narrative) and to his or her own and has to determine at which points to construct and convey an interpretation of the client's conflicts and struggles (S. A. Mitchell, 1988). This type of attunement requires an understanding of how privilege is interwoven with the expression of narratives in psychotherapy.

The way that narrative is constructed in an intersubjective space is illustrated in popular conceptions of mental health symptomology thought to be indigenous to a particular cultural group. For example, Soyoung Suh (2013) suggested that contemporary designations of *hwa-byung*, a culture-bound syndrome or cultural syndrome related to mood, particularly anger (fire illness), reflect a response to the rise of cultural psychiatry in the 1970s and 1980s, when medical professionals attempted to bring foreign recognition to an emotion-related disorder in Korea and secure Korea's position within a global context of mental health classification systems. According to Suh, although *hwa-byung* indicated a turn toward recognizing indigenous narrative in the 1980s, more recently the term has been revisited in Korea because some Korean mental health practitioners view *hwa-byung* as stress, whereas others view *hwa-byung* as depression, with variations in treatment approaches. Since the time that *hwa-byung* was identified as a culture-bound syndrome in the *DSM–IV* in 1994, Korean psychiatric research, especially biological research, and the development of a scale assessing *hwa-byung* have gained international recognition. Suh pointed out that contemporary Korean understandings of the nature of *hwa-byung* and its treatment are far from being conclusive. Yet *hwa-byung* continues to be described outside of Korea as a culture-bound syndrome in ways that do not consider contemporary variations in Korean constructions. The diversity of perspectives within Korea, in this case, thus remain invisible to much of the world because a Western, Euro American version of the illness is the only narrative that is seen.

In a related example, Dinesh Sharma (2003) revisited Sudhir Kakar's psychoanalytic theory concerning the mother–child relationship within Hindu joint family units in India. Kakar, an eminent Indian psychoanalyst, approached mother–child relationships within upper-middle–class Indian, Hindu homes through the lens of early psychoanalysts (e.g., Freud and Erickson) and through the lens of Hindu mythology and epics. Sharma argued that Kakar's constructions of the Hindu psyche do not consider changing cultural ideals concerning family structure, work, gender roles, marriage, education, child-rearing, and materialism in contemporary Indian society and also does not consider the variations of experiences across social class and caste lines (Bhatia, 2006). Sunil Bhatia (2006) further noted the lack of attention to globalization on intrapsychic and interpersonal experiences (e.g., self-concept, collective identity) in accounts of Indian family relationships. Bhatia suggested that an uncritical acceptance of Western psychological constructs within the Indian context has been shaped by British colonialism in India.

Nonetheless, Indian psychoanalysts and psychologists since the time of colonization have asserted that the Indian cultural context uniquely shapes internal life. One such example is the founder of the Indian Psychoanalytic Society, Girindrasekhar Bose, who in 1921 published his seminal work, *The Concept of Repression*. Bose maintained a 20-year correspondence with Sigmund Freud, who politely conversed with Bose but dismissed his culture-specific psychoanalytic conceptions. Although influenced by Freud's ideas, Bose developed an Indian psychoanalysis that emphasized Indian, Hindu philosophy and the Western notion of the unconscious (Akhtar & Tummala-Narra, 2005). It is important to consider that the exchange of narratives between Euro American psychological theories and non-Western theories is not a new by-product of globalization of the 21st century, although the dominance of Western narratives is reflective of colonization. In contemporary times, psychologists and psychoanalysts are revisiting the influence of the dominant Western narrative on the construction of indigenous narratives within their own sociocultural contexts and increasingly raising questions about the applications of dominant, colonizing perspectives.

Within the United States, questions about the validity of cultural attributes ascribed to particular racial and ethnic groups are being raised. Scholars such as Joseph Cervantes (2006) and Celia Falicov (2010) have challenged existing narratives concerning masculinity among Latino heterosexual men. Specifically, they have underscored the ways in which simplistic constructions of *machismo* must be expanded to move beyond negative stereotypes of Latino masculinity and include a wider and more complex range of masculinities. Cervantes (2006) suggested that the concept of *machismo* is connected with spiritual meanings and expectations concerning men's responsibilities within their families and communities. Falicov (2010) pointed out that traditional images of *machismo* that involve themes of power, seduction, and domination become primary descriptors of Latino men and internalized by men and women. The attribution of *machismo* as the defining characteristic or trait specific to Latino men contributes to a unidimensional view of masculinity and idea that Latino men are different than Western, Euro American heterosexual men in an essentialist way such that Latinos are seen as the "other," ignoring positive masculine attributes such as respect and responsibility in the family. A complete, indigenous narrative is either suppressed or lost in this case. Gender constructions within any broader cultural context are determined by region, migration history, ecological context, and family dynamics (Cervantes, 2006; Falicov, 2010; Tummala-Narra, 2013b). As such, local, indigenous narratives and personal stories are especially critical to deconstructing stereotypes in dominant narratives.

Homi Bhabha (1994), in his influential postcolonial critique *The Location of Culture*, recognized the unequal cultural representation of cultural narrative that facilitates social and political authority of one society over another. In his perspective, colonial constructions of the other's culture and race depend on the idea of "fixity," reflecting a sense of rigidity and disorder. These constructions pose challenges to oppressed and marginalized communities who attempt to assert their indigenous views. Critical psychologists have suggested that unequal power of narratives is sustained through "ideological persuasion" and through the assumption that the source of oppression is located in the individual or interpersonal and not societal and political inequities, fostering a sense of "false consciousness" or the acceptance of inaccurate beliefs about cultural groups (Fox, Prilleltensky, & Austin, 2009). Ellen Swartz (2013) wrote about the problem of "master-scripted" or "agreed-upon versions of knowledge" that either exclude or misrepresent African American narratives. She recognized that standard curricula in children's textbooks at school present selective historical accounts of people of African descent. For example, she pointed out that textbooks convey the message that slavery occurred without perpetrators because slave owners are not named, not even famous American leaders who were slave owners, such as George Washington and Thomas Jefferson. The counternarrative to master scripts is the "re-membered" narrative, and it involves marginalized individuals and communities as subjects and as agents rather than as objects of imposed storytelling (Swartz, 2013). It is often the case that girls, youth in poverty, and youth from racial, cultural, religious, and sexual minority communities contend with contradictory narratives about their sociocultural groups.

The incongruence between national identity as presented in dominant narratives and histories of various cultural groups within a nation is further evident in the experiences of Native peoples. For example, Haunani-Kay Trask (1999), a Native Hawaiian activist and professor of Hawaiian studies, wrote the following:

> When I was young the story of my people was told twice: once by my parents, then again by my school teachers. From my 'ohana' (family), I learned about the life of the old ones: how they fished and planted by the moon; shared all the fruits of their labors, especially their children; danced in great numbers for long hours; and honored the unity of their world in intricate genealogical chants. . . . At school, I learned that the 'pagan Hawaiians' did not read or write, were lustful cannibals, traded in slaves, and could not sing. Captain Cook had 'discovered' Hawai'i, and the ungrateful Hawaiians had killed him. (p. 113)

Trask drew on Frantz Fanon's (1952) analysis of the ways in which colonization distorts and destroys indigenous narrative, as evidenced in the rewriting and reordering of the history of Native Hawaiians by colonizers.

It is important to consider that divergent narratives do not exist only in the context of different cultures or nations but also permeate experiences of people within cultural groups. For example, the experiences of men and women within cultures often involve strong contrasts, as noted by feminist psychologists and feminist psychoanalytic scholars (Benjamin, 2011; Brown, 2006; Dimen, 2011; A. E. Harris, 2011). J. M. Smith (2003), in her poignant account of mothering, *A Potent Spell*, recognized that the internal experience of mothering is often significantly different from how it is described by those outside of the experience. She emphasized how mothers' efforts to protect their children from harm organize their day-to-day responses to the external world. In fact, J. M. Smith proposed that an intense vulnerability to loss of a child and/or separation from one's child contributes to women's disproportionately low access to economic, social, and political power.

J. M. Smith's analysis is significant for many reasons, one of which is that it recognizes the actual, complex lived experiences of mothers and challenges dominant narratives of mothers as "neurotic" or "overprotective." Relatedly, Daniel Stern (2005) addressed the relatively little attention given to the intrapsychic life of mothers. Similar to J. M. Smith (2003), Stern conceptualized the hypervigilance of the mother as indicative of her unambivalent wish to protect her baby. He further suggested that the experience of falling in love with the baby is an organizing state for mothers. Stern described falling in love in the mother–infant relationship as consisting of various components, such as the deep sense of attention between the mother and baby (e.g., gaze), a sense of mental submersion without loss of the self, the desire to have close physical contact, and the mother's sense of preoccupation with her baby. These efforts to understand parents' internal experiences are critical to understanding development. In fact, the paucity of theoretical development in psychology that includes subjective experiences of mothers and fathers is actually quite alarming.

Variations in narrative within cultural groups also exist across generation lines. Lisa Wexler (2014), in a recent examination of the meanings attached to culture and historical trauma across three generations of Inupiaq (Alaska Natives), including young people, adults, and elders, found some important overlaps and differences. The narratives of these three generations varied along the specific types of trauma they endured or continue to endure. Elders who were sent away to boarding high schools, where they were forbidden to engage in or express any aspect of their culture and language, talked about the impact of White colonialism and racist policies and their own attempts to retain the teachings of their parents and grandparents. Adults' narratives reflected experiences of the challenges they faced as a result of the punitive policies endured by their parents, who did not allow them to engage in their indigenous traditions in order to protect them. They experienced a strong awareness of social injustice and its negative influence on mental and physical health of family members (e.g., depression, alcoholism, suicide) and worked toward regaining a lost heritage and sense of cultural identity as a way to resist further colonization. In contrast to elders and adults, youth in the study located mental health challenges in their communities with family conflicts and individual issues, such as having depression or an addiction, rather than in historical and ongoing community trauma, and felt that culture once again was becoming lost. Wexler's study underscores the significance of attending to the dynamic nature of cultural narrative and the distinct collective memories across generation and time. It is this type of inquiry into the unique subjectivity of individual narrative and the accompanying unconscious and conscious affective experiences with which psychoanalytic theory is most concerned.

LISTENING TO INDIGENOUS NARRATIVE IN PSYCHOTHERAPY

Although psychoanalytic therapists have generally moved beyond the notion of the therapist as a "blank screen" (McWilliams, 2004), the tension between the therapist's role as an objective observer and as a subjective participant in the therapeutic process is inevitable. Contemporary psychoanalytic perspectives challenge essentialist constructions of social identity, namely the idea that constructs such as Black/White and male/female are distinct categories (Corbett, 2009; Dimen, 2011; A. Harris, 2005; Saketopoulou, 2011; Straker, 2004; Suchet, 2007). An essentialist approach ignores the multidimensional nature of narrative. From a psychoanalytic perspective, the problem of "false historical consciousness" (Carretero & Kriger, 2011), which supports essentialist thinking, is especially problematic when considering that ideology operates not only in the conscious mind but also in the unconscious. One way that a particular narrative can dominate another narrative in psychotherapy is through the overgeneralization of knowledge about a particular cultural group to attitudes and behaviors among all people who identify with that group, and the assumption that all people within a particular cultural group share the same experience of privilege and/or marginalization. The acceptance of the restructured, dominant narrative is rooted in power differences and is internalized unconsciously by people in majority and minority positions.

Attention to the dynamics of cultural domination and marginalization in narrative is a key aspect of culturally informed psychoanalytic practice. In addition, how a client and a therapist may resist being objectified and each seek recognition of his or her subjectivity from the other is of critical importance. Seeley (2000) noted that psychoanalytic conceptualizations have neglected the cultural nature of resistance in psychotherapy. Specifically, she suggested that resistances are similar to other features of psychotherapy, such as presenting problems, transference, and countertransference, because they are culturally embedded with regard to content and expression within the therapeutic relationship. Clients may experience psychotherapy as posing a threat to their "indigenous cultural identifications" (Seeley, 2000, p. 217) and therefore resist the therapist's approach, implicating potential power imbalances between the therapist and the client.

Conflicts concerning indigenous narrative that are left unaddressed in psychotherapy can have several negative effects on the client's experience of psychological distress and on his or her relational life. Transference and countertransference reactions that occur in the context of the therapeutic dyad are especially informative of the ways that the client's and therapist's worldviews and related narrative of the self and other shape therapeutic communication and process. For example, within an interethnic dyad, the client may experience the therapist as someone who negatively evaluates the client's perspective or that of his or her cultural group (e.g., ethnic, racial, gender, religious, sexual identity, ability status); the client then avoids talking about his or her cultural values or traditions with the therapist (Comas-Díaz & Jacobsen, 1991). In such a case, avoidance of any potential conflict that may erupt because of the expression of cultural differences may be a familiar strategy for coping with conflicts with people outside of the client's cultural group. In a different example, the therapist may be reluctant to explore issues of social identity with a client because the therapist is concerned about potentially offending the client or imposing the therapist's interest in sociocultural issues on the client, perhaps in a manner similar to how the therapist approaches issues of social context in his or her world outside of the therapeutic space. Many therapists are especially reluctant to address issues of sociocultural context when they are working with a client who is coping with severe distress, such as suicidal thoughts, because they believe contextual issues are secondary to the client's presenting concerns.

Comas-Díaz and Jacobsen (1991), Greene (2007), and Altman (2010), among others, have underscored the various forms of avoidance, excessive curiosity, and denial that can characterize therapeutic exchange concerning sociocultural context. Interactions involving these types of dynamics have profound consequences for the progression of psychotherapy. Specifically, when considering the importance of creating a therapeutic environment that facilitates an exploration of all aspects of the client's life circumstances and internal life, impasses in psychotherapy that mirror broader society conflicts with sociocultural issues create doubt, mistrust, and ambivalence in the experience of the client and that of the therapist. The client's hopes and expectations concerning the therapist's ability to attune to his or her lived experience are shaped by the experience of the social mirror (Suárez-Orozco, 2000). For example, a client of Indian origin may choose me as a therapist with the hope that I would be better able to understand his or her experiences, whereas another client of Indian origin may choose to work with a therapist who is not of Indian or South Asian origin because of the fear that it would not be possible to openly discuss certain topics that are stigmatized in the Indian community. In both situations, the client is influenced by layers of experience, such as those within the Indian community and outside of the Indian community, within the family, and within peer groups, all of which shape his or her fantasies about how it would feel to work with an Indian American therapist. In either case, the therapist must aim to create a therapeutic space in which the client can engage with different aspects of his or her identity in the fullest sense, with a sense of trust in the therapist's ability to bear and witness the client's whole experience.

Winnicott's (1986) framing of the holding environment is especially relevant to the type of therapeutic environment that facilitates an authentic engagement with indigenous narrative. For Winnicott (1986), at the core of the holding environment is mother's reliability in the experience of the child and specifically "human, not mechanical, reliability" (p. 62). Similar to the mother–child dyad, the therapist–client dyad must contain for the client a sense of the therapist's willingness to engage, remain curious, and maintain humility in the face of the unknown so that the client can come to experience his or her true self. From this perspective, attunement to the client's needs is not equated to absolute accuracy in interpretation of the client's conflicts but rather entails a process of continual empathic, genuine engagement with the client's experiences. In this type of therapeutic environment, the client comes to trust the therapist as someone who not only wants to help him or her but also wants to see him or her.

It is important to note that the quality of listening to a client's experiences with sociocultural context and identity is related to the importance of play in psychotherapy. The client and the therapist, when they both perceive that their relationship is one that is reliable, are more apt to reflect on, shape, and reshape their own narratives. In this way, psychotherapy provides a transitional space (Winnicott, 1971) for the client to symbolize lived experiences and imagine new possibilities of being and relating. One of the most challenging features of everyday life for people on the margins is the experience of never being fully seen by others who are in majority positions. It is often the case, for example, that racial minorities live dual or multiple existences as they navigate various cultural contexts. Individuals on multiple margins of race, gender, sexual identity, social class, and/or disability often face challenges in securing spaces where they can safely and reliably experience, voice, and make visible their narratives (Greene, 2007). One important consequence of the lack of such spaces is the disavowal of parts of one's experience and the necessary hiding of aspects of identity to survive in mainstream society. Clarisse Jones's and Kumea Shorter-Gooden's (2003) descriptions of the experiences of Black women in the United States are an important illustration of this type of disavowal. Jones and Shorter-Gooden note, "Black women are relentlessly pushed to serve and satisfy others and made to hide their true selves to placate White colleagues, Black men, and other segments of the community" (p. 7). They suggested, as such, that Black women's attitudes and behaviors often shift, unconsciously, as a function of what is needed from them by others.

Psychotherapy is a healing space in which a therapist can recognize the multiple locations of the client's identity and the life implications of these social locations. Recognizing the client's narrative, however, does not dismiss the relevance of the therapist's narrative. From a relational psychoanalytic perspective (A. E. Harris, 2011; S. A. Mitchell, 1988), the therapist must attend to his or her position concerning sociocultural difference and similarities between the therapist and the client. The exploration of narrative in the therapeutic dyad should proceed in a way that recognizes privilege of each narrative, as both client and therapist participate in the construction of meanings accompanying these narratives. Increasingly, therapists who identify as racial and ethnic minorities and/or sexual minorities have written about their unique positionality in the therapeutic relationship. For example, Janet Derrick (2005), a family therapist of Mohawk ancestry, described the sharp contrast between her Native values and traditions and those inherent to Western, Euro American perspectives. She spoke of having to relearn how to be a part of the circle system in her Native community after her years in graduate school. She recalled the difficult conversations concerning what characterizes a healthy family system in one of her graduate seminars and the lack of space to discuss her worldview, which diverged from that of her training institution. Derrick noted the reactions of non-Native professionals when she did reveal her worldview regarding family systems practice. Derrick (2005) wrote

> People feel overwhelmed by the complexity of the system and tell me they wish me well and that they would not know where to begin as a therapist; I am told to stop being dramatic or political; the circularity of our system is not recognized, nor is my language of the circle understood. (p. 48)

Salman Akhtar (2011), an immigrant, Indian American psychoanalyst, suggested that being an immigrant analyst poses unique challenges to psychoanalytic practice. Specifically, he emphasized the immigrant analyst's responsibility to maintain "cultural neutrality," in which the analyst takes a position that is equidistant between the cognitive and affective experiences rooted in his or her own cultural background and those of the client. Several psychoanalytic scholars (Akhtar, 2011; Holmes, 1992; Tang & Gardner, 1999; Tummala-Narra, 2007) have pointed out that if the therapist's physical features, such as skin color, hair texture, or eyelid shape, are distinct from those of the client, the therapist is not perceived by the client as a neutral figure but rather a screen upon which a range of stereotypes are projected. The voices of therapists from minority status backgrounds is particularly important in contemporary mental health practice because they indicate a shift in the ways that therapists develop their sense of professional and personal identities. In fact, the increasing numbers of racial, ethnic, linguistic, and sexual minority graduate students in the mental health professions raise questions about how multicultural issues are taught in graduate programs. In my experience of teaching graduate-level courses in multicultural issues in psychotherapy, each year more and more students from minority status backgrounds ask why psychology continues to assume that all therapists are White and heterosexual by focusing almost exclusively on the experiences of White therapists working with minority clients or of heterosexual therapists working with LGBTQ clients. With such practice, the racial, ethnic, or sexual minority therapist becomes an "outlier" in theories of psychotherapy.

Psychoanalytic theory, because of its emphasis on the subjective experience of the client, inherently values the perspectives of individual narratives that come to be seen as "outliers." Outliers are those whose life stories and circumstances do not neatly fit into categories that are generally recognized, represented, and/or accepted within mental health disciplines. Michelle Fine (2007) noted the problems implicated in positivistic approaches to psychological research in which the dismissal of data points considered to be outliers supersedes an active engagement with multiple interpretations of qualitative data, including those concerning the outliers. She aptly pointed out that in clinical and counseling psychologies, "the outlier holds the space of pathology, sickness, the other, the noncompliant" (p. 468). Too often in research and clinical practice, we witness the neglect of conceptualizing the experience of those individuals who are on the margins, the outliers, who stretch conventional ideas of what a person associated with a particular sociocultural group should think, feel, and behave. This is the potential risk of "cookbook" approaches that provide recommendations for working with clients from specific cultural groups, based on circumscribed information about these cultural groups. Similar to relational psychoanalytic scholars, Fine (2007) suggested that data are constructed through the relationship between the observed (participant) and the observer (researcher). In psychoanalytic psychotherapy, the therapist is responsible for listening to every aspect of the client's experience, including that which seems atypical, unusual, or unexpected. In fact, psychoanalysis from its inception did not aim to eradicate an individual's internal conflicts; rather, such conflicts were to be brought to the awareness of the client so the client could engage actively with the conflicts, gain insight, and develop an improved sense of agency in his or her life. In other words, conflict is seen as inevitable. The narrative of the client and that of the therapist are always intersecting and reshaping throughout the course of psychotherapeutic work.

The indigenous narratives of the client and of the therapist are fluid and intersectional. The presumption of either's experience as static or fixed contributes to a sense of falseness in the ways that the client and the therapist experience themselves and each other. Psychoanalytic theory's attention to dreams is especially relevant to the fluidity of cultural narrative. For Freud, dreams were the guide to the unconscious mind, providing a connection between the ancient and the modern, and inspiring visions of storytelling, art, poetry, and music within cultures (Lippmann, 2006). Paul Lippmann (2006) has cautioned that the ways in which dreams are perceived in broader society today indicate a declining emphasis on internal psychological life. Specifically, the centrality of dreams is thought to be replaced by physical screens, such as computers and films, limiting a more complex and nuanced view of internal life and the movement of private experience into public space (e.g., Internet, social media). Lippmann has also pointed out that dreams are open to various meanings and interpretations, and take time to explore.

Yet the growing emphasis on making the "correct interpretation" in a brief period of time constricts the therapist and the client from engaging in more creative experience in psychotherapy. Lippmann's work raises questions about dream interpretation and offers the alternative of "dream conversation," in which the client and therapist are involved in a joint exploration of the dream, which is perhaps the most private form of cultural narrative. The ability to play by engaging multiple possibilities of interpretation of wishes, fears, and conflicts (Winnicott, 1971) is an integral part of the client's and the therapist's experiences of feeling and being real in psychotherapy. Relatedly, the therapist's effort to contain his or her own anxiety in discovering, rather than evading, the client's lived experience and fantasy life is central to accurate understanding and interpretation (Bion, 1977; Charles, 2004).

Numerous scholars have called for collaboration, dialogue, and the use of perspective taking through "polyvocal" stories as a way to critically examine the dominant story presented in the mainstream (Diversi & Moreira, 2012; Lykes, 2013). Listening to indigenous narrative requires the therapist to create space for the client's perspective of healing, even when it stands in sharp contrast to the therapist's worldview in some way. Seeley (2005) suggested that therapists' subjectivities are "not only irreducibly personal, but also irreducibly cultural" (p. 435) and that therapists tend to listen to clients in ways that confirm their own existing cultural categories and experiences. She recommended that therapists routinely listen for key material that informs the client's indigenous perspective and explore the meaning and implication of these views. Otherwise, a client who recognizes the therapist's unwillingness to listen to indigenous narrative may not disclose the narrative fully, even though it may play a critical role in his or her distress (Seeley, 2005). Active dialogue is critical for identifying a full narrative, as experienced by the client. This is also critical for developing a relationship with the client that honors the client as an individual and as a member of broader communities (Cunsolo Willox, Harper, & Edge, 2013). In addition, it is important to recognize that the therapist's narrative inevitably interplays with that of the client. Thus, a collaborative approach is essential for what Chinua Achebe (2000) has called the "balance of stories" (p. 79).

CASE ILLUSTRATION: GINA

The following case vignette illustrates the ways in which similar and divergent cultural narratives in the therapeutic dyad (client, therapist) shape the nature of the therapeutic relationship and the course of psychotherapy.

Gina is a woman of African American and Native American ancestry in her early 30s who identifies as heterosexual and is from a lower-middle–class background. I met Gina after she was referred to see me by her physician, who had asked her to see a therapist to cope with her increasing anxiety over the course of several months. In this first session, Gina told me that she was unsure about whether or not being in psychotherapy was a good choice because such therapy was not the typical way for people in her community to deal with stress. In Gina's experience, African Americans in her community talked about their problems within the family and, in times of crisis, consulted with older members of the family. However, Gina did not have access to older family members (parents, grandparents) because she now lived far away from her home. She was willing to try psychotherapy after hearing that one of her friends benefitted from it. I worked with Gina in individual psychotherapy for approximately 3 years.

Gina was born and raised in a rural part of the United States. Her father's heritage is African American, and her mother's heritage is African American and Native American. During her early and middle childhood, Gina grew up primarily with her African American relatives and made regular visits with her mother's relatives who are Native American (Ojibwa). She described her parents as "hard working, lower middle class, and stressed." Her father worked several different jobs to financially support the family, and her mother worked part time and stayed home to care for Gina and her siblings (older sister and younger brother). Gina's older sister coped with a series of medical illnesses that frequently led to visits to the emergency room visits. Gina recalled feeling afraid that her sister would die every time she went to the emergency room or was admitted to the hospital. Her parents had little support from extended family or friends while caring for their children, and in Gina's view, were stressed out and tired. Gina also recalled that when she was 12 years old, the family relocated to live closer to a medical facility that could provide better care for her sister. They moved to a primarily White neighborhood, which felt alien to Gina because she had until then interacted primarily with African Americans both in her neighborhood and in school. She had trouble forming friendships in high school and felt as though people looked at her family with suspicion, as though they were "dangerous Black people." At school, although she felt that the other kids were not hostile to her, she felt different from them because she often felt like they didn't really know her. Gina stated, in one session, "I mean I liked that the other kids didn't see me as less than in some way, but I still never felt like I could be myself around them . . . like I never talked with them about my extended family or my culture."

In addition to adjusting to her new school, Gina spent less time with her maternal and paternal relatives and started to feel increasingly isolated. She remained involved in her sister's care and alternated between feeling hopeful about her sister's future and scared that her sister would die. Gina also remained close to her brother, who also helped the family with caring for their older sister. Despite having better medical care for her sister and the family's ability to access a higher income, Gina and her siblings became increasingly disengaged at school. Gina reported that a respite from her new school was time she spent with her relatives for a few weeks in the summer. As she grew older, however, she spent less time with her family, moved out of state for college, and eventually relocated to an urban area. She enjoyed seeing her family, but the visits became less frequent over the years because of the physical distance from her family. When she left home for college, Gina felt ambivalent about leaving her sister, on one hand wishing she could stay and care for her, and on the other hand, feeling guilty for wanting to leave. Gina hoped to find a new life where she could develop her professional interests and someday create a family of her own.

When I had met Gina, she had been dating Robert, a biracial African American and White man in his 40s, for about a year. Gina expressed that although she loved Robert, she was unsure about continuing her relationship with him because of what she perceived as a cultural difference between Robert and herself. She stated, "He comes from a pretty wealthy family. His dad is White, and always had a lot of money. I don't know how he would fit in with my family." Gina became increasingly anxious when Robert asked to spend more time with her, and she would attempt to keep him at a distance by telling him that she was busy with her work. Gina had few friends in whom she confided her conflicted feelings about Robert or, more broadly, information about her romantic relationships.

Our work in the first several months of psychotherapy centered on her feelings of anxiety, which most often concerned her relationship with Robert. She began to take walks, read, and spend more time with her friends, all of which she found to be grounding. During this time, Gina told me that she had always been scared and anxious, feeling as if something bad was going to happen to her or to someone she loved. In the course of these conversations, Gina stated, "I wish things could be easy in my mind, like the way my grandmother (maternal) used to teach me. She would say 'be calm and listen to yourself.' I wish I could be like her. I don't think I know how to stay calm and listen to myself." When I asked her to tell me more about her grandmother, she revealed that the ability to sit calmly, as she observed in her interactions with her Ojibwa community, seemed impossible at times when she was growing up. Gina expressed, "There wasn't much time to be calm with everything going on with my sister." We talked at length about her sister's condition and the fear that her sister would die, which continued to haunt her.

I asked her if there were other things that caused her to worry. Gina responded, "I was never sure how people would see me. I'm Black, but I'm also Ojibwa. Pretty much no one knows that I'm Ojibwa, too, not even Robert." I said, "Tell me why you don't tell people about your being Ojibwa." Gina stated, "Most people don't know what to do with it. They don't even know what it means." She worried that Robert's White, upper-middle–class upbringing would influence whether or not he would understand and accept her identifications with her Ojibwa heritage. In addition, over the course of several sessions, Gina spoke about Robert's wealthy upbringing and her fantasies about Robert's family. In one session, she stated, "I think he had it easy growing up. I know that his parents never had to struggle for money like mine did. We didn't do a lot of things like he did. He tells me sometimes about traveling to this place or that place. I can't imagine what it be like to do that."

Although I had been mindful of Gina's economic background, it was in this moment in our work together that I saw some of Gina's experience of social class in a more palpable way. I wondered about what she perceived and how she felt about my social class. My social class background changed over the course of my life, ranging across lower middle class (in childhood after migration) to upper middle class (in adulthood). The shifts in social class throughout my life positioned me to experience varying access to resources and lifestyles. These shifts have shaped my internal life of social class. However, my intrapsychic, affective experience of social class is not readily apparent to someone who may meet me today. Because of this, I wondered about Gina's fantasies of my life. When Gina told me that she couldn't imagine Robert's wealthy lifestyle and consequently felt distant from him, I felt torn about asking her whether she had experienced me in a similar way. On one hand, I did not want to interfere with her associations to Robert's and to her own class backgrounds. On the other hand, I felt as though my class background was already present in the room and that I was a silent third figure in the conversation.

In the next session, Gina said, "I am trying to figure out what Robert would like for his birthday. It's hard to get something for someone who has everything he needs." She, once again, talked about not being able to relate to Robert's world.

I then asked her, "As you talk about Robert and his background, I realize that you and I may have different experiences with money, having more or less access to it. I'm wondering if this has been on your mind."

Gina responded, "I don't know how much I think about it, but I know that you must have some money. I mean you have an office here and you dress nice. I guess I can't know what it's like for you though." I was relieved that

Gina could begin talking with me more openly about our class differences, yet I felt our deepening sense of connection was still precarious.

Our conversation eventually moved toward her feelings of not belonging with and resisting the "wealthy." She talked about how she longed to move out of her economic circumstances but that if she did, she would feel even more disconnection from her family, which she began experiencing after leaving her home for college. For Gina, her relationship with Robert posed a painful dilemma concerning separation. Engaging with me in psychotherapy presented a parallel dilemma. We continued our conversation about social class over the next several sessions, which included a discussion about her reduced fee for psychotherapy. She told me she wished she could pay my full fee but also wondered whether I was able to accept a reduced fee because I, like Robert, "didn't need the extra money." Gina's growing awareness and willingness to talk with me about her experience of money and class gradually helped her to explore her complex feelings about her self-image and images of and relationships with Robert, her family, and me.

Although we continued to talk about Gina's feelings about social class, in the subsequent weeks and months, our work began to focus more directly on Gina's reluctance to disclose her Native American heritage to others and her experience of being a biracial person and "on the outside." I remembered that when she told me in our first session that people in her community tended not to seek the help of therapists, I recognized only one of her communities (African American). Perhaps, this was a function of a shared mainstream social mirror in which visible physical features (e.g., skin color) continue to define cultural narrative. She had, in fact, been silent about her Native ancestry, and at the time, I failed to consider that there was more to her story. Her Ojibwa ancestry became the outlier or the unexpected story in the therapeutic encounter.

In one session, I stated to Gina, "I realize that I, too, like so many people in your life, asked you to tell me at first about only a part of yourself, and now I'm learning so much more about you." I then thanked her for talking with me and asked her to tell me about what it felt like to talk with me about being Ojibwa.

She responded, "It's strange to talk about it with you but good, too. I feel like I'm still learning to talk about it." Over the course of several weeks and months, Gina shared stories of her grandmother and her mother and her connection with various maternal relatives. She also reported that although her father respected her mother's Ojibwa ancestry, he did not follow any religious tradition or engage in spiritual practices, such as prayers, with her mother. Gina felt loved by her father but experienced him as someone who was disconnected with parts of her mother's life, mirroring Gina's own experiences with her African American and Ojibwa identities.

One of the most challenging aspects of Gina's psychotherapy was her reluctance to talk with me about Ojibwa healing practices (e.g., prayer, fasting) she learned from her mother and grandmother and that were an integral part of caring for her sister. I felt this reluctance even after I asked her specific questions about her family's healing practices. There were many times during the course of our work that I questioned my ability to ask the right questions to help Gina share her experience of her mixed ancestry and accompanying traditions and beliefs. I worried that I would inquire about her life in a way that might alienate her rather than encourage her to explore her experiences with depth. Perhaps there were spiritual and/or cultural reasons she was reluctant to share her experiences with me. I was aware that when I struggled with these questions, I often felt like an outsider in her life. There was a critical moment in our work, however, that brought both of our fears to the foreground.

During our sixth month of working together, Gina shared a dream with me. Gina dreamt that she had visited her sister in the hospital, where she had brought some herbs given to her by their grandmother to help her heal from her illness. Her sister then felt better and asked her to visit again soon. Gina interpreted the dream as a message from her grandmother that she had now passed on her knowledge of healing to Gina. Gina experienced the dream as a hopeful one, in which she had gained power to heal her sister, after which she felt relieved. In the course of our conversation, Gina explained to me that dreams have always been important to her and that she talked about them with her family but that whenever she told a friend about one of her dreams, the friend would usually interpret the dream as reflective of her conflicted feelings about her family members.

When I asked her what she thought of their interpretations, she said, "I can see why they think that, and yes, I sometimes feel like I need to be there for my sister, and I feel bad that I'm not there. Still, these dreams mean something else to me. They help me think about what I should be doing to help and how I should live my life." It was clear that for Gina, dreams were significant not only in terms of her anxiety concerning her sister's illness but also as a connection with her grandmother, mother, and her Ojibwa heritage, something she both longed for and hid beneath layers of other experience that was more visible to others. The dream also offered a way for Gina to allow me into her world, a transitional space in which I could imagine and witness her Ojibwa family and heritage with her.

As she discussed her dream life with me, she sometimes asked me questions such as, "Does this sound strange to you?" I experienced these questions as Gina's attempts to be reassured that I did not negatively evaluate her experience, and I responded by telling her that her dreams and her interpretation of her dreams did not seem strange to me, although I was unfamiliar with the ways she interpreted her dreams. Dreams were extraordinarily private experiences for Gina, and she took care to guard them carefully. The articulation of her narrative required both of us to take risks. For Gina, she had to bear the anxiety of letting someone know her more fully, and for me, I had to bear not knowing and fearing that I would not truly understand her.

As we continued to explore her dreams, we spoke increasingly of her relationship with Robert. Gina both wanted Robert to know about her Ojibwa ancestry and heritage and to protect this part of her life because she worried about being misunderstood and not accepted. In her view, silence about her heritage served to protect it from people who would not understand it. Silence was a form of resistance and resilience. While she had begun to talk with Robert more openly about her concerns about their social class differences, she wanted to do so with more depth and with the understanding that various aspects of her experience (e.g., class, race, culture, religion) were interconnected.

In my experience of being with Gina, at times, I felt as though I held the position of privilege and, at other times, the position of marginality. This was evident in that I connected with her valuing of her spiritual life and understood that my story was not the same as hers. Our differences were layered across race, ethnicity, religion, and social class. Gina's story is rooted in generations of social and economic oppression that had a particular course in the history of indigenous and African American communities in the United States. Psychotherapy entailed considering different possibilities of what Gina might do with her story and specifically which aspects of her story, and therefore herself, she would decide to voice and to whom. It was critical that she authored and commanded this narrative and that I witnessed the unfolding of her narrative with the awareness that she could experience me as one with or without privilege at different points in our work together. As her story unraveled, Gina gradually became more aware of how and why she consciously and unconsciously hid and disavowed parts of herself and how her anxiety was being contained through silence. Bringing voice to her story in psychotherapy and eventually to loved ones, including Robert, would both produce and contain her anxiety once again, but this time, she would be better able to speak on her terms rather than on the basis of a fear of losing love and acceptance. Listening to indigenous narrative creates profound tensions rooted in the client's and the therapist's life histories and circumstances, yet these tensions are necessary to bear and work through for an authentic engagement with all aspects of the client's story.

SUMMARY

This chapter addresses the issue of cultural constructions of psychological theory and the importance of attending to indigenous sociocultural narrative. Indigenous narrative refers to a person's subjectivity shaped by his or her sociocultural experience, including the narratives of cultural groups and the experiences of being associated with and/or identifying with these groups. Indigenous narrative is fluid and intersectional and develops along layers of sociocultural experiences and identities across the life-span. A theoretical emphasis on indigenous narrative challenges indiscriminate applications of Western, Euro American based conceptualizations of development, health, and pathology, and instead moves clinical understandings of narrative toward an analysis of complex interactions among the individual's sociocultural beliefs, sociohistorical conditions, and relational history. In addition, the context of authorship and ownership of narrative shape the criteria used to evaluate health and pathology. Indigenous narrative in psychotherapy is produced and processed in the context of an intersubjective relationship between the therapist and client who can, at varying moments, hold privileged and marginalized positions, as they may in their life outside of the therapeutic space. Therefore, the therapist should work to listen intently to the client's narrative while attending to his or her own cultural subjectivity. Transference, countertransference, dreams, and resistance can be informative of the ways in which the client's and the therapist's cultural narratives influence the therapeutic process. In the next chapter, I address a second feature of culturally informed psychoanalytic therapy that is closely connected with indigenous narrative: the consideration of language and affect.

5

CONSIDERING THE ROLE OF LANGUAGE AND AFFECT

Min, a 47-year-old, divorced, English-fluent woman, emigrated from Korea 5 years before I began seeing her in psychotherapy. She lived with her sister, who noticed that Min became increasingly isolated from others and urged her to seek help from a therapist. Min and I spent the first several meetings mostly in silence. I asked Min to describe her family relationships and her adjustment to living in the United States. I experienced Min's responses to my questions as brief and sometimes terse. In these initial meetings, I struggled with my inability to connect with Min and create a space where she could feel safe enough to talk openly with me. At times, I found myself wanting to end the session early because the silence felt prolonged and difficult to bear, both emotionally and physically.

The silence seemed less uncomfortable to Min. She continued to attend our sessions, always smiled at the end of our meetings, and confirmed our

http://dx.doi.org/10.1037/14800-006
Psychoanalytic Theory and Cultural Competence in Psychotherapy, by P. Tummala-Narra

next appointment. In our fourth session, I asked, "How are you feeling about coming to see me? I notice that when I ask you questions, you tend to be quiet."

"I'm ok, I think. Americans want to talk a lot about everything. This is not how I grew up." When I asked her if she could explain this further to me, she responded, "I don't know that I want to talk. How can talking help? In Korea, we don't have to talk about everything with someone to know how we feel."

In the remainder of our work together, which lasted until she relocated to secure employment (about 1½ years), Min and I negotiated our different approaches to communicating feelings. We recognized that we were unable to communicate in Korean, her heritage language because I don't speak Korean and did not have access to a Korean speaking interpreter. This, of course, left me wondering how this experience may have been easier for both of us if we could communicate in our primary languages. However, we discovered ways to talk about how our linguistic differences were connected with broader cultural values concerning the ways in which people communicate their suffering to others. Min and I began with a cognitive understanding of these differences. For example, I shared with her that my first language is Telegu, an Indian language, but that I speak almost exclusively in English, and she then disclosed that she continues to find it difficult to talk about her life in a language other than Korean. She also stated, "It's good to know that you understand what it's like to speak in another language."

As our work progressed, I could access her feelings of sadness not only because she had acculturated to my style of communication but also because I had acculturated to hers. I found myself increasingly able to sit with Min's quiet presence, which felt less and less distancing to me. Gradually, Min talked with me about her sadness, often through describing pain in her head and neck. She recognized that the pain in her body conveyed her sadness. Our verbal and nonverbal communication mirrored our cultural identifications, Min's as a Korean woman who was mourning her separation from her life in Korea and mine as an Indian American woman who identifies primarily with a Euro American style of communicating feelings. Perhaps Min experienced me as the American who talked too much but also as a fellow immigrant with a bicultural identity who shifted between American and Indian contexts.

Psychoanalytic psychotherapy, similar to other types of psychotherapy, relies heavily on language and verbal expression of affective material. The famous case of Anna O. (Bertha Pappenheim), written by Joseph Breuer and Sigmund Freud (1895), revealed the "talking cure" as a basic mechanism of change. In fact, one of Anna O.'s symptoms involved speech, in that she stopped speaking in her native language, German, and instead spoke in English, which was a second language to both her and to her analyst (Frie, 2013). Bilingualism, although common among early analysts and their patients, remained unexplored as a cultural matter. More recently, language is thought to be deeply embedded in culture, offering a critical space in which experience unfolds and becomes shared in the therapeutic dyad. It is through language that we hear cultural beliefs, identities, and histories (Frie, 2013). Culturally informed psychoanalytic practice attends to the conscious and unconscious communication inherent to language, bilingualism, and accompanying affects (Foster, 1996; Frie, 2013; Javier & Herron, 1996).

A nuanced, in-depth exploration of the client's emotions, including those that are conflictual and contradictory, is a defining feature of psychoanalytic work. Therapists make a distinction between emotional insight and intellectual (cognitive) insight; the former is thought to be a primary mechanism of therapeutic change. Emotional experience in psychotherapy can be more important than one's insight into past life experiences, and insight is often achieved through emotional experience (Ferenczi & Rank, 1924; Orfanos, 2006). Relatedly, psychoanalytic therapists attend to the ways in which painful emotions are avoided and managed through the use of defense mechanisms and aim to help clients develop an ability to tolerate a broader range of emotions by exploring various aspects of mental life, such as wishes, fears, fantasies, and dreams (Blagys & Hilsenroth, 2000; McWilliams, 2014; Shedler, 2010; Tomkins, 1991). The emphasis on free association or expression requires the client to openly discuss feelings, even when the process of talking about painful experiences is challenging. In addition, psychoanalytic therapists attend to what is not discussed in psychotherapy but is enacted by the client and the therapist in their relationship (McWilliams, 2014). There has also been increasing attention to the body and physical sensation in the internal experience of the client and the therapist and nonverbal communication between the client and the therapist as an important area of inquiry in psychotherapy (Lichtenberg, 2001; Lombardi, 2008).

Language and affect are inextricably tied to culture and indigenous narrative and thus require a close examination. In this chapter, I describe the importance of the individual meanings of language use and bilingualism and the complex use and interpretation of language in psychotherapy, such as language shifting. Then, I address how emotions may be expressed in ways that are consistent with the client's cultural identifications and at the same time contain a universal function of shaping the self and interactions with others. The nuances of verbal and nonverbal communication and accompanying meanings are discussed.

LANGUAGE

Language as Symbolic and Real

Language was conceptualized by Freud (1938) as an intermediary space between unconscious and conscious processes (Connolly, 2002). Rudolph Loewenstein (1956) suggested that language is the mechanism through which memories and emotions are externalized and symbolized such that they become a shared experience between the therapist and the client (Ainslie, Tummala-Narra, Harlem, Barbanel, & Ruth, 2013). In Loewenstein's view, the articulation of experience through language changes the nature of how one comes to understand this experience. The French psychoanalyst Jacques Lacan (1981) suggested that the "unconscious is structured like a language" (p. 20) and extended the concepts of the *signifier* and the *signified* introduced by the Swiss linguist Ferdinand de Saussure (1966). Lacan proposed that meanings of language are constructed through the relationship between the *signifier*, which is a sound or image, to the *signified*, which is a concept, and the relationships among *signifiers*, specifically through differences among *signifiers*. Lacan's perspective shifted language from an entity that lies inside a person to an intersubjective space rooted in culture (Connolly, 2002). A person's subjectivity is shaped through the interactions among *signifiers*, and situated in language. Lacan's emphasis on language and culture in structuring the unconscious supports the role of symbolism, myth, and metaphor in exploring subjectivity (Kristeva & Moi, 1986; Moncayo, 1998; Peña, 2003).

Psychoanalytic therapists attend to experience that is symbolized through unconscious life, as evident in dreams, myths, and metaphor. For example, the interpretation of dreams within any given cultural context connects one's private, internal life with one's community, with nature, and with spirituality (Lippmann, 2006). Spyros Orfanos (2006) noted that the myth can be conceived of as a sacred narrative, the interpretation of which can change with time and with the storyteller. Myth was connected with psychic life by Freud (e.g., Oedipus complex), who suggested that myth could be interpreted as a dream, using psychoanalytic understandings of symbolism (Orfanos, 2006). Myth is thought to hold the culture of a civilization, and metaphor, used interchangeably with myth, marks how individuals' realities are configured (Bion, 1977; Charles, 2004). Marilyn Charles (2004) described her reluctance to embrace a literal interpretation of the Oedipus complex and how Bion's (1977) conceptualization of the Oedipus story, among other myths, signified a way in which the act of knowing was prohibited. As such, the story of Oedipus and the myth more broadly provides a reference point, like a dream, from which we can more fully consider the complex feelings we have about the experience of prohibition. The American anthropologist and mythologist

Joseph Campbell (1974) suggested that if we read myths within our own religious traditions, we may interpret it factually, but when we read myths from other traditions, we understand the message that is symbolized in the myth. From his view, myths help us to connect with universal truths and with a feeling of aliveness.

In my therapeutic work with clients, I have found that myth serves a function of linking different linguistic and cultural contexts. For example, my Nepalese American client, Vinay, a man in his early 40s who had severe anxiety concerning his wife's illness, told me in one session that he had always imagined that their marriage would be everlasting, like that between Prince Rama and Princess Sita, the two main characters in one of the most revered epics of Hinduism, the *Ramayana*. Although I have read the *Ramayana*, an important text in my upbringing, I realized through my conversation with Vinay about Rama and Sita that he and I had extracted some shared and distinct meanings about life from this epic. In his view, the marriage between Rama and Sita embodied the sacredness of marriage, their deep love and admiration for each other, and the transcendence of this love beyond enormous obstacles they faced together and separately. I, too, resonated with the deep love that Rama and Sita shared but was also mindful about the tragic separation between them after Sita was abducted by the demon king Ravana. Sita, after being rescued by Rama and returning to their kingdom of Ayodhya, was abandoned by Rama as questions about her sexual purity were brought forth by people in their kingdom. Rama made the decision that Sita should leave the kingdom. Sita was once again separated from Rama, gave birth to their sons without Rama's knowledge, and later ended her life after Rama reconnected with their sons.

As I tried to link Vinay's perspective and mine, I wondered if Vinay was trying to communicate to me his fear of being separated from his wife through tragic loss. The discrepancy in focus within the *Ramayana* between my view and that of Vinay can be understood through multiple lenses. Although Vinay and I were both fully aware of the complete story of the *Ramayana*, our wishes and our fears, and our ability to verbalize them, influenced the parts of the story that were prominent for each of us. When I mentioned to Vinay that alongside the great love that Rama and Sita shared, there was tragedy, he initially reacted to my suggestion by stating, "Yes, but love doesn't die." We then were able to talk about his immense fear of losing his wife and his wish to keep her healthy and safe. The myth became the vehicle through which he talked about his painful feelings about his wife's illness, which he had difficulty articulating directly to me as he worked tirelessly to care for her, containing his own fears. The myth offered Vinay a path to express his wish to maintain a deep sense of connection to his wife, who died of her illness about 8 months later.

Language, through metaphor, myth, imagery, and symbolism, offers a view into cultural and spiritual beliefs and experiences. There are indeed words in each language that are difficult, if not impossible, to translate with the accompanying contextualized meaning into another language. Values and traditions of cultural groups are embedded in these words and terms, which provide a sense of continuity for individuals and communities. Thus, it is especially important for the therapist to understand how language expresses beliefs, values, and traditions (Roland, 1996). Although language and culture are intertwined, it is important to consider the variations in meanings that are shaped by the individual's life history and circumstances. In addition, as noted by Roger Frie (2013), all people are linguistic beings, and language should not be associated only with difference or minority or bilingual people but rather seen as a primary transmitter of culture for all people. Listening to the symbolism and linguistic context of the client allows for an understanding of the affective life that may in fact reflect shared or universal experiences alongside cultural differences (Kakar, 1995). The therapist must then attend to both the individual and the culture conveyed through language.

It is also critical to consider that language is dynamic and shifts with context. Numerous scholars have pointed out that the language the therapist uses in inquiring about certain topics, such as gender, culture, race, religion, sexual identity, social class, and dis/ability, affects the process of communication within the therapeutic relationship (Comas-Díaz, 2012; Drescher, 2007; Goodley, 2011; Olkin, 2002). For example, a therapist's assumption that a married female client has a male partner can manifest in language use in psychotherapy. Relatedly, the therapist's use of the word "homosexual" instead of "gay," "lesbian," or "bisexual" can contribute to impasses in communication. Specifically, the word "homosexual" is a medical term that has been associated with deviance and pathology and its use can intensify the client's experiences of disconnection and/or marginalization (Drescher, 2007; Lyons, Bieschke, Dendy, Worthington, & Georgemiller, 2010). Therapists may also convey a sense of what is considered "natural" or socially acceptable when they are not curious about the meanings accompanying language use (Drescher, 2007). In some cases, therapists worry about asking the meanings behind certain language use because they don't want to reify the disconnection they experience with their clients. Sometimes the therapist is unaware of language that is familiar to and more accurately descriptive of the experiences of cultural groups. For example, many therapists are less familiar with preferences for pronoun use among people with nonbinary genders, such as *zie*, which is used instead of *she* or *he*, or *hir*, which is used instead of *her* or *his*. Language that is self-defined captures the real experiences of the client and is critical to recognizing and seeing, rather than misgendering, the client (Mizock, Harrison, & Russinova, 2014).

It is important to note that attending to linguistic context does not mean that therapists should refrain from asking questions to clarify the client's language use or from admitting mistakes or lack of understanding. Too often, we operate in a world that is both immersed in and rejecting of politically correct language use, leaving us unsure about how best to clarify language confusion. Yet language use has profound implications for the nature of therapeutic work. In a study concerning helpful and harmful practices with boys and men among practitioners, Mahalik, Good, Tager, Levant, and Mackowiak (2012) noted the problem of gender bias among some clinicians who refused to inquire about histories of trauma among male clients because the clinicians assumed that men were really not victimized. These researchers (Mahalik et al., 2012) highlighted the problem of assessing men's psychological distress in a standard clinical language that neglected the ways in which many men communicate their emotions (e.g., metaphor, humor).

In addition, certain "insider terms" within a cultural group would be considered derogatory when used by those outside of the cultural group (Olkin, 2002). Therefore, the social location of the person communicating the message and the person receiving the message plays an important role in the meaning of language itself. Rhoda Olkin (2002), referring to the experiences of people with disabilities, pointed out that language conveys not only a description of a cultural group but also feelings about the group. The language used to describe a particular group has the power to determine which aspects of that group we focus our attention and thus shapes our realities. Recently, Dunn and Andrews (2015) noted the evolution of language used to describe disability and advocated for psychologists to adopt both person-first language (e.g., people with disabilities) and identity-first (e.g., disabled people) language. Psychologists have supported the use of person-first language to help reduce stigma, stereotyping, and prejudice, whereas the disability rights community and disability studies scholars within and outside of the United States have suggested that identity-first language allows individuals to value disability and claim disability from a position of pride. These developments highlight the importance of recognizing the fluid and dynamic aspects of language in descriptions concerning sociocultural identity and the meanings that language carries for individuals and communities.

Bilingualism

It is estimated that there are approximately 460 languages spoken in the United States (APA, 2012). The number of children speaking a second language at home is steadily increasing; among those who do, 62% speak Spanish, 19% speak an Indo-European language, and 15% speak an Asian or Pacific Island language (APA, 2012; Shin & Kominski, 2010). In addition, there is a wide range of English language proficiency among immigrant communities in the United States. The issue of bilingualism and multilingualism is undoubtedly of growing concern to mental health professionals. Research indicates that bilingualism has both advantages and disadvantages. There is evidence that supports the idea that bilingual people, when compared with monolingual individuals, have better executive functioning, with increased scores on tasks of selective attention and attention shifting, and are generally better able to perform on linguistic tests with ambiguous meanings (APA, 2012; Bialystok, 2009). Other studies, however, indicate that bilingual individuals tend to have a more limited range of vocabulary in each language and have lower scores on tests of verbal fluency when compared with monolingual individuals (APA, 2012; Bialystok, 2009). These mixed findings point to a complex picture of bilingual experience, with implications for mental health and psychotherapy.

Psychoanalytic perspectives on bilingualism emphasize the ways in which native or heritage language can facilitate a connection with early life experiences and reflect defensive functions, and how psychotherapy can function as a transitional space bridging old and new languages and cultural experiences. Psychoanalysts such as Edith Buxbaum (1949), Ralph Greenson (1950), and Eduardo Krapf (1955) were among the first in the discipline to describe their work with bilingual patients. Buxbaum (1949), a German psychoanalyst who practiced in the United States, reported that her female client who immigrated to the United States from Germany as an adolescent refused to speak in German in an attempt to cope with her negative experiences with a boy in Germany and establish a new identity in the United States (Santiago-Rivera & Altarriba, 2002). Greenson (1950) observed that each language spoken by his bilingual patients played a specific intrapsychic function, and that a dual sense of self emerged in the experiences of these patients. Krapf (1955), a multilingual psychoanalyst in Argentina, similarly observed that his multilingual patients unconsciously spoke in a specific language, and switched from speaking in one language to another, to avoid feelings of intense anxiety (Santiago-Rivera & Altarriba, 2002). The work of these scholars was especially influential as it brought to the forefront the complex ways in which clients negotiate each language in psychotherapy. Specifically, for some bilingual clients, the heritage language carries painful and/or traumatic childhood memories they may wish, either consciously or unconsciously, to avoid. Thus, they may find it easier to articulate these memories in the second language that carries less intense negative affect (Ainslie et al., 2013; Foster, 1996; Javier, 1995; Santiago-Rivera & Altarriba, 2002).

Over the past two decades, bilingualism has been explored more systematically by psychoanalytic scholars. Several combinations of language use exist within the therapeutic dyad, including when the therapist is an immigrant and works with a client whose heritage language is different from his or her own, when the client is an immigrant and works with a therapist who speaks English or the local language, when the therapist and the client are both immigrants but speak in a third language that is not either one of their heritage languages, and when the therapist and client are both immigrants and work in their shared heritage language (Ainslie et al., 2013; Amati-Mehler, Argentieri, & Canestri, 1990). These various possibilities raise important questions about the nuances of communication, affect, and defenses in the therapeutic relationship. Rafael Javier (1995) and RoseMarie Perez Foster (1996), in particular, called attention to the complications involved with psychotherapy when the therapist cannot access a client's memories that are encoded in a linguistic context that is unfamiliar to him or her. Foster (1996) elaborated on the organizing functions implicated in bilingualism. She suggested that language is a "characterological organizer," that is a culmination of social, object-relational, intrapsychic, and psycholinguistic factors. Bilingual individuals are thought to have "dual templates" that organize experiences of self and of others and two distinct verbal symbols used to express these experiences. For the bilingual or multilingual individual, each language is connected with a particular developmental period and context.

There is considerable variation in how people acquire different languages, such as through their parents and family members, through caregivers other than family members, and through teachers and peers at school. Sometimes a language is acquired in one's country of birth and other times in one's adopted homeland, where one becomes a member of a minority group. Psychotherapy offers a space in which the client can access memories of cognitive and affective experiences that are processed within a certain cultural, linguistic, and relational context. Javier (1995) referred to Freud's (1912) concept of *evenly suspended attention* as a critical element in being able to distinguish between the client's repression of painful affective experience and an unfamiliar linguistic encoding of an experience, as the therapist remains open to the possibility of multiple alternatives with regard to the client's experiences rather than focusing selectively on certain areas of the client's experiences at the cost of neglecting other areas.

In psychotherapy, language shifting occurs when the client chooses consciously or unconsciously to speak in a different language with a therapist who speaks both of the client's languages. The use of a certain language often reflects the client's interactions with caregivers and personal meanings connected with these early experiences (Frie, 2013). When language switching occurs, therapists and clients experience changes in the ways that they communicate with each other, particularly about affective experiences. For example, I have noticed that when I have asked my bilingual clients to talk about a painful experience, typically a traumatic event, in the heritage language, even when

CONSIDERING THE ROLE OF LANGUAGE AND AFFECT   119

I do not speak that language, they are more engaged and connected with that experience. The act of articulating their experience in the heritage language deepens our ability to communicate with each other. Each language reflects different self-states of the client and of the therapist (Bromberg, 1996; Foster, 1996). Language is intricately linked with affect, and it is often the case that bilingual and multilingual people feel differently when they retrieve and report memories in each language. The invitation of multiple languages in psychotherapy is often necessary to fully engage with the affective quality of clients' experiences, as is the analysis of enactments rooted in linguistic similarities and differences between the therapist and the client.

The dynamics of transference and countertransference are evident in the choice of language used in psychotherapy and in language switching. Ruth Lijtmaer (1999) outlined several possible reactions, spanning idealization to hostility, in the transference and countertransference. For example, when the therapist does not speak the client's heritage language, the client may doubt the therapist's ability to help him or her, potentially repeating past experiences of being misunderstood or disengaged with significant people. The same therapist may serve a different function, namely that as a transitional object through which the client bridges experiences from the heritage culture and those from the new cultural context, developing a new identity (Lijtmaer, 1999; Winnicott, 1971). Assuming the client has a choice of therapist, he or she may seek a therapist of a particular ethnic and linguistic background in the hope of learning about and acculturating to the new cultural context through interacting with this therapist. The therapist's countertransference in this situation may involve feelings of frustration and anger with his or her compromised attempts to communicate effectively with the client. On the other hand, when the client and therapist share a common language, the client and the therapist may idealize the heritage culture and language, with a potential of dismissing potential ambivalence about the heritage culture. The therapist may distance himself or herself from the client in an effort to minimize overidentification with the client. As such, language and language switching can serve defensive functions while also communicating a wish to connect with one's disavowed aspects of past experiences and/or with the therapist (Frie, 2013; Lijtmaer, 1999).

The loss of heritage language is an issue that is critical to many immigrants and refugees. The effort to communicate in a second language within a new cultural context is often experienced as challenging and becomes a mark of one's sense of imperfection and narcissistic wounds (Ainslie et al., 2013). This is evident in the realities of children and adolescents who migrate to a country with little exposure to the host language. In the United States, the acquisition of English is a key element in immigrant youth's academic adjustment. While research indicates that it usually takes between 4 and 7 years of "optimal academic instruction" for the acquisition of academic second language skills, children and adolescents are typically expected to complete second language learning programs by the end of 3 years (APA, 2012, p. 55). It is often the case that youth and adults experience a disconnection between their actual abilities and what they are able to express in a second language (Ainslie et al., 2013). The loss of language use among the second generation, those primarily raised in the new country, poses additional dilemmas for parents and children because language is a major mechanism of transmitting the nuances of cultural beliefs and traditions. For example, in many immigrant and refugee homes, it is typical to find varying degrees of English language fluency among older and younger members, attenuating the intergenerational gaps and loss (Grinberg & Grinberg, 1989). Fluency in the heritage language can also become an indicator of authenticity and sense of belonging within a particular ethnic group. This is exemplified in language, such as "off the boat" or "oreos" (Brown on the outside, White on the inside), used to describe an individual's primary identification with either the culture of origin or the new cultural context (Tummala-Narra, 2004).

Salman Akhtar (2011) observed the particular experiences of language use and loss of the bilingual, immigrant therapist. He recognized that because the bilingual, immigrant therapist often conducts psychotherapy in a language other than the heritage language, he or she may overlook the nuances of the language spoken by the client, such as puns and metaphors. Addressing linguistic differences in psychotherapy entails grieving the loss of or disconnection from the everyday use of and access to the heritage language. Akhtar called attention to the ways in which the immigrant therapist on occasion wishes to intervene with a client in his or her own heritage language. The therapist, in this case, must engage in self-inquiry to closely examine his or her wishes and needs to communicate in his or her own heritage language to the client, and the accompanying loss. The therapist's accent and ethnic-sounding name can further shape the nature of the client's transference. Specifically, Akhtar described a case of a woman who, upon some inquiry in psychotherapy, expressed that she felt anxious in pronouncing his name, and consequently, stopped in the middle of a sentence to switch her words such that she would not pronounce "Dr. Akhtar" in his presence. The client was concerned that if she mispronounced her therapist's name, he would view her as different from him, leaving her feeling "distant, rejected, and sad" (Akhtar, 2011, p. 224). In addition, the client attempted to protect her immigrant therapist from feeling like a foreigner by not stating his ethnic-sounding name. Akhtar's exploration of his client's word switching facilitated a deeper understanding of the client's long-standing feelings of unacceptability within her family.

Binomial Identities in the Immigrant Context[3]

The potential loss of heritage language is connected with the process of naming. For example, in the context of migration, names and changes in names across time and generations implicate cultural adjustment, ethnic identity, transition from "foreigner" or "other" to "American," loss of heritage culture, and the hope of remaking identity. Consequently, immigrants both work toward and away from "Americanization" of the self and of family, often with deep ambivalence concerning the choice to migrate. The optimism underlying the immigrant experience and the disillusionment that is shaped by experiences of discrimination and separation from loved ones coexist, contributing to divergent approaches to the transmission of culture to subsequent generations. This can manifest in the choice of names for oneself or one's children. Specifically, racial minority immigrants often contend with choosing a name that is "American" or more likely to be accepted by White Americans. In some cases, an immigrant or a refugee may attempt to protect his or her children by disconnecting from the heritage language and culture and more or less exclusively identifying and interacting within mainstream culture. On the other hand, immigrants and refugees may cope with discrimination by making active efforts to secure identifications with heritage language and culture and protect their children from becoming too "Americanized." In this latter case, they may be more likely to choose names for themselves and their children that indicate a sense of ethnic identity.

The naming process may also be influenced by histories of political and intergenerational trauma. Atrocities such as the forced separations of Native American children from their parents and communities, the forced migration of Africans to the United States and slavery, colonization, and the Nazi Holocaust are all experiences through which names and identities were transformed, either through force or choice. For many refugees and displaced individuals, experiences of torture and betrayal by governing groups in the country of origin may contribute to a desire to create a new identity that is associated with safety and survival (Foster, 2005). In the case of Jewish immigrants in the United States, name changes occurred in the context of escaping and/or surviving the Nazi Holocaust and continue to occur. Efforts to ward off anti-Semitism and obstacles to survival and success are often the reasons many Jewish Americans choose to change their birth names to Anglicized names. For many Jewish Americans, name changes may indicate a pragmatic assimilation in which they maintain a close connection to a Jewish

---

[3]From *Immigration in Psychoanalysis: Locating Ourselves*, edited by J. Beltsiou, 2016, New York, NY: Routledge. Copyright 2016 by Routledge. Adapted with permission.

identity and heritage but at the same time are perceived as White Americans. On the other hand, for immigrants who are seen as racial minorities, such as those from Africa, Asian, Latin America, and the Caribbean, visible features, such as skin color, hair texture, and eyelid shape, impede the ability to pass as White even when having Anglicized names.

There are many variations in how names are negotiated. Children of immigrants with a heritage birth name may choose to keep their birth name or to change it, and later in life decide to change it back to the birth name. It is important that the symbolism of naming and the renaming process be understood in terms of developing and shifting identity and that critical transitions and circumstances fuel decisions about the progression of naming across the life-span. This is illustrated in Jumpa Lahiri's (1999) novel *The Namesake*, in which an Indian immigrant father, Ashoke, names his son, Gogol, after the Russian author Nikolai Gogol. Ashoke's choice of his son's name is related to his survival of a train accident. Immediately before the train accident, Ashoke had been reading Nikolai Gogol's novel *The Overcoat*, and he associated the name Gogol with survival. His son, Gogol, is born and raised in the United States and grows up unaware of the reason for his unusual name as a person of Indian heritage. When Gogol turns 18 years old, he decides to change his name to Nikhil, a name that he associates with an Indian heritage. Gogol's decision to change his name to Nikhil perhaps represents his claim to a sense of belonging within Indian culture and, more broadly, just somewhere. Gogol is a name that is not typically given to Indians, and in the novel leaves this son of Indian immigrants without a sense of home. While his parents are unhappy with this decision, his father states, "In America anything is possible. Do as you wish." To Gogol's surprise, at the court, the process of changing his name legally seems anticlimactic. It is possible that Gogol may have hoped that the name change would provide more clarity concerning his identity; instead, he remains on the border between India and the United States.

The Namesake depicts the shifting of names and identities throughout the life-span across generations and the question of who defines the significance of the name itself. Names in the premigration context bear different meanings than in the postmigration context because circumstances, cultural values, and relationships transform. It is likely that Ashoke's intended meaning of choosing Gogol's name, from the viewpoint of an Indian who grew up in India, is disconnected from his son's experience of carrying this name as an Indian in the United States. The name, Gogol, holds different meanings in these two different cultural contexts and generations. For Ashoke, the name Gogol may have represented a connection to survival and a sense of connection to his family and home in India, whereas for Gogol, his name may have represented a sense of disconnection and alienation from his Indian ancestral home and his American home. Ashoke, upon Gogol's announcement that he will change his name, comes to accept that the meaning of the name had transformed for his son, who viewed himself as an American. Gogol, a few years after changing his name, meets a Bengali, Indian woman who he imagines as having a shared identity. However, he comes to realize that he shares only part of his new wife's identity and that she, too, is haunted by her own identity conflicts. Both Ashoke's and Gogol's experiences demonstrate the fluid nature of linguistic and cultural identity and the naming process, and how name change at one point in one's development does not necessarily mark the dissolution of one's identification with heritage culture or with mainstream culture.

The dilemma inherent to naming is illustrated in the experiences of migrants who adopt an Anglicized name that is used in public and retain a heritage name that is used at home and within their respective ethnic communities. The reasons for this binomial identity are varied, reflecting a wish to make it easier for others to pronounce names and be accepted by others while maintaining cultural identity (R. Thompson, 2006). Yet for many immigrants and refugees, binomial experiences continue to indicate a broader social expectation of the need to accommodate the mainstream at the cost of a more integrated experience that is driven by real choice. Increasingly, first and second generation individuals seem to choose names that reflect a hybrid identity, where chosen names are either translatable from heritage language to English (e.g., Pedro to Peter), or premigration linguistic traits are blended with Anglicized names (e.g., Lily, which can be Anglicized or Indian) (C. A. Sue & Telles, 2007).

In a social context in which heritage, Anglicized, or hybrid names are met with ambivalence, an individual may develop split off aspects of the self, and split-off identifications with cultural aspects of identity. Although many migrants may have access to different versions of the self, both real and imagined, across different cultural contexts (e.g., country of origin, adopted country), through their interactions with family and similar ethnic friends either in person or via the Internet, some migrants, such as refugees and those experiencing traumatic stress, may leave parts of the self behind (Bromberg, 1996; Harlem, 2010). This experience of missing or losing aspects of the self may also be pronounced in the case of international adoptees in the United States, who typically have no choice in names or access to their cultural heritage. Thus, it is important that psychotherapy involve the client's examination of multiple and sometimes forgotten and/or repressed experiences of the self via language. In addition, the significance of names along with the experiences steeped in specific sociocultural contexts can be remembered, forgotten, and remembered again.

EXPRESSION OF AFFECT

Exploring Affect

Affect or emotion, although an essential aspect of human experience, is a construct that is conceptualized differently across cultures. The ways in which affect is experienced, symbolized, and expressed vary significantly with context (Kleinman & Good, 1985; Seeley, 2005; Shweder, 1991). In addition, within societies, it may be more permissible for certain members of society to express painful emotions that might be stigmatized for other members of the same society. The expression of affect also can vary with the construction of implicit and explicit rules concerning interpersonal relating. For example, my client, a White, Greek American woman in her 60s, shared with me that she never talked with her male physician about her sadness about the loss of her husband, who was murdered, because she didn't think it was appropriate for a woman to openly share her sadness with a man. When I inquired more about her perspective, she stated, "We just don't do that kind of thing in my family. We were raised to talk to other women, not the men." Conversely, another client, a gay, African American man in his mid-20s, told me that he couldn't talk about his feelings when he was growing up because it would be assumed that he was "not a real man." He stated, "I couldn't begin to imagine talking to my folks about what I really feel or that I'm gay. I still can't. They would think that I'm not really gay but that I'm just too sensitive or something."

There are important cultural differences concerning the salience of sexuality and sexual identity and expressions of sexuality in private and public life. Some clients are unaware of words in their heritage languages referring to sexuality or that these words contain obscene connotations, therefore constraining the way that sexuality can be discussed in psychotherapy (Huang & Akhtar, 2005). For example, Akhtar (in Huang & Akhtar, 2005) described his work with a Hindu Indian woman in which she was not aware of the word for female genitals in Hindi; she later asked him to tell her the word, raising his anxiety about having to tell her this word despite cultural barriers shared by him and his patient. The discussion of other types of emotional experiences can be stigmatized, as well. Specifically, the client's socioeconomic background, particularly if the client is living in poverty, raises anxiety for many therapists, as evident in conscious and unconscious attempts to avoid or distance from the client's struggles. In a similar vein, physical disabilities can raise similar anxieties for able-bodied therapists, as they may feel anxious upon becoming aware of their assumptions about people with disabilities and/ or their own feelings of vulnerability.

Similar to verbal language, emotional expression symbolizes cultural ideals (Seeley, 2005). The expression of affect is inextricably linked with interpersonal space rooted in cultural values and beliefs. This is evident in the various conceptualizations of dissociative experiences, including the views of dissociation as a response to traumatic stress, spontaneous shifts in conscious experience, a part of religious and spiritual rituals and healing practices, and a culturally congruent and sanctioned way of expressing self-states and overwhelming affect (Seligman & Kirmayer, 2008). When the therapist and client differ across sociocultural identities (e.g., age, gender, race, ethnicity, religion, social class, sexual orientation, dis/ability), the expression of affect is further complicated by language barriers and stereotypes. In psychoanalytic therapy, the exploration of the client's full range of emotional experiences, such as love, sexual desire, sadness, anger, and aggression, is pivotal for therapeutic change. However, the degree to which these emotions are explored and expressed can vary significantly between the client and the therapist.

Roland (2006) described the difficulty in exploring anger experienced toward him by his Asian American patients, in contrast to many of his Euro American patients, who openly shared their disagreement or ambivalence about him more directly. He reported that his Asian American patients, while they expressed their anger toward others besides the therapist, they typically took longer to express any criticism of therapist even indirectly to him. Roland further pointed out that, among his Asian American patients, the anxiety connected with the prospect of expressing anger toward the therapist, was a function of a cultural value placed on relating within a hierarchal interpersonal space and with a fear of losing a nurturing relationship.

Although culture shapes emotions and even the nature of the self, it is dynamic, and continually reshapes internal and relational life. Markus and Kitayama (2010), in their review of cross-cultural understandings of the self, stated, "In an ongoing cycle of mutual constitution, people are socioculturally shaped shapers of their environments; they make each other up and are most productively analyzed together" (p. 421). Because individuals and social contexts are inseparable from each other, the capacity of individuals to influence and be influenced by their contexts is thought to be universal, despite cross-cultural differences in the expression of affect, cognition, and behavior (Markus & Kitayama, 2010). Thus, in psychotherapy, an exploration of affect as contextually driven must coexist with an exploration of affect as universal. In other words, cultural beliefs concerning emotion, its symbolization and expression, and individual constructions of emotional experiences should be considered, such that neither a psychic nor a sociocultural determinism dominates the exploration of affect in psychotherapy (Chodorow, 1999).

Psychoanalysis recognizes the privacy of emotions and the unique ways that emotions are experienced and constructed by individuals. Nancy Chodorow

(1999) observed that emotions may be expressed in particular ways across cultures but that emotions are experienced and constructed in different ways by different people within a cultural group. The personal meanings of emotions inform the client's experience of the self and others, including his or her sociocultural world. In fact, being genuinely engaged with the client's affective experience is thought to embody healing itself (McWilliams, 2004; Stark, 1999; Tomkins, 1991). Leston Havens (1986, p. 19) referred to *affective empathy* as the "experience of the patient's feeling state by the therapist," where the therapist determines "the other's feeling state by observing his expressions, tone of voice, posture, and the thousand objective expressions of affect the body produces, including autonomic ones." Such engagement requires an ability to attune to the client's emotional life and create a therapeutic space that is characterized by authenticity, mutuality, and collaboration (S. A. Mitchell, 1998b; Stark, 1999).

Psychoanalysts have further emphasized the importance of affect in transference and countertransference. Specifically, affect is thought to underlie the problem of repetition. Paul Russell (1998, p. 4 in Teicholz, Kriegman, & Fairfield, 1998), in his analysis of why people unconsciously repeat destructive patterns (e.g., repetition compulsion), suggested that "repetition occurs in lieu of something we cannot yet feel, a kind of affective incompetence." Russell proposed that the transference reflects the client's focus on certain aspects of the therapist that actually reenact past events. In this view, the therapist does, to some extent, mirror or reify the client's past experiences. Therefore, transference cannot be understood as encompassing only the client's conflictual relationships from the past. In fact, if we disavow our own potential entanglement in the client's transference, we risk diminishing our emotional connection with our clients (Russell, 1998). The therapist then must attend to the here-and-now moments occurring between the therapist and the client. Mitchell (S. A. Mitchell, 1998b, p. 53) expanded these ideas and stated that the "patient needs the analyst to feel and do things that the analyst is frightened to feel and do," serving a containing function in exploring painful affect. Steven Cooper (2000) further suggested that the therapist's containment of the client's affect is met with the client's efforts to contain the therapist's affect, even though the two processes are not equivalent. The process of mutual recognition and containment is thought to be essential to the client's ability to recognize and work with the nature of the limitations of psychotherapy, the therapist, and the self (Cooper, 2000).

Psychoanalytic perspectives focus on the importance of the client's discovery of his or her unconscious emotional experience. Symptom relief occurs as a function of this uncovering process. Freud's initial understanding concerning hysteria emphasized the split-off or repressed affect and emotional memories (e.g., reminiscences) associated with traumatic experiences that manifested in symptomology. Later in his work, Freud recognized that the analyst's attempts to remove symptoms undermined the reality that patients were both distressed by and attached to their symptoms (e.g., resistance), so the analyst should learn about the underlying conflicts creating the symptoms (Ogden & Gabbard, 2010). In this sense, symptoms are defenses protecting the client from experiencing overwhelming, distressing affect. Therefore, the full complexity of the symptom itself needs to be examined (Ogden & Gabbard, 2010). Psychoanalysts have further recognized that emotional experiences of the client and of the therapist intersect and shape the exploration of the client's affects, conflicts, and defenses. In fact, Nancy McWilliams (1999) pointed out that the initial stages of psychotherapy actually stimulate defenses, in which the therapist learns about the client's approach to coping with the stress of revealing private information to a stranger (e.g., therapist). People seek psychotherapy to both talk about difficult experiences and minimize them in the hope that the therapist will not negatively evaluate them, so they bear feelings of hope and shame (McWilliams, 1999).

Wishes and defenses can manifest in psychotherapy in ways that intersect with sociocultural identities. For example, when I first met my client, Laura, an African American woman in her 40s, she walked from the waiting room toward my office with the assistance of a cane. As we walked toward my office, we passed through two doorways, where the doors had been closed. While approaching the first doorway, she said, "I will get my own door. I don't need help."

After we were both seated in my office, I asked her to tell me what she hoped for in psychotherapy. She responded, "I'm tired of being a strong Black woman. I know I need help, but this is not going to be easy." In her statement, Laura revealed both her need for help and her reluctance to receive help from a stranger. In our work together, it became important for us to explore her identity as a Black woman and particularly how her self-reliance was both a source of strength and a burden that was perpetuated on a broader social scale, through stereotyping and discrimination. Despite her many accomplishments in her professional life, she spoke of being "tired," referring to a feeling of exhaustion from managing all of the stress of enduring a series of medical illnesses, the pain associated with her disability, family conflict, discrimination, and isolation. She felt that she had been there for everyone else in her life and that she had yet to find someone who could care for her.

Our work entailed a movement toward bringing her sadness into a safe space, where it could be voiced and heard fully. I found myself struggling with how to both respect her ability to do so much and help her to verbalize her wishes and fears about finding someone who would care for her without taking advantage of her. The negotiation of intimacy between us became a critical part of helping her to believe it was possible for her to be loved and cared for in the ways that she wished. In this case, it is also clear that the internalized stereotype of the "strong Black woman" operated such that Laura's feelings of vulnerability and longing for intimacy became masked and suppressed. Stereotypes carry both intensified and disavowed affective experiences. Some illustrations of the ways that stereotypes contain and arouse emotions include the labeling of minorities with terms such as "the violent Black man," "the asexual Asian man," "the angry Black woman," "the weak disabled person," or "the lesbian who hates men." Exploring internalized stereotypes is necessary for bringing painful affective experiences into the here-and-now interactions within the therapeutic dyad so that the client becomes better able to deconstruct his or her conflicts and defenses within a safe space.

Examining the meanings of feelings is a central task of psychoanalytic therapists, as is the recognition that these meanings are shaped by the interplay of social, interpersonal, and intrapsychic processes, including defenses. Therapeutic work involves attention to the "moment-to-moment microshifts" in the transference and countertransference, as meanings of language and affect are created through the dialogue and interaction between the client and the therapist (Boston Change Process Study Group & Nahum, 2008, p. 139). Arnold Modell (2005) noted that in psychoanalytic psychotherapy, the therapist and the client bring each of their own emotional memories to their relationship, shaping the nature of transference. This is evident when a client or a therapist reveals different aspects of himself or herself to a different therapist or client, respectively. Each person in the therapeutic dyad evokes a unique pattern of emotional reactions from the other person, depending on each individual's personality, emotional memories, values, and assumptions (Modell, 2005). Through empathic immersion, the therapist makes a genuine effort to understand the client, and through the facilitation of language, the client's affective experience becomes organized and conscious, and the client becomes seen and known. It is this ability to experience and express affects that is thought to be indicative of structural change in psychoanalytic psychotherapy (Ornstein, 2009).

In addition to verbal language and communication, the process of listening from an intersubjective perspective involves *implicit knowledge*, which refers to "knowing and memory that is nonverbal, nonsymbolic, and nonconscious, as compared to explicit or declarative knowledge" (D. B. Stern, 2008, p. 183). Implicit knowledge contains nonverbal processes, including affects, memories, and representation, and permeates transference, countertransference, the client's and the therapist's fantasies and relational experiences from the past (D. B. Stern, 2008). D. B. Stern (2009) suggested that when a client experiences therapy as beneficial or even lifesaving, he or she may not remember specific interpretations made by the therapist but rather specific important relational moments and how they felt sensorially, perceptually, and affectively.

Stern proposed that dissociated self states that have never been symbolized become *unformulated* in response to overwhelming or unbearable fear, shame, or humiliation. He further referred to enactments in psychotherapy as the "interpersonalization of the dissociation," when the client and therapist must grapple with their respective dissociated self-states (Bromberg, 1996; D. B. Stern, 2009, 2010).

The therapist must come to terms with his or her own feelings evoked through the enactment to preserve the ability to witness the client's *unformulated experiences* and help the client bring to awareness and express emotions that provide meaning to his or her narrative. This is especially true when the client has experienced traumatic stress in life, which is then relived within the therapeutic relationship. Philip Bromberg (2006) noted, "As the enactment continues, the patient's dissociated shame escalates, and the therapist finds himself feeling things about this patient and about his own role that make him increasingly uncomfortable, often triggering his own dissociative processes" (p. 123). The therapist then has to articulate his or her own experience of the enactment to facilitate the client's ability and willingness to verbalize his or her experience as well (Bromberg, 2006). Although affect often is communicated unconsciously in the therapeutic dyad, the therapist and the client must work collaboratively to deconstruct the enactment to discover what feels intolerable to recognize and acknowledge these feelings on a conscious level (Ehrenberg, 2010; I. Hoffman, 1998). Our ability to bear the anxiety of not knowing the client's *unformulated experience* and resisting the urge to make an interpretation as a function of our own anxiety with not knowing helps the client to know and feel that he or she and we can bear the intensity of affect and that meaning can be formed from such experiences (Charles, 2005).

Affect and the Body

Unconscious communication of affect between the therapist and the client has been thought to be an important feature of psychoanalytic therapy (Bollas, 1987; Charles, 2005; Ehrenberg, 2010; Knoblauch, 2005; D. B. Stern, 2009). Freud (1938) recognized the interdependence between intrapsychic and somatic phenomena, although he conceptualized the unconscious as an autonomous space between the physical and psychical (Carignani, 2012). In recent years, psychoanalysts have focused less on the body as anatomy and more on the body as experienced by the individual, shifting the client–therapist interaction to a focus on sensations and emotions (Carignani, 2012; Ferrari, 2001; Lombardi, 2008). Research in neuroscience indicates that the process of observing others' actions produces shifts in physical sensation within the observer (Arizmendi, 2008).

Psychoanalytic scholars have suggested that the therapist's empathic attunement is unconsciously grounded in his or her own bodily experiences, raising attention to the importance of body or embodied memories (Arizmendi, 2008; Elisha, 2010; Lemma, 2014; Leuzinger-Bohleber, 2008; Modell, 2005; Petrucelli, 2014).

Riccardo Lombardi (2008) observed that the therapist can experience bodily countertransference with clients who face challenges with the integration of bodily and psychic experiences, implicating the therapist's ability to contain the client's projections. He proposed that the therapist aims to engage in "a dialogue between body and mind" so that the client comes to recognize and relate to his or her own physical sensations, something that precedes his or her recognition of others (Lombardi, 2008). Lombardi (2013) has further noted that contemporary influences of access to and use of technology (e.g., Internet, texting) contribute to superficial object relations that foster dissociation and a discontinuity between sensations, emotions, and cognition. Relatedly, in recent years, there has been growing attention to the problem of youth and adults spending less time outdoors as a function of more time spent with technological devices, which is thought to contribute to a wide range of physical, behavioral, and relational problems (*nature-deficit disorder*) (Louv, 2005). Indeed, therapists today have the experience of working with clients who struggle with connecting with and communicating their actual emotional experiences in their intimate relationships. It is increasingly common that clients are challenged by developing relationships and being connected to others via online or texting and yet remain isolated and lonely, raising questions about how the body and intimacy are being redefined in the age of information technology and social media.

Judith Schore and Allan Schore (2014) pointed out that attachment develops through right brain communication between the infant and the caregiver, involving primarily nonverbal, visual, auditory, and tactile social–emotional interchanges. They proposed that these nonverbal communication patterns are used by the individual to regulate affect in interpersonal relationships throughout his or her life, including the therapeutic relationship. Thus, the therapist has to approach verbal and nonverbal communication with *evenly suspended attention* (Freud, 1912) so that he or she can connect on an implicit level with the client's experiences "from the inside out" (Bromberg, 2010; Schore & Schore, 2014). In this perspective, right brain, nonverbal interactions lie at the core of psychotherapy rather than left brain interactions (e.g., interpretation). Right brain interactions communicate body- and sensation-based emotional self-states and facilitate the client's growth and change in the presence of an empathically attuned therapist. Psychotherapy can provide a transitional space through which these bodily experiences are expressed and examined.

The significance of embodied memories is evident in the experiences of survivors of severe trauma. Specifically, traumatic events occurring in early childhood are typically not accessible through conscious communication and verbal language, but are expressed in sensations. My client Akila, an Egyptian American woman in her 30s, who sought help to cope with feelings of anxiety about conflicts with her husband, experienced spasms in her shoulder for as long as she could remember, with no known physiological cause despite numerous medical tests. Her shoulder would spasm during our sessions, particularly when she felt distressed. Well into a year of our work together, she revealed that she held a visual image in her mind about a maternal aunt. The aunt was naked in this image, and as Akila continued to verbalize her memory of her aunt, she multiple spasms and gradually revealed that the aunt had sexually molested her. Because her sense of shame and humiliation concerning the abuse was overwhelming to her, our conversations centered on her descriptions of her bodily pain inflicted through the spasms. Her spasms evoked my own feelings of helplessness because during sessions, I often wished I could relieve the pain she felt in her shoulder. Akila's expressions of psychic pain through her body allowed me to witness her sadness and rage, which was necessary for me to understand and engage with her internal life. In the coming months, Akila and I continued to negotiate how she could find words to describe her physical and psychological pain; she often felt safer showing me how she felt rather than telling me in words because talking about feelings felt prohibited and alien to her within her family and cultural contexts. It is important to note that bodily experience does not necessarily indicate a defense against painful affect but provides a space to express the traumatic event itself. There is now ample literature suggesting that somatization of psychological distress is a common phenomenon within cultures in which it is less acceptable to express negative emotions and distress through verbal language (Barnow & Balkir, 2013). However, the meanings underlying bodily symptomology vary significantly with the individual's cultural context, life history, and circumstances. Thus, therapists should be cautious in making broad interpretations inferring somatization of psychological distress.

CASE ILLUSTRATION: AMARO

The following case material from my work with my client Amaro, which spanned 2 years, illustrates the ways in which language and expression of affect play a critical role in the therapist's and client's exploration of sociocultural context and identity.

Amaro is a married Chilean American man in his mid-50s. He is the father of two sons who are both in their early 20s. He works full time as an architect. He was born and raised in an urban area of Chile and immigrated to the United States when he was 30 years old with his wife with the hope of securing better professional opportunities. Amaro was raised in a middle-class home, and his parents both worked in an architectural business. Through much of their lives, he and his two brothers attended competitive and elite educational institutions, which were fairly distant from their parental home. Amaro described his parents as intelligent and successful and said he always admired their dedication to their work. Amaro met his wife, Elana, while attending college in Chile. He described his wife as loving but at times emotionally distant. In the United States, he secured a stable position in architecture but began experiencing feelings of sadness periodically since immigrating. His sadness had progressed to depressive symptoms over the course of 6 months before our first meeting. He sought psychotherapy on his own to cope with his depressed mood and was familiar with psychotherapy because his younger brother had found psychotherapy to be helpful in dealing with substance abuse.

Amaro's first language is Spanish, and he is fluent in English. Amaro told me in our first session that he did not have a preference for speaking in Spanish and that he was comfortable working with me, even though I don't speak Spanish. In the initial stages of our work, he reported recent events that caused a great deal of stress to him and to his family, including his mother being diagnosed with cancer and the death of his maternal uncle. His mother had recently completed her medical treatment, and her illness was in remission when we met. When he described these stressful events, however, his emotions appeared to be disconnected from these events, although he told me that he felt sad about them. I found myself increasingly frustrated with not being able to hear or feel his sadness. I noticed that I began to feel more physically tired in our sessions. A few weeks later, I asked Amaro what it felt like for him to tell me about being sad. He said, "I never talk about it much with people. It is sometimes hard to really know what to say."

I asked, "Do you think that it would easier to know what to say if you spoke in Spanish?" Amaro responded by stating that the place of Spanish in his life had been diminishing over several years, and he didn't know whether it would make a difference for him if he spoke about his concerns in Spanish. I then requested him to speak in Spanish and then translate his words to me in English when he talked about his mother's illness and his uncle's death. I experienced Amaro's verbalization in Spanish strikingly different from that in English. His speech felt more alive to me, and within moments, I started to feel his sadness that was previously so inaccessible.

I shared with Amaro that I could hear his sadness more when he spoke in Spanish than when he spoke in English, to which he responded, "I think I feel like a different person in Spanish, too." Amaro connected with his sadness but also with a sense of hope when he spoke in Spanish. In English, he felt less sad but less hopeful. He reported feeling "more tired" in English, a feeling I absorbed in our initial sessions when his affect seemed invisible to me. Amaro and I talked about how English came to represent a dissociated space in which he felt mostly alone and different, even though this is the primary language through which he connected with his wife and children. In one session he stated, "I don't feel everything fully in English. It's like I'm half there. I don't know where the rest of me is."

We continued throughout the rest of our work with Amaro periodically speaking in Spanish and then translating his words into English, in an effort to engage different self-states in each language. At times, this process felt artificial because I could never completely enter his world. The projective identification in which I absorbed his feelings of being tired and alone in the room informed my own affective and bodily responses to our language gaps. Yet with the contrasting presence of both Spanish and English in our relationship, gradually we both felt increasingly emotionally alive and engaged with his affective life.

Several months into our work together, Amaro stated that he was increasingly sad about his life again and felt even more emotionally disconnected from Elana. When I inquired about their relationship, he stated, "I love my wife, but I don't think that she understands me very much." He revealed that his wife grew up under different circumstances that were unfamiliar to him. Elana had been raised primarily in Italy, and although her parents were born in Chile, they identified more with the Italian language and culture than with that of Chile. Amaro and Elana spoke primarily in English, and their sons learned only a small amount of Spanish and Italian through their parents. Amaro expressed that he worried that his sons would never know Spanish or relate to his life in Chile. Amaro and Elana traveled to Chile every 2 or 3 years to visit his parents, but over time, Amaro sensed that his sons were losing interest in their Chilean heritage. He mentioned to me in a session, "They [the sons] even have more American sounding names. They look like they could just be like Americans. Sometimes, I think what will they be like when they have their own families? What will they know about their culture to pass it on?" Amaro's fears about his sons' loss of connection with the Chilean culture were reified by his experience of losing Spanish as a language and as a representation of continuity with his family and with Chile.

In the course of our work, we further discussed Amaro's life in Chile. Amaro spoke at length about how he valued the importance of family and community in Chile and enjoyed various festivals throughout the year. Although he did not consider himself to be a religious person and is not a practicing Catholic, his family celebrated many of the Catholic festivals, and these festivals were an opportunity to connect with family members with whom Amaro did not regularly interact. Because Amaro attended high school and college far away from home, these festivals became the center of anticipation for him to reconnect with family. I asked Amaro whether he imagined himself living in Chile ever again. He stated, "The thing is that I love Chile more when I'm here, but when I'm there it is not simple either." At this point, Amaro moved away from a position of idealized imagery of his life in Chile to a position of strong ambivalence about his Chilean heritage. He expressed, "Some people in Chile are not so open-minded about things, like there is not as much respect for people who look like me." Amaro was referring to his skin color, a darker complexion when compared with the rest of his family. Amaro revealed that, although he felt that his parents loved him, he looked different from his lighter skinned brothers who passed for White Europeans, whereas his dark skin indicated his *Mestizo* (indigenous and European) ancestry. His darker skin color and *Mestizo* ancestry were further associated with lower social class of previous generations of family members. The word *Mestizo* was stigmatized in his community in Chile, and consequently Amaro, too, felt as though he was an outsider.

As Amaro talked about his experience of skin color, I was increasingly aware of my own skin color. Like Amaro, I thought about the ways in which I experienced my skin color in my family and Indian community. Specifically, I reflected on the devaluation of darker skin tones, particularly those of women, within my Indian community. Skin color in Chile and India, as in many other parts of the world, often is associated with racial ancestry, class and/or caste, and physical attractiveness. Although I have thought about and worked through the issue of skin color to a considerable extent in my life, Amaro's discussion of skin color triggered some memories of my upbringing that were painful, and I found myself feeling like I could relate to being in his world. I then wondered about how my shared experiences with Amaro had interplayed in our work and how it felt for Amaro to be working with a woman whose skin is darker than his. I also thought about how hard it can be to openly talk about a feature of one's physical body that, through socialization, comes to represent critical aspects of the self and of others.

I noticed that as Amaro talked about his skin color, he would look away from me for the first time in our sessions, as though he felt ashamed to reveal his feelings to me. When I remarked to him that perhaps he was feeling uncomfortable telling me about this part of his life, he said, "This is the hard part that I try not to think about. I know I can talk to you, but it's embarrassing."

I then responded, "What about this feels hard to talk about with me?"

Amaro stated, "I feel like it's a topic that is sensitive. Maybe, it feels offensive to you."

I said, "I'm wondering if it is hard to tell someone who is darker skinned than you."

Amaro, for the first time, held tears in his eyes, and said, "I'm afraid of how bad it sounds for me if I tell you the kinds of things that I heard about dark skinned people." In this moment, I could feel the depth of Amaro's distress.

I responded, "I understand that this is a difficult issue to talk about with me. People usually don't talk about skin color outside of their own communities. I can also see that you are worried about how I might feel or what I might think of you, if you tell me more." I also shared with him that I wanted to learn more about the messages about dark skinned people that he experienced and felt prepared to hear whatever he hoped to tell me. Over the next several weeks, Amaro gradually talked with me in both English and Spanish (when words and experiences felt nontranslatable from Spanish to English) about the negative comments concerning dark skin color he heard from his family members, peers, and teachers.

Our conversations also centered on Amaro's feelings of despair in missing his life in Chile and wishing to separate from the painful aspects of his life there. Later in our work, Amaro talked about how although he was perceived as less attractive in Chile because of his darker skin color, he became "raced" after arriving in the United States, where he was perceived as a racial and linguistic minority with an accent. In contrast, his wife and sons were perceived as White, Euro Americans. Amaro's feelings of disconnection from his family in the United States were related, in fact, to his feeling like and being perceived as the different one or the outsider in his family. Often, for Amaro, this experience of disconnection was interpreted as his wife's lack of interest in him. In a sense, Amaro was reliving the painful aspects of his life in Chile in the United States and needed to create a transition across his linguistic and cultural spaces to connect with the full complexity of his affective life, both physical and psychological. It had become increasingly clear that he was trying to negotiate his closeness and distance from his family in Chile and his family in the United States and, in essence, his bicultural, bilingual, and racial identities.

In our sessions, I was also aware that Amaro experienced me as both insider and outsider because he could connect with my dark skin status but not through a common ethnicity, first language, or accent. As I listened to Amaro talk in Spanish, I felt different physically and psychologically than when I listened to him talk in English. I related to his fears about losing Spanish in his life because I had already lost aspects of my own first language, which I typically speak only to family in India. I, too, imagined the loss of my heritage Indian language in my children's lives and all of the nuances of cultural values and customs contained in this language. I understood my countertransference as a necessary step in entering Amaro's world and that I gradually needed to work toward differentiating my loss of language from that in Amaro's experience.

Throughout our work, there was tension between separation and intimacy in our negotiation of language and exploration of affective states associated with language. Amaro unconsciously and consciously made efforts to contain my affective reactions to his life story, as he waited to tell me things that he thought would be upsetting to me, such as his Chilean community's views on people with dark skin color. Conversely, I made attempts to help him feel safe enough to tell me what he was really feeling both within and outside of our relationship. In addition, our discussions concerning the loss of language facilitated an exploration of Amaro's sadness concerning his mother's illness and his uncle's death. Amaro longed to spend time with his mother and eventually found ways to do so, taking time from his responsibilities at work and home. He also began to take initiative in developing ties with other Latin American immigrants in the United States, which provided him with a better sense of connection with the Spanish language. Amaro's wife's and children's involvement in gatherings with other Spanish-speaking immigrants further contributed to a growing sense of integration. Psychotherapy provided a space for bringing Amaro's narrative to a conscious level in multiple languages and for exploring his dissociated or disavowed feelings of loss across various layers of experience (e.g., family, culture, language). For Amaro, our work gradually facilitated the possibility of bearing a wider range of emotions and eventually experiencing himself more fully.

SUMMARY

Culturally informed psychoanalytic theory and practice attend to both conscious and unconscious communication in language. Language and the expression of affect, for people of all sociocultural backgrounds, are connected with context and related indigenous meanings. Importantly, the meanings attached to language are dynamic, shifting from one context to another. In a similar vein, the ways in which affect is communicated, such as through myth, metaphor, and the physical body, can vary across sociocultural contexts and across individuals within any particular cultural group. Psychoanalytic contributions to the area of bilingualism offer an understanding of language use and language shifting in psychotherapy that involves intrapsychic, relational, and social contextual factors. For bilingual and multilingual people, each language can reflect different self-states, with specific affective experiences. Therefore, it is important to attend to the dynamics of transference and countertransference in the client's choice of language use and language switching in psychotherapy. Understanding the nuances of language and affect further requires attention to the role of heritage language and the loss of heritage language in the client's life and in the therapist's life. The conflictual nature of heritage language use and loss under conditions of social oppression is evident in the naming process among immigrants who make efforts to acculturate to mainstream society. Psychoanalytic psychotherapy emphasizes the intersubjective quality of dialogue and interaction between the client and the therapist to more fully understand the client's affective life and, in particular, enactments in psychotherapy that challenge the therapist and the client to face disavowed or dissociated self-states. Relatedly, the therapist's attunement to the client's affective life relies in part on the therapist's ability to recognize his or her own affective states and bodily experiences. An understanding of indigenous narrative (previous chapter) and language and affect (this chapter) serves as important background to another defining area in culturally informed psychoanalytic psychotherapy, the issue of social oppression and traumatic stress, which is explored in the next chapter.

6

ADDRESSING SOCIAL OPPRESSION AND TRAUMATIC STRESS

Several years ago, I accepted an invitation to present a clinical case at a professional conference that was meant to focus on culture and psychotherapy. When I arrived at the conference, I noticed I was the only person of color. The audience, the moderator, and three discussants (one male, two female) were all White. I presented my work with a Pakistani American client with whom I had worked in individual psychotherapy. My client, an immigrant man from Pakistan, had sought help in coping with his sadness related to the ending of his relationship with his girlfriend. In the course of my presentation, among other issues concerning the client's relationships with his family and his former girlfriend, I described an impasse in my work with the client. Specifically, in one session, the client told me that he was reluctant to talk with me about some aspects of his schooling in Pakistan, where some of his teachers taught students that Hindu Indians were enemies of Pakistanis. I also shared in the presentation my thoughts about the challenges of discussing painful topics

http://dx.doi.org/10.1037/14800-007
Psychoanalytic Theory and Cultural Competence in Psychotherapy, by P. Tummala-Narra

with my client, such as the Partition of India at the end of British rule, which caused tragic losses for both Indians and Pakistanis.

Following my presentation, the two female discussants shared some helpful comments about the case. The third discussant began his discussion of the case by circulating to everyone in the meeting room copies of an article he had found on the Internet about the political conflicts between India and Pakistan. He then stated that people from South Asia, such as Indians and Pakistanis, had "weak egos," that the case I had presented was too "zipped up" without enough depth regarding the client's sexual life, and that he "couldn't get inside" me or the client. I felt stunned by his statements. The structure of the conference included an opportunity for me to respond to the discussants. My response to the male discussant was the following: "When you said that South Asians have weak egos, this is racist. I am offended." He stated, "I never actually said that." To my relief, one of the White female discussants directed her comments to the male discussant, "You are lying. We heard what you said." The male discussant continued to defend his position. No one in the audience, the moderator, or the other female discussant said anything. I continued to respond to the discussants' comments and argued for a perspective that respected the client's cultural background and recognized the tensions that transpired in the process of our work as a function of our shared and distinct South Asian identities. At the end of the conference, the female discussant who spoke out on my behalf and that of my client approached me and apologized for what had happened.

I left the conference in shock, disbelief, and sadness. I did have an opportunity in the coming weeks to process what had happened with the moderator. However, the enactment of racial and gender dynamics left me with several impressions about the state of clinical conceptualizations of culture, race, and more broadly social oppression. I wondered whether the conflicts the client and I had been working through were too difficult for the male discussant and perhaps others to bear. Was it too much to bear an ethnic minority woman's perspective in working with an ethnic minority man? I also wondered why it was so important for the male discussant to feel that he was a part of this case physically, sexually, and emotionally, and whether his experience of me as "zipped up" with my client reflected a feeling of being left out of something or a wish to dominate me and the client. In my view, his attempts of overtaking the case conference were palpable as he distributed "knowledge" (e.g., the article from the Internet) about India and Pakistan as though he knew something that neither my client nor I knew about ourselves or about each other.

The silence of one of the female discussants, the moderator, and the audience contributed to another enactment, one in which there was a lack of active witnesses who recognized and acknowledged the racism and sexism that permeated the discussant's comments. I want to underscore the significance of the one witness I did have in the conference, the female discussant who acknowledged what had happened. I chose to share this incident because of the explicit and implicit ways that certain narrative becomes privileged and other narrative becomes dismissed and marginalized as a function of broader social injustice (e.g., racism, sexism) that is enacted in academic and professional settings. For me, this incident raises concerns about conscious and unconscious processes in interpersonal interactions that shape the course of minority clients' and therapists' experiences.

Attending to narrative, language use, and affect in psychotherapy requires the recognition of the influence of social oppression, collective violence, and interpersonal violence on an individual's life conditions and intrapsychic experiences. Relational psychoanalysts, and feminist and multicultural psychologists have called for attention to the importance of sociohistorical context and the perils involved with removing historical knowledge and cultural context from the science and practice of psychology, including the derogation and traumatic injury of those who are most vulnerable and socially marginalized (Brown, 2006; Comas-Díaz, 2011; Greene, 2010; A. E. Harris, 2011). Although social justice is considered to be a core value for many practitioners from various theoretical orientations (Altman, 2010; Brown, 2006), there is less attention directed toward how the guiding principles of social justice (e.g., attending to power and privilege) are translated in therapeutic practice and experienced in the therapeutic relationship. Contemporary psychoanalytic approaches emphasize the need for addressing social justice in clinical practice with depth and complexity, with particular focus on the subjectivity and the narrative of the individual as a function of power, privilege, and cultural context. Generalizations about groups of people, such as racial and sexual minorities, reify structural inequalities with such power that even those of us (e.g., mental health professionals) who are trained to deconstruct the human experience cannot seem to escape the stronghold of unconscious and conscious discrimination. Although based in deeply embedded, rigid social structures, injustice is most often enacted in interpersonal or relational contexts.

I have found it helpful to consider issues of power and privilege through a psychoanalytic perspective that is informed by feminist and multicultural psychologies and considers the nuances of power across multiple levels (e.g., individual, interpersonal, societal). Power structures rooted in patriarchy and colonialism are key influences on the disempowerment of people along different dimensions (Brown, 2010). Feminist and multicultural perspectives overlap with psychoanalytic perspectives in challenging traditional views of the neutrality in the psychotherapeutic relationship, moving toward mutuality and an analysis of social location as experienced by the client and the therapist (Aron, 2001; Brown, 2010; A. E. Harris, 2011; I. Hoffman, 1998). All three perspectives have also challenged the nature of assessment, diagnosis, and treatment. For example, researchers in feminist and multicultural psychology have identified the relationship between social injustice (e.g., racism) and mental health outcomes. Feminist and multicultural scholars have suggested that the assessment of psychological issues in psychotherapy be based not only on the history of the individual but also on the history of the individual's groups of identification (e.g., ethnic, racial, sexual identity). Because issues of social justice often operate in unconscious communication between the therapist and client, contemporary psychoanalytic scholars emphasize the importance of the dynamics inherent to power differentials and privilege in broader society, with the understanding that the therapeutic relationship can mirror these dynamics. Relational psychoanalysts focus on the interaction between psychological, social, and political forces in human suffering (A. E. Harris, 2011) and the therapist's role as witness to injustice (Boulanger, 2009; D. B. Stern, 2010).

I recognize that stereotyping, discrimination, and violence directed against majority status individuals by minority status individuals have destructive effects on majority status individuals' psychological life. However, stereotyping, discrimination, and violence directed against minority status individuals by majority status individuals occurs at disproportionate levels, often implicating structural differences in power and privilege, with enduring traumatic stress. Thus, in this chapter I explore the effects of social oppression and traumatic stress on individuals, particularly those on the margins of mainstream society in the United States, and how a psychoanalytic lens helps the therapist and the client to address enactments in the therapeutic relationship that reflect dynamics of oppression in broader society.

EFFECTS OF SOCIAL OPPRESSION

Psychoanalytic theory offers a critical perspective on the experience of traumatic stress incurred from interpersonal violence, such as physical and sexual abuse. There is an emphasis on the importance of developmental challenges, such as the loss of basic sense of trust and safety, the internalization of negative messages from the abuser, dysregulation of affect, and fragmentation and dissociation in the face of traumatic experiences (Boulanger, 2007; J. M. Davies & Frawley, 1994; Fonagy & Bateman, 2008; Herman, 1992; Layton, 1995; A. Stein, 2012; Stolorow, 2003). Dissociation serves an adaptive function of coping with feelings of terror and helplessness, affects images of the self and of others, and presents itself as *unformulated experience*, in which traumatic material cannot be readily symbolized (D. B. Stern, 1997). Traumatic stress is understood as an amalgam of the actual violation by a perpetrator or perpetrators, relational disruptions, memories, bodily responses, and internal representations of the violations. Survivors of complex trauma tend to enact relational patterns rooted in a splitting of the external world into victims and perpetrators as they cope with dissociated self-states created through overwhelming feelings of terror (Boulanger, 2007; Herman, 1992). Bromberg (2006) elaborated on the disrupted sense of continuity of the self in the face of trauma. He noted that the denial or dismissal of physical and sexual violation has a great impact on the survivor's sense of self and that dissociation becomes an adaptive alternative to help with preserving one's sense of self. Relational analysts (Boulanger, 2007; Bromberg, 2001, 2006; J. M. Davies & Frawley, 1994) emphasize that the self is characterized by multiplicity, containing various self-states that develop in the context of relationships with caregivers and significant people in one's life. Self-states include representations of the self and of the other, including cognitions and affect. Bromberg (2001, p. 893) suggested that dissociation disrupts "the possibility of holding in a single state of consciousness two incompatible modes of relating" and the ability for "standing in the spaces" between self-states. Thus, psychoanalytic therapists aim to develop a safe, trusting relationship with the client and to help the client to access and explore unconscious traumatic material, integrate disavowed or dissociated self-experiences, and develop a positive, satisfying relational life.

More recently, psychoanalytic inquiry has expanded understandings of traumatic stress to social and contextual issues that shape experiences of violence and oppression. Interpersonal violence, collective violence, and systemic oppression often co-occur among people who are outside of mainstream culture. There is ample empirical and clinical evidence indicating the negative effects of social oppression (e.g., discrimination and violence based on gender, race, sexual orientation, social class, and dis/ability) on physical health outcomes and mental health outcomes, including but not limited to depression, anxiety, substance abuse, post-traumatic stress, and suicidal ideation and behavior (Brondolo, Libretti, Rivera, & Walsemann, 2012; Mizock, Harrison, & Russinova, 2014; Sellers, Copeland-Linder, Martin, & Lewis, 2006; Sirin, Ryce, Gupta, & Rogers-Sirin, 2013; Tummala-Narra & Claudius, 2013). Discrimination and stereotyping contribute to a powerful social mirror (Suárez-Orozco, 2000) and "social unconscious" (Dalal, 2006) that shape self-images and perceptions by others, both of which are recreated consciously and unconsciously in the therapeutic relationship. Attention to social oppression and its negative effects on intrapsychic processes in psychoanalytic literature has brought to the foreground the inextricable connection between what clients and therapists experience outside and what they experience within the therapeutic relationship (Altman, 2010; Layton, 2006). Therefore, it is worth examining more closely how different forms of social oppression influence identity and relationships.

Expressions of Social Oppression in Psychotherapy

The effects of unconscious, implicit, or aversive prejudice and discrimination (Baron & Banaji, 2006; Dovidio, Gluszek, John, Ditlmann, & Lagunes, 2010; Steele, 1997; Wachtel, 2002) are insidious, with lasting effects across the life-span. The experience of being raced has been thought to operate in everyday interactions because race and racism are part of our social fabric (Leary, 2007; D. W. Sue et al., 2007). Research on stereotype threat (Steele, 1997) underscores the importance of unconscious anxiety produced through the awareness of an operating stereotype concerning ability in a particular area (e.g., academics or athletics) under a testing or evaluative condition. Claude Steele's work (1997, 2010), for example, indicates that underperformance of female students in math and science classes compared with male students and of African American students in academic testing compared with White students occurs as a function of being primed with stereotypes attached to their respective cultural groups (e.g., girls or African Americans).

Stereotypes and their accompanying disavowing messages play a central role in the development of self-esteem and identity (Holmes, 2006; Wachtel, 2002). My client, a Dominican American woman in her 30s, reported that she never quite understood why she felt increasingly distant from her boyfriend, a White man, who she admired and with whom she fell in love. Months into our work, she remembered that her boyfriend had told her at the beginning of their relationship, in passing, that he never thought that he would be attracted to "a girl from the Caribbean" because he did not find women with darker skin attractive. I asked my client how she felt about his statement. She told me that, at the moment, she did not find this offensive, but over the course of the relationship, which lasted about 8 months, she was never quite able to settle in and be fully present with her boyfriend. We were then able to talk about racism that affected her identity and her life choices. This is an illustration of how injustice, in the form of stereotypes and discrimination, can manifest in the interpersonal realm in subtle and explicit ways, having a lasting effect on the individual's psyche. I want to note that had we not explored her experience of racism, I may have attributed the problems she faced in her relationship to only her conscious and unconscious fears of commitment and intimacy, which of course is a highly individualized and decontextualized conceptualization.

The negative effects of stereotyping can further present themselves in the transference and countertransference. A client may either seek or avoid a therapist of a particular cultural background as an attempt to find someone who will understand him or her completely, including his or her social identities and experiences of marginalization. In a different example, a client who has been targeted for racism within mainstream society may have a more difficult transition in working with a therapist who is affiliated with or perceived to be affiliated with the oppressing cultural group. In turn, the therapist may emotionally distance himself or herself from the client, perceiving the client to be disinterested in the therapist's desire to help. Indeed, our social identity positions shape unique realities and narratives that often diverge and conflict (Dovidio et al., 2010). Psychoanalytic scholars have advocated increasingly for exploration of the stress created by social inequality and the reasons this inequality persists in society and in psychotherapy. In fact, many scholars (Aron & Starr, 2013; Blechner, 2008; Dimen, 2006; Leary, 2012) have noted the importance of a psychoanalytic perspective in addressing the irrational aspects of social and political conflicts, such as those related to same-sex marriage, violence against women, and racial violence. Wachtel's (2002, 2014) framework of cyclical psychodynamics noted how specific patterns from early life experiences are perpetuated bidirectionally between one's internal life (e.g., fantasies, wishes, fears, images of self and other) and external realities created through history. In this view, the clinician's knowledge of history of social structures is critical, as is the exploration of the client's and the therapist's psychological processes (e.g., anxiety, conflict, defenses) that are both shaped by experiences of privilege and marginalization and potentially contribute to further inequality.

Ignacio Martín-Baró's (1994) vision of liberation psychology is highly relevant to a culturally informed psychoanalytic approach to the exploration of social oppression in psychotherapy. Martín-Baró (1994), a Salvadorian social psychologist, proposed that psychology holds a critical position in potentially supporting or resisting oppression by drawing the connection between "an unalienated personal existence and unalienated social existence, between individual control and collective power, between the liberation of each person and the liberation of a whole people" (p. 27). Specifically, the position of neutrality serves to preserve the status quo in which people on the margins of the mainstream are silenced and/or pathologized. In addition, the dominance of individualism in Euro American societies perpetuates the idea that social conflicts are rooted in individual traits and perceptions, thereby dehistoricizing and decontextualizing emotional distress. At the heart of liberation psychology is the recovery of historical and collective memory because a fictitious account of history results in the internalization of oppression within one's identity (Barratt, 2011). The therapist and client, from this perspective, engage in a dialectical dialogue that fosters a sense of critical consciousness or "concientizacion" (Freire, 1970). Liberation psychology suggests that we move beyond the exploration of dyadic relationships (e.g., parent–child) to the client's relationship to collectives and social structures to overcome a sense of "false consciousness" and develop a real sense of power (Martín-Baró, 1994). What results is the client's indigenous narrative, through which the client is the subject of his or her own experience. This is especially important in psychoanalytic psychotherapy when considering that a false existence reflects the overbearing dominance of social expectations on one's attitudes and behaviors (Winnicott, 1971).

It is often the case that mental health professionals contend with the question of whether it is in their purview to engage in dialogue about social oppression directly with clients. Sometimes therapists are concerned that they will be perceived by clients as racist, sexist, or perpetrators if they were to raise issues of social inequality in psychotherapy. In other cases, therapists refrain from discussing issues of gender, race, culture, religion, sexual identity, social class, dis/ability, and injustice because they worry they are being intrusive, imposing their own agenda on the client who may or may not be interested in discussing their experiences of social marginalization. Yet in many cases, these assumptions are not sufficiently explored by the therapist either in private or in dialogue with the client. Consequently, the client is left in a position to negotiate experiences of marginalization on his or her own, particularly when he or she recognizes the therapist's discomfort in engaging with these issues. Such experiences are all too familiar to many clients. Learning about the client's experiences of marginalization raises questions about existing dominant structures and what role the therapist plays in such structures. Listening to experiences of marginalization necessitates the therapist's recognition of the deep and enduring effects of oppression.

Oppression and Its Effects on Intrapsychic and Relational Life

Different types of social oppression (e.g., racism, sexism, heterosexism, classism, ableism) share common effects with respect to one's intrapsychic and relational worlds but also have distinct effects based on historical and cultural contexts. Colonization and slavery of people of color by Whites in the United States and elsewhere has left a painful legacy of distrust and disavowal. Frantz Fanon (1952), an Afro Caribbean psychiatrist born and raised in Martinique during French colonization, recognized that oppressed people are made to feel inferior systemically and thus internalize negative images of themselves and their cultural group. In his psychoanalytic conceptualization of the effects of colonization on internal life, he believed that it was his place to help the patient explore the unconscious and to respond to the patient with the aim of attending to change in social structure. Fanon (1952) stated

> The black man should no longer have to be faced with the dilemma 'whiten or perish,' but must become aware of the possibility of existence. . . . If I see in his dreams the expression of an unconscious desire to change color, my objective will not be to dissuade him by advising him to 'keep his distance'; on the contrary, once his motives have been

identified, my objective will be to enable him to choose action (or passivity) with respect to the real source of the conflict, i.e., the social structure. (p. 80)

More recently, challenges faced by people of color continue to be located almost exclusively within the confines of their individual characteristics or the attributes assigned to their specific cultural groups. For example, acculturation among immigrants traditionally has been thought to be a problem of conflicting values across cultural contexts (e.g., culture of origin and adopted culture). Although each individual negotiates acculturation in a new cultural context in unique ways based on his or her family history, it is important to consider that acculturation is also influenced by social inequality and traumatic stress. This is most prominent in the case of refugees who live in transitional states between the old and the new countries, immigrants with undocumented or unauthorized status, and survivors of human trafficking (APA, 2012). Immigrants who face the possibility of deportation are vulnerable to social, political, and economic instability, which then constricts the range of choices concerning acculturation to the new country. Relatedly, an immigrant who experiences loss of economic resources and academic and/or professional status after migration faces challenges in acculturation that are distinct from those of immigrants who obtain improved opportunities in the new culture. Many victims of trafficking, often women and children, are promised employment and education if they leave their homes, but they instead find themselves enduring sexual and/or commercial exploitation without documentation and any access to support (APA, 2012; Bernat & Zhilina, 2010).

Sunil Bhatia and Anjali Ram (2009) suggested that acculturation among immigrants is a product of the dynamic between broader social structure and the self, often involving a blend of privilege and marginalization. In a study with Asian Indians in the United States, they found that, before the terrorist attacks of September 11, 2001, many middle-class Asian Indians had experienced their racial positions as irrelevant to their adjustment to living in the United States. The participants, because of their professional, academic, and financial success, did not identify as people of color before 9/11. However, in the aftermath of 9/11, which included murder, physical assaults, and verbal harassment of Arab Americans, Middle Eastern Americans, and South Asian Americans, Asian Indians were perceived as foreigners, enemies, and terrorists. This turn of events promulgated a reexamination of racial positioning and the negotiation of acculturation in the United States. However, the attacks occurring after 9/11 were not the first against South Asians in the United States. Many South Asian Americans are unaware of the discrimination against South Asians in the United States that began with Asian Indians' migration to the United States in the 1820s and continues beyond 9/11, reflecting the broader mainstream narrative of the "model minority."

Relatedly, researchers and practitioners have observed the widespread problem of intergenerational conflicts in immigrant homes. Conflicts between immigrant parents and their children typically are thought to result from an *acculturation gap* (Birman & Simon, 2014; Prathikanti, 1997), which reflects cultural value differences across each generation. Although first- and second-generation immigrants have distinct and sometimes divergent trajectories in adjusting to and across cultural contexts, conflicts that arise between parents and children also are rooted in stress experienced outside the home. Intergenerational conflict and stress in immigrant homes are shaped by xenophobia and external demands that immigrants and their children face as they learn to navigate mainstream society. It is worth noting that the stress accompanying these external demands is largely unspoken among family members, contributing to the idea that family conflicts are purely culturally driven.

Social oppression operates in the psyche in profound ways. Chinua Achebe (2000, p. 59), in describing European colonization in Africa, pointed out that the "task of dispossessing others" requires a story that is fabricated by the colonizer that deems the colonized people intellectually inferior, uncivilized, and unable to care for themselves without the oversight of the colonizer. He also noted, "What is both unfortunate and unjust is the pain the person dispossessed is forced to bear in the act of dispossession itself and subsequently in the trauma of a diminished existence" (p. 70). In contemporary times, attempts to reclaim and repossess are not without danger because people of color often are perceived as ungrateful for the freedom they possess today or too sensitive to comments about race. In these cases, race and racism are thought to be problems of past generations, irrelevant or less relevant to modern society. The problem of dispossession further implicates the invisibility of "Whiteness" and the projection of racial otherness and accompanying undesirable human qualities onto people designated as "people of color" (Altman, 2010; Eng & Han, 2000; Suchet, 2004). Janet Helms and Donelda Cook (1999, p. 70) described the process of "de-culturation" experienced by members of oppressed groups, in which individuals are exposed to systematic "indoctrination" that members of their cultural groups are inferior, shaping racial identity development. They noted that internalized racial stereotypes and racism reflect individuals' psychological responses to systemic oppression. In addition, racism compromises the individual's ability to bear both positive and negative representations of the aggressive individual or group, contributing to a sense of alienation (Tummala-Narra, 2011) and *ethnocultural allodynia* (Comas-Díaz & Jacobsen, 2001) or a greater sensitivity to painful cultural and racial dynamics and invisibility in both ethnic and mainstream contexts (Espín, 2008). Anderson Franklin (2004) coined the term *invisibility syndrome* to describe African American men's reactions to past and ongoing racial insults and *microaggressions* (Pierce, 1970). The *invisibility syndrome* encompasses feelings, thoughts, and behaviors that impede one's ability to achieve goals and engage in fulfilling relationships, and it involves deep internal conflict and stress as identity development emerges in the context of racism.

The relationship of the individual to a broader social system that either protects or places the individual at risk for danger plays an important role in intrapsychic life. When institutions fail to protect individuals and communities, such as people in poverty, people with disabilities, racial minorities, LGBTQ individuals, and immigrants, they create traumatic stress and interfere with the individual's ability to develop safe object relations with the social environment (Hernandez de Tubert, 2006; Mizock et al., 2014; Suárez-Orozco, 2000). A psychoanalytic perspective recognizes that the inability for systems to secure basic human rights to all individuals in a society parallels the lack of containment in a parent–child dyad that fails to fulfill the basic physical and psychological needs of the child (Bion, 1977; Hernandez de Tubert, 2006). In addition, when a system denies or minimizes the occurrence of traumatic events and stress, the effects are more severe because they involve a sense of betrayal by forces that are meant to protect survivors.

Comas-Díaz's (2000) concept of postcolonization stress disorder, in contrast to the diagnosis of posttraumatic stress disorder (PTSD), locates pathology in social structures rather than in the individual survivor. She pointed out that PTSD does not capture the problem of racial trauma and proposed an alternative diagnosis of *postcolonization stress disorder* akin to the diagnosis of complex PTSD (Herman, 1992), referring to a process that is repeated, prolonged, and "ethnopolitically mediated" (Comas-Díaz, 2000, p. 1321). Paralleling the diagnosis of complex PTSD (Herman, 1992), postcolonization stress disorder alters group identity, relationships, and worldviews (Comas-Díaz, 2000). Intrapsychic consequences of politically driven trauma, such as exile, can also involve complicated mourning, remembering of the past, imagining a future, and a sense of not having a home (Harlem, 2010). Although numerous scholars, drawing on research and clinical evidence of the harmful and lasting effects of systemic violence, have called for the inclusion of racial trauma as an etiological factor in PTSD and complex PTSD (Bryant-Davis, 2007; Comas-Díaz, 2000; Daniel, 2000; Tummala-Narra, 2007), it continues to be excluded from our current diagnostic systems.

In previous work (Tummala-Narra, 2005), I've discussed the effects of racially and politically driven traumatic events on intrapsychic and interpersonal life, including identity shifts, the fear of annihilation, identification with and internalization of aggressive elements of trauma, and the formation of collective traumatic memories that are transmitted across generations. Scholars have further noted the generational effect of collective violence, such as slavery, genocide of Native Americans, the Nazi Holocaust, and

Japanese internment camps (Brave Heart & DeBruyn, 1998; Daniel, 2000; Faimberg, 2005; Gump, 2010; Kogan, 2002; Nagata & Cheng, 2003). For example, Ilany Kogan (2002) described the re-creation or enactment of parents' traumatic stress among children of Holocaust survivors. She noted that the children of these survivors experienced a "psychic hole" or a disconnection between identifying with the parents' traumatic stress and a sense of denial and repression of the trauma by the parents. Children of survivors are thought to be challenged by differentiating the self from the parent's sense of self, such that even when traumatic stress is not discussed overtly within the family, the child is able to discern aspects of the parent's traumatic past. Discovering and knowing the parent's traumatic history and the opportunity to speak about it can play a critical role in facilitating differentiation and the development of a separate sense of self (Kogan, 2002). At times, therapists may find it difficult to bear listening to the horrific nature of collective violence, such as that of genocide. Nevertheless, in psychotherapy, the client through sharing images of violence reveals unimaginable events that the therapist comes to witness (Ornstein, 2012).

Psychoanalytic scholars have noted other important intrapsychic consequences of cumulative racial trauma. Peter Fonagy (2001) described the concept of psychic equivalence as a survivor's lack of differentiation between external events and internal processes caused by traumatic stress. Specifically, a survivor of repeated racial trauma may come to become distrustful of the outside world and of his or her own experiences of racism. The ability to bear good and bad aspects of the object (e.g., cultural or racial group, institution) can also become compromised, leaving the individual alienated and marginalized (Holmes, 2001; Tummala-Narra, 2011). Each of these potential responses to racial trauma takes unique manifestation in the individual's identity and relational life, because they interact with family history, losses, life conditions, and access to resources. Traumatic stress rooted in social oppression (e.g., sexism, racism, xenophobia, homophobia, poverty, ableism, transphobia) poses challenges to a sense of safety and belonging and to one's sense of trust in one's own experience of reality. In fact, many of my racial minority clients, when describing experiences of discrimination, wonder whether these incidents actually were discriminatory or whether they are too sensitive, a perspective that they have partially internalized from mainstream society that keeps their actual experience at bay to maintain and perpetuate the status quo regarding racial hierarchies.

D. W. Sue and colleagues (2007) and John Dovidio (2009) have elaborated on the problem of subtle and ambiguous expressions of racism directed against people of color. D. W. Sue and colleagues (2007) described racial microaggressions as "brief and commonplace daily verbal, behavioral and environmental indignities, whether intentional or unintentional, that communicate hostile, derogatory or negative racial slights and insults" (p. 273). Research on microaggressions (Pierce, 1970; D. W. Sue et al., 2007) indicates that these types of interactions are pervasive and detrimental to the psychological well-being of racial minorities. D. W. Sue's description of microaggressions as a real phenomenon in the experience of racial minorities has been met with resistance from some psychologists (K. R. Thomas, 2008), who claim that the concept of microaggressions is "pure nonsense," arguing that all people experience verbal and behavioral insults. These psychologists have also drawn attention to the ambiguous nature of microaggressions, suggesting that cross-racial interactions interpreted as microaggressions may in fact reflect factors unrelated to race or racism (R. S. Harris, 2008). D. W. Sue and colleagues (2009) responded to these arguments by underscoring that people of color struggle with the ambiguity of microaggressions, often attribute unconscious or unintentional racism to personal reactivity or sensitivity, and yet are left wondering about the intention and behaviors of the individuals who directed the microaggressions toward them. The question of whose interpretation or narrative is privileged is raised again here. They posed the question, "If you want to understand oppression, do you ask the oppressor or the oppressed?" (D. W. Sue et al., 2009, p. 279).

Bhabha (1994) suggested that the construction of otherness relies on a dependency of "fixity," and stereotypes serve to simplify reality by ignoring the psychic experience of the subject. Stereotypes lie at the base of microaggressions and other forms of discrimination and serve to maintain the status quo of dominant systems. In fact, stereotypes embody the wish to get rid of social problems by locating them in individual deficits (Bhabha, 1994; Paschal, 1971). It is important to consider how stereotypes are projected and internalized. We are all socialized with stereotypes concerning groups with whom we identify and groups with whom we don't identify. Stereotypes reflect both curiosity and rejection of those considered to be the other. For example, Dan Goodley and Katherine Runswick-Cole (2011) recognized the cultural disavowal of disablism, as evident in society's ambivalence with disability. They described disablism as involving both a "fascination with and fear of disabled people" and "staring at and staring through" (p. 612). Ambivalence toward people outside the mainstream is further illustrated in current sentiment toward immigrants in the United States and other Western countries. Ricardo Ainslie (2009) suggested that the presence and increasing visibility of racial minority immigrants in the United States trigger a sense of collective anxiety, in which dissociative defenses maintain an emotional distance from a potentially threatening subgroup. As such, immigrants become scapegoats for economic and social problems (e.g., taking jobs away from "real Americans"). M. Fakhry Davids (2009) further suggested that *internal racism* reflects a "normal pathological organization" in mainstream society in which members of the marginalized group are recruited into a structure of defenses that protect against anxiety and fear of the marginalized group, maintain the racist position, and perpetuate the avoidance of personal responsibility. He argued, "In a racist mindset we remain convinced that our prejudiced view of the object is true, to the extent that contrary facts are assimilated in a way that, in essence, confirms that view" (p. 178). In other words, a paranoid interpretation about the marginalized group created by the dominant group becomes a part of internal life of members of the marginalized group, in which fantasies about specific cultural groups are mistaken to be facts.

Although culture is fluid and dynamic, stereotypes reflect rigid, fetishized perspectives of others and of the self, and depending on the needs of the dominant group, stereotypes morph into new ways to denigrate people (Bhabha, 1994; Lewes, Young-Bruehl, Roughton, Magee, & Miller, 2008). While designing a research study, I came upon one example of this. In the process of brainstorming current stereotypes of Asian Americans with a group of graduate students, I learned about a relatively new stereotype of South Asian women as asexual. This stands in contrast to earlier notions of South Asian women as exotic. The stereotype, in this case, is reinvented such that the derogation of South Asian women, manifested in both desexualization and hypersexualization, is perpetuated. In a similar vein, Fraley, Mona, and Theodore (2007) noted that people with physical disabilities and/or who identify as LGBTQ may be fetishized or sought out sexually by able-bodied people for a "novel" experience but not considered for a potential long-term relationship. Stereotypes remove subjectivity and disconnect us from feeling for the other.

The problem of removing subjectivity from the experience of individuals who are marginalized has been increasingly explored by researchers and practitioners focused on the issue of poverty and social class. Scholars have pointed out that one's inferences about people's internal experiences based on socially stratified groups, such as social class categories, overlook affective and relational experiences connected with these groups (Liu, 2002). Goodman, Pugach, Skolnik, and Smith (2013) noted that the stress, exclusion, and lack of access to structural power that people in poverty experience can contribute to a real and a perceived sense of powerlessness and that over the course of time, the experience of powerlessness can come to represent an aspect of one's identity, as evidenced in self-doubt and low sense of self-worth. In addition, categorical approaches contribute to the social exclusion and homogenization of people living in poverty (e.g., stereotypes such as unmotivated, criminal, uneducated) and serve to regulate the anxiety of people with economic power (e.g., middle class) (Goodman et al., 2013; Javier & Herron, 2002; L. Smith, 2013). Beverly Greene (2013) has argued that race and sexual identity can elicit discomfort and hostility because they reflect historically stigmatized or taboo issues in the United States. She pointed out that marriages across social lines (e.g., same-sex marriage, intercultural marriage) challenge both a historical interpretation of marriage and its accompanying privilege. Constructions of Whiteness, gender conformity, class (middle), heterosexuality, and able-bodiedness are then formed through the denunciation of those identities thought to be inferior or unnatural (racial minority, gender nonconforming, poor, LGBTQ, having a physical disability).

In addition to recognizing the realities of social oppression and its impact on internal life, a culturally informed psychoanalytic perspective emphasizes the importance of how oppression influences socialization processes within families, communities, and societies. In a recent study (Tummala-Narra & Sathasivam-Rueckert, in press) with 64 racial minority immigrant-origin (first- and second-generation Asian, Haitian, Latino/a, South Asian) high school students who participated in group interviews, my research team and I found that these adolescents struggled with messages at home and at school that contradicted each other. At home, they received positive messages about their cultural groups and about prioritizing education, whereas at school, many of the adolescents experienced microaggressions, stereotyping, and other types of discrimination by teachers and peers. For example, in one of the group interviews, a Cuban American student described a feeling of connection to other Latino/as:

> I feel really proud of being Latina because I remember after 9/11 a lot of people went to help clean up the city. The most people who went to help were Latinos. They made me feel very proud because we Latinos like to be together, harmony and help each other.

On the other hand, a different response from another student in the same group, a Guatemalan American student who is fluent in English, followed later in the course of the discussion: "My teacher came up to me, she grabbed my shoulder and she says loudly, 'Hello, How are you? Do you understand? Nod if you understand!'" The disparity between experiences at home and at school, in this case, is striking and raises questions about how the socialization experiences of children and adolescents either facilitate or impede a sense of belonging in mainstream society and how and from whom these adolescents seek help when coping with distress related to discrimination. In fact, in our study, many adolescents indicated that they would not seek help from adults at school (e.g., teachers, guidance counselors), particularly those who they perceived as uninterested in or disparaging of their cultural contexts.

Socialization related to gender and sexual identity is another illustration of the ways in which social oppression influences identity and relational life. For example, a "push-pull" dynamic characterizes mother–daughter relationships within the confines of patriarchy, in which mothers even when they want to encourage their daughters to define themselves independently of social expectations of women and girls, socialize their daughters to care for others at the cost of caring for themselves (Gutwill, Gitter, & Rubin, 2011; Tummala-Narra, 2004). Patriarchy also causes stress for boys and men, for whom gender role socialization constricts psychological possibilities. Research indicates that male and female practitioners often dismiss the significance of gender role socialization and stereotypes in their work with male clients, who are perceived as aggressive or abusive by nature or shamed for having dependency needs (Mahalik et al., 2012).

Diane Ehrensaft (2007) wrote about the challenges of parenting "girl-boys" (Corbett, 1996), or boys who don't experience themselves exactly as girls or as boys. She observed that parents, especially mothers, and the gender nonconforming child have both been blamed for their nonconformity to mainstream constructions of gender and sexual identity. In addition, she suggested that we consider what it may be like for a parent to effectively attend to a child's psychological development within the context of a society that demands and values binary thinking concerning gender. This issue is further complicated in cases of homophobic bullying of LGBTQ and heterosexual youth perceived to identify as LGBTQ (Poteat, Scheer, DiGiovanni, & Mereish, 2014). Minority parents and parents of minority children then struggle with a parallel problem of socializing and preparing their children for a society that may be hostile to them.

Multiple Marginalization

Certain subgroups of people are more vulnerable to social oppression than are others. This is evident in the disproportionate numbers of racial minorities (e.g., African American, Latino/a, Native American) and people with disabilities who live in poverty, the disproportionate number of people with disabilities who are African American and Native American, the disproportionate number of homeless people who are victimized by interpersonal violence, and the disproportionate number of sexual minority and transgender youth who are victimized by hate crimes (Cornish, Gorgens, Monson, Olkin, Palombi, & Abels, 2008; Duncan & Hatzenbuehler, 2014; Farrell, 2012). An example of the ways in which social policy affects particular subgroups disproportionately is evident among immigrant women who have undocumented or unauthorized status. Policies such as the immigration legislation (2010) in the state of Arizona, which allowed police to detain anyone suspected of being undocumented and not carrying immigration documentation, place women at risk. Specifically, immigrant women are vulnerable not only to rape, physical assault, separation from children, lack of access to care, detention, and deportation but also to exploitation by police and immigration authorities (Comas-Díaz, 2010).

Many individuals face multiple forms of oppression occurring within the mainstream context and their communities. Interpersonal trauma occurring within the family and within one's cultural group can coexist with collective oppression and trauma, contributing to compounded stress. It is important to note that all aspects of a person's identity are intertwined, and each aspect of identity, such as race, gender, or spirituality, does not develop independently of any other aspect of identity. Relatedly, oppression related to any one aspect of identity can be "mutually reinforcing" (Greene, 2013, p. 36). For example, Beverly Greene (2013) suggested that, because of social and religious stigma, LGBTQ people face harm similar to that faced by people of color. She highlighted the problem of clergy in communities of color who speak out against LGBTQ members and noted that "marginalized people who scold their own enjoy wide media exposure and support, whereas those who put forth a systemic and more complex analysis are not routinely afforded that exposure" (Greene, 2013, p. 39).

People facing multiple forms of marginalization are also typically more vulnerable to being victimized by violence (Bodnar, 2004; Greene, 2013; Olkin, 2002; Tummala-Narra, 2011). They cope with conflicting loyalties to the different communities with whom they affiliate and identify. For example, many women of color develop a gendered racial identity (A. J. Thomas, Hacker, & Hoxha, 2011) as they negotiate closeness and distance with social groups in the context of ongoing sexism and racism, facing challenges in establishing a sense of security and belonging within any social group (Tummala-Narra, 2011). This conflict is illustrated in my Iraqi American client's experience, as she revealed to me in a session: "It's hard for me to talk about sometimes how the men in my family are more dominating. If I tell outsiders, they will think that our men are all terrorists." For this client, her experience of being dominated by men in her family is compounded by her experience with racism and stereotyping outside the home, limiting the possibility of openly voicing her distress in either context.

These conflicting loyalties are further complicated in the case of interpersonal violence that occurs within one's cultural group, as the survivor's compromised sense of safety shapes his or her cultural identity (Tummala-Narra, 2014a). Scholars (Tummala-Narra, 2014a; Yi, 2014a) have described the experience of sexism and sexual violence among women of color who develop ambivalence about their heritage cultures and feel compromised in developing a positive ethnic identity. Recently, Kris Yi (2014a) introduced the concept of *cultural dissociation* as an experience of merging between the suffering of the traumatized person and his or her heritage culture. A person who experiences cultural dissociation may distance himself or herself from participating in his or her cultural traditions, speaking in a native language, and interacting with similar ethnic people, and instead identify with mainstream cultural norms. According to Yi, cultural dissociation is untenable because the experience of trauma inevitably reappears in relational life, disrupting a person's sense of psychological stability. Cultural dissociation involves an inability to "stand in the spaces between" dissociated self-states associated with distinct cultures (Bromberg, 2006; Yi, 2014a). As such, Yi (2014a) cautioned therapists to carefully attend to the problem of differentiating between a client's traumatic experiences and normative experiences within his or her heritage culture and community to effectively explore ethnic identity.

It is important to consider that people who are marginalized within their cultural groups also face challenges in developing a sense of authenticity and belonging in multiple contexts. When people of color are told by members of their communities that they are not "real" members of the group (e.g., "not Black enough," "White identified") and face discrimination from people outside of their cultural groups, they experience compounded stress that invalidates their sense of self (Gaztambide, 2014; Tummala-Narra, 2007). The internalization of beliefs concerning race, gender, social class, and other social identities from dominant society is enacted within cultural groups. For example, as mentioned, the problem of colorism or the devaluation of dark skin color or light skin color, depending on the context, within families and communities has significant negative effects on individuals' intrapsychic and relational life, including the development of a sense of goodness and badness and a sense of belonging (Tummala-Narra, 2007). Members of a cultural group can become screens of projection for a cultural group's fears of losing a sense of collective identity that protects against the discrimination by those outside of the cultural group. In fact, individuals may be accused of being disloyal or disrespectful, or seen as a threat to the integrity and positive social image of the cultural group (Mahalingam, Balan, & Haritatos, 2008). Yet for many individuals, upholding only a positive image in the context of oppression masks the challenges faced by individuals within a community, such as issues related to mental health and traumatic experience (Tummala-Narra, 2014a).

MOURNING AND ENACTMENT IN PSYCHOTHERAPY

Mourning of loss is a central feature of psychoanalytic psychotherapy. Freud (1917) defined mourning as "the reaction to the loss of a loved person, or to the loss of some abstraction which has taken the place of one, such as one's country, liberty, an ideal" (p. 243). Mourning was conceptualized as a process with an end, involving the mourner's withdrawal of libido from the loved object, such that he or she can develop relationships with new objects. On the other hand, melancholia was described by Freud (1917) as a form of pathological, unresolved mourning in which an individual is unable to resolve his or her ambivalence toward the lost loved object and therefore unable to invest in new relationships. Eng and Han (2000) extended Freud's conception of melancholia as connected with an individual disposition to an intersubjective context to describe the experience of race and racism among Asian Americans. They suggested that even when Asian Americans are born in the United States, they are treated as foreigners because of phenotypical markers. The myth of the model minority or the notion that Asian Americans are economically, academically, and professionally successful and immune to personal problems works to dismiss the reality of discrimination against Asian Americans and serves as a "melancholic mechanism facilitating the erasure and loss of repressed Asian American histories and identities" (Eng & Han, 2000, p. 673).

Racial melancholia involves the internalization of the model minority stereotype, which becomes a partial success in that it serves as a way of being seen in mainstream society and a partial failure in that Asian Americans contend with an unattainable ideal of Whiteness. The hope of the American dream and related assimilation is further transferred across immigrant generations, such that parents imagine that their children will succeed in achieving the American dream in ways that were not possible for them. Yet this places children of Asian immigrants in an impossible bind in which racism and othering permeate their efforts to achieve the American dream. The mourning of identifications with heritage Asian cultures and Whiteness becomes critical in addressing racial melancholia (Eng & Han, 2000).

The problem of unresolved mourning has been described as intrinsic to the experience of various minority communities. Another illustration of unresolved grief is that of indigenous people. Brave Heart and DeBruyn (1998) underscored that the stereotypes of indigenous people as stoic and savage have contributed to the notion that indigenous people lack feelings and either are incapable of grieving or lack the right to grieve. Thus, they experience *disenfranchised grief*, which involves feelings of sadness, anger, guilt, shame, and helplessness that are more intense than comparable feelings accompanying a typical mourning process. This type of unresolved, traumatic grief is transmitted across generations and shapes identity and emotional distress, as manifested in problems such as substance abuse, depression, and suicide. The recognition of traumatic stress and the ability to mourn losses are essential aims of psychoanalytic psychotherapy.

Working through unresolved grief and melancholia resulting from social oppression (Brave Heart & DeBruyn, 1998; Eng & Han, 2000; Herman, 1992) by recognizing and validating the connection between past atrocities and present day stress lies at the heart of culturally informed psychoanalytic psychotherapy. Remembering traumatic events experienced by cultures and communities and understanding the depth of their effects facilitates the recovery of strength in coping with traumatic stress among individuals, families, and communities, and helps to avoid a repetition of the events themselves (Ainslie & Brabeck, 2003; Harney, 2007; Harvey, 2007; Harvey & Tummala-Narra, 2007; Lear, 2007; Tummala-Narra, 2013a; Twemlow & Parens, 2006). Accounts of silence concerning traumatic events across generations, compounded by experiences of discrimination, have been noted among families of survivors of collective violence, such as in the case of survivors of the Nazi Holocaust and those of the Japanese internment camps in the United States (Nagata & Cheng, 2003; Ornstein, 2010).

Anna Ornstein (2010) wrote about the silence of survivors of the Holocaust after World War II as necessary for recovery and movement toward a new life and consolidation of the self. She pointed out that it would have been too soon for survivors to speak about the unbearable loss experienced in the Holocaust and that the access to collective mourning holds important meanings for survivors. In addition, creating *memorial spaces*, such as those evident in art and literature, can facilitate connections among those who were victimized by the collective trauma, those who were witnesses, and those who were unexposed to the trauma (Ornstein, 2010). Ornstein referred to the example of the Vietnam War Memorial in Washington, DC, as a *memorial space* where survivors can exert choice in whether they remain in the physical periphery of the memorial, and therefore the trauma, or make contact with the traumatic grief, sometimes for the first time since the war. Psychotherapy is still another space in which survivors alternate between disavowing the painful affect associated with collective trauma and attempting to make contact with this affect and the traumatic memories.

Unresolved grief can contribute to a *community character*, which consists of internalized patterns of behavior and implicit rules that help communities to manage anxiety, including stereotyping and hostility toward cultural groups (Borg, 2004). In addition, collective trauma produces a shared anxiety within a community that reinforces group identity and an intensification of "us" and "them" and "good" and "bad" delineations (Ainslie & Brabeck, 2003; Aviram, 2009; Davids, 2009; Hollander & Gutwill, 2006; Volkan, 1998). Although Freud's model of mourning is dyadic, involving the mourner and the mourned, a triadic model of mourning has been thought to be necessary for more adequately understanding the problem of collective loss (Moglen, 2005). In the latter approach, social oppression and loss involve the mourner (individual or group), the mourned (an ideal or sociocultural formation), and social forces that have destroyed the ideal. This third component of mourning raises questions about responsibility and related anger and aggression. Seth Moglen (2005) noted the importance of naming the sources of grief and mourning because the mourned objects do not disappear on their own but instead re-appear in the face of ongoing oppression and inequality. Remembering and naming collective trauma works toward owning individual and collective dissociative defenses used to cope with sadness, guilt, shame, and anger (Lewes et al., 2008).

When the therapist is unable to recognize and validate the client's history of social oppression, he or she creates a therapeutic space that potentially reproduces traumatic experiences. In this case, the therapist communicates unconsciously a disavowal of the oppression faced by the client and perpetuates the status quo of sociopolitical systems and their effects (Comas-Díaz, 2012). Numerous psychoanalytic scholars have written about the role of remembering and witnessing social oppression in the therapeutic relationship (Ainslie & Brabeck, 2003; Altman, 2010; Benjamin, 2011; Boulanger, 2007; Frosh, 2011; Powell, 2012). Jessica Benjamin (2011) emphasized the importance of mutuality in the therapist–client interaction concerning dialogue on injustice and the therapist's ability to take responsibility by recognizing and acknowledging the client's experiences of oppression and suffering. She conceptualized the *moral third* in psychotherapy as the therapist's honest recognition of defensiveness and misattunement to the client. Mutuality in the therapeutic relationship, which involves the recognition of the client's experience, signifies an attempt to decolonize destructive narratives about the self and about one's cultural groups. Ghislaine Boulanger (2012) noted that therapists are "morally obligated to bear witness" (p. 319) to oppressive events that disrupt the client's sense of self and relationships with others. This witnessing is viewed as necessary for the client to remove doubt concerning the meaning and importance his or her experience. Boulanger suggested that when we, as therapists, cannot connect with our client's histories of social oppression directly, we must witness the traumatic events through "an act of imagination" (p. 321) by suspending our subjectivity to enter the internal experience of the client while remaining separate. This type of witnessing that recognizes the subjectivity of the client and that of the therapist as both separate and related facilitates the movement from making unspoken experiences heard in the therapeutic relationship.

Witnessing requires us to examine our feelings and reactions to our clients' histories of oppression. Witnessing engages conflict rather than contributing to further repression (Comas-Díaz, 2000). As therapists, we consciously or unconsciously choose whether or not to explore experiences of social oppression and marginalization with our clients. Despite the decision to initiate or deepen dialogue concerning social oppression, the client's experiences remain (Greene, 2007). It is important to recognize that experiences of social oppression may have more significance in the everyday life of the client than of the therapist, or the reverse may be true. Nevertheless, there are critical moments when the effects of social oppression must be examined by the client and the therapist for the therapeutic process to be effective. The therapist's personal worldview and commitment to addressing inequities and oppression is an important factor in whether or not these issues will be explored and whether or not the therapist initiates discussing these issues with the client.

Culturally informed psychoanalytic psychotherapy addresses how broader social structures influence the perceptions and feelings that the client and the therapist have toward each other. Although conceptualizations of transference initially assumed that the client's reactions to the therapist were distorted as a function of feelings accompanying early object relations, contemporary understandings of transference reflect a view of the therapist as a real figure whose subjectivity interplays with that of the client (Javier & Herron, 2002; S. A. Mitchell, 1998b; Russell, 1998). For example, Javier and Herron (2002) suggested that many therapists from middle-class backgrounds who work with clients who are poor or from low-income backgrounds experience feeling confused or frozen by a lack of familiarity of the client's life circumstances and struggle with how to be helpful to the client. The therapist's acknowledgement of discrimination against the poor is a critical part of examining transference and countertransference, in which the therapist has to consider how he or she feels about the client's economic and social conditions, including any inclination to avoid identifying with being poor, and how the client feels about the economically privileged therapist (Javier & Herron, 2002; L. Smith, 2005). In this case, recognition and witnessing involve empathic attunement to the client's lived realities of economic struggle and/or poverty, his or her internal and relational experiences of these struggles, and his or her efforts to cope with stress (Farrell, 2012; Kohut, 1984).

Even when comfortable discussing financial issues with a client who is unemployed, the therapist may focus entirely on the client's lack of income or employment rather than addressing a full range of issues relevant to the client's concerns about work itself. David Blustein (2006) recognized the importance of exploring the experience of working as it connects the individual with economic, social, cultural, and political structures. Specifically, Blustein suggested that work serves multiple functions, including a means of survival and power, a means of social connection, and a means of self-determination. This more complex view of working as it intersects with social class is especially important in psychoanalytic psychotherapy because the influence of social structures, interpersonal processes, and individual psychology all contribute to an individual's distress and resilience.

As therapists, we must consider our willingness to engage with differences and similarities in privilege and marginalization with our clients concerning issues of gender, race, ethnicity, sexual identity, social class, religion, dis/ability, language, and immigration status. Privilege is at times invisible to the therapist and to the client, with each individual making assumptions about the other's sociocultural background and life circumstances, such as when a client imagines that his or her therapist has always been economically and socially privileged, when in reality the therapist grew up in poverty or currently faces economic struggles. In a different example, a White therapist may assume that an ethnic minority client from a middle-class or upper-middle–class background is protected from discrimination. In addition, for most people, privilege and marginalization coexist and become either more or less salient across different relational contexts. The issues of privilege and marginalization often are met with ambivalence because they evoke feelings of sadness, guilt, shame, and anger by people among majority status and minority status backgrounds. Yet as Wachtel (2014) noted, psychoanalytic therapists aim not to dismiss their clients when they experience negative reactions, such as anger, toward the therapist but rather make efforts to understand the reasons their clients experience these negative feelings.

Psychoanalytic accounts of *Whiteness* are important to examine. The melancholy of the White person has also been described as involving feelings of emptiness associated with an ideal of Whiteness (Straker, 2004). Melanie Suchet (2004) noted that race remains in today's world as a "melancholic structure, disavowed and unacknowledged" (p. 436) and for Whites carries shame and guilt that are dissociated. Neil Altman (2006) called attention to the ways in which many White people tend not to reflect on what it means to be White. Whiteness, from his perspective, is presumed to be a lack of color but carries a feeling of specialness and creates a standard against which other racial groups are measured. When guilt accompanying Whiteness becomes intolerable, many White people deny that they contribute to social inequality or blame ethnic minorities (Altman, 2006). Adrienne Harris (2012) described White identity as involving a feeling of guiltiness or a "hysterical form of attachment and narcissism, not a break with colonizing gaze and structure" that "makes for ruptured, anxious dissociated speech" (p. 205). Harris further suggested that a therapist's work should reflect growth from guiltiness to remorse. Suchet (2007) described her own "unraveling" of Whiteness in an effort to deconstruct her White privilege and feelings of shame and guilt. In each account, these White analysts have acknowledged their ambivalence concerning the undoing of White privilege. Suchet (2007), for example, wrote, "I wonder too, if there is a small part of me that wishes to remain white, the white I abhor" (p. 880). This type of honest reflection, in which the typical defenses are used to manage anxiety, is critical for the mourning of Whiteness. In addition, this type of reflection is relevant not only to Whiteness but also to other identities that mark social privilege and power (e.g., gender, social class, sexual identity, dis/ability).

Mourning of social oppression is an ongoing process, one that manifests in different permutations depending on life circumstances and transitions. Mourning is also relevant to the recognition of oppression within cultural groups. It is important to understand that validation of oppression within groups does not negate the effects of oppression by those outside of one's cultural group. Witnessing social oppression in psychotherapy requires that the therapist and the client engage with the complexity of marginalization and privilege and their effects on various aspects of the client's life.

A culturally informed psychoanalytic approach requires the therapist to bear the likelihood that he or she will make, recognize, and admit mistakes, and understand the effects of these mistakes on the client and the therapeutic relationship (Benjamin, 2011; Cushman, 2000; Gaztambide, 2012; Summers, 2014). Therapists and clients unconsciously enact dynamics related to social identity and oppression (Berzoff, 2012; Ogden, 1994). Clients who have experienced collective trauma and social marginalization may experience the therapist as victimizer, victim, or bystander at varying times in the course of psychotherapy (Herman, 1992). The therapist may respond to the client's experiences in ways that reify the client's conscious and unconscious expectations of the therapist. Kimberlyn Leary's (2000) described racial enactments as "interactive sequences that embody the actualization in the clinical situation of cultural attitudes toward race and racial difference" (p. 639). An example of a racial enactment is the therapist's and the client's silence concerning racial difference in the therapeutic relationship. She noted that racial enactments involve a complex negotiation of internal responses (e.g., idealization, envy, devaluation) experienced by the therapist and the client and of the interpersonal interactions between the therapist and the client.

Working through enactments requires a collaborative approach in which the client is encouraged to discuss his or her perspective concerning the therapist's attitudes and behavior. Kris Yi (1998) referred to the empathic–introspective mode of inquiry (Stolorow, Brandchaft, & Atwood, 1987) in addressing racial issues in psychotherapy. This type of inquiry involves the therapist's efforts to simultaneously empathize with the client's experiences and engage in introspection concerning his or her subjectivity influencing the therapeutic relationship. In deconstructing racial enactments, the therapist must be able to listen openly to the client's perspective, even those things that are painful to hear. The enactment is deconstructed and examined carefully by the therapist and client so that an understanding of its function can be achieved through an open dialogue rather than a closed system in which silence is perpetuated (Leary, 2000, 2007).

The nature of enactments related to sociocultural context can be further understood through examining *normative unconscious processes*, which have been described by Lynne Layton (2006) as "the psychological consequences of living in a culture in which many norms serve the dominant ideological purpose of maintaining a power status quo" (p. 239). Normative unconscious processes lie at the core of enactments related to social identity, as the therapist and the client are pulled into reifying destructive norms concerning gender, race, social class, and sexuality. According to Layton, social inequities and oppressive ideologies produce narcissistic wounds that are enacted by the client and the therapist, often in the form of idealization and devaluation of cultural groups. The ability to deconstruct such enactments is necessary not only for a corrective emotional experience, in which the client feels validated and understood by the therapist, but also for a "corrective relational experience," in which the client experiences mutuality and reciprocity in his or her relationship with the therapist (Stark, 1999).

In some cases, enactments allow for the opportunity to examine the client's and therapist's stereotypes about other cultural groups. For example, an African American client may tell her White therapist that she does not feel comfortable with her Japanese American colleague at work, and describing the colleague as a "foreigner" even though the colleague was born in the United States. The therapist is faced with a dilemma of whether and how to explore the client's stereotyping of the colleague. This type of dilemma raises questions about the therapist's own conscious and unconscious beliefs about the client's and the colleague's racial and cultural backgrounds and how he or she conceptualizes why the client has shared this experience with the therapist at a particular moment in the course of psychotherapy. For example, it is possible that the client's colleague becomes a container for the client's frustration with her workplace, where the client feels marginalized, or that the client is speaking in displacement about her own feelings of being a "foreigner" in her relationship with the therapist. There are, of course, various other possibilities that can be explored in the deconstruction of this enactment and require attention to both conscious and unconscious processes rooted in the client's life history and circumstances and in the dynamics of the therapeutic relationship.

CASE ILLUSTRATION: FARAH[1]

In the following case illustration, I present some ways in which social oppression and traumatic stress are experienced by a client in an immigrant context and addressed in psychotherapy. I worked with this client, Farah, weekly for approximately 3 years.

---

[1]Adapted from "Cultural Identity in the Context of Trauma and Immigration From a Psychoanalytic Pespective," by P. Tummala-Narra, 2014, *Psychoanalytic Psychology*, *31*, pp. 403–406. Copyright 2014 by the American Psychological Association.

Farah is a 38-year-old, Muslim, heterosexual woman who immigrated to the United States from a rural village in India with her husband when she was 23 years old. She and her husband, both from working-class backgrounds in India, initially moved to a large city in the United States and later to a suburb of the same city. Farah has the equivalent of an associate's degree from a college in India and works in a retail store. Her husband earned an undergraduate degree in engineering from a university in India and works as a manager of a small business. They have a 14-year-old daughter and a 10-year-old son. Farah decided to seek psychotherapy to help with addressing her increasing anxiety and isolation over a course of several months, acting upon the suggestion of a friend at her workplace. She was referred to me by her friend's physician.

Farah's mother died when she was 7 years old of injuries sustained in a bus accident. For several years, her sister, who is several years older than Farah, became a maternal figure. Her father remarried when Farah was 11 years old. Farah described her stepmother as a cruel woman who "manipulated" her father and lied to him. Farah and her sister were physically abused by their stepmother through their adolescence. In addition to the physical violence, her stepmother's brother who stayed with their family on several occasions sexually molested her and her sister. Farah and her sister never told their father about the sexual abuse, although they suspected that their stepmother was aware of the abuse. The sexual abuse ended when her stepmother's brother moved away to another region of India.

Farah described her father as depressed, withdrawn, and unable to grieve the death of her mother. She stated that although her father was aware of the physical violence in their home, he did little to protect his daughters other than occasionally sending them on visits to their maternal grandparents' home to get a break from his wife. Farah remains close to her sister, but since getting married, she has maintained a distant relationship with her father and no contact with her stepmother. In our initial meetings, Farah reported that she had trouble sleeping for most of her life and was apprehensive about getting married, especially since she had known her husband for only a few weeks before their marriage. Much to her relief, she has experienced her husband as a safe figure, and described her in-laws as kind people who treat her with respect. Her in-laws reminded her of her own mother, who she described as soft-spoken and caring. At times, she feels guilty for being happy in her marriage because her sister, who also immigrated to the United States, had been coping with a stressful marriage, in which she was emotionally abused by her husband. Farah reported that her brother-in-law blames her sister for not being able to have children. Over the course of several years, she has felt increasingly helpless in supporting her sister and anxious about her sister's future.

Farah had also been struggling as a mother to her adolescent daughter, who had begun to express interest in dating boys, something that was forbidden in Farah's family and community in India. Farah's adjustment to living in the United States involved mixed emotions. On one hand, she looked forward to starting a new life away from her adolescent years with her father and stepmother. On the other hand, she knew little about American society and culture and worried about losing her connection with her Indian, Muslim heritage. After moving to the United States, she and her husband attended mosque more regularly than they had while living in India, although they did not consider themselves to be religious people. She found herself wanting to find ways to stay connected with the Muslim community yet felt different from other people in this community because she had little or no contact with her family in India. She had disclosed her experience of sexual abuse and physical violence to her husband. However, she felt as though she could not talk about these experiences with anyone else, especially others in her mosque or in the broader Indian community. She worried that such a disclosure would negatively affect perceptions of her family, particularly her children.

The adjustment to living in the United States was also influenced by her interactions in several work environments where she felt hostility toward South Asians. Although she was fluent in English and had taken pride in her educational background, she felt as though others viewed her as having inferior intelligence. She reported that a few coworkers asked her questions about whether her husband was "good to her" because they assumed South Asian men dominate and/or abuse women. The stereotypes of South Asian men and women felt offensive to Farah because they stood in contrast to her experience of her father's relationship with her stepmother and that of her own marriage. She also felt conflicted about the stereotype because she struggled with memories of sexual abuse by a man and experienced anxiety about her sister's troubled marriage. She also worried about her daughter's interest in boys and the possibility of her daughter being hurt sexually in some way.

In the course of our work together, Farah expressed feeling "alone in the world," especially when she imagined the worst for her sister and daughter. She strongly identified with her mother, who she constructed through her early childhood memories and stories told by her maternal grandparents. She wanted to be a "good" mother like her mother had been to her and her sister. Our work focused on working on some ways to relieve her anxiety more immediately, such as relaxation and breathing exercises. Several months into our work together, after she was able to sleep more regularly and her anxiety felt more manageable to her, we shifted our conversations to her grief over her mother's death. In one session, when I asked her to tell me about her mother, she stated

> I never got to talk about her when I was growing up. My dad never wanted to deal with it. Just move on, he would say. Just my sister and I would talk about her sometimes. It's too much to think about her sometimes. If she didn't die, then none of the bad things would have happened. She would have helped my sister now. She would have been here to help with my kids.

Farah continued to talk about her profound sense of loss as she talked about her mother and her anger toward her father and stepmother. However, she also missed her father, in part because he was a link to her mother.

She increasingly talked about the silence imposed on her and her sister after their mother's death. When I asked her what it was like to talk with me about the violence in her home in India, she stated, "It's hard to talk about it. Maybe you will find it hard to listen to what that man (stepmother's brother) did to us. It's too shameful."

I responded, "Tell me what feels hard about telling me more about what happened."

Farah then talked about her apprehension of telling another Indian person about "family matters" and the guilt she felt for speaking negatively about her family.

I stated, "I understand that it is unusual to talk about things like abuse and violence inside the home to someone like me, an Indian. I wonder if you are concerned that I won't believe you or that I may think negatively of you or your family in some way."

Farah stated that she did at times have all of these concerns. Farah later proceeded to talk more about what she imagined about my reactions to the violence in her home and her feelings of ambivalence about her father, who she sometimes missed and other times felt enraged by his silence and apathy.

During these moments in psychotherapy, Farah experienced me as a bystander, like her father, and a potential perpetrator, like her stepmother and her stepmother's brother, and at times, I worried that I would somehow embody these positions and retraumatize her. In particular, I wondered about how she experienced my inquiry into her experience with sexual and physical abuse and whether it reflected my own wish for her to talk about it in more depth rather than her need to discuss the details of her trauma. I could identify with her fear of breaking silence around physical and sexual violence in the Indian community because these are topics that typically are stigmatized and avoided. I was also aware, at least in part, that I wished she would overcome her fear and break her silence within her family and community. I understood that my internal reactions were reflective of my own struggles as an Indian immigrant woman who identifies with both Indian and Euro American cultural systems.

I noticed that Farah and I both shifted positions at different moments in our work, during which we would take turns backing away from discussing her traumatic experiences and then reengage with this material. Deconstructing this enactment became critical to the process of uncovering Farah's feelings about her traumatic experiences. In one session, I asked Farah how she imagined our conversation about abuse and violence might have felt if we had been living in India and how this conversation may be different in the United

States. It was when I could talk with her about our shared experiences as Indian immigrant women and recognized that her fears about disclosing her trauma history to other Indians did indeed involve a risk of disconnecting from the community that Farah began to take the risk of telling me the details of her traumatic experiences.

Our discussions about her traumatic history were further complicated by language. Farah internally recalled her traumatic memories in her native language, Hindi, and then relayed them to me in English. I often felt as though I could not enter her world sufficiently because we did not share a native Indian language. Sometimes I experienced Farah's descriptions of severe violence as disconnected from the emotional aspects of the trauma. I asked her in these moments to describe the events in Hindi and then translate them to English. Over the course of several sessions, I could hear her sadness and fear connected with her experiences of sexual and physical abuse. Gradually, she also spoke about feeling silenced after moving to the United States, particularly at her previous workplaces, where her coworkers assumed that she was a submissive South Asian woman. In these interactions, Farah felt "frozen," not able to respond, which reminded her of experiences of being "held down" by her abusers (stepmother and her brother).

In our work, she continued to explore her conflicted feelings of immigration to the United States. Until her daughter became an adolescent, Farah felt hopeful about her family's future in the United States. However, as her daughter became more "Westernized," Farah's concerns for her safety and her growing disconnection with her family in India and with India itself left her feeling overwhelmed and confused. She was unsure again about her own safety and sense of belonging and was terrified for her daughter. Farah felt supported by some of her friends in the mosque but did not feel that she could ever tell them about her whole self. This became a central focus in psychotherapy, in which she examined her identifications as a Muslim, Indian woman in the context of migration, cultural shifts in the family, and her trauma history. For Farah, moving to the United States marked a rescue from a terrifying childhood and adolescence, yet she experienced the ongoing effects of her early trauma and new forms of oppression in her new American cultural context.

Farah is both empowered and disempowered in her move to the United States as she copes with traumatic stress, a sense of disconnection from her Indian home, a negative reception in the United States toward Muslims, and opportunities for creating new, more-hopeful relationships. A relational psychoanalytic perspective in which individual, interpersonal, and sociocultural issues are thought to be intricately tied is especially important to a deeper understanding of how cultural identity can transform throughout one's life (Boulanger, 2004; Layton, 2004). This is evident in Farah's ambivalence toward her Indian and American cultural contexts. Her negotiation of cultural identity is situated in her experience as a Muslim, Indian woman in a traumatic context in India and as a Muslim, Indian woman in new cultural context in the United States, where she is victimized by racism and loved and cared for by her family. Because trauma is inextricably tied to both contexts, she developed split-off aspects of the self (Bromberg, 2006) that interfered with her ability to experience herself as a whole person and establish a sense of home. It is important to note that the demands of her external world (e.g., Indian and non-Indian communities) support the shifting from one cultural context to another such that existing structures of oppression are unchanged.

The therapeutic relationship offered a space in which Farah could challenge the idea that she had to hide aspects of her experience to survive being victimized. Through the exploration of her trauma history before and after migration, she came to have a better understanding of how this history shaped her feelings about living in the United States. She also came to realize that her fears of her daughter's, sister's, and her own future were connected with her traumatic experiences, exacerbated by an uncertain sense of belonging in the United States. She was able to more deeply consider the role of stereotypes of women, men, and South Asians within her Muslim, Indian community and within mainstream American society, in her cultural identity. Farah's reluctance to talk with other Indians about her history of abuse was evident in the transference because she was reluctant to disclose details of her abuse to me. I believe that our willingness to address her apprehension helped her to break her silence in psychotherapy and begin to consider experiencing herself more fully outside of psychotherapy in her relationships with family and friends. Farah gradually began to define her own unique experience of herself as a Muslim, Indian woman in the United States as she mourned the loss of her mother, her relationships with her father and stepmother, and the loss of a wish to belong fully in mainstream American context.

Despite our shared experiences as Asian Indian immigrant women, we clearly had unique experiences (e.g., traumatic history, religious background, social class background) and developed unique meanings of these experiences in India and the United States. The recognition of similarities and differences in social location between the therapist and the client can be critical for the client's exploration of identity in the immigrant context. By the end of our work together, Farah had told a couple of close friends about her trauma history in India and found ways to talk with her daughter about her fears concerning dating and becoming too "Westernized." She also had begun to talk to her children and her husband about her mother in more depth. I, too, was transformed through our work. Although my immigrant background has always been important personally and professionally, I had grown increasingly aware of the artificial dichotomy that is all too often drawn between individual and sociocultural experience. Farah had brought to the foreground the ways in which this false dichotomy serves only to create theoretical splits that potentially can have damaging effects for clients coping with trauma in an immigrant context. Witnessing and bearing the complexity of the various layers of experience inside and outside was, in fact, imperative to her healing.

SUMMARY

Psychoanalytic perspectives on traumatic stress provide a critical lens for understanding the impact of social oppression on intrapsychic and relational life. Culturally informed psychoanalytic psychotherapy emphasizes the role of unconscious and implicit stereotyping, prejudice, and discrimination on the client's and the therapist's experiences of the self and of each other. The experience of discrimination contributes to various challenges to a sense of safety, belonging, and integration, as evidenced, for example, in an individual's or a group's difficulty in bearing both positive and negative representations of the aggressive individual or group. This chapter further calls attention to the intergenerational effects of collective violence and the experience of multiple marginalization, particularly as it relates to vulnerable communities (e.g., racial minorities, women of color, people with disabilities, people living in poverty, LGBTQ individuals, gender nonconforming). There is an emphasis on the therapist's ability to witness the client's narrative in psychotherapy, during which unimaginable events can be spoken about and heard. Culturally informed psychoanalytic practice attends to the mourning of loss, unresolved grief related to social oppression, and the role of enactments in psychotherapy, which reflect cultural attitudes toward race and other aspects of social identity in broader society. The ability to deconstruct enactments is an essential part of addressing social oppression and related traumatic stress in psychotherapy. Experiences of social oppression and traumatic stress have important implications for one's identity. The next chapter addresses the complexity of cultural identification, as shaped by sociocultural context, relational experiences, and intrapsychic life.

7

RECOGNIZING THE COMPLEXITY OF CULTURAL IDENTIFICATIONS

I met Vira, a 16-year-old Hindu, Indian American girl, and her parents in a consultation precipitated by escalating conflict at home. Vira's parents were born and raised in what they described as a "religiously conservative home" in India and moved to the United States to find employment as software engineers. Vira was born and raised in a suburban area of the United States. Her parents had convinced her to meet with a therapist after learning that she had been sending sexually revealing pictures of herself to boys in school via text messages. Although Vira reluctantly came to see me, she gradually became more willing to talk about her feelings of disconnection from her parents, who she viewed as "out of touch with kids and technology." In one session, she stated, "Why can't I be a girl who is Hindu and a girl who boys like?" For Vira, sexual attention from boys was linked with having to please them in whatever way they requested, including sending pictures of herself when they asked her to do so. Vira referred to texting these pictures as

http://dx.doi.org/10.1037/14800-008
Psychoanalytic Theory and Cultural Competence in Psychotherapy, by P. Tummala-Narra

something that "everyone does" and as "no big deal." Although she dismissed any meanings attached to her texting, she spoke about her Hindu religious beliefs with great fervor, taking pride in her knowledge of Hindu scriptures. In fact, she studied these scriptures regularly and attended religious classes every week. Interestingly, Vira did not connect her interest in Hinduism to her parents' values. Vira's immersion into Hinduism and her texting interactions with boys were separated, disavowed from each other, and did not seem to present any conflict for her in conscious life; instead, they reflected a sense of defiance toward her parents.

Later in our work, Vira revealed that she did not want to be as conservative as her mother and thought of her mother as someone who was not attractive to her father. She proceeded to tell me that her father made disparaging comments about her mother's "ugly" appearance periodically, leaving her mother feeling demoralized. Vira coped with hearing these comments by her father by distancing herself from her mother and by responding to sexual attention from boys in a way that ensured that she did not receive the same type of message that her mother received from her father. Vira's desire to be seen as an attractive young woman can be understood in the context of the negative sexual images of women in her home. Her feelings can also be understood through the dynamics of her peer environment. Vira eventually told me that she was the only Indian girl whose photos White boys in her school were interested in seeing. She said, in one of our sessions, "I don't want to be just another smart, nerdy Indian girl. I want them to see me another way. I don't want to date them or anything. I really am religious, you know." In these moments, Vira began to more openly express her confusion about her identity as an Indian American girl. When I listened to Vira's conflicts, I found myself identifying with her and her mother, reminiscent of my own conflicted, layered identities growing up as an Indian immigrant girl in the United States. I believe that Vira could sense my thoughts because she began to make comments about my identity. For example, she stated, "You sound like you grew up here. You probably know what it's like to have strict parents." I did let her know that, similar to her, I did grow up primarily in the United States and that I am Hindu but that I imagined our experiences were unique from each other in some ways, too.

My discussions with Vira concerning cultural identity involved a delicate balance between recognizing our shared experiences and differentiating ourselves from each other. Vira needed to define herself in the context of feeling constricted by home and school. Psychotherapy offered a space in which she could explore her identity with the broadest range of possibilities about who she would decide to become and also explore the barriers she faced in having her self-definition recognized by others. Creating such a space required that I continually examine my feelings about Vira's life at home and school and the broader social messages absorbed by young Asian Indians in the United States.

Ethnic identity has been defined as one's sense of belonging to a specific ethnic group and the perceptions and meanings connected with this affiliation (Phinney, 1996; Schwartz, Unger, Zamboanga, & Szapocznik, 2010). Numerous studies indicate that a strong, positive ethnic identity is associated with psychological health and academic adjustment, particularly among adolescents and young adults (T. B. Smith & Silva, 2011). However, it is unclear that having a stronger ethnic identity protects against certain stressors, such as racism and discrimination (G. L. Stein, Kiang, Supple, & Gonzalez, 2014; Tummala-Narra, Inman, & Ettigi, 2011). In addition, even when parents and caregivers encourage their children to connect with their ethnic communities, young people may not develop positive feelings because as other factors, such as interactions within schools and neighborhoods, influence ethnic identity formation (Supple, Ghazarian, Frabutt, Plunkett, & Sands, 2006). In recent years, researchers have called for a multidimensional, socioecological approach to ethnic identity that addresses the complexity of how people construct their ethnic or cultural identities in relation to their sociocultural contexts (García Coll & Marks, 2012; T. B. Smith & Silva, 2011; Umaña-Taylor, Diversi, & Fine, 2002).

Although research on ethnic identity has emphasized the role of mainstream context on ethnic minorities' cultural identities, it is important to consider how individuals' interactions within their families and ethnic groups shapes cultural identity and that cultural identity reflects a mutual influence of the individual and his or her social context. Cultural identity is also an amalgam of multiple group memberships that interact with one another and change over the course of one's life. The multiplicity of identity also implicates an interaction of oppression, marginalization, and privilege across multiple dimensions (Greene, 2007). A culturally informed psychoanalytic framework considers the influence of layers of experience, including those occurring within families, communities, institutions, and societies, to understand the development and significance of cultural identity. Thus, this approach challenges simplistic conceptualizations of cultural identity development and considers the role of cultural narrative, language, affects associated with interactions in different contexts, and experiences of social oppression and privilege. A contemporary psychoanalytic perspective contrasts with other psychological models that largely support linear, sequential, and conscious level processes in racial and cultural identity development (Yi, 2014b). There is also increasing recognition that cultural identity is relevant to all people, not just those who identify as people of color or minorities. An emphasis on unconscious conflict and subjectivity of internal experience contributes to a more complex understanding of cultural identity and the development of coexisting, divergent cultural identifications.

In this chapter, I describe some conflicts inherent to the development of cultural identity and the intrapsychic and interpersonal implications of intersectional, hybrid identities in everyday life and the therapeutic relationship. I emphasize a conceptualization of cultural identity as encompassing not only ethnic identity but also its intersections with other aspects of social location and identity, such as age, gender, race, religion, social class, sexual orientation, and dis/ability. In addition, each aspect of identity is associated with experiences of marginality and privilege. I underscore the therapist's and the client's ability to bear anxiety related to the ambiguous and conflictual nature of negotiating a complex, hybrid cultural identity and attend to the interpersonal dynamics in the therapeutic relationship that produce this anxiety.

CULTURAL IDENTITY AND CONFLICT

The term "identity" was introduced in 1919 to psychoanalysis by Victor Tausk and later elaborated by Erik Erikson (1950), who suggested that identity develops from self-objectification and is defined by the relationship of a soul to its existence, implicating both a sense of self and the sharing of specific traits of the self with others (Akhtar, 2009). Erikson emphasized the role of individual, family, and social factors in identity formation, an idea that was criticized by his contemporaries. Heinz Lichtenstein (1964) extended identity to encompass two aspects: the identity principle or the individual's drive to assert and maintain his or her individuality, and metamorphosis or the urge to resist assigned roles in society (Akhtar, 2009; Lachmann, 2004). Since the 1970s, psychoanalytic theory on identity has shifted to a focus on a sense of self as fluctuating between an intrapsychic and a relational view of sense of self or identity. An intrapsychic focus (Jacobson, 1964) suggests that a sense of self or identity develops in a linear way through an individual's response to his or her environment, whereas a relational focus (D. N. Stern, 1995) suggests that a sense of self develops in a cumulative and transformative way through interactions between the individual and others (Lachmann, 2004).

Psychoanalytic scholars have conceptualized identity as providing an intrapsychic experience of "subjective self-sameness" that allows people to feel and behave in ways that feel true to themselves (Mann, 2006). In recent years, relational psychoanalysts have emphasized the ways in which identity is transformed throughout one's life. In addition, psychotherapy is thought to provide an opportunity to rediscover aspects of the self or of identity through a reconstruction and coconstruction in the therapist–client relationship. Psychoanalytic psychotherapy aims to help clients with the integration of past and present conflictual and disavowed experiences of the self. The development of cultural identity from a psychoanalytic perspective requires attention to the realities of the client's social environment, the client's affective experience of his or her social environment, the intrapsychic meanings associated with these experiences, and the client's response to others.

Structural Issues

Cultural identity develops in a society characterized by structural inequalities. Social oppression diminishes an individual's access to agency and choice within political, economic, social, and interpersonal spheres. Laura Smith (2005) called oppression "prejudice plus power" (p. 688). Through her analysis of social class and poverty, she noted that although people in dominant and nondominant groups are capable of classism against others, people in dominant groups have institutional and cultural power to enforce their oppressive attitudes, in contrast to people in nondominant groups. Social oppression can distort not only one's identity and self-worth but also one's perceptions of one's own and other cultural groups. In addition, oppression and marginalization shape the individual's sense of safety and belonging, which is essential to ensuring access to a full range of cultural identifications.

In recent years, there has been increasing media attention to racial profiling and violence against Black adolescent boys and men in the United States, although racial profiling and violence occur with far greater frequency than what is reported in mainstream media. The tragic, fatal shooting of Trayvon Martin, a 17-year-old African American boy, by George Zimmerman, a biracial (Latino/White) neighborhood watch volunteer, in 2012, sparked national debate on the role of race in violence against Black boys and men. In 2014, the fatal shooting of Michael Brown, an 18-year-old African American man, by a White police officer, Darren Wilson, in Ferguson, Missouri, retraumatized African American communities. Also in 2014, Eric Garner, a 43-year-old African American man, was killed by a White police officer, Daniel Pantaleo, in Staten Island, New York; Pantaleo placed a banned tactic, a chokehold, on Garner. Garner was suspected by police officers of selling loose cigarettes. In the cases of Michael Brown and Eric Garner, grand juries decided not to indict the police officers. The deaths of Michael Brown and Eric Garner brought to the foreground historical and ongoing racial tensions that permeate the interactions between African American community members and White authorities.

These traumatic events incite fear, sadness, frustration, and anger within communities of color, where group and individual identities cannot be negotiated independently of oppression, particularly when there are minimal or no consequences for offenders. Parents are in a position of having to prepare children to protect themselves in a potentially dangerous environment, so children develop their identities within the parameters of oppression. In addition, as Greene (2010) has pointed out, narratives that contrast with that of the dominant group are often dismissed. This is evident in figures in the media who insist that race is no longer an issue in the United States since the presidential election of Barack Obama or who use terms such as "playing the race card" when describing racial minorities who openly challenge racist ideologies and institutions.

The ways in which individuals cope with negative social messages and oppression vary considerably. However, these variations unfortunately often are attributed solely to an individual's capabilities or competence rather than to the interplay among individual, community, and societal dynamics. The negotiation of a negative social mirror (Suárez-Orozco & Suárez-Orozco, 2001) involves complex processes related to interpersonal interactions both within and outside of one's cultural group. For example, many minorities believe that they need to portray a positive image of their cultural groups to cope with their marginalized positions (Mahalingam, Balan, & Haritatos, 2008). In other cases, when individuals experience marginalization and/or trauma within their families and/or cultural group, positive images of the cultural group may be challenging to develop and sustain (Yi, 2014a). Both the internalization of an idealized image and a devalued image of one's cultural group present dilemmas and constrict the range of options available to an individual with respect to cultural identity development.

The negotiation of the model minority stereotype among many Asian Americans illustrates such a dilemma. For example, a Japanese American client whose academic performance is lower than that of his or her peers not only may feel demoralized by his or her relatively lower performance but also may question his or her authenticity as a person of Japanese ancestry and sense of belonging among other Japanese Americans who excel academically. For another Japanese American client, the model minority stereotype may be internalized in way that reifies his or her academic and professional success but in a way that his or her success is attributed to being Asian rather than to his or her individual abilities and efforts. In both cases, the stereotype plays an important role in how one comes to define himself or herself as a Japanese American person. The stereotype, particularly when it is marked as a "positive" stereotype, is not actively questioned but rather locates itself in individual strengths and deficits. Importantly, this stereotype, similar to other "positive" stereotypes, marks both privilege and marginalization. Specifically, the notion of model minority contains an explicit message that Asian Americans carry a privileged economic status in contrast to other racial minorities and simultaneously an implicit message that Asian Americans are inherently different from other minorities and Whites, placing them in a position of otherness. As such, identifying with the model minority stereotype can serve to secure privilege in the face of marginalization. However, such identifications can contribute to the minimization or denial of the structural inequalities faced by Asian Americans.

The internalization of social oppression in the formation of identity is evident among people marginalized across different sociocultural lines. For example, researchers and clinicians are increasingly reporting incidents of hate crimes, bullying, and emotional violence endured by people with disabilities. A child with a physical disability absorbs attitudes and behaviors toward his or her disability not only from parents and caregivers but also from his or her school environment. Many children and adolescents with disabilities find schools, where an emphasis on preparing students for developing skills for a capitalist market society and the management of student and teacher performance can override attention to strengths and vulnerabilities of students, to be stressful environments (Goodley & Runswick-Cole, 2011). The policing of youth on the margins (e.g., minorities) in schools has become a serious threat to young people's trust in adults who hold positions of authority (e.g., teachers, law enforcement) and in youth's access to safe public spaces (Fine, Freudenberg, Payne, Perkins, Smith, & Wanzer, 2003; Tummala-Narra & Sathasivam-Rueckert, 2013). Michelle Fine (2010), in particular, wrote extensively on the problem of *structural and psychic circuits of dispossession*, referring to the failure of public and private institutions to address the needs of people on the margins, especially those with little or no economic resources, which have profound implications for choice in identity.

For example, listening to youth's narratives about the microaggressions and/or explicit racial slurs they encounter on a daily basis at school is a key element in engaging with how cultural identity develops. In the group interview study (Tummala-Narra & Sathasivam-Rueckert, in press) referred to in chapter 6, immigrant-origin adolescents consistently reported struggling with negative images of their cultural groups. They were often typed by peers and teachers as carrying certain traits, such as "intelligence," "laziness," or being "dirty," all of which were attributed to their cultural groups (e.g., Asian, Haitian, Latino/a, South Asian). A majority of our participants told the group facilitators (undergraduate and graduate student assistants and me) they wished people outside their home would see all of their experience and not just certain characteristics determined by the lens of typologies. As much as they wished to dismiss stereotypes about their cultural groups, they wondered whether or not these stereotypes reflected something that was real or true about them. In other words, these youth face an impossible dilemma of how to define themselves outside of the parameters that have been set in place for them by dominant discourse.

In the course of our meetings with these adolescents, we learned about the importance of their desire to have people in their school see the "whole" culture or cultures with which they identify, not just partial images of a culture that are portrayed in stereotypes. Many of the adolescents told us that they just wanted people to see more of their cultures, families, and in essence, more of what they feel inside. Through collaboration with the research team, several adolescents who participated in the group interviews and teachers organized a "culture fair," a week-long series of events at the school that highlighted the pride and sense of connection adolescents felt toward their cultural groups. This type of engagement helped to bridge a necessary gap between the adolescents' positive affect associated with their cultural groups and the negative associations linked with their cultural groups in their school context. They also wanted a space in which they could discuss what they did not like about being a member of their cultural groups. For example, although many adolescents respected their parents for their hard work and dedication, they expressed feeling as though their parents did not understand the social demands of being an adolescent in the United States or enforced too many social restrictions. In addition, some adolescents felt they could not disclose these conflictual experiences to anyone within their families or school and tended to rely on friends from similar ethnic backgrounds with similar conflicts for emotional support. Upon the recommendation of these students, my research team continued to develop ideas for creating more spaces in which the students could talk openly about their social identities and the coexistence of multiple, contradictory affective experiences concerning their cultural groups and mainstream settings. We implemented dialogue groups, facilitated by graduate student assistants, in which adolescents could talk with each other and the facilitator about experiences of stereotyping and discrimination. It is unfortunate that most young people do not have access to safe public spaces in which such conversations can occur. Nevertheless, it was clear from the responses of our participants that they needed a safe space to talk about conflicting messages about their cultural groups to facilitate a sense of cultural identity they felt they could own rather than having their identities defined only through the demands of others.

In addition to the problem of societal oppression, marginalization of subgroups of individuals within a cultural group further imposes conflict in the formation of cultural identity. For example, LGBTQ individuals may face homophobic reactions and alienation from family, friends, and members of an ethnic or religious community in addition to that from mainstream society. A person with a physical disability may be considered by his or her family as carrying stigma for the family and thus experience himself or herself as a burden to others. A second-generation, immigrant-origin person may be ridiculed within his or her ethnic community for not being able to speak in his or her parents' heritage language. A person from a low-income background within an ethnic community may be excluded from social events and gatherings. In some cases, experiences of privilege are intertwined with experiences of marginalization. For example, a person who grows up in a working-class background and later shifts to a middle-class lifestyle and secures a position of economic privilege may be rejected by his or her child-hood community as someone who is no longer an "authentic" member of that group. Yi (2014b) observed that an individual's experiences within his or her cultural groups should be considered in ethnic identity development. Specifically, she described the problem of sexism-related trauma among ethnic minority women, which can contribute to negative and idealized images of the culture in the face of contradictory experiences within the culture. Therefore, therapists must carefully examine the extent to which experiences of marginalization within a cultural group and/or outside of the cultural group shape an individual's cultural identifications.

Diverging Identifications and Conflicting Loyalties

People develop cultural identities through interactions across multiple contexts, with different and sometimes contradictory narratives. Specifically, cultural identity formation often occurs through the navigation across cultures with divergent beliefs and traditions. Shifting unconsciously from one context to another is common, yet burdensome, because it involves the suppression and disavowal of affects, memories, and sensibilities rooted in cultural experience. For example, my client, Crystal, a Jamaican American woman who moved to the United States with her family when she was in her late teens, told me

> It's like you have to act a certain way when you are with certain people. That's true for everybody I guess, but it's also different. People see me and they think this is a Black woman. I have to act a certain way so they don't see me as negative. So, I try to act like them. Then, I go home and I'm Jamaican, not Black or anything, just Jamaican, just me.

In a similar vein, my client, Sheila, who identifies as a White lesbian, stated

> Sometimes you have to do things to make other people comfortable with the fact that you are a lesbian. You have to show them that it's not such a terrible thing. So, I don't really talk to them (coworkers) about who I date.

Hiding aspects of the self, such as sexual orientation, can be used to protect against anticipated discrimination but comes at the cost of increased vigilance and anxiety related to a sense of falseness and invisibility (Croteau, 2008).

Shifting, for many people, does not rely on real choice but rather operates through a dual sense of self that is necessary for surviving and thriving in multiple contexts (Roland, 1996, 2006). A person must develop creative solutions to the dilemma of managing public and private selves to cope with the stress that accompanies shifting. Despite the seamless nature of shifting, largely because it lies in the unconscious, shifting poses a risk for the individual's experience of being without a home. In some cases, an individual can develop split identifications with important people in their lives who remain separated as a way of bearing the anxiety of two or more contradictory cultural beliefs that clash with each other. For example, my client, Ravi, a first-generation, Indian American man in his early 30s, told me that he had not introduced his White, Irish American girlfriend to his parents although he and his girlfriend had talked about the possibility of getting married. Ravi, since moving away from home to attend college, gradually revealed less and less about himself to his parents and family members. However, when he went home to visit his family, he felt "happy" and "grounded." He described similar feelings about his experience of being with his girlfriend, yet he could not imagine bringing his two disparate worlds together because he expressed different parts of his identity when he was with her than when he was with his parents. Specifically, Ravi felt that he was more "American," independent, and adventurous when he was with his girlfriend and more "Indian" and oriented toward family when he was with his parents. He imagined that his parents and his girlfriend would not connect with each other and that they were too different from each other. He fantasized that if his parents and girlfriend "knew about each other," they would not approve of each other and consequently would be disappointed with him. In essence, Ravi, in an effort to cope with the anxiety of divergent cultural identifications that had developed in multiple contexts, had lived a dual existence in which self-states associated with each aspect of his cultural identity (e.g., American and Indian) were disconnected. He seamlessly shifted across Indian and mainstream American contexts and, over the course of time, began to feel as though there was little continuity in his sense of self. In psychotherapy, our work focused on developing an ability to imagine a safe way to bring his worlds together and mourn the ways in which his worlds perhaps would not be able to merge as he had wished.

Inherent to the shifting across multiple contexts are dilemmas concerning loyalty to one or more cultural groups. For example, a lesbian, gay, or bisexual ethnic minority may be challenged with the demands of his or her ethnic community and those of the LGB community, which may contradict each other, creating "conflicts of allegiance" (American Psychological Association, 2000; Morales, 1989). Conflicting loyalties play themselves out in intrapsychic and interpersonal spaces. Specifically, a person may be conflicted consciously or unconsciously about how he or she feels about a particular worldview and then realize this conflict in his or her interactions with others. For example, individuals who, because of their religious upbringing, believe that same-sex marriage is morally unacceptable but also believe that lesbian, gay, and bisexual people should have the same legal rights as heterosexual people may be deeply conflicted about their identification with and loyalty to different communities. Depending on whether they interact with people who align with one of these two views, they may express a singular, nonconflicted image of their true feelings as a way of securing a sense of safety in each setting.

Understanding the dynamics of loyalty and conflict requires understanding that privilege and marginalization can coexist and vary in their expression across contexts. It is a common experience that people manage their discomfort with a privileged status by minimizing its significance or emphasizing the privileged status of others who they perceive as having more social or economic power, rendering the relevance of their own privilege invisible. This may be particularly challenging for minority and majority status therapists who, by virtue of their professional status, may have ambivalent feelings about their privileged position in their interactions with clients. Therapists and clients experience a complex matrix of privilege and marginalization in their lives, which can have important implications for transference and countertransference dynamics and their ability to openly discuss various aspects of their cultural identifications with each other.

Shifting Loyalties Among Immigrants and Their Children

The experiences of immigrants and their children offer another illustration of dilemmas concerning loyalty to multiple cultural groups. The process of cultural identity development involves splitting, with fluctuating feelings of idealization and devaluation of one's cultural group and other mainstream groups (Akhtar, 2011; Lijtmaer, 2001). Akhtar (2011) noted that immigrants may affiliate exclusively with people within their own cultural groups (e.g., ethnocentric withdrawal) or develop an "as-if" (Deutsch, 1965) identity in their attempt to quickly identify with the new culture by disengaging with the culture of origin (e.g., counterphobic assimilation). These processes of negotiating cultural identity can operate in the experiences of immigrants and their children, the first and second generation, respectively. One's family is thought to be a transmitter of culture and a mediator between the individual and broader society. As culture is transmitted from one generation to the next, it tends to become increasingly removed from its origins and over several generations may become more symbolic (Sherry & Ornstein, 2014). However, the observance of cultural and religious traditions helps to maintain a sense of continuity across generations, particularly when there are external supports (e.g., similar ethnic or religious communities and institutions, recognition in mainstream society) that bridge the individual with his or her cultural heritage and ancestry.

The dilemmas inherent to cultural identity formation for the first and second generation can be distinct. First- and second-generation individuals experience loyalty to the new country and the country of origin in different ways because external symbols of an "American" identity coexist with internal conflicts concerning loyalty to the country of origin and the adopted country. For example, for many first-generation immigrants (e.g., those born outside of the United States who come to the United States as adults), the experience of becoming naturalized as a U.S. citizen can be a conflictual process. The official submission of loyalty to the United States is both an important milestone that recognizes the immigrant as a "real" American and an indicator of further psychological separation and disloyalty to one's country of origin. Relatedly, a first-generation immigrant's sense of home and a second-generation immigrant's sense of home can vary in important ways. It is more likely that first-generation immigrants experience nostalgia in the face of separation from the country of origin and fantasize about returning to the country, especially as they enter older age (Akhtar, 2011). In fact, many first-generation immigrants who have access to economic resources and are able to travel to their birth countries spend greater amounts of time in the country of origin in later stages of life (e.g., older age). Second-generation immigrants (e.g., those born in or primarily raised in the United States) are less likely to experience their parents' countries of origin as "home" and instead develop a multicultural, hybrid identity in which the United States is the reference point of "home" (Tummala-Narra, 2009a).

These types of distinctions across immigrant generations can bear a significant influence on cultural identity development and related feelings of loyalty. In a study with Muslim American youth, Sirin and Fine (2008) found that these youth experienced a sense of loyalty to the United States even though they were targets of verbal harassment in a post-9/11 society. The researchers noted that "being American" provided a frame of reference through which youth could criticize the United States. Notably, these youth claimed their rights as citizens, becoming valid critics of U.S. policies, and engaged in civic activities within mainstream circles. In addition, Sirin and Fine (2008) found that Muslim American youth were as engaged within mainstream society as within their Muslim communities, indicating a desire to identify with both cultures and secure a "peaceful coexistence at the hyphen of Muslim and American identities" (p. 129).

It is important to consider that first- and second-generation immigrant-origin individuals face unique struggles in cultural adjustment that affect identity. Research over the past two decades has supported the phenomenon of the immigrant paradox, which indicates that second-generation or U.S.-born individuals have worse mental health and educational outcomes than do first-generation or foreign-born individuals (Alegría et al., 2008; APA, 2012; García Coll & Marks, 2012; Suárez-Orozco, Suárez-Orozco, & Todorova, 2008). However, it would be naïve to assume that the first generation does not experience stress. On the contrary, the first generation often faces tremendous barriers in social and economic survival, which may be experienced and expressed in ways that are distinct from that of the second generation. Both first- and second-generation individuals tend to underuse mental health services, despite greater exposure to Western culture among the second generation.

Although research highlights these trends in mental health and access to care, the mechanisms underlying these disparities have remained unclear. A closer examination of the unique dilemmas of the first and second generation and their relevance to cultural identity can elucidate some potential reasons mental health and educational outcomes may be more problematic for the second generation. Specifically, the second generation develops cultural identity through the support and demands of parents and family members. Many adolescents feel that they cannot turn to their parents to help navigate the demands of mainstream society because immigrant parents struggle with their own anxiety and ambivalence related to cultural adjustment and identity formation and may not be adequately accessible to their children (Mann, 2004). First-generation parents may be stressed because of marital conflicts and/or decreased access to support from extended family. Second-generation individuals often occupy a position of translating language and culture to their parents and other older members of the family, face pressure to excel academically and professionally, and feel constrained by parental restrictions in socializing with others outside of their ethnic and religious communities (Akhtar, 2011). The second generation also maintains a close emotional connection with their family and ethnic and/or religious community. It is often the case that second-generation individuals experience ambivalence throughout their lives about their hybrid cultural identifications, which manifest in important life decisions, such as choice of career, romantic partners, spouses, and friends and parenting. Although the first generation also engages with these dilemmas, they may be more engaged with a negotiation of separation from loved ones in the country of origin and transnational living as they age in the adopted country. The guilt of separating or leaving loved ones behind in the country of origin may be transmitted to the second generation who, in adulthood, face the challenge of separating from their parents (Akhtar, 2011). These distinct developmental trajectories of the first and second generation set the stage for a unique set of cultural identifications for each group that transform throughout the life-span.

The access to multiple sources of support, such as that from family and similar ethnic and different ethnic friends, plays a key role in cultural adjustment and identity formation (Akhtar, 2011; Sirin & Fine, 2008; Tummala-Narra & Sathasivam-Rueckert, in press). Friendships serve an important mirroring function for first- and second-generation immigrants as they mourn the losses incurred in migration and negotiate the challenges of acculturation and separation and closeness with the culture of origin. Friends within and outside of one's cultural group can serve distinct but necessary functions, such as when a friend within one's ethnic community facilitates a sense of connection or reconnection to the culture of origin and a friend outside of one's ethnic community helps with connection to mainstream or less-familiar cultural perspectives and experiences (Akhtar, 2011). In addition, similar ethnic friendships for the first generation provide a sense of community, resembling family networks in the country of origin, whereas similar ethnic friendships for the second generation provide support as they define themselves along cultural lines that overlap and contrast with those of their parents. As such, the exploration of friendships in psychotherapy can help illuminate the ways in which cultural identity develops and transforms over time.

Technology and Transnational Space

The fluidity of sociocultural identity is increasingly situated in a technological age that has shifted individuals' access to transnational and transcultural spaces. The high prevalence in the use of the Internet and social networking sites has marked an important cultural change in how people interact with each other and define themselves. It has been estimated that 69% of adults who have access to the Internet use social networking sites, 66% use Facebook, and more than 25 million adults use online dating services every month (Duggan, 2013; Finkel, Eastwick, Karney, Reis, & Sprecher, 2012). The Internet provides a space for many people to communicate self-states in ways they are unable to in face-to-face interactions. Thus, the therapist plays an important role in exploring the client's online relational life to address the contrasts and tensions implicated in the negotiation of private and public selves. Sherry Turkle (2004) has called for psychoanalytic theory to develop a theoretical understanding of the role of computers in individuals' intrapsychic and relational life. She suggested that the computer has become a screen upon which thoughts and feelings are projected and that children develop emotional attachments to computers similar to the way we may expect attachments to people. The Internet stretches the range of possibilities for self-definition, and provides a space to experiment with different personas and play with identities in a presumed safe space. On the other hand, online spaces can become precarious ground for bullying, racism, sexism, homophobia, and other types of oppression.

The technological age has also challenged previously held notions of diaspora and transnational space. The term *diaspora* has shifted from a reference to displacement between nations to a reference to "out of culture," "out of language," and "out of oneself experience" (Jin, 2007; Lam, 2011). Diaspora has increasingly been conceptualized as a transnational space or an open system in which an individual can simultaneously exist in multiple spaces (Lam, 2011; Morawska, 2011). In this perspective, culture, race, and gender are no longer confined within fixed boundaries, such as national borders or binary constructions of gender (Bhatia & Ram, 2009). The ability to shift across spaces can facilitate a sense of transcendence over binary constructions of identity and also contribute to a sense of psychic homelessness. Ewa Morawska (2011) has argued that people in diasporas have complex, contradictory, and dynamic relationships with their countries of origin and adopted countries, which vary with social context (e.g., gender, social class). Access to the Internet and social media is a bridge to transnational life for many diasporic individuals who negotiate physical and psychological distance between the country of origin and the adopted country.

It is important to consider that transnational space is experienced in unique ways depending on the reasons for displacement from the country of origin. For example, refugees' ability to engage with fantasies of returning to their country of origin may differ significantly from those of immigrants because of starkly different social and political circumstances and experiences of trauma. Another variation in engagement with transnational space concerns the experience of transnational adoptees, which calls attention to the sense of isolation inherent to the negotiation of cultural identity among this subgroup. Specifically, David Eng and Shinhee Han (2006), in a case study with a Korean transnational adoptee, found that although Asian immigrant parents and their children negotiate cultural adjustment as "intergenerational and intersubjective conflicts," transnational adoptees "struggle with these issues in social and psychic isolation" (p. 142). There are other important variations in youth migration, such as unaccompanied minors who make treacherous journeys to the U.S. border to escape extreme poverty and violence, unaccompanied refugee children who are sent by parents to live with relatives or friends in the United States to escape natural disasters, and parachute children, who are sent to live with relatives or family friends to obtain a better education in the United States by parents who typically are wealthy. Each of these trajectories has implications for distinct types of physical and emotional stress, access to appropriate care and support, and identity development (APA, 2012; Lee & Friedlander, 2014).

INTERSECTIONALITY, CULTURAL HYBRIDITY, AND PSYCHOANALYTIC PSYCHOTHERAPY

Contemporary psychoanalytic scholars have increasingly written about their work with clients with multiple minority identities (Ruth, 2012). These writers (Bonovitz, 2009; Greene, 2010; Ruth, 2012; Suchet, 2004; Tummala-Narra, 2009a) have emphasized the importance of attending to the unique subjective experiences of people with intersecting identities. Kimberle Crenshaw (1989) first introduced the term *intersectionality* to highlight the marginalization of Black women's experiences and of violence against women of color in feminist theory, politics, and law, on the basis of gender and race. Since its inception, studies on intersectionality in critical race theory, sociology, and psychology have expanded to the examination of various social identities, power dynamics, and broader systemic issues within and beyond national boundaries (Carbado, Crenshaw, Mays, & Tomlinson, 2013). For example, the sociologist Patricia Hill Collins (2000) argued that oppression is influenced by interrelated or intersectional social structures and hierarchies (e.g., race, social class, gender). In recent years, intersectionality has referred to "the way in which an individual embodies within the self, multiple, cultural, ethnic, and group identities" (Ecklund, 2012; Mahalingam et al., 2008). Conceptualizations of intersectionality allow for an understanding of how certain aspects of cultural identity are experienced as more salient than others in a particular context. From a psychoanalytic perspective, how we experience key figures and their responses (e.g., *inner objects*) forms identity (Ruth, 2012). Kathryn Ecklund (2012) noted that children's cultural identity development relies on the value of cultural identity among others within and outside the home, institutional contexts, and family dynamics. In other words, children learn which identities are most valued by others and which are most adaptive for survival and success, and they consequently learn to express these aspects of identity in the presence of others. Thus, multiple layers of an individual's ecology are implicated in his or her adaptation to external demands concerning identity (Harvey, 2007; Tummala-Narra, 2014a; Yakushko, Davidson, & Williams, 2009).

Intersectionality implicates the creation of a new form of cultural identity rather than only the additive effects of different identities. The concept of cultural hybridity is related to intersectionality in that it both recreates a sense of self, drawing on various cultural experiences, and creates a set of new meanings and a sense of "cultural newness" (Bhabha, 1994; Davis, 2010, p. 661). Many people consider their intersected, hybrid identities as more prominent than any one aspect of identity (Parent, DeBlaere, & Moradi, 2013). For example, my client, Jesse, a biracial man (African American/White) in his 40s, who had lived in low-income housing while growing up told me that he does not want to define himself along typical racial and social class terminology. Rather, he described himself as a "guy who people think is White, but really I'm a poor Black man. It's not the same as a poor White man." His self-identification reflects an intersected identity distinct from any singular aspect of his identity (man, African American and White (biracial) person, someone who has lived in poverty). Jesse's identity is one that is situated in a complex and layered sociopolitical context (Settles, 2006), one in which some parts of his identity are more visible than others to the external world.

Richard Ruth (2012) suggested that a psychoanalytic perspective on multiple minority identities is influenced by Anna Freud's (1967) conceptualization of development, which emphasized the progression of several autonomous functions or lines. Specifically, each aspect of identity is thought to be

> . . . complex, conflictual, and interacting to various degrees, as part of a loose assembly (A. E. Harris, 2005) with other aspects of identity, some more conscious, positively valued, and well developed, and others more unconscious, more conflictual, perhaps less accepted, and less well developed. (Ruth, 2012, p. 172)

Although hybrid, intersectional identities produce hope for potentially new self-experiences, such identities also may be experienced as inviable (Sonntag, 2011). Certain aspects of identity may be associated with negative feelings and conflicts and become dissociated, whereas other aspects of identity are associated with positive feelings and personal strengths. These include aspects of identity that carry marginalized or privileged positions. Purdie-Vaughns and Eibach (2008) suggested that a person with multiple "subordinate identities" challenges the norms of the "subordinate" groups with whom he or she identifies and experiences *intersectional invisibility*, which refers to the lack of recognition of the person and the distortion of the person to make him or her fit into a group's expectations. Many people who are minorities across multiple social dimensions (e.g., gender, race, ethnicity, religion, sexual orientation, social class, dis/ability) are marginalized within oppressed groups and experience invisibility in dominant and subordinate groups (Purdie-Vaughns & Eibach, 2008). Cultural expectations and norms can vary considerably across communities, leaving individuals who identify with two or more communities with dilemmas of how to reconcile different forms of bias and incompatible norms (Leigh, 2012). For example, transgender people of color are vulnerable to violence, racism, and gender discrimination outside of the trans community and to racism within the trans community (Ziegler & Rasul, 2014). Identifying with any community in this case can be precarious, yet securing acceptance within and/or identifying with multiple communities can be critical to identity development.

Intersectional, hybrid identities often pose tremendous uncertainty and anxiety as people attempt to secure a sense of belonging within and across cultural groups. External definitions of identity constrict the range of possibilities for an individual's self-definition. Thus, cultural identifications are negotiated in ways that are adaptive or damaging or both. The complexity of cultural identifications raises questions about how one determines the adaptiveness versus the destructiveness of specific identifications and beliefs. Susannah Sherry and Anna Ornstein (2014), from a self-psychological perspective, noted that values and ideals hold an idealized position in the psyche, which "explains why both socially beneficial and socially destructive behavior are pursued with the same high level of passion and commitment" (p. 454). They argued that it is not the "content, but rather, their idealized position in the psyche that arouses our love and admiration" (p. 454). Relatedly, Vamik Volkan (1998) suggested that collective victory and defeat experienced by cultural groups can be internalized as "chosen glories" or "chosen traumas," respectively, and become expressed in individual cultural identifications (Ainslie, 2011). When we consider that processes of idealization and devaluation both characterize cultural identifications and are shaped by family, community, and society, it is critical that therapists attend to how clients develop their collective and individual cultural identifications and the affective and relational experiences associated with these identifications. This exploration helps the client and therapist to distinguish distress and pathology from health and resilience.

Therapeutic Implications

Bhabha (1994) suggested that cultural hybridity is formed amid "in-between spaces" that "provide the terrain for elaborating strategies of selfhood— singular or communal—that initiate new signs of identity, and innovative sites of collaboration and contestation" (p. 2). Drawing on Winnicott's (1971) idea that the essential aim of psychotherapy is to create transitional space for creative engagement, therapists must consider how different contextual realities of the client shape complex sociocultural identities. Winnicott's notion of culture, although focused on the contextual space between the mother and the child, connected the past, present, and future (Boulanger, 2004). A culturally informed psychoanalytic perspective challenges the view that cultural identity is simply a product of a particular strategy, such as assimilation or the integration of multiple cultural identifications with all of the cultural groups with which one is affiliated. This perspective further emphasizes that cultural identity is not a fixed end point in development (Berry, 1997; Bhatia & Ram, 2009). It emphasizes that cultural identity reflects fluid and dynamic intrapsychic and interpersonal conflict shaped by family relationships, positive and negative interactions within communities, social oppression, interpersonal and collective traumatic stress, asymmetry in social power, privilege, access to support, and developmental transitions (e.g., developmental stage, loss).

A psychoanalytic approach recognizes the multiplicity, hybridity, and fluidity of identity; the role of ambivalence and loss in the formation of cultural identifications; and the importance of securing a sense of continuity across cultural contexts, time, and self-states (Benjamin, 2002b; Boulanger, 2004; Bromberg, 1996; A. E. Harris, 2002; Ipp, 2010; Layton, 2006). For example, Jessica Benjamin (2002b) argued that a child develops multiple identifications of gender through his or her parents or caregivers and a person's identification with a specific sex does not imply that he or she has a fixed and coherent sense of gender identity and experience. Thus, psychoanalytic perspectives recognize the murky nature of identity development that progresses throughout one's life. There is also a recognition that some clients, particularly those with multiple minority identities, may experience certain aspects of identity as more salient than others at different points in time and therefore focus on exploration of particular components of identity, such as race or dis/ability, that feel more conflictual in their lives (Ruth, 2012). In addition, there is a value placed on understanding the consequences of the therapist and the client living in and working together in a particular cultural context with specific social hierarchies during a particular time in history and how norms mirroring these social realities are unconsciously maintained, legitimized, and enacted in the therapeutic relationship (e.g., normative unconscious processes) (Layton, 2006).

Addressing intersectionality and hybridity in psychoanalytic psychotherapy also involves an examination of how people negotiate a personal sense of reality in the face of marginalization within and outside of cultural groups. People with multiple minority identities are often in the position of developing a personal set of meanings that do not quite fit with collective ideologies. For example, many women of color transform competing and conflictual experiences of religious teachings concerning the role of women to a spiritual life that is personally fulfilling and empowering. This type of transformation is illustrated in the writings of feminist psychologists from various theoretical orientations who have challenged in their own lives dominant narratives of spirituality within their religious traditions and those imposed by mainstream society (Espín, 2008; Rayburn & Comas-Díaz, 2008; Tummala-Narra, 2008). These scholars, who vary in race, ethnicity, religion, and sexual orientation, have reimagined, reinterpreted, and challenged institutional exclusion of women, images of God as male and/or White, and attempts to displace women from their position as carriers of spiritual practices and traditions. In doing so, they each emphasize the importance of a private spiritual life and personal meanings of religion and spirituality in their personal lives and their therapeutic work with clients.

Some aspects of identity may be more visible and explicitly discussed in psychotherapy than are others. For example, a client's or therapist's ethnicity may be less visible to the other when compared with race and thus may be less likely to be seen or heard in psychotherapy (Summers, 2014). Attending to intersectionality in psychotherapy links the client's and the therapist's understandings of visible and invisible aspects of identity. Laura Brown (2009) noted how intersectionality in the therapeutic process fosters an engagement with "self-invention through the disentanglement of the strands of the self, including those that have generated psychological distress and problematic behaviors" (p. 345). Engaging with intersectionality facilitates the shift away from a "handbook style" of conceptualizing the other and toward a nuanced conceptualizing of the self and the other, and the relationships among the self, the other, and broader social structures (Brown, 2009; Ruth, 2012). From the latter perspective, the self and the other refer to the therapist and the client as both individuals' social locations and identities configure and reconfigure the therapeutic process. In addition, the therapist is challenged by the task of exploring cultural identifications in ways that neither pathologize nor idealize the client's values and beliefs (Tummala-Narra, 2009a).

Therapists, through the exploration of their own sociocultural identities and experiences of privilege and marginalization and by bearing the anxiety of the unknown aspects of the client's identity, help the client to play and engage with new possibilities of self-definition, recognize the external and internal constraints within which these possibilities can be negotiated, and mourn losses incurred in these negotiations. The therapist attends to transference and countertransference to disentangle the intrapsychic, interpersonal, and societal influences on the client's sense of self and well-being and recognize how these interdependent influences shape the client's shifting cultural identifications.

Transference and countertransference reflect the expression of the client's and the therapist's hybrid identities and related conflicts. The therapist may be experienced as someone who is a minority, someone with privilege, and someone marked by a particular gender, ethnicity, religion, social class, or sexual orientation all by the same client at different points in the course of psychotherapy. The client may be experienced as marked by all of these different identities by the therapist as well. In my practice, there are times when I struggle with the impact of my experiences of privilege and marginality on my work with clients. I am aware of my privilege with regard to my immigration status (U.S. citizen), sexual orientation (heterosexual), social class (upper middle class), and ability status (able-bodied). I am also aware of my position as a woman of color, Asian Indian immigrant, and Hindu. The ways in which my privilege and marginality interact with those of the client are revealed in the transference and countertransference and in the moment-to-moment interactions in psychotherapy.

Reflecting on the complexity of my identifications has been a critical part of developing an ability to listen to the complexity of cultural identifications experienced by my clients. It is important to recognize that the therapist interacts and communicates with the client in a way that reflects the therapist's cultural identifications and his or her unconscious and conscious beliefs about which aspects of the client's identity are most salient. Thus, it is important for the therapist to assume a position of *evenly hovering attention* or an attitude that involves empathic listening and a type of observation in which the therapist does not assume the client's conscious statements are necessarily fully reflective of his or her cognitive and affective experience (Ruth, 2012). This approach requires a suspension of assuming to know what the client may feel or sound like initially as an affirmation of a particular interpretation. The therapist must listen with openness to the narratives that are continually shifting and to the narratives that seem to be rigidly fixed in the client's experiences.

Muriel Dimen (2002) wrote about the "space of paradox" as essential to psychoanalytic work, referring to the variations in the client's constructions of the therapist's identity (e.g., female, male, gender-free). It is often the case that the therapist and the client occupy contradictory sociocultural locations in each other's eyes at different points in the therapeutic work, requiring both the therapist and the client to examine their cultural identities. Engaging with these paradoxical moments and contradictory images of the therapist is critical for the client to deepen his or her connection with the therapist, for his or her understanding of the complexity of identity, and for him or her to bear the emotional stress associated with the ambiguity of cultural identifications.

CASE ILLUSTRATION: JEFF

Jeff is a gay Chinese American man in his mid-20s who was referred to me by a psychiatrist in his university's counseling services. Several weeks before I met Jeff, he had a series of panic attacks and had begun taking medication to help cope with his anxiety. He also had experienced periods of depression since late adolescence. Jeff had never seen a therapist before meeting with me and was eager to meet with someone because he had become increasingly anxious and felt he couldn't talk to anyone about his stress. The initial stages of our work focused primarily on Jeff's panic attacks, which improved with the help of medication and breathing exercises he practiced in and outside of session. He continued to feel anxious, although his panic symptoms reduced considerably over the course of 2 months.

Jeff revealed that he had come out to some of his friends but that he was terrified about coming out to his parents. His parents had immigrated to the United States from China soon after getting married. His maternal and paternal grandparents were persecuted during the Cultural Revolution and later escaped to Taiwan with their children. Jeff's parents grew up in China and Taiwan and made a decision to move to the United States to pursue better educational opportunities. They struggled economically for many years before settling into a middle-class neighborhood in a rural part of the United States, where there were very few ethnic minorities, particularly Asian Americans. Jeff was born in the United States and is an only child. He grew up hearing stories of their grandparents' escape from persecution in China and of their survival. He remained close to his grandparents, maintained regular contact with them through e-mail and phone calls, and visited Taiwan every other year. Jeff reported that he felt loved and cared for by his parents but often felt that he could not share details of his personal life with them. He stated that his parents prioritized his education and expected him to excel academically and professionally, particularly because they grew up with few economic resources. In a session early in our work together, he stated, "For them, education was a way out of chaos. So, I can see why they care so much about it. It makes sense." Jeff valued his parent's emphasis on academics and was driven to do well in school. He was also an outstanding athlete in high school. His academic success, in particular, was celebrated by his parents in the United States and by his grandparents in Taiwan. As the only child, he felt a sense of duty to fulfilling his parents' expectations and dreams for a better life.

However, there were parts of his life that remained suppressed and hidden from his parents. Specifically, when Jeff was in high school, he became aware that he was attracted to boys, a realization that terrified him. He worried this would never be accepted by his family, especially his father. Jeff kept his growing awareness of his sexual identity a closely guarded secret and became increasingly isolated even though he felt connected to his family and friends in other ways. As he became more aware of his sexual identity, he also became more aware of the racial tensions in his school, where he witnessed racial minority peers being teased by some White peers. By the end of high school, he began to experience depressed mood and withdrew from his friends at school. He enrolled in a prestigious college, where he continued to do well academically. In his sophomore year, he attended a meeting of an LGBTQ student organization on campus, where he met some friends who became an important source of support. Over the next 2 years, Jeff came to identify as a gay man and briefly dated a few men. During this time, he typically met men online because he felt anxious in approaching them in person. He would then meet his dates in person, after which he would lose interest in them or find they were not interested in him. Jeff reported that although online dating sites did not lead to him meeting anyone "special," they provided an opportunity to learn more about himself and what he liked and did not like about people without feeling "pressured" to know what to say and do in an in-person interaction. He felt increasingly more comfortable with in-person meetings, particularly with men on his college campus. Although he began to feel more like himself, he felt a tremendous degree of shame and guilt about not revealing his sexual identity to his parents and grandparents.

In his senior year of college, Jeff met Max, with whom he fell in love. Max is a 24-year-old, third-generation Filipino American man, who had come out to his family and friends as an adolescent. Jeff felt that he had found a loving partner but felt "pressured" to talk with his family about his sexual identity and Max. After college, Jeff began medical school. He became depressed, anxious, and overwhelmed by the stressful demands of school and maintaining his relationship with Max. When I initially talked with Jeff about his relationship with Max, he stated, "He (Max) doesn't always get how stressed out I get. He is not as busy as I am, and things are easier for him. His parents are not as traditional as mine." He proceeded to talk about Max's ability to feel "more free" with his family who has accepted his sexual identity. In one session, Jeff stated, "Max is not like any Asian person I know. He is different. He doesn't believe that he has to live up to someone else's expectation of him. The family, too, is more American than mine."

Although most of Jeff's friends in high school and college are White, since meeting Max, many of his friends are from different Asian American backgrounds (e.g., Chinese, Filipino, Asian Indian). When I asked Jeff about why he thought he had developed friendships with more Asian Americans since college, he responded, "I thought that I didn't really want to be around Asians. Even though I'm Asian, I never believed that I could be gay and Asian." Jeff further stated that before he met Max, he learned that some of his friends talked behind his back: "I heard from this one friend that a couple of guys who I thought I was really close with were saying things like no one would want to date Jeff—he's got Asian parents and they don't even know he's gay." Jeff felt betrayed by these friends and found that once again he was emotionally isolated, until he met Max. In many ways, Max embodied what Jeff wished for in his own life, especially a sense of comfort with his identity. Meeting Max had facilitated Jeff's exploration of his friendships with other Asian Americans, including Chinese Americans. Yet he felt frozen in his ability to talk with his family about his sexual identity.

In psychotherapy, Jeff discussed feeling as though he was confronted with difficult decisions throughout his life, and had never felt comfortable with major decisions concerning relationships. He felt most "competent" when he accomplished something, such as gaining admission to medical school and winning athletic awards in high school. He felt proud of himself at such moments. These victories were also connected with a deep sense of love and obligation for his parents and his ability to secure a position of economic security, which allayed his parents' anxiety about living in the United States. Yet Jeff's contradictory experiences left him feeling confused and despondent. He asked me in one session, "How can I feel so good sometimes with my family and then sometimes feel so different from them that it makes me want to get away from them?" We spoke over the course of our work together about what he feared the most about his parents' possible response to learning about his sexual identity. He responded, "They had to go through so much more than me. They gave up a lot for me. They left their parents in Taiwan. What if they lost me, too?"

I responded, "Your parents gave up something very important for you. What do you feel that you have to give up for them?"

Jeff stated, "A lot I guess, but I don't want to give up Max. He is too important."

In the following weeks, we explored Jeff's fears about disappointing his parents, particularly his father. He worried about his father's religious beliefs because his father grew up in a religious community that denounced homosexuality. Jeff imagined that his father would "disown" him for committing a sin or that he would never quite see him the same way. Either outcome felt overwhelming and unbearable at times to Jeff, leaving him feeling hopeless. In our work, we continued to talk through different scenes he imagined playing out if he were to talk with his parents, with little progress toward Jeff forming a decision.

In these moments, I felt unsure about Jeff's ability to imagine a different outcome other than being disowned by his family if he were to tell them he is gay. At times, I wondered whether we were not talking about something important that could have been related to an impasse in our work. We spent many sessions feeling stuck in a rigid position with little to no hope of engaging with any other possibilities. In a session during our fifth month of working together, I asked Jeff, "What has it felt like for you to talk with me about being gay and not feeling like you can tell your parents about it?" He stated

> I feel really scared. It's hard to think that they would respect me. I don't want them to lose their respect for me. Family is everything to me. This is one of the things I love about being Chinese. You must know what that's like. Indians and Chinese are similar in that way. I mean I don't want to say that everything about being Asian is great, but this part about family is a good thing.

As I listened to Jeff, I felt as though I could relate to his longing for family, but I realized that he was talking about a family that was both connected and disconnected. The former involved the interactions that gave him a sense of love, pleasure, and security, and the latter consisted of anxiety related to the unknown and the unspoken, despite Jeff's wish for his family to know and accept him fully. I also recognized that Jeff perhaps struggled with a similar conflict in his interactions with me. Perhaps, I had not seen him fully either, and he was unsure as to whether I would accept him. His comment made explicit both similarities and differences in our cultural identities.

I responded to Jeff, "I feel like I can relate to your feelings about how important family and being close to them is, and this is something similar between many Chinese and Indian families. I'm wondering what it is like for you to talk to someone who is Indian about being gay."

Jeff stated, "Well, I guess what other people think means a lot to me."

I said, "I'm wondering if you sometimes worry about what I think about you, too."

He told me that he sometimes worried that I saw him as someone who is "fake" and "not brave enough to face them (parents)," and other times, he wondered whether I had religious beliefs that homosexuality is sinful. In the transference, Jeff experienced me as fluctuating between a first-generation Asian parent with particular religious beliefs who judged his sexual identity negatively and a second-generation Asian American who judged his reluctance to come out to his family negatively.

My countertransference involved feeling concerned that, as a heterosexual woman, I would not be able to fully understand Jeff's experiences or be able to secure his trust. I was also aware of how difficult it is for many LGBTQ Asian Americans, including Chinese Americans and Indian Americans, to cope with the stress of being marginalized within and outside of their cultural groups. I responded to Jeff by telling him I did not have any beliefs about homosexuality being sinful and that I believed being gay is an important and valuable part of his identity and who he is. I also told him that I did not see him as "fake" or "not brave," but in fact, in this conversation, I had begun to feel more connected to his real self. I thanked him for sharing more of himself and told him I understood that this had involved a risk but one that was necessary for us to move forward in our work.

In subsequent sessions, Jeff began to role-play with me different conversations he might have with his father, and over the course of several more months, he decided that he wanted to visit his parents and tell them he is gay. His decision coincided with a conversation with his mother who asked him via telephone why he never seems to "bring home a girl" for them to meet. During our session before he met with his parents, he told me that he could no longer be gay in secret. When he told his parents, they told him they were in shock and needed time to think through what he had revealed to them. Over the next several months, they talked in person and via phone, and reached a point when his parents expressed a willingness to meet Max.

In our work together, Jeff engaged in a process of mourning his feeling of disappointing his parents and recovery from a place of silence and invisibility toward voice and visibility. He continued to discuss the contradictory positions that each aspect of his identity held, such as his self-image as a gay man, a caring son, and a Chinese American with grandparents and parents who suffered political persecution. In the initial part of our work, he engaged with questions such as, "How can you be a model minority if you are gay?" and over time, began to grapple with questions such as

> When I go for the visit to Taiwan, I want my grandparents to know
> that I've become all of these great things that they wanted for us, and
> I'm gay. I wonder if they can see that being gay is part of what makes
> me a good person.

Jeff's increasing willingness to engage with and work through these new questions in psychotherapy contributed to less anxiety and depressed mood, a more coherent sense of self, a sense of continuity with his Chinese heritage, and greater emotional intimacy with Max.

Jeff's cultural identifications as a second-generation Chinese American and as a gay man are inseparable, although for much of his adolescence, they remained separated as he negotiated racist and homophobic responses. Different aspects of identity held different meanings about the self and others. He both consciously and unconsciously avoided interacting with Chinese and other Asian Americans while growing up as a way to protect himself from racism, yet he continued to experience racist insults despite his efforts. These attempts to ward off hate reflected Jeff's internalization of the notion that he had control over what others perceived of him and that he, in fact, was responsible for other's negative projections. He also faced the challenge of disclosing his sexual identity to his family whose beliefs contrasted with an accepting attitude toward LGBTQ people. The fear of disclosing his sexual identity was rooted in a real possibility that he would lose a loving, secure space in his life, even if it was a space in which he could not entirely be himself. His parents' love and support were critical for Jeff to maintain a sense of continuity and his ability to bear the complexity of his identity.

Jeff's dilemmas concerning his identity underscore the conflictual and fluid nature of culture and its associated affective experiences and meanings. Working through transference and countertransference facilitated the exploration of cultural identity in ways that challenged rigidly held beliefs about who Jeff thought he had to be in order to relate to the most important people in his life. In this case, the willingness of the therapist and of the client to engage in the contradictions within their own sociocultural experiences was essential to understanding so that the client could begin to disentangle the various aspects of his identity in a safe space.

Early in our work, Jeff did not ask me directly about my sexual identity. However, toward the end of our work, he did ask me whether I am heterosexual. I responded, "Yes, I am." He thanked me for directly answering his question and told me he had assumed I am heterosexual but at times wondered if I was not heterosexual. We then explored his feelings about my sexual identity and what it meant for him. Jeff stated there was a part of him that wished I could really know exactly what it feels like to be gay but there was another part of him that was less concerned with my sexual identity and more concerned with whether I would be willing to know and understand him. In one of our last sessions, he stated

> Being gay is one part of me, and being straight is one part of you. I couldn't see that at first because it was just not where I was at. I've moved a long way from there and know so much more about who I am. I guess I have to keep thinking about who I'm still becoming.

SUMMARY

Cultural identifications form through the exposure to and socialization within multiple contexts, which implicate experiences of marginalization and privilege. Culturally informed psychoanalytic practice emphasizes various layers of experience within families, communities, institutions, and broader society as shaping conscious and unconscious processes in identity development. Structural problems, such as racism, can restrict the range of possibilities in choosing one's identifications. For individuals who are identified with multiple groups or communities, shifting across these contexts can involve a disavowal of affects and memories. It is important to consider that many individuals experience alienation and discrimination from people within and outside of their cultural groups. Shifting across cultural contexts can implicate dilemmas concerning loyalty to different cultural groups, as exemplified in conflicts related to acculturation gaps between immigrant parents and their children. The expansion of Internet use, social media, and transnational spaces on a global scale has posed yet another level of complexity in how people relate to one another, come to know themselves, and create and recreate identity. Individuals have multiple identities that intersect with each other and negotiate cultural identifications in adaptive and self-damaging ways. Psychoanalytic therapists recognize the multiplicity, hybridity, and fluidity of identity and attend to the conscious and unconscious processes underlying the experience of identity development. Attention to conflict and subjectivity is critical to understanding divergent, contradictory cultural identifications. The exploration of cultural identifications in psychotherapy entails the therapist's ability to examine his or her own sociocultural identity and related privilege and marginality and bear the anxiety of not always seeing or knowing the client's experiences. Thus, the issue of the therapist's self-examination is an essential part of engaging with the client's sociocultural experiences. In the following chapter, I explore the issue of self-examination as the fifth area of emphasis in a culturally informed psychoanalytic framework.

8

EXPANDING SELF-EXAMINATION: CULTURAL CONTEXT IN THE LIFE AND WORK OF THE THERAPIST

John is a White, Jamaican American man in his mid-30s. When I met John, he had recently ended his marriage with his high school sweetheart. From John's perspective, the marriage ended because he had felt as though his wife had treated him more like a child than a partner. Although there was a part of him that needed her to be in this maternal role, over time he began to feel hopeless about the future of their relationship. He eventually grieved the ending of his relationship and wished to work on meeting a woman he would find more compatible. Toward the end of the first year of our working together, John endured a series of traumatic events within a course of several months, including the sudden death of his maternal grandfather who he adored. His grief was profound, and he readily shared his sadness in session, where he would often cry for his grandfather. John "idolized" his grandfather as someone who was a responsible and caring man. John's parents died of complications of two different illnesses within the same year when he was

http://dx.doi.org/10.1037/14800-009
Psychoanalytic Theory and Cultural Competence in Psychotherapy, by P. Tummala-Narra

an adolescent in Jamaica. His grandfather had been his primary caregiver for most of his life. When his grandfather died, he told me, "I lost the most important person in my life." He would later find ways to connect with memories of his grandfather, most typically by spending time with his maternal relatives.

John and I developed a strong connection in the course of several months in psychotherapy. During the times that John talked about his grandfather's death, I felt myself experiencing deep sadness, sometimes to the extent that I would tear up in session. I also noticed that I had dreams about my grandfather in India who had died several years earlier. Mostly, I dreamt of the disbelief I experienced when I learned of his death, which felt sudden and unexpected to me. I also dreamt of spending time with him. John's sadness was inside me, manifesting itself in a way that sometimes felt overwhelming. I realized I had been missing my first home, in India, where I spent my early childhood. John's expression of sadness reminded me of a young child longing for a parent figure to comfort him. For me, these feelings of sadness also encompassed a separation from home that felt irreconcilable because I chose to live in an independent space away from my family's home in India and my parents' home in the United States, even though I was deeply connected to both places. John's losses brought to the foreground of my mind suppressed longings for parents and family who I missed greatly at that time in my life.

I believe that immersing in John's sadness and that in my own life was necessary to understand, to the degree that it was possible, the nature of John's experience. It was also important that I recognize my own anguish as separate and distinct from John's conscious and unconscious experience for John to grieve and emerge from his grief with a sense of hope concerning his future and ability to find a loving relationship. There were times when I wondered whether or not seeing the sadness of a therapist, particularly a female therapist, would help or interfere with John's trust in me that I could manage and contain my feelings and maintain a position of authority as the therapist. I also realized, however, that our clients need us to authentically feel some of what they feel so that the feelings themselves become bearable and the clients can further examine unconscious material. John, in fact, did tell me, "It helps when I can see that you understand what I'm feeling." The termination phase of our work evoked feelings of sadness as John struggled with feeling as though he was left again. Yet he also felt that he had time to anticipate the ending of our work. Our work had a transformative effect on me because I reconnected with feelings of loss that were disavowed for many years. These moments of deep immersion into the client's emotional experiences raise questions about whether the therapist has gone too far in his or her involvement with the client. I do think, however, that this is an inevitable part of being a therapist.

Increasingly, psychoanalytic perspectives have embraced the idea that the therapist's own life history, interests, and passions are relevant to psychotherapeutic work and, in fact, inform the ways in which the therapist becomes an instrument of therapeutic change. The therapist's neutrality generally is not conceptualized as one of a "blank screen" but rather as a guiding principle to secure the client's ability to free associate and develop transference without the interference of the therapist (Gediman, 2006). Some analysts, however, have questioned whether neutrality is possible in the therapeutic relationship (Renik, 1996). Interpersonal psychoanalysts, such as Edgar Levenson and Merton Gill, in part influenced by Harry Stack Sullivan, emphasized a nonhierarchical relationship between the therapist and the client. An emphasis on the dynamics of transference and countertransference supported by contemporary theorists, such as Stephen Mitchell, Irwin Hoffman, and Donnel Stern, has facilitated a "demystification of power within the therapy hour" (Cushman, 1995, p. 291). Although asymmetry in the therapist–client relationship may be an inherent part of psychotherapy, these theorists suggest that it must be understood through a historical and sociopolitical lens (Cushman, 1995). This perspective calls attention to the therapist's self-inquiry and the engagement of his or her own social context in the therapeutic relationship. Therapists hold the position of listening to their clients' painful, sometimes heart-wrenching experiences, bringing to awareness or triggering their own personal challenges and tragedies. Irwin Hirsch (2008) suggested that, in fact, how therapists practice "in a professional context has both theoretical-conceptual significance and personal significance" (p. 46). The therapist's understandings of and engagement with his or her own history, conflicts, and passions are thought to provide meaning and life to his or her work (Aronson, 2007).

Relational psychoanalysts view transference and countertransference as interconnected and the therapist's emotional involvement as integral to therapeutic process and change (Bonovitz, 2005). They also conceptualize transference and countertransference as inseparable from culture and context. Over the past several decades, mental health professionals have contended with the issue of racial/ethnic matching in the therapeutic dyad (S. Sue, 1998; Zane & Ku, 2014). Although a similar racial/ethnic therapist–client dyad has been found to be associated with trust and credibility of the therapist in the initial stages of treatment (Meyer, Zane, & Cho, 2011), racial/ethnic matching seems to have few lasting effects on psychotherapy outcome (Cabral & Smith, 2011). However, it is likely that many clients hope and imagine that working with a therapist of a similar sociocultural background would secure the likelihood of being better understood and helped. Dynamics of transference and countertransference early in therapeutic interactions may be especially significant for the client's decision to continue treatment and engage fully with the therapist. Racial/ethnic matching in the therapeutic dyad does not determine long-term therapeutic effectiveness, a fact that should help reduce therapists' anxiety about working with clients from different sociocultural backgrounds.

Therapists' emotional investment in a sociocultural perspective, an understanding of the self as a cultural being, and the ability to engage in inquiry into their own sociocultural histories, professional training, and life circumstances are critical to engaging effectively with all clients. D. W. Sue (2001) identified several barriers to therapists' "personal cultural competence." First, he noted the difficulty that we all have in recognizing and acknowledging our biases because doing so can challenge our sense of morality and fairness. Second, we tend to interact in a socially polite manner that precludes an honest exploration of difficult and painful issues, such as discrimination. Third, we tend to minimize our personal responsibility and direct or indirect contributions to injustice. Fourth, we tend to avoid painful affect associated with racially charged memories, images, and events (D. W. Sue, 2001).

Working toward overcoming these barriers is essential to overcoming feelings of powerlessness and helplessness, which are embedded in the experiences of many therapists who feel overwhelmed by social injustice and sociocultural differences. These barriers contribute to the therapist either dismissing or inappropriately magnifying the role of social context in the client's life. In this chapter, I explore the therapist's engagement with his or her own experiences with sociocultural identity and trauma and/or oppression, both within and outside of the psychotherapeutic relationship. In chapters 4 through 6, I presented case illustrations, all of which involved the role of the therapist's self-examination. In this chapter, I elaborate this concept as one that involves lifelong learning and transformation, as the therapist, like the client, negotiates conflict and stress both within and outside of the therapeutic relationship. The chapter further elaborates on psychoanalytic self-examination as being critical for developing a sense of authenticity and for listening to culture because the therapist's subjectivity influences his or her attention to the client's experience and what he or she hears in the client's words.

SOCIOCULTURAL CONTEXT IN THE PERSONAL AND PROFESSIONAL LIFE OF THE THERAPIST

Personal Investment in Issues of Diversity

The therapist's personal investment in issues of sociocultural diversity plays an important role in the implementation of culturally informed practice. Numerous studies indicate that the therapist's racial and ethnic attitudes predict cultural competence in psychotherapy (Lee & Tracey, 2008). It has also been noted that ethnic minority therapists tend to be more likely to attend to issues of culture and race in psychotherapy (Berger, Zane, & Hwang, 2014; Sodowsky, Kuo Jackson, Richardson, & Corey, 1998). This is especially concerning when considering that most mental health service providers are White. Therapists' attitudes toward diversity, including an awareness and appreciation of similarities and differences between themselves and others and an interest in seeking diversity in contact with others in their daily lives (personal and professional), are associated with their comfort in addressing sociocultural issues with clients (Miville, Gelso, Pannu, Liu, Touradji, Holloway, & Fuertes, 1999; Tummala-Narra, Singer, Li, Esposito, & Ash, 2012). In an interview study (Singer & Tummala-Narra, 2013) focused on White, Euro American therapists' perspectives on working with racial minority immigrant clients, therapists differed considerably with respect to whether or not race is an important issue to explore in psychotherapy. Some therapists worried that bringing up the issue of race would be experienced by the client as an imposition of the therapist's agenda, and other therapists felt that race is an important issue that is "always in the room" (p. 293). Many of these therapists further struggled with their own limitations in knowledge of the cultural groups of these clients and sometimes referred clients to colleagues but other times remained uncomfortable throughout their work with their clients. In addition, many therapists indicated that they did not have an opportunity for reflecting on their work with colleagues and thus remained isolated in their practice.

The therapist's personal orientation to diversity is influenced by several different factors, such as personal life history, history of interpersonal and collective traumas, social location, professional training, and the atmosphere of one's workplace or institution. The therapist's cultural beliefs and narratives and his or her privilege or lack of privilege in sociocultural location has a great impact on interpretation, enactments, and interactions with clients (Bodnar, 2004). The therapist's own experiences with gender, race, ethnicity, religion, dis/ability, language, sexual identity, social class, and immigration come to life explicitly and implicitly in therapeutic work. Because the psychic and social are intertwined, the therapist's social location, cultural beliefs, familial stress and conflict, loss, and trauma all shape his or her personal and professional identities. Therapists who have experienced marginalization experience shifting across multiple sociocultural contexts and sometimes struggle with starkly different realities embedded in each context. The processes of disavowal and disconnection in the lives of clients who suffer oppression, which I have previously described, are also relevant to therapists. Susan Bodnar (2004) described the discontinuity in her experience as a well-educated Jewish psychoanalyst contrasted with her experience of growing up in a working-class family in which many relatives faced problems such as depression, alcoholism, learning issues, anorexia, and multiple divorces. She recalled working hard to fulfill the dreams of her grandparents and parents and her grandmother telling her, "Remember where you come from" (p. 581). Bodnar elaborated, "Reconciling the profound tension between one's roots and one's ambition is a life's work" (p. 581).

Experiences of Trauma

The therapist's experiences of trauma and loss can have important implications for the client and the therapist. Although secondary traumatic stress can be experienced by all therapists, it is of particular concern for therapists who have endured interpersonal and collective trauma. Kaethe Weingarten (2010) called attention to mental health experts focusing far more on helping therapists develop "empathic stress reactions" while listening to their clients' traumatic experiences than on helping therapists address their own trauma histories. The effects of traumatic transference and countertransference can be profound. For example, projective identification can occur when the client's split-off or disavowed transference reactions are projected onto the therapist. The therapist then identifies with the client's reactions, which can leave the therapist feeling disorganized and disoriented (J. M. Davies & Frawley, 1994). Judith Herman (1992) wrote extensively about the ways in which survivors' traumatic transference reflects feelings of terror and helplessness that pervade relationships with others, including that with therapist. The therapist may become an idealized figure who protects the survivor from the potential of reexperiencing the trauma, and when the therapist inevitably does not meet the idealized expectations, the survivor experiences disappointment, anger, and sometimes rage toward the therapist. Simultaneously, the therapist can begin to experience feelings of terror and rage, in some ways similar to the client's traumatic stress, and identify with the feelings of the survivor and of perpetrator.

Enactments can develop as the therapist's own personal traumas are evoked while listening to the client's traumatic story, which in turn affects therapeutic communication. For example, the therapist's own sense of safety and faith in justice and fairness can become compromised, or the therapist may assume the role of a rescuer as a way to cope with feelings of guilt and helplessness (Herman, 1992). Thus, access to support for the therapist is critical to his or her ability to fully bear witness to the client's traumatic experiences. In addition, this support is necessary not just in the training years but throughout one's career (Yassen, 1995). Therapists who are committed to working with survivors of trauma and have adequate support are able to develop a greater ability to understand themselves and others and a higher sense of purpose and integrity in their lives (Herman, 1992).

The therapist's experiences with sociocultural context can be further understood by attending to the intersection of interpersonal and collective traumas and sociocultural location. The therapist's conscious reactions to the client and countertransference should be examined with a consideration of his or her own privilege and social marginalization. For example, a heterosexual therapist may worry that he or she may not be able to speak with authority about sexuality with a gay or lesbian client (McNamara, 2013). In fact, many therapists struggle with exploring clients' sexual identities and with the prospect of disclosing their own sexual identity to their clients (Drescher, 2007; M. King, 2011). In another example, a therapist may find it difficult to listen to a client with a physical disability who describes experiences of physical pain or loss. The therapist, rather than fully listening to the client, may make an interpretation too quickly in an attempt to manage his or her own feelings (e.g., helplessness, fear of dependency) (Watermeyer, 2012).

Although the therapist's experiences of loss and marginality can facilitate empathic listening to a client facing marginalization, they also can elicit the therapist's unconscious dissociation from painful affect. The therapist's dissociation in psychotherapy, similar to that for the client, occurs as a function of maintaining a sense of personal continuity and coherence when faced with overwhelming affect, many times linked with perceived sociocultural differences (Bromberg, 1996; Cohen, 2007; Ipp, 2010). Engaging with our own traumatic past and ongoing experiences of social oppression is critical for identifying when we are able to be present with our clients and when we find it difficult, if not impossible, to connect with a client's beliefs and perspectives. Giselle Galdi (2007) described her countertransference issues in her work with a client who is a veteran of the Vietnam War. She noted how her experience as a political refugee from Hungary was intertwined with her client's traumas, evoking her own feelings of hopelessness. She stated

> His seeming deadness, his tendency to withdraw, to be unreachable, often made me feel shut out, unimportant. . . . I tried to overcompensate for my helplessness in face of seemingly unsurmountable difficulties— and feeling under the gun, so to speak—when I made more aggressive interpretations, and pointed out his resistances. (Galdi, 2007, p. 15)

These interpretations contributed to impasses in the work, which were addressed only after Galdi recognized her need to feel alive in her interactions with her client and her role in the impasses with her client. Galdi further recognized that she and her client had different political perspectives concerning war, again calling to question whether and how she would maintain a present, empathic position in her work with him.

Experiences of Minority Therapists

Over the past decade, therapists from minority backgrounds have begun to write about their experiences of marginality within their profession and their therapeutic work with clients. Douglas Haldeman (2010) wrote about the complexity of being a White, gay male therapist who has experienced oppression as a gay man and privilege as a White, Euro American, able-bodied, married, and financially stable man. He examined his experience of concealing his sexual identity as a young adult and working through the coming out process and how these painful experiences are connected with his empathic attunement to the experiences of his gay clients. Haldeman further emphasized the importance of recognizing and working through his own heterophobic biases, which were rooted in his experiences of oppression as a gay man. His candid account of the effects of his minority status and identity on his psychotherapeutic work called attention to the importance of facing and monitoring our own shame and recognizing our biases and/or lack of knowledge about certain communities (e.g., LGBTQ, racial, cultural, religious).

Other minority therapists have written about various dilemmas that are evoked in the process of working with clients. Fanny Chalfin (2014) described her dilemma, as a therapist with a visual impairment, of how much to disclose about her disability to her clients at the beginning of treatment and how self-disclosure may affect the client's initial transference. Some clients may feel as though they have been "cheated" or misled by the therapist with a disability or by the person referring the client to the therapist (Chalfin, 2014). Chalfin recognized that clients may interact in politically correct ways to avoid facing feelings of being "damaged" or feelings of guilt. Interestingly, when she disclosed in her initial phone calls with potential clients that she has a visual impairment and that there would be a guide dog present in session, they responded that this would not be a problem for them. Yet several clients did not come to the first session or called to cancel the session. Chalfin observed that some of the clients who did work with her had family members with disabilities, and in their cases, Chalfin's disability facilitated an exploration of their feelings concerning disability. Thus, the therapist's dis/ability status became a ground for the client's projections, at least in the beginning of treatment.

The minority therapist is often in the position to negotiate the client's projections linked with sociocultural context and position. Along with past and current relational dynamics, the client's stereotypes and fantasies about the therapist's sociocultural background influence transference reactions. Comas-Díaz and Jacobsen (1995) suggested that therapists of color represent a "colored screen," the opposite of the "blank screen," in that the client's projections are intensified because of the therapist's physical features. The racial minority therapist often is seen as the "other" by a racial majority client who may come to work through his or her own feelings of alienation by consciously and unconsciously identifying with the minority therapist's otherness (Comas-Díaz & Jacobsen, 1995). In my practice, I have worked with clients who, during the initial stages of treatment, have commented that they were relieved to be working with someone who is an immigrant, assuming that I was not born here despite that I have a mainstream American accent. Some non-Asian Indian clients have mentioned they believe Asian Indians are smart and therefore they could trust me or that they had always thought of Indian women as passive, but they don't see me as a passive person. I understand that at times these initial impressions are projections of the client's disavowed parts of the self. Other times, they reflect a client's effort to manage the anxiety he or she feels in an interaction with someone who is culturally and/or racially unfamiliar. Such projections also reflect socialization processes in broader society, where categorical notions of racial and ethnic minorities (e.g., Asian Indians as model minorities, Asian Indians as submissive or passive) have far greater presence than do actual narratives of people within these communities.

Clients may also interact with a minority therapist either in ways to compensate for oppression that they perceive has been directed toward the therapist's racial and/or cultural groups or in ways that project hostility and aggression toward the therapist. Additionally, the client's negative and aggressive feelings toward the therapist and the therapist's cultural groups may evoke feelings of guilt (Tang & Gardner, 1999). The client's projections related to sociocultural context and location can leave minority therapists feeling vulnerable and frustrated. They can also shift the dynamics of power in the therapist–client dyad because the therapist's minority status challenges his or her sense of authority and sometimes credibility. The therapist may cope with these challenges by striving to affirm or assert competence and authority, which can either facilitate the therapeutic process or create further impasses, depending on the nature of the therapeutic dyad.

Ali and colleagues (2005), among others (Rastogi & Wieling, 2005), wrote about her experiences as an ethnic minority therapist after hearing comments from clients such as "My mom and I were talking about how Mexican men are so loud and drunk all the time, not all of them, but most of them," or "This guy at work is a tightwad; he's Jewish, you know how they are." Ali described her feelings of confusion and vulnerability when her clients made these statements in her presence, knowing that she is not White. The therapist, in these cases, faces various dilemmas because he or she is typically not consciously prepared to hear these types of comments from a client. There is a reversal of power and vulnerability in the therapeutic relationship in these moments. The client's perceptions of the therapist's experiences of marginalization are linked with perceptions of the therapist's lack of power and competence. Comas-Díaz and Jacobsen (1995) noted that therapist of color and White client dyads involve contradictions involving processes of projection and identification and a collective racial unconscious. In my experience, it is often the case that the client is communicating both a wish and a fear of relating intimately with a therapist he or she perceives as different in a significant way. I have found that when clients make comments that initially feel offensive to me, and as I further examine their implicit and explicit communications with them, I learn that they are conflicted about how to interact with me. In an effort to connect with me, they either convey their knowledge about Asian Indians and Hindus or minimize any potential cultural differences between us. Internalized feelings of hostility and prejudice may be embedded in these communications.

Relatedly, in therapeutic dyads with the client and therapist of similar ethnic background, a positive transference and sense of trust in the therapist that is attributed to the belief the therapist will be versed in the client's cultural context does not exclude the possibility of coexisting negative and hostile projections onto the therapist. Open and honest dialogue concerning race, gender, religion, dis/ability, social class, sexual identity, and ethnicity in broader society (e.g., schools, neighborhoods, workplaces) is limited, and the therapeutic encounter is a space in which this constricted engagement with sociocultural issues becomes reproduced. As therapists, we work toward helping clients expand their engagement with complex and conflicting layers of experience within themselves, their families, relationships with friends and romantic partners, and peers. We explore these experiences through examining transference and countertransference and the nature of the therapeutic process and communication. In a similar vein, we must work toward helping our clients deconstruct their complex sociocultural lenses and identities so that they are better able to experience others and themselves more fully. The examination of our own sociocultural identities and histories of oppression is an essential part of this unfolding process.

Institutional Challenges

The therapist's self-examination should include an analysis of the institutions in which he or she trains, practices, and teaches. Institutions, despite explicit mission statements that indicate a valuing of diversity and social justice, can reflect broader social inequities. Many therapists are trained in dominant, decontextualized theories of psychotherapy that hold authority and privilege over more nuanced and sophisticated approaches to the role of sociocultural context in psychotherapy. Dominant theories also have complex histories. The history of psychoanalysis in the United States and elsewhere is one that encompasses a dissociation from sociocultural realities of the inner world and dismissal of concerns of women; racial, ethnic, linguistic, and sexual minorities; people living in poverty; people with disabilities; and transgender people. Psychoanalysis is not alone in this problem because all major psychological theories have historically neglected sociocultural issues in psychotherapy. In addition, the pressures of conforming to a medical model that tends to categorize symptomology without integrating social context and a push to work with more clients in less time contribute to the location of illness within the individual without serious consideration for his or her ecology.

As mentioned in chapter 1, psychoanalytic theory in the United States and elsewhere developed in the context of trauma, war, and exile. In fact, psychoanalysis has been conceptualized as a survivor of the Holocaust (Aron & Starr, 2013; Cushman, 1995; Hale, 1995; Prince, 2009). Lewis Aron and Karen Starr (2013) have called attention to the influence of persecution and marginalization of Jewish analysts in Europe and of Jewish émigré analysts in the United States, the subsequent fight for safety, survival, and identification of Jews as Whites, and the medicalization of psychoanalysis. These historical realities have a great impact in the ways that psychoanalysis and psychoanalytic psychotherapy have been conceptualized and taught to subsequent generations. In fact, Aron and Starr (2013) noted that psychoanalysis has been viewed both privately (within psychoanalytic institutions) and publicly as a Jewish science or discipline. They pointed out that contemporary psychoanalysis demands that we recognize and understand our vulnerabilities related to historical trauma. They stated, "In its grandiosity, psychoanalysis dissociated its vulnerability by projecting it onto other psychotherapies and onto patients, leaving it and its practitioners overly identified with the heroic and masterful" (Aron & Starr, 2013, p. 29).

Increasingly, contemporary psychoanalytic scholars recognize the disavowal of social context in the history of psychoanalysis and emphasize a "moral and ethical sensibility" (Aron & Starr, 2013, p. 29) and the importance of bearing witness to injustice (Boulanger, 2012). Nancy Hollander (2006) observed that therapists conduct their work in a culture in which they unconsciously align with capitalist systems, reinstate hegemonic ideology, and constrict their critical consciousness as a way of coping with feelings of helplessness and fear. Paradoxically, therapists become bystanders to injustice, when they limit their sense of agency through the use of defenses such as denial, splitting, projection, and disavowal. Thus, it is of critical importance that therapists attend to their feelings of anxiety and experiences of trauma to effectively engage with social injustice. Hollander (2006, p. 159) further supported a position of "ethical nonneutrality" in which institutions and individuals can privately and publicly recognize that it is impossible to remain neutral under conditions of human rights violations and extreme social conflict and take ownership of this position in the implementation of services and collaboration with marginalized communities.

The therapist should attend to the implicit and explicit values inherent to the cultural contexts of institutions. Understanding the impact of the history and culture of institutions on the therapist's personal and professional life involves a consideration of mourning processes in which the therapist must contend with conflicts and sometimes irreconcilable differences between his or her personal worldviews and those inherent to dominant theoretical perspectives in the mental health professions. The recognition of the historical and ongoing disavowal of sociocultural context by psychotherapists, both psychoanalytically and nonpsychoanalytically oriented, marks a collective mourning that is necessary to address stereotypes and assumptions concerning gender, race, ethnicity, religion, social class, sexual orientation, and dis/ability that are embedded in psychological theories. Specifically, we can examine at a metacognitive level the impact of context on the development of our theoretical ideas, clinical and research training in graduate programs, and interventions.

Clinical supervision, in particular, is a critical institutional mechanism for learning how to conduct psychotherapy. In previously published work (Tummala-Narra, 2004), I have suggested that clinical supervision is a practical means through which conscious and unconscious thoughts and feelings concerning the client's, therapist's, and supervisor's sociocultural location and identity can be explored. The therapist and supervisor must be open to addressing transference and countertransference that is rooted in sociocultural issues; developing an ability to tolerate and engage with anxiety, fear, and shame in discussing issues such as race, social class, and sexual orientation; and discussing relevant power dynamics. Ideally, the supervisor can help the supervisee examine feelings of vulnerability when addressing sociocultural differences and similarities in psychotherapy and supervision. This is especially important because supervisees must secure a reasonable sense of safety to honestly engage with difficult, and often personal, material in a supervisory relationship that is inherently evaluative.

Too often, minority therapists in training are in the position of initiating discussions on diversity and becoming "holders of cultural information" (Tummala-Narra, 2004, p. 304). This is illustrated in supervision when a lesbian therapist in training consistently initiates conversations about her client's sexual identity with a heterosexual supervisor who avoids talking about sexual identity. Many therapists in training who are racial and ethnic minorities experience a disconnection between the value systems emphasized in their personal and professional circles and a sense of loneliness within their training and practice circles, in which their perspectives are invisible or silenced within institutions. The loneliness and invisibility experienced by many ethnic minority therapists can become burdensome over the course of their careers (Wyche, 2012). In addition, like other minority therapists (e.g., sexual minorities, religious minorities), they are at risk of being perceived as the representatives of their cultural and/or racial groups. It is a common concern among therapists of color that they will be referred clients of their particular cultural or racial background by colleagues and supervisors without consideration of the therapist's preferences and/or professional training. Unfortunately, these practices, in addition to categorizing the skills of minority therapists into a specific area of "cultural expertise," mask and minimize the complexity of minority therapists' work with minority and majority status clients. One such illustration is the experience of many bilingual therapists who feel as though their ability to speak in a particular language, such as Spanish, is seen as the primary reason for referrals and that differences in ethnicity and national origin may be disregarded by colleagues who refer clients to them. In these instances, the actual nature of therapeutic work is overlooked because an emphasis on language similarity precludes attention to the nuances of working bilingually in psychotherapy. For example, bilingual or multilingual therapists whose heritage language is not English often face the challenge of communicating as mental health professionals in the heritage language with a client, when their professional training was conducted in English (Aguirre, Bermúdez, Parra Cardona, Zamora, & Reyes, 2005).

Clinical supervision, therefore, should address not only the client–therapist interactions within sessions but also the experiences of the therapist in training within an institutional context. Therapists in training (both minority and majority status) are in the process of developing a professional identity, and often they struggle with seemingly disjointed knowledge concerning sociocultural issues in their academic training, clinical supervision, and psychotherapy practice. As with minority therapists, minority supervisors often are sought out by minority supervisees for consultation with the hope of their perspectives being understood and the provision of help bridging multiple cultural and professional contexts. However, supervisor–supervisee matching based on minority or cultural background does not ensure a safe and effective engagement with issues of diversity. For example, a client, supervisee, and supervisor who share a common immigrant background may experience a "fellow immigrant transference," in which they avoid exploring potential sociocultural differences because of the assumption of similarity as immigrants (Mehta, 1997).

Conscious and unconscious processes within the supervisory triad influence which content, affects, and meanings are explored in psychotherapy and supervision (Brown & Miller, 2002; Debiak, 2007). The supervisor's degree of comfort in discussing sociocultural context is a key factor in whether or not the supervisee will feel prepared to address the complexity of the client's narrative. Shelly Harrell (2014) noted that the supervisee and supervisor must confront emotionally charged material related to sociocultural issues within a space of compassion and empathy for difficult feelings, such as anxiety, ambivalence, and anger. In addition, supervision and mentoring of minority trainees are especially helpful when they involve conversations about the interaction of the trainees' sociocultural and professional identities and when they expand curiosity and reflection about the self and others (Harrell, 2014; Millán, 2010; Watkins, 2013). This is important to consider because dialogues on diversity and psychotherapy continue to be located in restricted spaces, although training programs have required course work concerning these issues.

The access to institutional resources, such as culturally competent supervision, ongoing training and dialogue on issues of diversity, translators and colleagues with knowledge and experience, and available literature concerning sociocultural issues and mental health, facilitates therapist's self-examination and engagement with culturally informed practices with clients (Tummala-Narra et al., 2012). Sometimes the clinical setting is not conducive for therapists to access these resources or does not provide the time to effectively address the client's needs. The supervisor, in these circumstances, plays an important role as an advocate who can help the supervisee negotiate these institutional challenges that affect the client's well-being. In addition, openness to exploring impasses in psychotherapy and supervision is critical to a safe and effective learning environment.

There are times when the therapist in training and the supervisor cope with overwhelming feelings by avoiding difficult material either in their own lives or in that of the client. These defenses are often produced and supported institutionally. For example, many therapists are reluctant to disclose the impact of painful emotional experiences, such as a history of trauma, in the presentation of their clinical work in professional meetings or publications because they face potential backlash for revealing too much vulnerability (Weingarten, 2010). Some psychoanalytic scholars have recognized their reluctance to openly write about and discuss the importance of personal beliefs, such as their religious and spiritual beliefs and practices, because they feared colleagues would perceive them as lacking objectivity (Aron, 2004; Rizzuto, 2004; Roland, 2005; Tummala-Narra, 2009b). Therapists receive contradictory messages in the mental health professions about how open they should be about their personal experiences. We are encouraged to examine our feelings, but we also are advised to contain them so that we do not impose ourselves inappropriately in our work with clients and, in professional settings, so that we maintain an "objective" position in our clinical formulations and interpretations. Nevertheless, our internal experiences play an important role in our ability to listen to our clients and formulate their concerns, and unless we receive support in honestly discussing these experiences, we are at risk of isolating ourselves, disavowing our experiences, and potentially engaging with clients in destructive ways. For therapists well beyond their training years, peer consultation serves an important purpose of reducing isolation and maintaining an ability to critically listen to the client and remain open to alternative perspectives (Riquelme, 2007).

The Therapist's Responsibility of Exploring Sociocultural Issues

Relational psychoanalytic perspectives increasingly have recognized that the therapeutic process is socially constructed through the interactions between the therapist and the client and that the interpersonal is intertwined with the cultural (S. A. Mitchell, 1997; Walls, 2004). Gary Walls (2004) pointed out that, from this perspective, an understanding of the client's intrapsychic and interpersonal life requires an examination of the therapist's inner life. The therapist's subjective experiences are thought to interact with those of the client such that a third presence in psychotherapy represents the social context of the client and of the therapist (Aggarwal, 2010; Altman, 2010; Ogden, 1994). Specifically, conflicts and impasses in the therapeutic dyad may reflect racial, ethnic, gender, class, or other types of sociocultural conflicts that are internalized by the client and the therapist (Altman, 2010; Dimen, 2006; Walls, 2004). In addition, these conflicts often reflect the client's and the therapist's dissociative processes, which operate to manage the stress imposed by structural inequalities and injustice, interpersonal trauma, and institutional challenges that are reenacted in the therapeutic dyad.

Neil Altman (2010, p. 86) suggested that clinical material that manifestly concerns drive issues may actually be "displaced commentary" on sociocultural differentials or injustice and that the reverse also may be true. In considering the issue of social class differences between the client and the therapist, Altman (2010, p. 86), described the following example:

> [A] patient's anger at the analyst may be seen as secondary to his plausible attribution of a condescending attitude to his higher-class analyst. Alternatively, the patient's attribution of contempt to his analyst on social class grounds may be seen as a derivative of a more basic aggressive or competitive attitude toward the analyst.

This three-person perspective attends to the therapeutic dyad and the client's and the therapist's relationship with broader social context (Altman, 2010). Thus, there is an interaction and mutual influence between sociocultural context and basic drives, needs, and affects that become expressed or enacted in the therapeutic dyad.

The three-person perspective further allows for a wider range of possibilities for interpreting the client's experiences because it considers how social context interacts with the client's and the therapist's dispositions in the here-and-now moments in psychotherapy. Altman used the example of working in a community mental health clinic in an inner city setting to underscore the tensions that arise for therapists who must negotiate the push to see more clients and complete more documentation in shorter amounts of time while continuing to provide quality services. These tensions contribute to polarization within clinics between administrators, who may be primarily concerned with financial challenges, and therapists, who are concerned primarily with the quality of the services provided to clients. In contrast, therapists in private practice are both therapists and administrators of their practice.

Therapists' dilemmas concerning the provision of services raise important questions about their personal beliefs and motives concerning money (Dimen, 2006). Therapists must examine how their institutional settings (e.g., community mental health, inpatient unit, outpatient clinic, college counseling center) influence their engagement with the client's sociocultural context. Therapists must also ask themselves whether working with middle-class clients reflects an interest in earning a particular income or whether their resistance to working in public clinics reflects a sense of elitism or a conscious decision to not work in a system that they perceive as delivering inadequate services to clients (Altman, 2010). The therapist's inquiry into his or her own history with social class and related affects is a necessary step to listening with attunement to the client's experiences with socioeconomic issues.

A personal engagement with issues of diversity helps the therapist develop a capacity to initiate discussions concerning sociocultural context and identity with clients. When a therapist depends only on the client to become educated about the client's cultural group(s), he or she risks positioning the client as the other or as a representative of an entire cultural group. The client then may not trust the therapist to value the importance of contextual issues or may come to see the therapist as someone who is incapable of bearing witness to his or her experience. Although it is important to be attuned to the client's experiences with his or her sociocultural context by listening to the client's words, it is also critical that the therapist take a genuine interest in the client's context and invest time and effort in learning about the client's cultural groups outside of sessions (e.g., consulting with colleagues, reading relevant literature). This learning is lifelong because culture and identity are dynamic and fluid. In addition, a therapist's understandings of a particular client's experiences of his or her culture should not become the sole template for approaching other clients from a similar cultural background.

From a culturally informed psychoanalytic perspective, it is the responsibility of the therapist to critically examine how he or she listens to the client and may influence the client's responses in the therapeutic process. In addition, psychoanalytic knowledge informs us that the process of understanding our own subjectivity and that of others is complex and unpredictable. In interacting with the client, the therapist should be open to unconscious, unarticulated experiences in his or her own life that may not have been previously accessible to him or her (J. E. Davies, 2011; Slavin, 1998). In other words, therapists must examine their own disavowal of painful experiences. J. E. Davies (2011, p. 557) wrote eloquently about the ways in which listening in psychotherapy involves the ability to "locate and experience" her client's experiences within herself, some of which were difficult to bear emotionally. The therapist's ability to live with discomfort, otherness, aloneness, confusion, and disorientation, among other feelings experienced by the client, is both an essential part of the process and an outcome of self-examination. The therapist is emotionally transformed through listening fully to the client, and this transformation allows for authentic engagement and therapeutic change for the client.

COUNTERTRANSFERENCE AND SELF-DISCLOSURE

Transference initially was conceptualized by Freud (1905) as a phenomena describing the way in which a patient's relationship to an early object, such as a parent, becomes unconsciously transferred or displaced onto the analyst. The analysis of the transference allows for an understanding of the nature of a patient's conflicts associated with these early relationships. Freud (1910) later conceptualized countertransference as the emotional reactions of the analyst, resulting from the patient's transference or influence on the analyst's unconscious. Countertransference, in Freud's view, was something to be recognized and overcome because it would interfere with the patient's ability to free associate. As such, self-analysis, ongoing self-examination, and entering analysis periodically throughout one's career as an analyst was recommended as a way to minimize the potential intrusion of the analyst's countertransference on the patient's analysis and the analyst's overinvolvement in the patient's life. Countertransference has undergone many revisions in psychoanalysis since Freud's introduction of the concept. It is beyond the scope of this chapter to review all of these changes, but here I highlight several conceptualizations of countertransference that are especially relevant to the consideration of sociocultural issues.

Sándor Ferenczi (1932) challenged Freud's initial conceptualization of countertransference by exploring the analyst's sense of openness to the patient. Ferenczi, emphasizing the individuality of each analyst–patient dyad, suggested that the analyst and the patient engage in a transmission of thoughts and feelings, a sense of knowing the other, without verbally communicating these thoughts and feelings (Boschan, 2011; Hirsch, 2008). Using a radically different approach, he sought to evoke intense transference reactions from his patients, including negative transference, as a way to help the patient access unconscious feelings that were "de-symbolized by trauma" (Boschan, 2011, p. 313). In Ferenczi's perspective, the analyst's recognition and acceptance of his or her participation in the patient's transference is critical to helping the patient fully access unacceptable, repressed thoughts and feelings and address pathological defenses. The notion of mutuality in transference and countertransference is inherent to Ferenczi's conceptualization.

Heinrich Racker (1957) suggested that the analyst's experience consists of a countertransference predisposition rooted in past events and of present and real experiences with the client. Racker (1957) wrote

> It is precisely this fusion of present and past, the continuous and intimate connection of reality and fantasy, of external and internal, conscious and unconscious, that demands a concept embracing the totality of the analyst's psychological response, and renders it advisable, at the same time, to keep for this totality of response the accustomed term *counter-transference*. (p. 310)

In his view, a *concordant* type of countertransference originates from an earlier period in the analyst's life. However, the patient's transference can trigger the analyst's countertransference, which is seated in the analyst's identification with the patient's internal objects, and countertransference, in this case, is *complementary* to the client's transference. Harold Searles (1988) noted the importance of the therapist's personality and unconscious life on patients, especially those with severe mental illness, such as schizophrenia. For example, he described his feelings and fantasies while working with patients with schizophrenia, which felt alien to his typical experiences. For Searles, these experiences of introjection by the therapist reflected empathic attunement to the patient's experiences, which benefits both the patient and the analyst.

Over the course of a century, psychoanalysts increasingly have conceptualized countertransference as the therapist's total experience of and response to the client; it is a response that remains in the unconscious and varies depending on the nature of the client's problems (e.g., neurotic, psychotic) (Little, 1960; Winnicott, 1947). D. W. Winnicott (1947) discussed the complex unconscious feelings of hate and guilt as a response to the projected affect by patients suffering from "psychosis" and noted that the analyst experienced such patients as difficult. James Anderson (2014, p. 377), in his interview with Margaret Little, a contemporary of Winnicott, noted that the word "psychotic" referred in fact to "anxieties being concerned with identity and existence," in contrast to a definition of "psychotic" as being out of touch with reality. Winnicott, like other analysts, emphasized the importance of consciously recognizing and working through these negative feelings so that they do not become unconsciously enacted in the relationship with the patient and interfere with the emergence of the patient's true self. Winnicott's struggle with negative affect concerning these clients raises questions about whether and how therapists explicitly or implicitly address difficult feelings with their clients.

Questions regarding the degree of involvement of the analyst in the patient's analysis have persisted throughout the history of psychoanalytic theory. Harry Stack Sullivan (1953), despite his emphasis on the participant–observer role of the therapist, cautioned against overinvolvement of the therapist because it could indicate a pathological self form of countertransference. In more recent years, interpersonal and relational psychoanalysts challenged previous notions of the therapist's involvement with the client and the distinction between transference and countertransference. These analysts suggested that the client's unconscious responses to the therapist and the therapist's unconscious responses to the client are interconnected (Gill, 1983; Gill & Hoffman, 1982). Ferenczi's perspective, which supported the emotional involvement of the analyst, mutuality, and less asymmetry in the therapeutic dyad, anticipated these developments.

Contemporary interpersonal, relational, and intersubjective theorists focus on the ambiguous nature of interpersonal reality and assume that the client's intrapsychic life can be understood through "interpretive construction" (S. A. Mitchell, 1997). Therefore, the therapist's involvement in transference and countertransference is inevitable. Merton Gill (1983), from an interpersonal perspective, suggested that the therapist must be prepared to inquire into the client's experience of his or her relationship with the therapist because the immediate here-and-now interactions within the therapeutic dyad inform the client's distress and conflicts. Gill proposed that the client's associations that are not explicitly connected with the therapeutic relationship may still contain allusions to it and that the therapist should prepare for falling within the client's expectations of him or her to some extent. According to Gill, the therapist is unconsciously pressured to experience the client in ways that align with the client's conflicted expectations. This perspective clearly implicates a bidirectional influence of the therapist's and the client's conscious and unconscious responses to one another.

Many contemporary psychoanalytic scholars have rejected the notion of the therapist's anonymity. Instead, there is an emphasis on the coexistence of mutuality and asymmetry in the therapeutic dyad (Aron, 2006; I. Z. Hoffman, 2009). A. E. Harris (2011) noted that relational psychoanalysis conceptualizes the human mind as both individuated and interpersonal. Therefore, the mutual influence of the therapist and the client becomes the location of inquiry in understanding the client's intrapsychic and interpersonal concerns (Aron, 2006; A. E. Harris, 2011; I. Hoffman, 1998; S. A. Mitchell, 1998a; Stolorow, Brandchaft, & Atwood, 1987). The recognition of the therapist's subjectivity changes how power dynamics in the therapeutic relationship are structured. It also calls attention to the therapist's self-scrutiny that should be supported through disclosure and dialogue with colleagues (A. E. Harris, 2011). S. A. Mitchell (1998a) suggested that it is impossible for a therapist to achieve a neutral and value-free position. The therapist, in his view, understands the client's experience through examining his or her own experiences and the dynamics of transference and countertransference. According to S. A. Mitchell, the therapist's expertise reflects an ability to understand the therapeutic process and hold and protect the process of the client's reflection and self-inquiry.

The Therapist's Needs

The therapist's examination of how he or she influences the client's responses must involve a consideration of his or her own personal desires and passions. Philip Bromberg (2006) suggested that enactments produce shame that is experienced by the client and the therapist and thus destabilizes both individuals. The client and the therapist need something from each other, and enactments position each individual to deny the legitimacy of his or her own needs. Bromberg proposed that self-states that experience need and those that contain shame become dissociated and communication between the therapist and client is suspended. He recognized that despite the challenge of facing one's feelings of shame, the therapist must make explicit his or her own experience of the enactment to facilitate the client's ability to do the same. In this way, the therapist's self-revelation is necessary for the client to engage in the intersubjective space that previously may have been inaccessible (Bromberg, 2006). Relatedly, Hirsch (2008, p. 113) observed that although the therapist may be aware that therapeutic change is facilitated through "new and unpredictable affective relational experience," in his or her relationship with the client, the therapist may be reluctant to explicitly identify to the client what may have been helpful in a particular interaction in the process of psychotherapy. Hirsch noted the importance of the therapist's willingness to share his or her understanding of particular relational moments that occur between the therapist and the client in psychotherapy as a way of recognizing the therapist's and client's affective experiences and the uniqueness of each client–therapist relationship.

The therapist's attitudes and responses in psychotherapy are shaped by individual or characterological, cultural, moral, and countertransferential factors (I. Z. Hoffman, 2009). I. Z. Hoffman (2009) suggested that the recognition of the intersubjective nature of psychotherapeutic work fosters a sense of modesty regarding the therapist's influence and an appreciation for the client's sense of agency and a capacity to differ from and agree with the therapist's conceptualization of the client's life. The client's experiences of loss, suffering, trauma, discrimination, poverty, and marginalization can evoke profound anxiety for the therapist that must be examined, contained, and thoughtfully worked through to help the client feel safe enough to explore these experiences with depth and without carrying the responsibility of managing the therapist's feelings. It is important to recognize that at times the client's emotional life may overwhelm the therapist, as evidenced in the therapist's emotional and physical states (Frankel, 2006; Lombardi, 2013). The therapist, in this case, has to monitor the extent to which it is possible for him or her to remain involved with the client. For example, the therapist who listens to a client's homophobic or racist attitudes may feel trapped as he or she attempts to hear the client's struggles despite feeling angry and frustrated with the client. Therapist's feelings of anger and/or hostility may be understood as a response to the client's internalized homophobia or racism and also to his or her own shame and helplessness in being unable to change the client's attitudes. This type of dilemma is especially challenging for the therapist who values the importance of inclusion, diversity, and social justice in his or her personal and professional lives. Therapists' needs are multiply determined through personal and professional experiences, in that the need to advance justice and fairness can be rooted in early life experiences of injustice and/or in a moral sensibility cultivated independently of these earlier experiences.

Listening to a client's struggles can evoke not only anxiety and despair for the therapist but also intense, passionate feelings (I. Z. Hoffman, 2009). The therapist may experience pleasure, joy, excitement, and love in his or her interactions with a client. Therapists can also feel ambivalently about their loving feelings toward their clients, in ways that they do not about other affective experiences such as sadness. There is a concern, of course, that loving feelings may become enacted in ways that may violate the client's personal boundaries or impose a sense of compliance or coercion in the client's attitudes and behaviors toward the therapist (Rabin, 2003). The types of loving feelings held by the therapist can vary considerably; such feelings can be connected with maternal or paternal caring, idealization of the client, and sexual attraction. It is of critical importance for the therapist to understand these feelings, where they are rooted, and the dynamics in the interactions with the client that may contribute to these feelings. Andrea Celenza (2007) wrote about the complicated nature of love in the psychoanalytic therapeutic dyad, one that consists of power imbalance and asymmetry. The structure of psychoanalytic psychotherapy has important implications for the therapist's and the client's feelings for and fantasies about one another. Celenza (2007) pointed out that the structure of psycho-analytic therapy:

> . . . creates a universally wished-for context—a context in which one's needs and wishes are continuously placed in the foreground despite one's best (conscious and unconscious) efforts to keep them buried, unexpressed, or denied. . . . On a practical level, it is a necessary structure that is defining of the therapeutic context. On an experiential level, however, it is highly seductive. (p. 289)

The therapist bears great responsibility in disentangling dynamics of love, attention, and power through careful attention to the structure of the psychotherapy encounter and his or her personal wishes and needs (Celenza, 2007).

The decision to become a therapist reflects a personal and professional choice and, for many, an unmet need. Many therapists attempt to satisfy unmet needs through connecting and empathically resonating with clients, and most of these therapists do so with great respect for the client's suffering (Celenza, 2010). Having these needs is not necessarily problematic unless the therapist loses the capacity to recognize and differentiate his or her needs and wishes and those of the client and/or fails to protect the well-being of the client. It is important to consider that the therapist's needs, similar to those of the client, change over the course of time, depending on the nature of his or her personal life at any given developmental period. For example, a therapist with extensive experience working with traumatized clients may choose not to work with children after becoming a parent. Therapists' life histories also consist of experiences associated with fixed notions and stereotypes of people from various sociocultural groups, which may influence how they interact with clients. The therapist must nondefensively acknowledge and explore his or her associations to gender, race, ethnicity, social class, sexual identity, and dis/ability and his or her resistance in seeking new knowledge that informs his or her understanding of these issues. It is also imperative that the therapist not become or remain isolated because being alone with these types of assumptions can compromise the therapist's ability to authentically engage with clients.

Remaining open to dialogue and reshaping one's long-standing understandings of people from a particular cultural group can feel difficult and requires the ability to accept that one may not be an expert and to bear the unknown. It also requires that the therapist recognize his or her privilege in not knowing certain experiences, such as not knowing what it is like to live in poverty, have a physical disability, be a racial minority, or be bilingual. In addition, the therapist must be prepared to feel uncomfortable and at times emotionally unsafe because therapeutic dialogue on the reality of social injustice exposes feelings such as shame, guilt, anger, and helplessness and challenges the defenses protecting the therapist and the client from identifying and engaging with these feelings.

Engaging in one's own analysis has been a necessary part of psychoanalytic work since Freud's inception of this perspective. Today, psychoanalysts and psychoanalytic therapists continue the tradition of engaging in a long-term psychoanalysis or psychotherapy. Unfortunately, in some cases, the therapist's own analysis or psychotherapy experience does not address the connection between the social world and the individual, and there are aspects of the therapist's experience that remain unexplored and unprocessed. This is a serious problem when therapists then work with clients without having an in-depth personal understanding of how their sociocultural contexts shape and are shaped by other aspects of their life, such as their internal dispositions and relationships with people. However, it is important to consider that many therapists find their personal therapeutic work is transformative and engage in such work at various points in their lives to examine their identities and cope with life transitions, losses, and traumas. Rose Marie Perez Foster (1996), in reflecting on her experiences of bilingualism, stated, "Although I have lived these language habits all of my life, they did not become clear and conscious to me until my own bilingual analysis" (p. 142). Nancy McWilliams (2013b) wrote about the significance of her personal analysis in accessing joy and vitality in her emotional life, transforming her internal images of gender and power, her work life, her marriage, and her decision to become a parent.

Like Foster and McWilliams, I have found my personal psychotherapy experiences to be critical to various aspects of my life, such as recognizing and working through traumatic experience, intimate relationships, marriage, and parenting. I have also found that being in my own therapy has helped me to understand the unfolding nature of the healing process and the importance of being emotionally held by a therapist such that I could work through my resistance to uncovering painful experiences. I came to recognize that my feelings about my immigration, experiences of racism and sexism, conflicts within my family of origin, becoming a wife and a mother, and professional life were far more complex than I had understood them to be earlier in my life. My personal therapy also helped me to understand the courage required of my clients to trust me enough to tell me about experiences that are prohibited and stigmatized. I learned to empathize with my client's experiences of oppression in a way that honored the reality and complexity of what oppression feels like and the implications it holds for one's inner life and one's relational life. As McWilliams (2013a) noted, psychotherapy is concerned with emotional honesty. A good personal therapy recognizes a full range of cognitive and emotional experiences and helps us to develop "faith in the process" (p. 623) of this uncovering and the ability to expand the range of options of how we engage with ourselves and with others.

Self-Disclosure

As conceptualizations of countertransference have shifted over the past century, many relational and intersubjective psychoanalysts have challenged the notion of the therapist's neutrality and anonymity in psychotherapy. These scholars (I. Z. Hoffman, 2009; S. A. Mitchell, 1998a; Orange, Atwood, & Stolorow, 1997; Renik, 2006) have argued that therapists convey information about themselves to their clients in implicit and inadvertent ways. For example, a predoctoral trainee may reveal that he or she does not have a doctoral degree and thus has fewer years of experience practicing psychotherapy (Davis, 2002). A therapist may wear a ring on his or her finger, which may indicate to a client that the therapist is either married or in a committed partnership with someone. A racial minority therapist may not be perceived by a client as a "neutral" figure but rather as a screen upon which various unconscious feelings and images are projected by the client. In addition, the therapist's interpretations of the client's concerns reveal the therapist's worldview and personal beliefs. Therapists also deliberately and inadvertently socialize their clients into a particular way of relating in psychotherapy. Specifically, therapists socialize clients about the importance of open dialogue and free association to access hidden emotional experiences, the role of attachment in development, the influence of stress and trauma, the complexity of intimacy and sexuality, and the impact of external messages from families, communities, and societies (e.g., superego) on self-esteem (McWilliams, 2003).

Because it may be impossible to achieve a neutral and anonymous position as a therapist, it has been suggested the therapist recognize his or her subjectivity to achieve an objective stance (Renik, 1996, 2006). Several analysts have argued it is helpful for the therapist to disclose his or her approach to understanding the client's issues and disclose certain aspects of the countertransference to the client as a way of understanding here-and-now interactions between the therapist and the client (J. M. Davies, 1994; Ehrenberg, 2010; Renik, 2006). Timothy Davis (2002) pointed out that although rejecting the notion of anonymity may allow the therapist to be more authentically present with the client, it does not necessarily imply that the therapist's explicit self-disclosure is always in the best interest of the client. Indeed, there is a risk of self-disclosing at times when it is not useful to the client, and other times withholding information may actually be helpful to the client. The timing and content of the disclosure and how the disclosure is then explored and understood by the therapist and the client are critical in evaluating its effectiveness (Davis, 2002). In some cases, the therapist may consciously make a decision not to disclose something about himself or herself and upon later reflection realize he or she withheld from disclosing as a way to cope with intense transferential reactions from the client or countertransference that is evoked in the process of interacting with the client. For such reasons, the therapist must reflect on these moments and accept and learn from mistakes in psychotherapy.

From a relational perspective, the emphasis is on understanding what transpires between the therapist and the client. Christopher Bonovitz (2006) noted that the term "self-disclosure" may be misleading in that it suggests that the subjective experience of the client can always be differentiated from that of the therapist. He suggested that "who is who may sometimes become muddled, and it may not be so clear cut where the sources of our subjective experience are coming from: analyst, patient, or some combination" (Bonovitz, 2006, p. 303). In this view, self-disclosure is not merely a technique; it also entails a process of recognizing the ways in which a therapist may reveal himself or herself to the client. Therapists must examine carefully all aspects of the therapeutic process to evaluate the nature and content of the disclosure, how the disclosure takes place, and whether or not self-disclosure would benefit the client (Gediman, 2006; Kantrowitz, 2009; Meissner, 2002; Renik, 2006; Zayas & Torres, 2009). There are various forms of the therapist's self-disclosure, such as disclosing personal feelings about the client's material, sharing experiences from the therapist's personal life, and answering the client's questions about the therapist's personal life (Meissner, 2002). Bruce Smith and Nadine Tang (2006) have observed that therapists, like clients, have unconscious and conscious needs to be known and must develop the ability to refrain from disclosing themselves to their clients in ways that are not beneficial to the client. In considering whether a therapist should reveal an aspect of himself or herself, Bromberg (2006) suggested that when the therapist authentically believes the client's knowing would facilitate the therapeutic process and remains curious about the client's experience of his or her disclosure, he or she is less likely to implicitly or explicitly demand that the client accept the therapist's subjectivity in place of the client's experience.

With regard to sociocultural differences and similarities, the issue of the therapist's self-disclosure is complicated by the therapist's identity sometimes being invisible to clients even when the therapist has visible physical features that are different from those of the client. For example, the client may have fantasies about the therapist's race, social class, sexual identity, and religion that may strongly contrast with the internal experience of the therapist. Minority therapists, in particular, are perceived as holding positions of both authority and disadvantage (B. L. Smith & Tang, 2006). There have been times when I have listened to clients who spoke with hostility about different minority groups. Listening entailed refraining from disclosing everything I felt in those moments. However, I needed to recognize the validity of my feelings, which stood in sharp contrast to those of the client. I have found that exploring the underlying meanings of my clients' communications with me and sharing my personal feelings about these communications are important to understanding the transference and countertransference and developing a more authentic engagement. With regard to responding to a client's questions, the therapist has to consider the nature of questions. Clients have asked me questions about where I am from, or where I was born, whether my husband is Indian, and whether I have children. I struggle with these questions in terms of when it makes sense to respond and when it does not, and when I feel comfortable answering these questions and when I do not. I also recognize that sometimes answering these questions facilitates a connection with the client, and other times, the client is ambivalent about hearing a response from me. There are also times when I feel protective of my private life and thoughts, which comes into tension with the client's wish and fear about a potential disclosure on my part.

Yet in our contemporary society, many clients access information about their therapists via the internet (Kantrowitz, 2009). Although disclosure via the Internet (e.g., Google) reveals certain aspects of the therapist's life, the therapist's deliberate disclosure in his or her own words embodies a different type of experience for the client and the therapist. For example, when a therapist wears a religious or cultural symbol (e.g., necklace with a cross, yarmulke, heritage dress); speaks with an accent that does not sound "American" to the client; or discloses he or she is suffering from an illness or the death of a loved one, grew up in poverty, is gay or lesbian, is biracial, or grew up in a country outside of the United States, the therapist's words carry important affective meanings for the client. These disclosures have the potential to expand the client's ability to examine meanings of various aspects of his or her own identity that have been unexplored or partially explored. This is particularly important because one of the aims of psychotherapy is to help the client identify new ways of being and relating that have not been actively considered (Summers, 2013). These types of disclosures can also indicate to the client that the therapist is comfortable to some degree in being himself or herself in the professional setting and is comfortable with and willing to address sociocultural difference and similarities with the client. However, the client's needs are primary in the therapeutic relationship, and the therapist's self-disclosure should be followed up by inquiry about the effects of the self-disclosure on the client and the therapist, their interactions with each other, and the structure of the therapeutic relationship (e.g., power, asymmetry).

There are times when nondisclosure can help the client access fantasies about the self and others that otherwise would not be possible. As such, the therapist must maintain a position of open-mindedness, curiosity, and humility. The client is best served when the therapist has a capacity for *mentalization* or the ability to remain open to multiple possibilities and perspectives (Jurist, 2014). Elliot Jurist (2014, p. 497) wrote about the significance of the superego as a "vehicle for how individuals evaluate themselves, imagine them in the future, and for how cultures reproduce themselves." He pointed to the ambivalence that underlies the superego, in which the individual struggles with the tensions between wishes and obligations. I have come to see that clients and therapists contend with this tension in the type of dialogue they have with each other, as they imagine and anticipate what the other person may feel and think about themselves and about each other and work toward moving beyond politically correct, socially acceptable conversation and toward genuine dialogue and collaboration. Mistakes in psychotherapy are inevitable because the therapist may fail to recognize certain aspects of the client's subjective experience. Mistakes replayed through enactments can lead to impasses that are retraumatizing to the client and become destructive to the therapeutic alliance. However, when mistakes are recognized, acknowledged, and subject to reparation, and it is understood that reparation may endure for a prolonged period of time, they often have the potential to deepen psychotherapy (Benjamin, 2004; Gaztambide, 2012; Gilhooley, 2011). Bertram Karon (2002) suggested that it is not always "accurate empathy" that helps clients but the therapist's attempts at accurate empathy that are curative in psychotherapy. In the best of possible relational outcomes, the client internalizes his or her experience of the therapist in a way that models what may constitute an authentic, caring, and emotionally intimate relationship in which mistakes and enactments are recognized and worked through.

CASE ILLUSTRATION

Karen is a single, heterosexual, White woman in her early 40s, who sought help to address her sadness after the death of her stepfather. Karen's stepfather died about one year before our first session. Karen is of French, German, and English ancestry, and her maternal grandparents emigrated from England to the United States as young adults. In my first meeting with Karen, I asked her to describe her ethnic background, a question I pose routinely to my clients. She told me that she is White and that she has no ethnic background. I did not learn about her grandparents' immigration history or her parents' ethnic backgrounds until several weeks passed. She did not ask me about my ethnicity. She described the previous year of her life as one of the worst years of her life. She stated, "My stepfather was the most important person in my life. He was the person I would always turn to." After her stepfather died, Karen began drinking alcohol (e.g., wine and vodka) more and more frequently. Her drinking concerned her friends, who often reminded her of her problems with substance abuse earlier in her life. Karen felt that she may again "be out of control" and therefore wanted to address her problems.

Karen was born and raised in a middle-class family in the Southern part of the United States and relocated to a Northeastern city to attend college. Her parents divorced when she was 8 years old, after which she lived with her mother. Her father had a history of substance use, which was the primary reason for her mother filing for divorce. Karen's father continued to abuse alcohol and remained distant from her. She had a difficult relationship with her mother, who suffered from depression and compulsive hand washing. Her mother did receive psychotherapy and took medications to help with her distress, and there were periods of time in Karen's childhood that her mother was more present in her life. Karen reported having a close relationship with her mother when her mother was well. When Karen was 12 years old, her mother married a man who would become a role model for her. Karen described her stepfather as a "stable, happy man," who never "checked out" from her life. Her mother's marriage to her stepfather brought economic and emotional stability to her life. Karen's sense of isolation in her home before she met her stepfather was compounded by a sense of loneliness at school. She described herself as an "average" student in school who didn't have many friends in school. Her father, typically while intoxicated, would make derogatory comments about her weight and, more generally, her physical appearance. In contrast, her stepfather told her that she is beautiful. When I asked her about her mother's attitude toward her appearance, she said, "My mother wouldn't say anything, like she didn't have an opinion about how I look. I always just thought she agreed with my dad, but didn't want to hurt my feelings."

Karen dated several men briefly in college and fell in love with someone in her senior year of college. She and her boyfriend lived together for 5 years, and she ended the relationship after learning that he had been involved with another woman for several months. Karen was overwhelmed by the breakup of her relationship and had since had brief relationships with men. In her early 30s, she drank alcohol excessively when she felt depressed and eventually decided to seek help from a therapist and attended Alcoholics Anonymous (AA), both of which she found helpful. She had remained sober for many years, until her stepfather died. When I met Karen, she socialized with a few female friends and maintained periodic contact with her parents, mostly by e-mail and phone calls. Early in our work together, Karen told me that she worries about being single for the rest of her life and that she did not want to lose hope as many of her friends had in their own lives. After college, she pursued a fulfilling career. Although she enjoyed her job, she worried that she was consumed with it and recognized that she "hid behind the work" to cope with her anxiety about relationships with men.

While Karen was in treatment with me, she rejoined AA and was able to maintain her sobriety. Initially, our work focused on Karen's ability to feel more stable in her life and reconnect with friends she found to be supportive.

We met twice weekly because she indicated she wanted to be sure she was not isolating herself or avoiding her problems. When I began working with Karen, I noticed how removed she seemed from her feelings. Her responses to my questions were brief, leaving me unsure as to whether she was interested in forming a connection with me. She usually entered my office with an observation about the way I was dressed that day. She made statements such as, "You look nice today" and "I like your sweater." At first, I replied with a simple "thank you." I did notice, however, that I was more consciously aware of my clothing and the way I looked when I met with Karen, which is not something that is typical of my experience with other clients. I did wonder whether her comments indicated deeper meanings attached to physical appearance, and in fact, I learned later in our work that her parents emphasized the importance of physical beauty in ways that devalued her sense of attractiveness to others.

In a session in our third month of working together, after commenting on my clothes, Karen said, "I'm sorry. I feel like I'm always saying something about the way you look. I won't do that anymore."

I asked her whether there was something in my response to her that indicated to her that I wasn't comfortable with her commenting on my clothes.

She responded, "I don't know. I'm just used to saying things about how people look when I first get to know them, and so, I just say what people say I guess—like a compliment. Maybe it's a way of getting to know you better."

I stated, "Like with a friend?"

Karen stated, "Yes, I wish I could know more about you."

I asked her what she would like to know about me, to which she responded, "I actually don't know that I want to know anything specific about you. I've never worked with an Indian doctor before."

At this moment, I remember touching my necklace which was in Karen's view. My necklace has an "Om," a sacred symbol in Hinduism. Almost immediately, I felt anxious as Karen and I moved from a space of polite conversation about clothing style to a far more complicated space of difference between us. I had worn my necklace every day at that time in my life, partly as a way to keep my faith as I coped with my anxiety concerning my son's illness. Not long before I met Karen, my son had been diagnosed with a medical illness, and I was preoccupied with his well-being. Karen had seen my necklace and noticed that it symbolized my Hindu, Indian identity. This was Karen's first explicit recognition of our ethnic and racial differences. Yet I was consciously unaware of what the Om symbol may have meant for her; for me, it reflected hope in the face of stress in my personal life.

Returning to Karen's statement that she had never worked with an Indian doctor, I did respond to her by asking whether she had any particular feelings about working with me. She told me that she felt comfortable in working with me but that being with me felt unfamiliar to her because most of the people with whom she interacted are White. In one session, she stated, "I always wanted to be around people who weren't just like me, or White, but growing up in a small town in the South didn't help with that." I asked her to tell me how she imagined Indian people to be different than White people. Karen responded to me by saying, "I guess I always just heard that people from India are smart, and they do really well here, like get good jobs. I always thought that the clothes that Indian women wear are pretty. I hope I'm not saying something to offend you."

For Karen, Whiteness carried both privilege and disadvantage. The privilege involved the identification with a "standard" racial group against which people outside of this standard group, like me, were compared. The disadvantage was related to her long-standing feeling that there was "nothing special" about her. Her associations to my Indian ethnicity involved the fantasy that there was something special about me, although my specialness was connected with otherness.

I told Karen that I wasn't offended and that I welcomed any questions she may have, although I can only speak to my experience of being Indian.

Karen appeared relieved as she stated, "I'm glad that you said that. I worry that I'm going to say something wrong."

In the following weeks, Karen and I talked explicitly about the necklace I wore. I explained to her that it carried a sacred meaning in Hinduism, and she appreciated that I shared this information with her and that I was honest with her in my response. The necklace became a springboard for our exploration of Karen's grief. She began to talk with me more openly about a sense of emptiness she felt in her life with her parents and how she feared that she would return to this space of loneliness without the presence of her stepfather. I began to experience her as someone who was trying to connect to an experience of profound loss, disappointment, and alienation.

At the beginning of a session during our seventh month of working together, I let her know that I would have to answer my phone if it rang during our session. On that particular day, I had been awaiting a phone call from my son's physician, who was going to tell me the results of my son's lab results. I told Karen that I would need to answer the phone because it concerned one of my children. I was aware of how unusual this was for me as I told a client about something that felt so personal to me.

Karen asked, "Is everything ok?"

I responded, "I am waiting to hear from my son's doctor, and I'm hoping that everything is ok."

Sensing my anxiety and perhaps feeling anxious herself, she asked whether I would be "up to" our session. I assured her that I felt well enough to be with her in the session and that I would like to continue. The phone never rang during this session. Nevertheless, Karen and I were both clearly affected by the anticipated phone call. I asked Karen whether she felt as though she had to take care of me in the session.

She responded, "I think I want everything to be ok for you. Taking care of people is something I'm used to." We then discussed her ambivalence about taking care of someone who is supposed to be in the position of caring for her (e.g., mother, father). Our conversation deepened Karen's ability to talk about her fears of connecting in intimate friendships and relationships, as she imagined herself as someone who no one would love enough to care for her. Learning that my son was ill evoked other fears for Karen. Karen told me that she had been afraid of becoming like her mother and father. She worried that she would become dependent on someone or something else such that she would damage the person or thing or herself.

There were many times during the course of our work together that I revealed aspects of my personal life to Karen, sometimes explicitly and other times inadvertently. In these moments, I experienced myself in various ways: special, vulnerable, othered, and invisible. Sometimes I wondered about how much authority and power I held in my interaction with her when I disclosed that my child was suffering (as was I). I thought about my ambivalence about Karen's privilege of not having to know Indian people, whereas there was no choice for me as an Indian woman to know White people. Other times, I recognized her feelings of vulnerability and shame as she often worried about offending me or of being seen by me as an oppressor. I believe that Karen's fantasies of me as the minority individual in the room facilitated her exploration of her feelings of marginality and lack of specialness in her life, despite her White privilege. The power dynamics in our relationship continually shifted and had to be examined to help Karen connect with her feelings of vulnerability and aggression. The realities we both brought with us to our work at a particular time in our lives were unavoidable, although we both unconsciously and consciously made efforts to contain feelings we feared would overwhelm our relationship or each other.

I believe that in Karen's case, my willingness to reveal aspects of my life did help her to become more engaged with her emotional experiences. As we explored her associations to my Indian ethnicity, she began to wonder about and imagine her grandparents' journey to the United States and to see herself as someone with an ethnic ancestry. Karen had spent much of her life hiding her emotional life from others because when she attempted to reveal herself, she was often disappointed. She struggled with internalized messages from all three parents (e.g., father, mother, stepfather), and hiding provided a way to cope with the contradictions within these messages. Karen wondered whether she would be able to take in or internalize her stepfather's unconditional love, despite his death. Mourning the loss of her stepfather gradually gave way to a sense of hope that she would be able to meet someone like him or someone with whom she could feel like herself. Knowing that her therapist was also experiencing grief in her personal life may have helped her to connect more deeply with her own grief. In addition, my ability to bear and work through the stress I experienced in my personal life, which by no means was simple, was critical to helping her mourn the physical loss of her stepfather and the psychological losses of her mother and father.

SUMMARY

The therapist's self-examination is essential for his or her sense of authenticity and ability to listen and attend to the client's subjective experience. The therapist's commitment to engaging with sociocultural context both personally and professionally contributes to the recognition of cultural differences and similarities in psychotherapy. Therapists should attend to their own experiences of traumatic stress and loss in order to be present and bear painful affective experiences related to the client's traumatic history. Therapists often face unique challenges of working through their own experiences with oppression and marginalization as they may become a screen for the client's projections associated with sociocultural identity. The therapist's self-examination should involve an analysis of his or her training in and exposure to dominant theories of psychotherapy, such as psychoanalytic theory, which developed in part under traumatic circumstances. Culturally informed psychoanalytic practice recognizes the importance of attending to therapists' vulnerability to historical trauma and neglect of sociocultural issues on present-day therapeutic approaches. Contemporary psychoanalytic conceptualizations concerning countertransference and self-disclosure emphasize the mutual influence of therapists and clients, and the therapist's willingness to critically examine how his or her sociocultural identifications and experiences of privilege and marginality may influence the client's responses in psychotherapy. The therapist's conflicts concerning sociocultural identity and personal needs and desires and his or her influence on therapeutic work with clients can be explored effectively in his or her own personal psychotherapy or analysis and through clinical supervision and peer consultation. Self-examination is a critical aspect of culturally informed psychoanalytic practice because it shapes what is heard by the therapist and how the therapist may approach issues of diversity in psychotherapy. The five areas of emphasis that compose a psychoanalytically informed approach to cultural competence in psychotherapy, which I describe in chapters 4 through 8, have important implications for future directions in psychoanalytic theory and practice and, more broadly, for the applications of cultural competence in the mental health professions. In the final chapter, I explore some thoughts on future directions concerning this framework.

9

IMPLICATIONS OF A CULTURALLY INFORMED PSYCHOANALYTIC PERSPECTIVE: SOME THOUGHTS ON FUTURE DIRECTIONS

Years ago, during a professional meeting, I presented on the topic of race in the context of clinical supervision. Following the end of my presentation, a colleague introduced himself to me and after discussing my efforts to integrate multicultural and psychoanalytic perspectives, he stated, "Good luck with your mission. It's not easy to do."

At first, I appreciated his goodwill but later reflected on his comment. I thought about his apprehension and began to wonder whether my aims were realistic. I was also struck by a feeling of being alone because his words conveyed encouragement but also a message that this was *my* mission, not his. The implicit message was that people who look like me (ethnic minorities), on the margins in a sense, are the ones to carry forth this "mission."

I have since met colleagues and students who have been invested in this process of bringing social context into the foreground of psychoanalysis and those who have been interested in learning about the relevance of psychoanalytic

http://dx.doi.org/10.1037/14800-010
Psychoanalytic Theory and Cultural Competence in Psychotherapy, by P. Tummala-Narra

ideas in understanding our contemporary world. I have learned that we must move beyond the idea that cultural competence is located among a relatively small number of mental health professionals who happen to care more about diversity than do their counterparts. We also need to move beyond an *us* and *them* dichotomy in theoretical approaches to human experience to actualize a complex approach to people's lived realities.

Cultural competence in psychoanalytic theory entails an extension from an emphasis on the caregiving environment to multiple social contexts that provide important mirroring functions for individuals and communities. This inclusion of cultural competence as a core emphasis of psychoanalytic psychotherapy is important not only to practitioners interested in social issues but also to practitioners whose goal is to help clients with complexity and depth. Within the context of an increasingly pluralistic society and significant disparities in mental health care for marginalized communities, it behooves psychoanalytic practitioners to seriously and consistently engage with cultural competence and all practitioners to engage with conceptualizations of social identity that attend to conscious and unconscious processes. Challenges to our current mental health care system and the multilayered needs of clients require nuanced conceptualizations and techniques that respect the breadth and depth of sociocultural issues in the lives of clients and therapists and within institutions that provide training and services.

The framework I have presented focuses on cultural competence as a core area of emphasis in psychoanalytic theory and calls for the application of psychoanalytic ideas to existing conceptualizations of culturally competent practice. A psychoanalytic perspective on cultural competence aims to move away from reductionistic and cookbook-style approaches to psychotherapy and toward a complex, process-oriented model of practice. Culturally informed psychoanalytic practitioners, researchers, and educators are concerned with social injustice and human rights and understand the inextricable connection between the sociocultural, relational, and intrapsychic. Although psycho-analytic theory has been scrutinized since the time of Freud's introduction of his ideas concerning the unconscious, it remains highly relevant to our contemporary world, in which we contend with major changes in technology, social media, globalization, and migration, all against the backdrop of social oppression and injustice. A belief in the effectiveness of the "talking cure" continues to persist across all psychoanalytic work, despite the plural-ism in psychoanalytic theory (Leavy, 2010). In addition, young people from diverse backgrounds are increasingly interested in psychoanalytic perspectives, hoping to gain more in-depth understanding of human attitudes, motivation, and behavior. In this chapter, I present some recommendations for training, research, and practice that are drawn from a culturally informed psychoanalytic perspective. This chapter addresses the importance of attending to necessary changes within the culture of psychoanalysis and the growing disconnection of psychoanalytic thought from academic psychology and that between disciplines. In addition, I discuss some recent developments in the application of psychoanalytic concepts in "mainstream" psychology, such as community and other nonclinical domains, that challenge conventional notions of psychoanalysis and psychoanalytic therapy as being located only within the confines of the analyst's or the therapist's office.

ISSUES IN THE CULTURE OF TRAINING AND PSYCHOANALYTIC RESEARCH

Psychoanalysis has a complex standing in the mental health professions (Aron & Starr, 2013; Rubin, 1999). Some predict that psychoanalysis will become obsolete, and others predict the longevity of psychoanalysis in its ability to inform us of the depth of the human experience and conflict. Jeffrey Rubin (1999) pointed out that psychoanalysis can pose a threat to a society in which a "quick-fix mentality reigns and a greater premium is placed on conspicuous consumption than self-examination" (p. 62). Although psychoanalysis offers a unique approach to understanding human experience, specifically issues such as conflict, development, and identity, it continues to face challenges in systematically addressing issues of social context. The culture of psychoanalysis should be further explored in an effort to imagine the future of psychoanalytic theory, training, practice, research, and education. We must examine the remnants of historical biases, such as racism, sexism, heterosexism, classism, and ableism. We also should critically examine the attempts of nonpsychoanalytically oriented academicians and clinicians to marginalize psychoanalytic ideas on the basis of historical and political conflicts and a lack of knowledge concerning contemporary psychoanalytic perspectives.

Rigid and authoritarian positions within training programs and professional organizations should be replaced with an attitude of humility and respect for diverse psychoanalytic and nonpsychoanalytic theoretical perspectives so that more sophisticated understandings of development, psychopathology, and identity can be developed. In addition, it is important to keep in mind that there is variation among psychoanalytic theorists about which aspects of psychoanalysis should be prioritized and emphasized. Aron and Starr (2013) noted the contrast between a practical approach to psychoanalytic therapy that focuses on symptom relief and day-to-day realities of the client and an approach that emphasizes dreams, fantasy, and imagination. Splitting that occurs between these two conceptualizations of psychoanalytic therapy can be problematic because it does not recognize that psychoanalytic therapy can be used "short-term to problem-solve, as well as long-term, to bring to life someone who is deprived of vitality" (Aron

& Starr, 2013, p. 391). The pluralism within psychoanalytic theories (e.g., classical, object relations, self-psychology, intersubjective, relational) is desirable because it allows for the possibility of exploring various aspects of client's lives, the therapeutic process, and the integration of knowledge needed to help clients whose realities do not reflect discrete categories of experience but rather dynamic and continually shifting experience.

Culturally informed psychoanalytic practice involves the specific approaches detailed in this book and addresses institutional and systemic barriers, such as lack of access to interpreters and lack of ongoing training or access to consultation. From this perspective, psychoanalytic education and training would need to involve a curriculum that reflects the valuing of sociocultural issues. Typically, there are no standard curricula in psychoanalytic training institutes that formally include educational modules on social context and identity. There are few faculty members who are of racial, sexual, or other minorities. It is not surprising that psychoanalytic institutes tend to recruit few minority candidates. Academic programs in psychology (e.g., clinical, counseling) typically do not include psychoanalytic contributions to the study of sociocultural diversity in their curricula. Most students in graduate training programs have little formal access to psychoanalytic ideas, so the idea of psychoanalytic theory addressing sociocultural issues feels foreign to them. In addition, there are gaps between supervisees and supervisors (psychoanalytic and nonpsychoanalytic in orientation) with respect to exposure to training in cultural competence and social justice issues, contributing to challenges in the supervisory relationship when addressing issues of social identity and context. Trainees and early career professionals are often caught between negotiating contradictory messages about the importance and relevance of sociocultural context in practice.

Several psychoanalysts have written about the problem of shame experienced by candidates in psychoanalytic training who must navigate a rigid hierarchy, at times leaving their training with feelings of uncertainty about their expertise (Buechler, 2008; Eisold, 2004). Sometimes the structure and power dynamics inherent to analytic training prohibit trainees from actively collaborating with their supervisors and meeting their training needs. In addition, experiences of alienation and marginalization of racial and sexual minority psychoanalysts during psychoanalytic training are well documented (Corbett, 2002, 2008; Drescher, 2008; Wyche, 2012). Clearly, the problems of a rigid and exclusive hierarchical system of training contradict the goals of a culturally informed psychoanalytic approach that requires an open system of dialogue and collaboration. These problems within psychoanalytic institutes in the United States and elsewhere have been recognized, and efforts continue to be made across different institutes toward an honest examination of systemic exclusion of perspectives relevant to people on the margins.

A culturally informed psychoanalytic perspective requires self-examination at the individual and institutional levels. The access to resources, such as having colleagues to talk with about issues of diversity and how their theoretical formulations are shaped by attention to these issues, is related to clinicians' multicultural practices in psychotherapy (Tummala-Narra et al., 2012). Mental health practitioners, especially those with training responsibilities, can either obstruct or facilitate the integration of cultural competence in education. The issue of access to psychoanalytic knowledge is also an important issue to consider. For example, the financial cost of psychoanalytic training is prohibitive for most individuals, and language that is used in psychoanalytic literature is experienced by many researchers and practitioners as difficult to translate to daily practice. In addition, psychoanalytic ideas typically are published in journals that specialize in psychoanalysis, so there is little crossover of these ideas into mainstream academic journals.

Despite solid evidence that psychoanalytic psychotherapy is effective (Blatt & Zuroff, 2005; Shedler, 2010; Westen, Novotny, & Thompson-Brenner, 2004), psychoanalytic researchers continue to face challenges in securing funding to conduct studies. Typically, funding agencies do not support psychoanalytic researchers because of the belief that there is no empirical validity for psychoanalytic treatment. However, without resources, these researchers often are unable to conduct their research (McWilliams, 2013a). There is a long history of controversy concerning the relationship between psychoanalysis and research, with scholars debating whether or not psychoanalysis should be considered a science (Chiesa, 2010; McWilliams, 2013a; Rubin, 1999; Wallerstein & Fonagy, 1999). Marco Chiesa (2010) suggested that, historically, there have been several positions regarding research within psychoanalysis. These positions are represented across the following lines: some psychoanalysts who view scientific research and psychoanalysis as inherently incompatible (rejectionistic stance); academicians and educators who are actively involved in conducting research and view research as necessary to the development and survival of psychoanalysis; and clinicians who are not actively involved in research but not averse to research in psychoanalysis. It is especially problematic when some analysts who hold the rejectionistic position also carry authority in psychoanalytic training institutes and perpetuate a disconnection between clinicians and researchers and among disciplines. However, many clinicians find that the focus and language of research studies is too far removed from their day-to-day clinical practice (Chiesa, 2010).

In my view, psychoanalytic concepts and research in psychology inform each other. Although there are researchers who define scientific research as only those studies that involve randomized clinical trials and quantitative methodology, many other researchers value multiple research methodologies, including those used in quantitative studies, qualitative studies, process-outcome studies, epidemiological studies, historical studies, ethnographic studies, participatory action research (PAR), and case studies (Chiesa, 2010; Wallerstein, 2009). There is a clear need for research programs that value different methodologies, address the complexities of clinical problems (e.g., multiple coexisting diagnoses and life stressors), systematically examine issues of social and cultural diversity, and include research participants from diverse backgrounds. In addition, psychoanalytic research, testing, and assessment should address constructs related to sociocultural identity, social injustice, and the heterogeneity of experience within sociocultural groups.

It is important to consider that evidence-based practice (EBP) is defined as "the integration of the best available research with clinical expertise in the context of patient characteristics, culture, and preferences" (American Psychological Association Presidential Task Force on Evidence-Based Practice, 2006, p. 273). This is not incompatible with a psychoanalytic paradigm, in which research is understood to encompass a variety of different methodologies and the concerns of a socioculturally diverse society are regarded to be of primary importance. The assessment of variables such as race, ethnicity, religion, gender, income, education, employment, sexual orientation, and dis/ability are of great importance in contemporary society because each of these variables has direct implications not only for the generalizability of research findings but also for disparities in physical and mental health and in accessing adequate mental health care (Watkins, 2013).

ADDRESSING THE DISCONNECTION BETWEEN PSYCHOANALYTIC THEORY AND ACADEMIC PSYCHOLOGY

There is a long-standing disconnection between psychoanalytic theory and broader academic psychology. Over the past two decades, in particular, we have witnessed a transformation in graduate education in clinical psychology from a focus on psychoanalytic theory to a focus on clinical neuroscience, cognitive–behavioral theories, and developmental theories that largely neglect or devalue psychoanalytic perspectives. It is the common experience of graduate students to not have been exposed to primary sources from any theoretical orientation (McWilliams, 2005). Most students, for example, have not read the works of Freud, Sullivan, Winnicott, Kohut, Mitchell, or contemporary psychoanalytic authors. Instead, their knowledge of psychoanalytic theory is derived primarily from undergraduate or graduate textbooks that provide incomplete or distorted information concerning psychoanalytic theory. These students may have also been told by faculty or other students that psychoanalytic theory is irrelevant to contemporary practice with individuals from diverse sociocultural backgrounds. However, in my experience, when my students have been given the space to read and discuss primary sources and clinical case material from a psychoanalytic perspective, they have found it to be a relevant, practical, and important lens through which they come to understand, sit with, and work through painful affect, difficult interpersonal dynamics, and complex interactions between the individual and his or her social context.

Psychoanalytic concepts can inform the process of multicultural education in the classroom and in clinical settings. Specifically, issues such as race, sexual orientation, social class, and dis/ability evoke feelings of anxiety, relief, guilt, shame, and anger that can manifest implicitly or explicitly in educational settings (Tummala-Narra, 2009c). Typically, mandatory courses on diversity in counseling psychology and clinical psychology graduate programs are taught by minority faculty, and even when programs integrate issues of diversity in their curricula, these courses become a core location of multicultural education. Ethnic minority supervisors have been found to spend more time discussing multicultural issues with their supervisees than do White supervisors, even though the former have not had a formal education in multicultural issues during their training years (Hird, Tao, & Gloria, 2004). In addition, many ethnic minority supervisors have written about their experiences of racial and cultural insensitivity throughout their training and professional life (Rastogi & Wieling, 2005; Tummala-Narra, 2004).

A psychoanalytic perspective draws on the significance of affective and interpersonal processes that underlie training in multicultural competence from the perspective of the instructor and that of the student. Scholars have noted that affective reactions of students and instructors can mobilize or impede multicultural learning (Spanierman, Poteat, Wang, & Oh, 2008; Utsey & Gernat, 2002). A psychoanalytic perspective is well suited to an in-depth understanding of the interpersonal nature of multicultural education. From this lens, multicultural education involves a mutual influence of students and instructors. Thus, course work and supervision should attend to the instructor's and students' self-inquiry, active and explicit reflection on the process of learning and relational patterns that develop through dialogue, and ability to tolerate painful affect that is evoked in the process of engaging in these dialogues (Tummala-Narra, 2009c).

Psychoanalytically oriented clinicians and academicians have an ambivalent relationship with broader academic psychology, and this tension is reflected in professionals who practice and teach across academic institutions and clinical settings. As a professor in a doctoral program in counseling psychology who conducts research on immigration, race, and traumatic stress and as a psychoanalytic practitioner who works with clients from diverse sociocultural backgrounds, I directly experience and witness the rifts between research and practice. Finding a professional home as a minority, psychoanalytically oriented psychologist is complicated. For many minority psychologists, the process of securing a professional home involves shifting across multiple professional spaces. It is often the case that minority psychologists join multiple committees and divisions of professional organizations so that their lived realities as minority individuals and those of the communities with which they identify are represented. This process, of course, adds burden to minority psychologists because they typically invest more emotional and financial resources in finding a professional home than do other psychologists. However, it has been my experience that psychoanalytic organizations, such as the American Psychological Association's Division of Psychoanalysis (Division 39), increasingly have recognized the problem of bifurcating sociocultural issues and individual psychology and expanded efforts to bridge these gaps from a theoretical standpoint and a practical one of welcoming and engaging students and professionals from diverse backgrounds.

Clinicians and academicians, especially those with training responsibilities, can obstruct or facilitate the integration of psychoanalytic concepts and cultural competence in education. Faculty in universities and psychoanalytic institutes and educators in clinical settings bear great responsibility for teaching students about the importance of insight, learning from clients and their experiences within a particular sociocultural and historical context, and social justice in practice. They also bear the responsibility of helping students to critically analyze literature that claims or predicts the "decline" of psychoanalytic psychotherapy (Norcross, Pfund, & Prochaska, 2013) because much of this literature does not consider contemporary developments in psychoanalytic theory or the real experiences of clients who benefit from psychoanalytic psychotherapy (Jurist, 2013). Elliot Jurist (2013) suggested that we embrace a pluralism that "urges us toward a tolerance that is based upon knowing something about and engaging views that differ from one's own" (p. 222). When we fail to engage with multiple perspectives, we are unable to teach future generations to engage with diverse viewpoints, and therefore create an atmosphere in which students feel as though they must identify with only one particular set of ideas to be sound clinicians and researchers. For many students, this is challenging because their lived realities and those of their clients require a more complex engagement. In fact, many of my students have asked me, particularly over the past decade, whether or not it would be acceptable for them to reveal their psychoanalytic orientation to directors of psychology internship programs for which they are invited to interview for an internship position. Other students have asked me whether they could openly discuss their psychoanalytic interests in a research conference focused on race and immigration without being negatively evaluated for having an interest in psychoanalytic ideas.

The message that these students receive repeatedly is that psychoanalytic theory is outdated, nonscientific, and incompatible with attention to socio-cultural context. My concern with these messages is that we commit a dis-service to our students when we foreclose possibilities for them by not exposing them to multiple theoretical perspectives in a sophisticated way. In my experi-ence, students are interested in securing a safe learning space in which they can explore theory and freely ask questions without being penalized for having an interest in a particular theoretical orientation or conceptualization. This is critical for the future of culturally informed practice because students either learn to respect multiple perspectives or dismiss the complexity of gender, race, religion, ethnicity, class, sexual identity, and dis/ability.

Students in psychology training programs reflect the future of the profes-sion. They look to faculty in their academic and clinical institutions to model their future practice, research, and teaching. Therefore, it is the responsibil-ity of faculty, supervisors, and mentors to initiate and foster dialogue with practitioners and researchers across theoretical orientations and disciplines so that political divisions underlying theoretical differences do not progress into rigid, anti-intellectual positions that stifle developments in theory, research, and practice and ultimately fail individuals and communities in need of urgent attention. It is important that faculty and supervisors rely on primary sources to inform themselves of science and practice. It is also important that students read primary sources, discuss their developing understandings of theory with faculty and supervisors, and learn to resist prematurely forming conclusions about theories. In other words, there is no substitute for direct dialogue and communication among professionals and students. The term *cultural humility* is relevant here in that it reflects a "lifelong process of self-reflection, self-critique, continual assessment of power imbalances, and the development of mutually respectful relationships and partnerships" (Gallardo, 2014, p. 3). It is indeed easier to glorify conflict and difference than to delve into real intellec-tual exchange of ideas. Jack Drescher (2009) noted that the media highlights conflict among professionals by presenting conflict between scientists and pro-fessionals and confusing the public with selective data. As scientists and prac-titioners, we are at risk of creating and perpetuating artificial splits that come at a high price to the public. A culturally informed psychoanalytic perspective emphasizes a respect for the pluralism within psychoanalysis and the mental health professions. This perspective also supports collaboration between clini-cians and researchers so that knowledge produced by both sets of professionals can be used to benefit clients. The tendencies to devalue research by clinicians and clinical practice by researchers are important barriers to overcome if we are to make the progress needed to better serve marginalized communities.

A collaborative approach is critical to developing a vision of psycho-therapy and mental health that is driven by an ethical stance of improving access to appropriate care rather than by external demands, such as those from third-party payers (McWilliams, 2005). Collaborative advocacy by practitioners from different theoretical orientations is urgently needed to meet new service demands that are expected with the passage of the Affordable Care Act (ACA) in the United States and ensure the Parity Act (Clemens, Plakun, Lazar, & Mellman, 2014). Although the ACA provides health care access to uninsured Americans, the problems of underfunding and understaffing of mental health care facilities remain largely unaddressed. As psychological treatment becomes increasingly integrated with medical care, it is important that mental health professionals collaborate with each other to provide culturally informed practice in an environment in which sociocultural issues may again become "streamlined" because of limitations of time and increases in caseloads.

PSYCHOANALYTIC THEORY AND NONCLINICAL DOMAINS

In recent years, several psychoanalytic practitioners have advocated for a progressive discipline that is socially and politically active across diverse communities. Psychoanalytic practitioners have drawn on knowledge from disciplines outside of psychology and the social sciences, such as neuroscience, arts, and humanities, to improve understanding of human experience and develop more nuanced interventions that prioritize the individual's connection to his or her social world (Charles, 2015; Knafo, 2012; Nagel, 2013; Orfanos, 2006; Summers, 2011). There have also been expanding applications of psychoanalytic concepts in community interventions and nonclinical domains within and outside of the United States. These approaches call attention to the need to voice the experiences and concerns of marginalized communities and modify existing psychoanalytic theory. Interventions have been collaborative efforts with a wide range of communities, such as schools, psychosocial and economic rehabilitation services, programs serving refugees, communities coping with racial trauma, communities directly affected by war and the aftermath of 9/11, and children exposed to community violence (Ainslie, 2013; J. L. Darwin & Reich, 2006; Gourguechon, 2013; Hollander, 2010; Liang, Tummala-Narra, & West, 2011; Rogers, 2014; Sklarew, Twemlow, & Wilkinson, 2004; Twemlow, Fonagy, Sacco, Vernberg, & Malcom, 2011; Twemlow & Parens, 2006; Volkan, 2004).

There is a dire global need for community-based interventions that are accessible to poor and socially marginalized individuals and communities. Psychoanalytic practitioners emphasize interventions focused on interpersonal processes and reflection, and lasting, meaningful changes that occur through these processes (Sacco, Campbell, & Ledoux, 2014; Twemlow et al., 2011). Collaboration between practitioners and community members involves an examination of collective trauma (e.g., racial trauma, hate crimes, discrimination), transference and countertransference, enactments, painful affect, and defenses (Borg, 2004; J. L. Darwin & Reich, 2006; Tummala-Narra, 2013a). A culturally informed psychoanalytic framework recognizes that the interactions between practitioners or consultants and community members reflect broader societal dynamics concerning minority status, marginalization, and oppression. For example, practitioners and community members must reflect on their own anxieties, assumptions, and biases, which can interfere with establishing a sense of trust and safety. Mark Borg (2004) coined the term *community character* to describe the unconscious internalization of behavior and implicit rules that communities use to manage anxiety. Stuart Twemlow and Henri Parens (2006) emphasized the importance of listening to the narratives of all stakeholders, privileging the narratives of marginalized individuals in community level conflict, and holding and containing difficult affect in community interventions. Psychoanalytic approaches to community-based intervention foster cognitive and emotional insight and bring to conscious awareness individual and collective meanings of traumatic experiences (Tummala-Narra, 2013a). As psychoanalytic practitioners in individual psychotherapy develop and modify theory based on intensive work with clients, they also develop and modify theory based on their collaborations with communities who typically have little voice among mainstream mental health professions. A culturally informed psychoanalytic perspective emphasizes the importance of dynamic shifts in theoretical understandings of psychological distress and the practitioner's and the researcher's flexibility and openness to new information discovered through community collaborations.

Psychoanalytic approaches to community collaborations are informed by knowledge of historical context and its impact on everyday realities. Ricardo Ainslie (2013), a psychologist–psychoanalyst and professor, delineated some major features of psychoanalytic theory that inform community interventions, including a reengagement with trauma by eliminating barriers of repression and other defenses and translating experience into language that facilitates catharsis and organizes affect. In addition, Ainslie suggested that collective remembering and testimony are essential for healing at the community level. Through his work as a psychoanalytic ethnographer of communities in Texas and Mexico, he uses films, books, and photographic exhibits to communicate the affective experiences of communities who are coping with historical and ongoing racism and political violence. For example, Ainslie described the process of conducting interviews in Hempstead, Texas, with an African American community who experienced the closing of the Sam Schwarz School (established in 1928), a "cornerstone" for the community. The closing of the school signified an erasure of a collective history of the African American community in Hempstead. The interviews eventually were documented in his film *Crossover: A Story of Desegregation*. Ainslie noted that many more people than could possibly be included had hoped to be interviewed for the documentary. The interviews became testimonies of a community whose narratives were never heard in the mainstream. His approach to the interviews involved a psychoanalytic sensibility with an "open-ended, free associative stance" (p. 144). He stated

> Viewed in this light, 'activism' includes the process of articulating insights, of putting into words and, sometimes, into representational form (through a variety of media), the understandings that one has drawn from what one has seen, heard, and felt as a psychoanalyst. (p. 144)

Ainslie's interviews provided a mechanism for collective mourning through providing testimonials of racial segregation and trauma. The documentary, a "public document or representation" (p. 146) of the trauma of Jim Crow, was screened in various communities in Texas and conferences and public events in different states. Ainslie's work with the residents of Hempstead eventually led to "The Sam Schwarz Reunion and Retrospective," which involved both the African American and White communities, an important milestone in bearing witness to the experiences of alumni of the Sam Schwarz School (Ainslie, 2013).

Ainslie's work is an exemplary extension of a culturally informed psychoanalytic theory beyond the clinical dyad. Many other psychoanalytic researchers and practitioners have continued to find ways to address collective traumas within marginalized communities and help bring voice to those who hold little social and economic power (J. L. Darwin & Reich, 2006; Gourguechon, 2013; Sklarew, Twemlow, & Wilkinson, 2004; Tummala-Narra, 2013a). Mental health professionals who are engaged in community-based interventions benefit significantly from a psychoanalytic emphasis on unconscious bias as it influences social injustice and the lasting effects of traumatic stress on interpersonal and intrapsychic processes. Looking to the future, practitioners and researchers can benefit from training that integrates psychoanalytic concepts in preparation for engaging in community interventions and social advocacy, particularly an understanding of traumatic stress and unconscious processes and their expression in transference and countertransference (Goren & Alpert, 2013).

CONCLUDING THOUGHTS

A psychoanalytic lens is critical for understanding the effects of the social realities of our daily lives. In an era of intense social and political conflict, injustice, marked debates concerning social policy, such as those related to immigration and same-sex marriage, attending to sociocultural context is not optional, and when clinicians, researchers, and educators move toward collaborating with marginalized communities, they reduce the likelihood of becoming or remaining bystanders (Hollander, 2006). Significant gaps in theory and research concerning the complexity of sociocultural identity continue to persist in the mental health professions. The future of psychoanalytic theory and practice and that of culturally competent practice rely on an active interchange across frameworks and communities. The voices of individuals and communities experiencing social marginalization are at the crux of diversity issues, so a culturally informed psychoanalytic perspective moves us toward recognizing and hearing these voices so that they do not remain on the margins but become mainstream.

REFERENCES

Achebe, C. (2000). *Home and exile*. Oxford: Oxford University Press.

Aggarwal, N. K. (2010). Cultural formulations in child and adolescent psychiatry. *Journal of the American Academy of Child & Adolescent Psychiatry, 49*, 306–309.

Aguirre, C., Bermúdez, J. M., Parra Cardona, J. R., Zamora, J. A., & Reyes, N. A. (2005). The process of integrating language, context, and meaning: The voices of bilingual and bicultural therapists. In M. Rastogi & E. Wieling (Eds.), *Voices of color: First-person accounts of ethnic minority therapists* (pp. 189–209). Thousand Oaks, CA: Sage Publications.

Ainslie, R. C. (1998). Cultural mourning, immigration, and engagement: Vignettes from the Mexican experience. In M. Suárez-Orozco (Ed.), *Crossings: Immigration and the socio-cultural remaking of the North American space* (pp. 283–300). Cambridge, MA: Harvard University Press.

Ainslie, R. C. (2009). Social class and its reproduction in the immigrant's construction of self. *Psychoanalysis, Culture & Society, 14*, 213–224. http://dx.doi.org/10.1057/pcs.2009.13

Ainslie, R. C. (2011). Immigration and the psychodynamics of class. *Psychoanalytic Psychology, 28*, 560–568. http://dx.doi.org/10.1037/a0025262

Ainslie, R. C. (2013). Intervention strategies for addressing collective trauma: Healing communities ravaged by racial strife. *Psychoanalysis, Culture & Society, 18*(2), 140–152. http://dx.doi.org/10.1057/pcs.2013.3

Ainslie, R. C., & Brabeck, K. (2003). Race murder and community trauma: Psychoanalysis and ethnography in exploring the impact of the killing of James Byrd in Jasper, Texas. *Psychoanalysis, Culture & Society, 8*(1), 42–50. http://dx.doi.org/10.1353/psy.2003.0002

Ainslie, R. C., Tummala-Narra, P., Harlem, A., Barbanel, L., & Ruth, R. (2013). Contemporary psychoanalytic views on the experience of immigration. *Psychoanalytic Psychology, 30*, 663–679. http://dx.doi.org/10.1037/a0034588

Akhtar, S. (1999). *Immigration and identity: Turmoil, treatment, and transformation*. Northvale, NJ: Jason Aronson.

Akhtar, S. (2006). Technical challenges faced by the immigrant psychoanalyst. *The Psychoanalytic Quarterly, 75*, 21–43. http://dx.doi.org/10.1002/j.2167-4086.2006.tb00031.x

Akhtar, S. (2008). *The crescent and the couch: Cross-currents between Islam and psychoanalysis*. Lanham, MD: Jason Aronson.

Akhtar, S. (2009). Identity in the contemporary world. *The American Journal of Psychoanalysis, 69*(1), 1–3. http://dx.doi.org/10.1057/ajp.2008.41

Akhtar, S. (2011). *Immigration and acculturation: Mourning, adaptation, and the next generation*. New York, NY: Jason Aronson.

Akhtar, S., & Tummala-Narra, P. (2005). Psychoanalysis in India. In S. Akhtar (Ed.), *Freud along the Ganges* (pp. 3–28). New York, NY: Other Press.

Alegría, M., Chatterji, P., Wells, K., Cao, Z., Chen, C. N., Takeuchi, D., . . . Meng, X. L. (2008). Disparity in depression treatment among racial and ethnic minority populations in the United States. *Psychiatric Services, 59*(11), 1264–1272. http://dx.doi.org/10.1176/ps.2008.59.11.1264

Ali, S. R., Flojo, J. R., Chronister, K. M., Hayashino, D., Smiling, Q. R., Torres, D., & McWhirter, E. H. (2005). When racism is reversed: Therapists of color speak about their experiences with racism from clients, supervisees, and supervisors. In M. Rastogi & E. Wieling (Eds.), *Voices of color: First-person accounts of ethnic minority therapists* (pp. 117–133). Thousand Oaks, CA: Sage Publications.

Altman, N. (2000). Black and White thinking: A psychoanalyst reconsiders race. *Psychoanalytic Dialogues, 10,* 589–605.

Altman, N. (2006). Whiteness. *The Psychoanalytic Quarterly, 75*(1), 45–72. http://dx.doi.org/10.1002/j.2167-4086.2006.tb00032.x

Altman, N. (2010). *The analyst in the inner city: Race, class, and culture through a psychoanalytic lens* (2nd ed.). New York, NY: Routledge.

Amati-Mehler, J., Argentieri, S., & Canestri, J. (1990). The babel of the unconscious. *The International Journal of Psychoanalysis, 71,* 569–583.

American Psychiatric Association. (1994). *Diagnostic and statistical manual of mental disorders* (4th ed.). Washington, DC: Author.

American Psychiatric Association. (2013). *Diagnostic and statistical manual of mental disorders* (5th ed.). Washington, DC: Author.

American Psychological Association. (2000). *Guidelines for psychotherapy with lesbian, gay, and bisexual clients.* Washington, DC: Author.

American Psychological Association. (2003). Guidelines on multicultural education, training, research, practice, and organizational change for psychologists. *American Psychologist, 58,* 377–402.

American Psychological Association. (2012). *Crossroads: The psychology of immigration in the new century, report of the APA Presidential Task Force on Immigration.* Washington, DC: Author.

American Psychological Association Presidential Task Force on Evidence-Based Practice. (2006). Evidence-based practice in psychology. *American Psychologist, 61,* 271–285. http://dx.doi.org/10.1037/0003-066X.61.4.271

Anderson, J. W. (2014). How D. W. Winnicott conducted psychoanalysis. *Psychoanalytic Psychology, 31,* 375–395. http://dx.doi.org/10.1037/a0035374

Arizmendi, T. G. (2008). Nonverbal communication in the context of dissociative processes. *Psychoanalytic Psychology, 25,* 443–457. http://dx.doi.org/10.1037/0736-9735.25.3.443

Aron, L. (2001). Intersubjectivity in the analytic situation. In J. C. Muran (Ed.), *Self-relations in the psychotherapy process* (pp. 137–164). Washington, DC: American Psychological Association.

Aron, L. (2004). God's influence on my psychoanalytic vision and values. *Psychoanalytic Psychology, 21,* 442–451. http://dx.doi.org/10.1037/0736-9735.21.3.442

Aron, L. (2006). Analytic impasse and the third: Clinical implications of intersubjectivity theory. *The International Journal of Psychoanalysis, 87,* 349–368.

Aron, L., & Putnam, J. (2007). Commentary: Tapping the multiplicity of self-other relationships. In J. C. Muran (Ed.), *Dialogues on difference: Studies of diversity in the therapeutic relationship* (pp. 64–72). Washington, DC: American Psychological Association. http://dx.doi.org/10.1037/11500-006

Aron, L., & Starr, K. (2013). *A psychotherapy for the people: Toward a progressive psychoanalysis.* New York, NY: Routledge.

Aronson, S. (2007). Balancing the fiddlers on my roof: On wearing a yarmulke and working as a psychoanalyst. *Contemporary Psychoanalysis, 43,* 451–459.

Arredondo, P., & Perez, P. (2003). Expanding multicultural competence through social justice leadership. *The Counseling Psychologist, 31,* 282–289. http://dx.doi.org/10.1177/0011000003031003003

Arredondo, P., & Toporek, R. (2004). Multicultural counseling competencies=Ethical practice. *Journal of Mental Health Counseling, 26,* 44–55.

Atkinson, D. R., Morten, G., & Sue, D. W. (Eds.). (1998). *Counseling American minorities* (5th ed.). Boston, MA: McGraw-Hill.

Atlas, G. (2013). What's love got to do with it? Sexuality, shame, and the use of the other. *Studies in Gender and Sexuality, 14,* 51–58. http://dx.doi.org/10.1080/15240657.2013.756778

Atwood, G. E., Orange, D. M., & Stolorow, R. D. (2002). Shattered worlds/psychotic states: A post-Cartesian view of the experience of personal annihilation. *Psychoanalytic Psychology, 19,* 281–306. http://dx.doi.org/10.1037/0736-9735.19.2.281

Aviram, R. B. (2009). *The relational origins of prejudice: A convergence of psychoanalytic and social cognitive perspectives.* Lanham, MD: Jason Aronson.

Barlow, D. H., & Durand, V. M. (2005). *Abnormal psychology: An integrative approach.* Belmont, CA: Wadsworth.

Barnow, S., & Balkir, N. (2013). *Cultural variations in psychopathology: From research to practice.* Cambridge, MA: Hogrefe.

Baron, A. S., & Banaji, M. R. (2006). The development of implicit attitudes. Evidence of race evaluations from ages 6 and 10 and adulthood. *Psychological Science, 17*(1), 53–58. http://dx.doi.org/10.1111/j.1467-9280.2005.01664.x

Barratt, B. B. (2011). Ignacio Martin Baro's writings for a liberation psychology. *Psychoanalytic Psychotherapy in South Africa, 19,* 121–134.

Benjamin, J. (1988). *The bonds of love: Psychoanalysis, feminism, and the problem of domination.* New York, NY: Pantheon Books.

Benjamin, J. (1998). *Shadow of the other: Intersubjectivity and gender in psychoanalysis.* New York, NY: Routledge.

Benjamin, J. (2002a). The question of sexual difference. *Feminism & Psychology, 12,* 39–43.

Benjamin, J. (2002b). Sameness and difference: An "overinclusive" view of gender constitution. In M. Dimen (Ed.), *Gender in psychoanalytic space: Between clinic and culture* (pp. 181–206). New York, NY: Other Press.

Benjamin, J. (2004). Beyond doer and done to: An intersubjective view of thirdness. *The Psychoanalytic Quarterly, 73*(1), 5–46.

Benjamin, J. (2011). Facing reality together discussion: With culture in mind: The social third. *Studies in Gender and Sexuality, 12,* 27–36. http://dx.doi.org/10.1080/15240657.2011.536052

Berger, L. K., Zane, N., & Hwang, W. C. (2014). Therapist ethnicity and treatment orientation differences in multicultural counseling competencies. *Asian American Journal of Psychology, 5,* 53–65. http://dx.doi.org/10.1037/a0036178

Bernal, G., & Scharrón-del-Río, M. R. (2001). Are empirically supported treatments valid for ethnic minorities? Toward an alternative approach for treatment research. *Cultural Diversity and Ethnic Minority Psychology, 7,* 328–342. http://dx.doi.org/10.1037/1099-9809.7.4.328

Bernat, F. P., & Zhilina, T. (2010). Human trafficking: The local becomes global. *Women & Criminal Justice, 20*(1-2), 2–9. http://dx.doi.org/10.1080/08974451003641289

Berry, J. W. (1997). Immigration, acculturation, and adaptation. *Applied Psychology: An International Review, 46,* 5–34.

Berzoff, J. (2012). *Falling through the cracks: Psychodynamic practice with vulnerable and oppressed populations.* New York, NY: Columbia University Press.

Bhabha, H. K. (1994). *The location of culture.* London, United Kingdom: Routledge.

Bhatia, S. (2006). Reinterpreting the inner self in global India: "Malevolent mothers," "distant fathers" and the development of children's identity. *Culture & Psychology, 12,* 378–392. http://dx.doi.org/10.1177/1354067X06064601

Bhatia, S., & Ram, A. (2009). Theorizing identity in transnational and diaspora cultures: A critical approach to acculturation. *International Journal of Intercultural Relations, 33,* 140–149. http://dx.doi.org/10.1016/j.ijintrel.2008.12.009

Bialystok, E. (2009). Bilingualism: The good, the bad, and the indifferent. *Bilingualism: Language and Cognition, 12,* 3–11. http://dx.doi.org/10.1017/S1366728908003477

Bion, W. R. (1977). *Second thoughts: Selected papers on psycho-analysis.* New York, NY: Jason Aronson.

Birman, D., & Simon, C. D. (2014). Acculturation research: Challenges, complexities, and possibilities. In F. T. L. Leong (Ed.), *APA Handbook of Multicultural Psychology: Vol. 1. Theory and Research* (pp. 207–230). Washington, DC: American Psychological Association.

Blagys, M. D., & Hilsenroth, M. J. (2000). Distinctive features of short-term psychodynamic-interpersonal psychotherapy: A review of the comparative psychotherapy process literature. *Clinical Psychology: Science and Practice, 7,* 167–188. http://dx.doi.org/10.1093/clipsy.7.2.167

Blatt, S. J., & Zuroff, D. C. (2005). Empirical evaluation of the assumptions in identifying evidence-based treatments in mental health. *Clinical Psychology Review, 25,* 459–486. http://dx.doi.org/10.1016/j.cpr.2005.03.001

Blechner, M. J. (2008). The political is psychoanalytic: On same-sex marriage. *Studies in Gender and Sexuality, 9,* 146–154. http://dx.doi.org/10.1080/15240650801935164

Blustein, D. L. (2006). *The psychology of working: A new perspective for career development, counseling, and public policy.* Mahwah, NJ: Lawrence Erlbaum.

Bodnar, S. (2004). Remember where you come from: Dissociative process in multicultural individuals. *Psychoanalytic Dialogues, 14,* 581–603. http://dx.doi.org/10.1080/10481880409353128

Bollas, C. (1987). *The shadow of the object: Psychoanalysis of the unthought known.* New York, NY: Columbia University Press.

Bonovitz, C. (2005). Locating culture in the psychic field. *Contemporary Psychoanalysis, 41,* 55–75. http://dx.doi.org/10.1080/00107530.2005.10745848

Bonovitz, C. (2006). The illusion of certainty in self-disclosure: Commentary on paper by Helen K. Gediman. *Psychoanalytic Dialogues, 16,* 293–304.

Bonovitz, C. (2009). Countertransference in child psychoanalytic psychotherapy: The emergence of the analyst's childhood. *Psychoanalytic Psychology, 26,* 235–245. http://dx.doi.org/10.1037/a0016445

Borg, M. B., Jr. (2004). Community intervention as clinical case study. *Clinical Case Studies, 3,* 250–270. http://dx.doi.org/10.1177/1534650103259636

Borg, M. B., Jr. (2005). "Superblind": Supervising a blind therapist with a blind analysand in a community mental health setting. *Psychoanalytic Psychology, 22,* 32–48. http://dx.doi.org/10.1037/0736-9735.22.1.32

Boschan, P. J. (2011). Transference and countertransference in Sándor Ferenczi's clinical diary. *The American Journal of Psychoanalysis, 71,* 309–320. http://dx.doi.org/10.1057/ajp.2011.36

Boston Change Process Study Group, & Nahum, J. P. (2008). Forms of relational meaning: Issues in the relations between the implicit and reflective–verbal domains. *Psychoanalytic Dialogues, 18,* 125–148. http://dx.doi.org/10.1080/10481880801909351

Boulanger, G. (2004). Lot's wife, Cary Grant, and the American dream: Psychoanalysis with immigrants. *Contemporary Psychoanalysis, 40,* 353–372. http://dx.doi.org/10.1080/00107530.2004.10745836

Boulanger, G. (2007). *Wounded by reality: Understanding and treating adult onset trauma.* Mahwah, NJ: Analytic Press.

Boulanger, G. (2009). Witnesses to reality: Working psychodynamically with survivors of terror. *Psychoanalytic Dialogues, 18,* 638–657.

Boulanger, G. (2012). Psychoanalytic witnessing: Professional obligation or moral imperative? *Psychoanalytic Psychology, 29,* 318–324. http://dx.doi.org/10.1037/a0028542

Bowlby, J. (1969). *Attachment and loss.* New York, NY: Basic Books.

Brave Heart, M. Y. H., & DeBruyn, L. M. (1998). The American Indian Holocaust: Healing historical unresolved grief. *American Indian and Alaska Native Mental Health Research, 8,* 56–78.

Breuer, J., & Freud, S. (1895). Studies in hysteria. *The standard edition of the complete psychological works of Sigmund Freud* (Vol. II). London, United Kingdom: Hogarth Press.

Bromberg, P. M. (1996). Standing in the spaces: The multiplicity of self and the psychoanalytic relationship. *Contemporary Psychoanalysis, 32,* 509–535. http://dx.doi.org/10.1080/00107530.1996.10746334

Bromberg, P. M. (2001). Treating patients with symptoms—and symptoms with patience: Reflections on shame, dissociation, and eating disorders. *Psychoanalytic Dialogues, 11,* 891–912. http://dx.doi.org/10.1080/10481881109348650

Bromberg, P. M. (2006). *Awakening the dreamer: Clinical journeys.* Mahwah, NJ: Analytic Press.

Bromberg, P. M. (2010). Minding the dissociative gap. *Contemporary Psychoanalysis, 46*(1), 19–31. http://dx.doi.org/10.1080/00107530.2010.10746037

Brondolo, E., Libretti, M., Rivera, L., & Walsemann, K. M. (2012). Racism and social capital: The implications for social and physical well-being. *Journal of Social Issues, 68,* 358–384. http://dx.doi.org/10.1111/j.1540-4560.2012.01752.x

Brown, L. J., & Miller, M. (2002). The triadic intersubjective matrix in supervision: The use of disclosure to work through painful affects. *The International Journal of Psychoanalysis, 83,* 811–823. http://dx.doi.org/10.1516/TDHV-GWPP-4HX7-VM9X

Brown, L. S. (2006). Still subversive after all these years: The relevance of feminist therapy in the age of evidence-based practice. *Psychology of Women Quarterly, 30,* 15–24. http://dx.doi.org/10.1111/j.1471-6402.2006.00258.x

Brown, L. S. (2009). Cultural competence: A new way of thinking about integration in therapy. *Journal of Psychotherapy Integration, 19*(4), 340–353. http://dx.doi.org/10.1037/a0017967

Brown, L. S. (2010). *Feminist therapy.* Washington, DC: American Psychological Association.

Bryant-Davis, T. (2007). Healing requires recognition: The case for race-based traumatic stress. *The Counseling Psychologist, 35,* 135–143. http://dx.doi.org/10.1177/0011000006295152

Bryant-Davis, T., Chung, H., & Tillman, S. (2009). From the margins to the center: Ethnic minority women and the mental health effects of sexual assault. *Trauma, Violence, & Abuse, 10*(4), 330–357. http://dx.doi.org/10.1177/1524838009339755

Buechler, S. (2008). Shaming psychoanalytic candidates. *Psychoanalytic Inquiry, 28,* 361–372. http://dx.doi.org/10.1080/07351690801962430

Butler, J. (1995). Melancholy gender—refused identification. *Psychoanalytic Dialogues, 5,* 165–180. http://dx.doi.org/10.1080/10481889509539059

Butler, J. (2000). *Antigone's claim: Kinship between life and death.* New York, NY: Columbia University Press.

Buxbaum, E. (1949). *The role of a second language in the formation of ego and superego.* Albany, NY: Psychoanalytic Quarterly Pr.

Cabral, R. R., & Smith, T. B. (2011). Racial/ethnic matching of clients and therapists in mental health services: A meta-analytic review of preferences, perceptions, and outcomes. *Journal of Counseling Psychology, 58*(4), 537–554. http://dx.doi.org/10.1037/a0025266

Campbell, J. (1974). *The mythic image.* Princeton, NJ: Princeton University Press.

Carbado, D. W., Crenshaw, K. W., Mays, V. M., & Tomlinson, B. (2013). INTERSECTIONALITY: Mapping the Movements of a Theory. *Du Bois Review: Social Science Research on Race, 10,* 303–312. http://dx.doi.org/10.1017/S1742058X13000349

Carignani, P. (2012). I. The body in psychoanalysis. *British Journal of Psychotherapy, 28,* 288–318. http://dx.doi.org/10.1111/j.1752-0118.2012.01299.x

Carretero, M., & Kriger, M. (2011). Historical representations and conflicts about indigenous people as national identities. *Culture & Psychology, 17,* 177–195. http://dx.doi.org/10.1177/1354067X11398311

Casas, J. M., & Corral, C. V. (2000). Multicultural counseling. In A. E. Kasdin (Ed.), *Encyclopedia of psychology* (Vol. 5, pp. 337–339). Washington, DC: American Psychological Association and Oxford University Press. http://dx.doi.org/10.1037/10520-143

Celenza, A. (2007). Analytic love and power: Responsiveness and responsibility. *Psychoanalytic Inquiry, 27,* 287–301. http://dx.doi.org/10.1080/07351690701389478

Celenza, A. (2010). The analyst's need and desire. *Psychoanalytic Dialogues, 20,* 60–69. http://dx.doi.org/10.1080/10481880903558981

Cervantes, J. M. (2006). A new understanding of the macho male image: Exploration of the Mexican American man. In M. Englar-Carlson & M. A. Stevens (Eds.), *In the room with men: A casebook of therapeutic change* (pp. 197–224). Washington, DC: American Psychological Association. http://dx.doi.org/10.1037/11411-010

Chalfin, F. (2014). The role of a visible/visual disability in the clinical dyad: Issues of visibility/invisibility for the client and clinician. *Psychoanalytic Social Work, 21*(1-2), 121–132. http://dx.doi.org/10.1080/15228878.2013.834265

Charles, M. (2004). *Learning from experience: A guidebook for clinicians.* Hillsdale, NJ: Analytic Press.

Charles, M. (2005). Patterns: Basic units of emotional memory. *Psychoanalytic Inquiry, 25,* 484–505. http://dx.doi.org/10.2513/s07351690pi2504_5

Charles, M. (2011). What does a woman want? *Psychoanalysis, Culture & Society,* *16,* 337–353. http://dx.doi.org/10.1057/pcs.2010.20

Charles, M. (2015). *Psychoanalysis and literature: The stories we live.* Lanham, MD: Rowman & Littlefield.

Chiesa, M. (2010). Research and psychoanalysis: Still time to bridge the great divide? *Psychoanalytic Psychology, 27,* 99–114. http://dx.doi.org/10.1037/a0019413

Chodorow, N. (1989). *Feminism and psychoanalytic theory.* New Haven, CT: Yale University Press.

Chodorow, N. (1999). *The power of feelings: Personal meaning in psychoanalysis, gender, and culture.* New Haven, CT: Yale University Press.

Clarkin, J. F., Levy, K. N., Lenzenweger, M. F., & Kernberg, O. F. (2007). Evaluating three treatments for borderline personality disorder: A multiwave study. *The American Journal of Psychiatry, 164,* 922–928. http://dx.doi.org/10.1176/appi.ajp.164.6.922

Clemens, N. A., Plakun, E. M., Lazar, S. G., & Mellman, L. (2014). Obstacles to early career psychiatrists practicing psychotherapy. *Psychodynamic Psychiatry, 42,* 479–495. http://dx.doi.org/10.1521/pdps.2014.42.3.479

Cohen, E. (2007). Enactments and dissociations driven by cultural differences. *The American Journal of Psychoanalysis, 67,* 22–29. http://dx.doi.org/10.1057/palgrave.ajp.3350002

Cohler, B. J., & Galatzer-Levy, R. M. (2013). The historical moment in the analysis of gay men. *Journal of the American Psychoanalytic Association, 61,* 1139–1173. http://dx.doi.org/10.1177/0003065113514607

Collins, P. H. (2000). *Black feminist thought: Knowledge, consciousness, and the politics of empowerment.* New York, NY: Routledge.

Comas-Díaz, L. (2000). An ethnopolitical approach to working with people of color. *American Psychologist, 55,* 1319–1325. http://dx.doi.org/10.1037/0003-066X.55.11.1319

Comas-Díaz, L. (2006). Latino healing: The integration of ethnic psychology into psychotherapy. *Psychotherapy: Theory, Research, Practice, Training, 43,* 436–453. http://dx.doi.org/10.1037/0033-3204.43.4.436

Comas-Díaz, L. (2010, Summer). *Sin nombre:* Female immigrants and the anti-immigration laws. *The Feminist Psychology, 37*(3), 7; 14.

Comas-Díaz, L. (2011). Multicultural approaches to psychotherapy. In J. C. Norcross, G. R. VandenBos, & D. K. Freedheim (Eds.), *History of psychotherapy: Continuity and change* (2nd ed., pp. 243–267). Washington, DC: American Psychological Association. http://dx.doi.org/10.1037/12353-008

Comas-Díaz, L. (2012). *Multicultural care: A clinician's guide to cultural competence.* Washington, DC: American Psychological Association. http://dx.doi.org/10.1037/13491-000

Comas-Díaz, L., & Greene, B. (2013). *Psychological health of women of color: Intersections, challenges, and opportunities.* Westport, CT: Praeger.

Comas-Díaz, L., & Jacobsen, F. M. (1991). Ethnocultural transference and counter-transference in the therapeutic dyad. *American Journal of Orthopsychiatry, 61*, 392–402. http://dx.doi.org/10.1037/h0079267

Comas-Díaz, L., & Jacobsen, F. M. (1995). The therapist of color and the white patient dyad: Contradictions and recognitions. *Cultural Diversity and Mental Health, 1*, 93–106. http://dx.doi.org/10.1037/1099-9809.1.2.93

Comas-Díaz, L., & Jacobsen, F. M. (2001). Ethnocultural allodynia. *Journal of Psychotherapy Practice & Research, 10*, 246–252.

Connolly, A. (2002). To speak in tongues: Language, diversity and psychoanalysis. *The Journal of Analytical Psychology, 47*, 359–382. http://dx.doi.org/10.1111/1465-5922.00325

Constantine, M. G., & Ladany, N. (2001). New visions for defining and assessing multicultural counseling competence. In M. G. Constantine & N. Ladany (Eds.), *Handbook of multicultural counseling* (2nd ed., pp. 482–498). Thousand Oaks, CA: Sage Publications.

Cooper, S. H. (2000). *Objects of hope: Exploring possibility and limit in psychoanalysis.* Hillsdale, NJ: Analytic Press.

Corbett, K. (1996). Homosexual boyhood: Notes on girlboys. *Gender & Psychoanalysis, 1*, 429–461.

Corbett, K. (2002). The mystery of homosexuality. In M. Dimen & V. Goldner (Eds.), *Gender in psychoanalytic space: Between clinic and culture* (pp. 21–39). New York, NY: Other Press.

Corbett, K. (2008). Gender now. *Psychoanalytic Dialogues, 18*, 838–856. http://dx.doi.org/10.1080/10481880802473381

Corbett, K. (2009). Boyhood femininity, gender identity disorder, masculine presuppositions, and the anxiety of regulation. *Psychoanalytic Dialogues, 19*, 353–370. http://dx.doi.org/10.1080/10481880903088484

Cornish, J. A., Gorgens, K. A., Monson, S. P., Olkin, R., Palombi, B. J., & Abels, A. V. (2008). Perspectives on ethical practice with people who have disabilities. *Professional Psychology: Research and Practice, 39*, 488–497. http://dx.doi.org/10.1037/a0013092

Courtois, C. A., & Ford, J. D. (2014). *Treating complex traumatic stress disorders: Scientific foundations and therapeutic models.* New York, NY: Guilford Press.

Crenshaw, K. W. (1989). Demarginalizing the intersection of race and sex: A Black feminist critique of antidiscrimination doctrine, feminist theory and antiracist politics. *University of Chicago Legal Forum, 1989*, 139–167.

Cross, W. E. (1978). The Thomas and Cross models of psychological nigrescence: A review. *Journal of Black Psychology, 5*, 13–31. http://dx.doi.org/10.1177/009579847800500102

Croteau, J. M. (2008). Reflections on understanding and ameliorating internalized heterosexism. *The Counseling Psychologist, 36*, 645–653. http://dx.doi.org/10.1177/0011000008319285

Crown, N. J. (2008). Slips of the tongue, sleights of the hand: Observation on psychotherapy in sign language. *Psychoanalytic Psychology, 25,* 356–362. http://dx.doi.org/10.1037/0736-9735.25.2.356

Cunsolo Willox, A., Harper, S. L., & Edge, V. L. (2013). My word. Storytelling in a digital age: Digital storytelling as an emerging narrative method for preserving and promoting indigenous oral wisdom. *Qualitative Research, 13,* 127–147. http://dx.doi.org/10.1177/1468794112446105

Cushman, P. (1995). *Constructing the self, constructing America: A cultural history of psychotherapy.* New York: Addison-Wesley Publishing Company, Inc.

Cushman, P. (2000). White guilt, political activity, and the analyst: Commentary on paper by Neil Altman. *Psychoanalytic Dialogues, 10,* 607–618. http://dx.doi.org/10.1080/10481881009348570

Dalal, F. (2006). Racism: Processes of detachment, dehumanization, and hatred. *The Psychoanalytic Quarterly, 75,* 131–161. http://dx.doi.org/10.1002/j.2167-4086.2006.tb00035.x

Dalal, F. N. (1993). "Race" and racism: An attempt to organize difference. *Group Analysis, 26,* 277–290. http://dx.doi.org/10.1177/0533316493263008

Daniel, J. H. (2000). The courage to hear: African American women's memories of racial trauma. In L. C. Jackson & B. Greene (Eds.), *Psychotherapy with African American women: Innovations in psychodynamic perspectives and practice* (pp. 126–144). New York, NY: Guilford Press.

Danto, E. A. (2005). *Freud's free clinics: Psychoanalysis and social justice, 1918–1938.* New York, NY: Columbia University Press.

Darwin, C. (1859). *The origin of species by means of natural selection.* London, United Kingdom: John Murray.

Darwin, J. L., & Reich, K. I. (2006). Reaching out to the families of those who serve: The SOFAR project. *Professional Psychology: Research and Practice, 37,* 481–484. http://dx.doi.org/10.1037/0735-7028.37.5.481

Davids, M. F. (2009). The impact of Islamophobia. *Psychoanalysis and History, 11,* 175–191. http://dx.doi.org/10.3366/E1460823509000397

Davies, J. E. (2011). Cultural dimensions of intersubjectivity: Negotiating "sameness" and "otherness" in the analytic relationship. *Psychoanalytic Psychology, 28,* 549–559. http://dx.doi.org/10.1037/a0022393

Davies, J. M. (1998). Multiple perspectives on multiplicity. *Psychoanalytic Dialogues, 8,* 195–206. http://dx.doi.org/10.1080/10481889809539241

Davies, J. M. (2001). Erotic overstimulation and the co-construction of sexual meanings in transference-countertransference experience. *The Psychoanalytic Quarterly, 70,* 757–788. http://dx.doi.org/10.1002/j.2167-4086.2001.tb00620.x

Davies, J. M. (2004). Whose bad objects are we anyway? Repetition and our elusive love affair with evil. *Psychoanalytic Dialogues, 14,* 711–732.

Davies, J. M., & Frawley, M. G. (1994). *Treating the adult survivor of childhood sexual abuse: A psychoanalytic perspective*. New York, NY: Basic Books.

Davis, J. T. (2002). Countertransference temptation and the use of self of self-disclosure by psychotherapists in training: A discussion for beginning psychotherapists and their supervisors. *Psychoanalytic Psychology, 19*, 435–454.

Davis, T. (2010). Third spaces or heterotopias? Recreating and negotiating migrant identity using online spaces. *Sociology, 44*, 661–677.

Debiak, D. (2007). Attending to diversity in group psychotherapy: An ethical imperative. *International Journal of Group Psychotherapy, 57*, 1–12. http://dx.doi.org/10.1521/ijgp.2007.57.1.1

Demos, J. (1997). Oedipus and America: Historical perspectives on the reception of psychoanalysis in the United States. In J. Pfister & N. Schnog (Eds.), *Inventing the psychological: Toward a cultural history of emotional life in America* (pp. 63–78). New Haven, CT: Yale University Press.

Derrick, J. M. (2005). When turtle met rabbit: Native family systems. In M. Rastogi & E. Wieling (Eds.), *Voices of color: First-person accounts of ethnic minority therapists* (pp. 43–64). Thousand Oaks, CA: Sage Publications. http://dx.doi.org/10.4135/9781452231662.n4

Deutsch, H. (1965). *Neuroses and character types: Clinical psychoanalytical studies*. Madison, CT: International Universities Press.

Dimaggio, G., & Lysaker, P. H. (2014). Supporters of a single orientation may do less for science and the health of patients than integrationists: A reply to Govrin. *Journal of Psychotherapy Integration, 24*(2), 91–94. http://dx.doi.org/10.1037/a0036996

Dimen, M. (1991). Deconstructing difference: Gender, splitting, and transitional space. *Psychoanalytic Dialogues, 1*, 335–352.

Dimen, M. (2002). Deconstructing difference: Gender, splitting, and transitional space. In M. Dimen & V. Goldner (Eds.), *Gender in psychoanalytic space: Between clinic and culture* (pp. 41–61). New York, NY: Other Press.

Dimen, M. (2006). Money, love, and hate: Contradiction and paradox in psychoanalysis. In L. Layton, N. C. Hollander, & S. Gutwill (Eds.), *Psychoanalysis, class and politics: Encounters in the clinical setting* (pp. 29–50). London, United Kingdom: Routledge.

Dimen, M. (2011). *With culture in mind: Psychoanalytic stories*. New York, NY: Routledge.

Dimen, M., & Goldner, V. (2002). *Gender in psychoanalytic space: Between clinic and culture*. New York, NY: Other Press.

Diversi, M., & Moreira, C. (2012). Decolonizing constructions of childhood and history: Interrupting narratives of avoidance to children's questions about social injustice. *International Journal of Qualitative Studies in Education, 25*, 189–203. http://dx.doi.org/10.1080/09518398.2011.649703

Doi, T. (1989). The concept of amae and its psychoanalytic implications. *International Review of Psycho-Analysis, 16*, 349–354.

Dovidio, J. F. (2009). Psychology. Racial bias, unspoken but heard. *Science, 326*(5960), 1641–1642. http://dx.doi.org/10.1126/science.1184231

Dovidio, J. F., Gluszek, A., John, M., Ditlmann, R., & Lagunes, P. (2010). Understanding bias toward Latinos: Discrimination, dimensions of difference, and experience of exclusion. *Journal of Social Issues, 66,* 59–78. http://dx.doi.org/10.1111/j.1540-4560.2009.01633.x

Drescher, J. (2007). From bisexuality to intersexuality. *Contemporary Psychoanalysis, 43,* 204–228. http://dx.doi.org/10.1080/00107530.2007.10745905

Drescher, J. (2008). A history of homosexuality and organized psychoanalysis. *The Journal of the American Academy of Psychoanalysis & Dynamic Psychiatry, 36,* 443–460. http://dx.doi.org/10.1521/jaap.2008.36.3.443

Drescher, J. (2009). When politics distort science: What mental health professionals can do. *Journal of Gay & Lesbian Mental Health, 13,* 213–226. http://dx.doi.org/10.1080/19359700902964222

Duggan, S. B. (2013). Becoming "I": "Orientation" interactions with online blogs. *Narrative Inquiry, 23,* 214–226. http://dx.doi.org/10.1075/ni.23.1.11dug

Duncan, D. T., & Hatzenbuchler, M. L. (2014). Lesbian, gay, bisexual, and transgender hate crimes and suicidality among a population-based sample of sexual-minority adolescents in Boston. *American Journal of Public Health, 104,* 272–278. http://dx.doi.org/10.2105/AJPH.2013.301424

Dunn, D. S., & Andrews, E. E. (2015). Person-first and identity-first language: Developing psychologists' cultural competence using disability language. *American Psychologist, 70,* 255–264. http://dx.doi.org/10.1037/a0038636

Eagle, M. N. (2011). *From classical to contemporary psychoanalysis: A critique and integration.* New York, NY: Routledge.

Ecklund, K. (2012). Intersectionality of identity in children: A case study. *Professional Psychology: Research and Practice, 43,* 256–264. http://dx.doi.org/10.1037/a0028654

Ehrenberg, D. B. (2010). Working at the "intimate edge." *Contemporary Psychoanalysis, 46,* 120–141. http://dx.doi.org/10.1080/00107530.2010.10746043

Ehrensaft, D. (2007). Raising girlyboys: A parent's perspective. *Studies in Gender and Sexuality, 8,* 269–302. http://dx.doi.org/10.1080/15240650701226581

Ehrensaft, D. (2014). Found in transition: Our littlest transgender people. *Contemporary Psychoanalysis, 50,* 571–592. http://dx.doi.org/10.1080/00107530.2014.942591

Eisold, K. (2004). Psychoanalytic training: The "faculty system." *Psychoanalytic Inquiry, 24,* 51–70. http://dx.doi.org/10.1080/07351692409349070

Elise, D. (2000). Woman and desire: Why women may *not* want to want. *Studies in Gender and Sexuality, 1,* 125–145. http://dx.doi.org/10.1080/15240650109349151

Elisha, P. (2010). *The conscious body: A psychoanalytic exploration of the body in therapy*. Washington, DC: American Psychological Association.

Eng, D. L., & Han, S. (2000). A dialogue on racial melancholia. *Psychoanalytic Dialogues, 10*, 667–700. http://dx.doi.org/10.1080/10481881009348576

Eng, D. L., & Han, S. (2006). Desegregating love: Transnational adoption, radical reparation, and racial transitional object. *Studies in Gender and Sexuality, 7*, 141–172.

Epstein, M. (2001). *Going on being: Buddhism and the way of change: A positive psychology for the West*. New York, NY: Broadway Books.

Erikson, E. H. (1950). *Childhood and society*. New York, NY: W. W. Norton.

Espín, O. M. (2008). My "friendship" with women saints as a source of spirituality. In C. A. Rayburn & L. Comas-Díaz (Eds.), *WomanSoul: The inner life of women's spirituality* (pp. 71–84). Westport, CT: Praeger.

Faimberg, H. (2005). Après-coup. *The International Journal of Psychoanalysis, 86*, 1–13. http://dx.doi.org/10.1516/MDY4-GMDH-C1BW-MW8E

Falicov, C. J. (2010). Changing constructions of machismo for Latino men in therapy: "The devil never sleeps." *Family Process, 49*, 309–329. http://dx.doi.org/10.1111/j.1545-5300.2010.01325.x

Fanon, F. (1952). *Black skin, White masks*. New York, NY: Grove Press.

Farrell, D. (2012). Understanding the psychodynamics of chronic homelessness from a self-psychological perspective. *Clinical Social Work Journal, 40*, 337–347.

Ferenczi, S. (1932/1988). *The clinical diary of Sándor Ferenczi*. J. Dupont (Ed.). Cambridge, MA: Harvard University Press.

Ferenczi, S. (1949). Psycho-analysis and education. *The International Journal of Psychoanalysis, 30*, 220–224.

Ferenczi, S., & Rank, O. (1924). *The development of psychoanalysis*. New York, NY: Nervous and Mental Disease Publishing.

Ferrari, A. (2001). Individuo-universo dos mitos. *Revista Brasileira de Psicanálise, 35*, 305–316.

Fine, M. (2007). Expanding the methodological imagination. *The Counseling Psychologist, 35*, 459–473. http://dx.doi.org/10.1177/0011000006296172

Fine, M. (2010). The breast and the state: An analysis of good and bad nipples by gender, race, and class. *Studies in Gender and Sexuality, 11*, 24–32. http://dx.doi.org/10.1080/15240650903445849

Fine, M., Freudenberg, N., Payne, Y., Perkins, T., Smith, K., & Wanzer, K. (2003). "Anything can happen with police around": Urban youth evaluate strategies of surveillance in public places. *Journal of Social Issues, 59*, 141–158. http://dx.doi.org/10.1111/1540-4560.t01-1-00009

Finkel, E. J., Eastwick, P. W., Karney, B. R., Reis, H. T., & Sprecher, S. (2012). Online dating: A critical analysis from the perspective of psychological science. *Psychological Science in the Public Interest*, *13*, 3–66. http://dx.doi.org/10.1177/1529100612436522

Flores, J. (2007). Social conflict and subjectivity: The analyst's involvement. *International Forum of Psychoanalysis*, *16*, 254–258. http://dx.doi.org/10.1080/08037060701745733

Fonagy, P. (2001). *Attachment theory and psychoanalysis*. New York, NY: Other Press.

Fonagy, P., & Bateman, A. (2008). The development of borderline personality disorder—a mentalizing model. *Journal of Personality Disorders*, *22*, 4–21. http://dx.doi.org/10.1521/pedi.2008.22.1.4

Foster, R. P. (1996). What is a multicultural perspective for psychoanalysis? In R. P. Foster, M. Moskowitz, & R. A. Javier (Eds.), *Reaching across boundaries of culture and class: Widening the scope of psychotherapy* (pp. 3–20). Northvale, NJ: Jason Aronson.

Foster, R. P. (2005). The new faces of childhood perimigration trauma in the United States. *Journal of Infant, Child, and Adolescent Psychotherapy: JICAP*, *4*, 21–41. http://dx.doi.org/10.1080/15289160409348486

Fowers, B. J., & Richardson, F. C. (1996). Why is multiculturalism good? *American Psychologist*, *51*, 609–621. http://dx.doi.org/10.1037/0003-066X.51.6.609

Fox, D., Prilleltensky, I., & Austin, S. (2009). *Critical psychology: An introduction*. Los Angeles, CA: Sage Publications.

Fraley, S. S., Mona, L. R., & Theodore, P. S. (2007). The sexual lives of lesbian, gay, and bisexual people with disabilities: Psychological perspectives. *Sexuality Research & Social Policy: A Journal of the NSRC*, *4*, 15–26. http://dx.doi.org/10.1525/srsp.2007.4.1.15

Frankel, S. A. (2006). The clinical use of therapeutic disjunctions. *Psychoanalytic Psychology*, *23*, 56–71. http://dx.doi.org/10.1037/0736-9735.23.1.56

Franklin, A. J. (2004). *From brotherhood to manhood: How Black men rescue their relationships and dreams from the invisibility syndrome*. New York, NY: Wiley.

Freeman, M. (2002). Charting the narrative unconscious: Cultural memory and the challenge of autobiography. *Narrative Inquiry*, *12*, 193–211.

Freire, P. (1970). *Pedagogy of the oppressed*. New York, NY: Continuum International Publishing Group.

Freud, A. (1967). *Psycho-analysis for teachers and parents*. Boston, MA: Beacon Press.

Freud, S. (1905). Three essays on the theory of sexuality. In J. Strachey (Ed. & Trans.), *The standard edition of the complete psychological works of Sigmund Freud* (Vol. 7, pp. 123–246). London, United Kingdom: Hogarth Press.

Freud, S. (1910). The future prospects of psycho-analytic therapy. In J. Strachey (Ed. & Trans.), *The standard edition of the complete psychological works of Sigmund Freud* (Vol. 11, pp. 139–152). London, United Kingdom: Hogarth Press.

Freud, S. (1912). Recommendations to physicians practicing psycho-analysis. In P. Gay (Ed.), *The Freud reader* (pp. 356–363). New York, NY: W.W. Norton & Company.

Freud, S. (1915). The unconscious. In J. Strachey (Ed. & Trans.), *The standard edition of the complete psychological works of Sigmund Freud* (Vol. 14, pp. 159–225). London, United Kingdom: Hogarth Press.

Freud, S. (1917). Mourning and melancholia. In P. Gay (Ed.), *The Freud reader* (pp. 584–589). New York, NY: W.W. Norton & Company.

Freud, S. (1927). The future of an illusion. In P. Gay (Ed.), *The Freud reader* (pp. 685–722). New York, NY: W.W. Norton & Company.

Freud, S. (1930). Civilization and its discontents. In P. Gay (Ed.), *The Freud reader* (pp. 722–772). New York, NY: W.W. Norton & Company.

Freud, S. (1938). Interpretation of dreams. In P. Gay (Ed.), *The Freud reader* (pp. 129–142). New York, NY: W.W. Norton & Company.

Frie, R. (2013). Culture and language: Bilingualism in the German-Jewish experience and across contexts. *Clinical Social Work Journal, 41,* 11–19.

Fromm, E. (1956). *The art of loving.* New York, NY: Harper & Row.

Fromm, E., & Suzuki, D. T. (1960). *Zen and psychoanalysis.* New York, NY: Harper & Row.

Frosh, S. (2011). The relational ethics of conflict and identity. *Psychoanalysis, Culture & Society, 16,* 225–243. http://dx.doi.org/10.1057/pcs.2010.31

Gabbard, G., Miller, L., & Martinez, M. (2008). A neurobiological perspective on mentalizing and internal object relations in traumatized borderline patients. In E. L. Jurist, A. Slade, & S. Bergner (Eds.), *Mind to mind: Infant research, neuroscience and psychoanalysis* (pp. 202–224). New York, NY: Other Press.

Galdi, G. (2007). The analytic encounter, a scene of clashing cultures. *The American Journal of Psychoanalysis, 67,* 4–21. http://dx.doi.org/10.1057/palgrave.ajp.3350001

Gallardo, M. E. (2014). *Developing cultural humility. Embracing race, privilege and power.* Thousand Oaks, CA: Sage Publications. http://dx.doi.org/10.4135/9781483388076

Gallardo, M. E., Yeh, C. J., Trimble, J. E., & Parham, T. A. (2012). *Culturally adaptive counseling skills: Demonstrations of evidence-based practices.* Thousand Oaks, CA: Sage Publications. http://dx.doi.org/10.4135/9781483349329

García Coll, C., & Marks, A. K. (Eds.). (2012). *The immigrant paradox in children and adolescents: Is becoming American a developmental risk?* Washington, DC: American Psychological Association. http://dx.doi.org/10.1037/13094-000

Gaztambide, D. J. (2012). Addressing cultural impasses with rupture resolution strategies: A proposal and recommendations. *Professional Psychology: Research and Practice, 43,* 183–189. http://dx.doi.org/10.1037/a0026911

Gaztambide, D. J. (2014). I'm not Black, I'm not White, what am I? The illusion of the color line. *Psychoanalysis, Culture & Society, 19*, 89–97. http://dx.doi.org/10.1057/pcs.2013.22

Gediman, H. K. (2006). Facilitating analysis with implicit and explicit self-disclosures. *Psychoanalytic Dialogues, 16*, 241–262.

Ghent, E. (1995). Interaction in the psychoanalytic situation. *Psychoanalytic Dialogues, 5*(3), 479–491. http://dx.doi.org/10.1080/10481889509539087

Gilhooley, D. (2011). Mistakes. *Psychoanalytic Psychology, 28*, 311–333. http://dx.doi.org/10.1037/a0023080

Gill, M. M. (1983). The interpersonal paradigm and the degree of the therapist's involvement. *Contemporary Psychoanalysis, 19*, 200–237. http://dx.doi.org/10.1080/00107530.1983.10746605

Gill, M. M., & Hoffman, I. Z. (1982). A method for studying the analysis of aspects of the patient's experience of the relationship in psychoanalysis and psychotherapy. *Journal of the American Psychoanalytic Association, 30*, 137–167. http://dx.doi.org/10.1177/000306518203000106

Goldner, V. (1991). Toward a critical relational theory of gender. *Psychoanalytic Dialogues, 1*, 249–272. http://dx.doi.org/10.1080/10481889109538898

Goldner, V. (2011). Trans: Gender in free fall. *Psychoanalytic Dialogues, 21*(2), 159–171.

Gone, J. P., & Trimble, J. E. (2012). American Indian and Alaska Native mental health: Diverse perspectives on enduring disparities. *Annual Review of Clinical Psychology, 8*, 131–160. http://dx.doi.org/10.1146/annurev-clinpsy-032511-143127

Goodley, D. (2011). *Disability studies: An interdisciplinary introduction.* Los Angeles, CA: Sage Publications.

Goodley, D., & Runswick-Cole, K. (2011). The violence of disablism. *Sociology of Health & Illness, 33*, 602–617. http://dx.doi.org/10.1111/j.1467-9566.2010.01302.x

Goodman, L. A., Pugach, M., Skolnik, A., & Smith, L. (2013). Poverty and mental health practice: Within and beyond the 50-minute hour. *Journal of Clinical Psychology, 69*, 182–190. http://dx.doi.org/10.1002/jclp.21957

Goren, E., & Alpert, J. (2013). Conclusion to special issue on psychoanalysis, trauma and community: Psychoanalysts out of the office. *Psychoanalysis, Culture & Society, 18*, 217–221. http://dx.doi.org/10.1057/pcs.2013.7

Gourguechon, P. (2013). Typology of applied psychoanalysis. *International Journal of Applied Psychoanalytic Studies, 10*, 192–198.

Greenberg, J. R., & Mitchell, S. A. (1983). *Object relations in psychoanalytic theory.* Cambridge, MA: Harvard University Press.

Greene, B. (2007). How difference makes a difference. In J. C. Muran (Ed.), *Dialogues on difference: Studies of diversity in the therapeutic relationship* (pp. 47–63). Washington, DC: American Psychological Association. http://dx.doi.org/10.1037/11500-005

Greene, B. (2010). 2009 Carolyn Wood Sherif Award Address: Riding Trojan horses from symbolism to structural change: In feminist psychology, context matters. *Psychology of Women Quarterly, 34*, 443–457. http://dx.doi.org/10.1111/j.1471-6402.2010.01594.x

Greene, B. (2013). The use and abuse of religious beliefs in dividing and conquering between socially marginalized groups: The same-sex marriage debate. *Psychology of Sexual Orientation and Gender Diversity, 1*(S), 35–44. http://dx.doi.org/10.1037/2329-0382.1.S.35

Greene, B., & Brodbar, D. (2010). A minyan of women: Family dynamics, Jewish identity, and psychotherapy practice. *Women & Therapy, 33*, 155–157. http://dx.doi.org/10.1080/02703141003766282

Greenson, R. R. (1950). The mother tongue and the mother. *The International Journal of Psychoanalysis, 31*, 18–23.

Grinberg, L., & Grinberg, R. (1989). *Psychoanalytic perspectives on migration and exile*. New Haven, CT: Yale University Press.

Grossmark, R. (2009). Two men talking: The emergence of multiple masculinities in psychoanalytic treatment. In B. Reis & R. Grossmark (Eds.), *Heterosexual masculinities: Contemporary perspectives from psychoanalytic gender theory* (pp. 73–87). New York, NY: Taylor & Francis.

Gump, J. P. (2010). Reality matters: The shadow of trauma on African American subjectivity. *Psychoanalytic Psychology, 27*, 42–54. http://dx.doi.org/10.1037/a0018639

Guntrip, H. (1956). Recent developments in psychoanalytical theory. *British Journal of Medical Psychology, 29*, 82–99. http://dx.doi.org/10.1111/j.2044-8341.1956.tb00906.x

Guss, J. R. (2010). The danger of desire: Anal sex and the homo/masculine subject. *Studies in Gender and Sexuality, 11*, 124–140. http://dx.doi.org/10.1080/15240657.2010.491001

Gutwill, S., Gitter, A., & Rubin, L. (2011). The Women's Therapy Centre Institute: The personal is political. *Women & Therapy, 34*, 143–158. http://dx.doi.org/10.1080/02703149.2011.532703

Haldeman, D. C. (2010). Reflections of a gay male psychotherapist. *Psychotherapy (Chic), 47*, 177–185. http://dx.doi.org/10.1037/a0019757

Hale, N. G., Jr. (1995). *The rise and crisis of psychoanalysis in the United States: Freud and the Americans 1917–1985*. New York, NY: Oxford University Press.

Hamer, F. M. (2006). Racism as a transference state: Episodes of racial hostility in the psychoanalytic context. *The Psychoanalytic Quarterly, 75*, 197–214. http://dx.doi.org/10.1002/j.2167-4086.2006.tb00037.x

Hansen, J. T. (2010). Counseling and psychoanalysis: Advancing the value of diversity. *Journal of Multicultural Counseling and Development, 38*, 16–26. http://dx.doi.org/10.1002/j.2161-1912.2010.tb00110.x

Harlem, A. (2009). Thinking through others: Cultural psychology and the psychoanalytic treatment of immigrants. *Psychoanalysis, Culture & Society, 14*, 273–288. http://dx.doi.org/10.1057/pcs.2009.12

Harlem, A. (2010). Exile as a dissociative state: When a self is "lost in transit." *Psychoanalytic Psychology, 27*, 460–474. http://dx.doi.org/10.1037/a0020755

Harney, P. (2007). Resilience processes in context: Contributions and implications of Bronfenbrenner's person-process-context model. *Journal of Aggression, Maltreatment & Trauma, 14*(3), 73–87. http://dx.doi.org/10.1300/J146v14n03_05

Harrell, S. P. (2014). Compassionate confrontation and empathic exploration: The integration of race-related narratives in clinical supervision. In C. A. Falender, E. P. Shafranske, & C. J. Falicov (Eds.), *Multiculturalism and diversity in clinical supervision: A competency-based approach* (pp. 83–110). Washington, DC: American Psychological Association. http://dx.doi.org/10.1037/14370-004

Harris, A. (2005). *Gender as soft assembly*. Hillsdale, NJ: Analytic Press.

Harris, A. (2012). The house of difference, or White silence. *Studies in Gender and Sexuality, 13*, 197–216. http://dx.doi.org/10.1080/15240657.2012.707575

Harris, A. E. (2002). Gender and contradiction. In M. Dimen (Ed.), *Gender in psychoanalytic space: Between clinic and culture* (pp. 91–115). New York, NY: Other Press.

Harris, A. E. (2011). The relational tradition: Landscape and canon. *Journal of the American Psychoanalytic Association, 59*, 701–736. http://dx.doi.org/10.1177/0003065111416655

Harris, R. S., Jr. (2009). Racial microaggression? How do you know?—Revisited. *American Psychologist, 64*, 220–221. http://dx.doi.org/10.1037/a0014749

Hartnack, C. (1987). British psychoanalysts in colonial India. In M. G. Ash & W. R. Woodward (Eds.), *Psychology in twentieth century thought and society* (pp. 233–251). New York, NY: Cambridge University Press.

Harvey, M. R. (2007). Towards an ecological understanding of resilience in trauma survivors. *Journal of Aggression, Maltreatment & Trauma, 14*, 9–32. http://dx.doi.org/10.1300/J146v14n01_02

Harvey, M. R., & Tummala-Narra, P. (Eds.). (2007). *Sources and expressions of resiliency in trauma survivors: Ecological theory, multicultural practice*. Binghamton, NY: The Haworth Press.

Havens, L. L. (1986). *Making contact uses of language in psychotherapy*. Cambridge, MA: Harvard University Press.

Hays, P. A. (2007). *Addressing cultural complexities in practice: A framework for clinicians and counselors* (2nd ed.). Washington, DC: American Psychological Association.

Hays, P. A. (2009). Integrating evidence-based practice, cognitive–behavior therapy, and multicultural therapy: Ten steps for culturally competent practice. *Professional Psychology: Research and Practice, 40*, 354–360. http://dx.doi.org/10.1037/a0016250

Hays, P. A. (2016). *Addressing cultural complexities in practice: Assessment, diagnosis, and therapy* (3rd ed.). Washington, DC: American Psychological Association.

Helms, J. E. (1990). *Black and white racial identity: Theory, research, and practice.* Westport, CT: Greenwood Press.

Helms, J. E., & Cook, D. A. (1999). *Using race and culture in counseling and psychotherapy: Theory and process.* Boston, MA: Allyn and Bacon.

Helms, J. E., Nicolas, G., & Green, C. E. (2010). Racism and ethnoviolence as trauma: Enhancing professional training. *Traumatology, 16*(4), 53–62. http://dx.doi.org/10.1177/1534765610389595

Herman, J. L. (1992). *Trauma and recovery.* New York, NY: Basic Books.

Hernández de Tubert, R. H. (2006). Social trauma: The pathogenic effects of untoward social conditions. *International Forum of Psychoanalysis, 15,* 151–156. http://dx.doi.org/10.1080/08037060500526037

Hinshelwood, R. D. (2007). Intolerance and the intolerable: The case of racism. *Psychoanalysis, Culture & Society, 12,* 1–20. http://dx.doi.org/10.1057/palgrave.pcs.2100103

Hird, J. S., Tao, K. W., & Gloria, A. M. (2004). Examining supervisors' multicultural competence in racially similar and different supervision dyads. *The Clinical Supervisor, 23,* 107–122. http://dx.doi.org/10.1300/J001v23n02_07

Hirsch, I. (2008). *Coasting in the countertransference: Conflicts of self interest between analyst and patient.* Hillsdale, NJ: Analytic Press.

Hoffman, I. (1998). *Ritual and spontaneity in the psychoanalytic process: A dialectical constructivist point of view.* Hillsdale, NJ: Analytic Press.

Hoffman, I. Z. (2009). Therapeutic passion in the countertransference. *Psychoanalytic Dialogues, 19,* 617–637. http://dx.doi.org/10.1080/10481880903340141

Hollander, N. C. (2006). Psychoanalysis and the problem of the bystander in times of terror. In L. Layton, N. C. Hollander, & S. Gutwill (Eds.), *Psychoanalysis, class and politics: Encounters in the clinical setting* (pp. 154–165). London, United Kingdom: Routledge.

Hollander, N. C. (2010). *Uprooted minds: Surviving the politics of terror in the Americas.* New York, NY: Routledge.

Hollander, N. C. (2013). Social trauma, politics and psychoanalysis: A personal narrative. *Psychoanalysis, Culture & Society, 18,* 167–183. http://dx.doi.org/10.1057/pcs.2013.8

Hollander, N. C., & Gutwill, S. (2006). Despair and hope in a culture of denial. In L. Layton, N. C. Hollander, & S. Gutwill (Eds.), *Psychoanalysis, class and politics: Encounters in the clinical setting* (pp. 81–91). London, United Kingdom: Routledge.

Holmes, D. E. (1992). Race and transference in psychoanalysis and psychotherapy. *The International Journal of Psychoanalysis, 73,* 1–11.

Holmes, D. E. (2001). Race and countertransference: Two "blind spots" in psycho-analytic perception. In D. E. Scharff (Ed.), *Freud at the Millennium* (pp. 251–268). New York, NY: Other Press.

Holmes, D. E. (2006). The wrecking effects of race and social class on self and success. *The Psychoanalytic Quarterly, 75,* 215–235. http://dx.doi.org/10.1002/j.2167-4086.2006.tb00038.x

Horney, K. (1937). *The neurotic personality of our time.* New York, NY: W.W. Norton & Company.

Huang, F. Y., & Akhtar, S. (2005). Immigrant sex: The transport of affection and sensuality across cultures. *The American Journal of Psychoanalysis, 65,* 179–188. http://dx.doi.org/10.1007/s11231-005-3625-1

Hurley, E. J., & Gerstein, L. H. (2013). The multiculturally and internationally competent mental health professional. In R. L. Lowman (Ed.), *Internationalizing multiculturalism: Expanding professional competencies in a globalized world* (pp. 227–254). Washington, DC: American Psychological Association. http://dx.doi.org/10.1037/14044-009

Inman, A. G., & DeBoer Kreider, E. (2013). Multicultural competence: Psychotherapy practice and supervision. *Psychotherapy (Chic), 50,* 346–350. http://dx.doi.org/10.1037/a0032029

Ipp, H. (2010). Nell—A bridge to the amputated self: The impact of immigration on continuities and discontinuities of self. *International Journal of Psychoanalytic Self Psychology, 5,* 373–386. http://dx.doi.org/10.1080/15551024.2010.508197

Isay, R. A. (1988). Homosexuality in heterosexual and homosexual men. *Psychiatric Annals, 18,* 43–46. http://dx.doi.org/10.3928/0048-5713-19880101-13

Isay, R. A. (1991). The homosexual analyst. Clinical considerations. *The Psychoanalytic Study of the Child, 46,* 199–216.

Jacobson, E. (1964). *The self and the object world.* New York, NY: International Universities Press.

Javier, R. A. (1995). Vicissitudes of autobiographical memories in a bilingual analysis. *Psychoanalytic Psychology, 12,* 429–438.

Javier, R. A. (1996). In search of repressed memories in bilingual individuals. In R. P. Foster, M. Moskowitz, & R. A. Javier (Eds.), *Reaching across boundaries of culture and class: Widening the scope of psychotherapy* (pp. 225–241). Northvale, NJ: Jason Aronson.

Javier, R. A., & Herron, W. G. (2002). Psychoanalysis and the disenfranchised: Countertransference issues. *Psychoanalytic Psychology, 19,* 149–166. http://dx.doi.org/10.1037/0736-9735.19.1.149

Jefferson, K., B. Neilands, T., & Sevelius, J. (2013). Transgender women of color: Discrimination and depression symptoms. *Ethnicity and Inequalities in Health and Social Care, 6*(4), 121–136. http://dx.doi.org/10.1108/EIHSC-08-2013-0013

Jin, H. (2007). *A free life.* New York, NY: Pantheon Press.

Jones, C., & Shorter-Gooden, K. (2003). *Shifting: The double lives of Black women in America*. New York, NY: HarperCollins.

Jung, C. G. (1938). *Psychology and religion*. New Haven, CT: Yale University Press.

Jurist, E. L. (2013). Commentary on Norcross and Karpiak's "Clinical psychologists in the 2010s: 50 years of the APA Division of clinical psychology." *Clinical Psychology: Science and Practice, 20*, 221–223. http://dx.doi.org/10.1111/cpsp.12036

Jurist, E. L. (2014). Whatever happened to the superego? Loewald and the future of psychoanalysis. *Psychoanalytic Psychology, 31*, 489–501. http://dx.doi.org/10.1037/a0038060

Kaftal, E. (1991). On intimacy between men. *Psychoanalytic Dialogues, 1*, 305–328. http://dx.doi.org/10.1080/10481889109538902

Kakar, S. (1995). Clinical work and cultural imagination. *The Psychoanalytic Quarterly, 64*, 265–281.

Kantrowitz, J. L. (2009). Privacy and disclosure in psychoanalysis. *Journal of the American Psychoanalytic Association, 57*, 787–806. http://dx.doi.org/10.1177/0003065109338599

Kardiner, A. (1941). *The traumatic neuroses of war*. Washington, DC: US National Research Council. http://dx.doi.org/10.1037/10581-000

Karon, B. P. (2002). Analyzability or the ability to analyze? *Contemporary Psychoanalysis, 38*, 121–140. http://dx.doi.org/10.1080/00107530.2002.10745809

Kassoff, B. (2004). The queering of relational psychoanalysis. *Journal of Lesbian Studies, 8*, 159–176. http://dx.doi.org/10.1300/J155v08n01_10

Kernberg, O. F. (1996) The analyst's authority in the psychoanalytic situation. *Psychoanalytic Quarterly, 65*, 137–157.

King, M. (2011). The queer relationship between psychoanalysts and their gay and lesbian patients. *Psychoanalytic Psychotherapy, 25*, 308–318. http://dx.doi.org/10.1080/02668734.2011.627147

King, R. A., & Shelley, C. A. (2008). Community feeling and social interest: Adlerian parallels, synergy and differences with the field of community psychology. *Journal of Community & Applied Social Psychology, 18*, 96–107. http://dx.doi.org/10.1002/casp.962

Kirmayer, L. J. (2012). Rethinking cultural competence. *Transcultural Psychiatry, 49*, 149–164. http://dx.doi.org/10.1177/1363461512444673

Kleinman, A. (1995). *Writing at the margin: Discourse between anthropology and medicine*. Berkeley, CA: University of California Press.

Kleinman, A., & Good, B. (1985). *Culture and depression: Studies in the anthropology and cross-cultural psychiatry of affect and disorder*. Berkeley, CA: University of California Press.

Knafo, D. (2012). Dancing with the unconscious: The art of psychoanalysis. *Psychoanalytic Inquiry, 32*, 275–291. http://dx.doi.org/10.1080/07351690.2011.609081

Knoblauch, S. H. (2005). Body rhythms and the unconscious: Toward an expanding of clinical attention. *Psychoanalytic Dialogues, 15*, 807–827. http://dx.doi.org/10.2513/s10481885pd1506_2

Kogan, I. (2002). "Enactment" in the lives and treatment of Holocaust survivors' offspring. *The Psychoanalytic Quarterly, 71*, 251–272. http://dx.doi.org/10.1002/j.2167-4086.2002.tb00013.x

Kogan, I. (2010). Migration and identity: Different perspectives. *The International Journal of Psychoanalysis, 91*, 1206–1208. http://dx.doi.org/10.1111/j.1745-8315.2010.00329.x

Kohut, H. (1971). *The analysis of the self.* Chicago, IL: Chicago University Press.

Kohut, H. (1984). Introspection, empathy, and semicircle of mental health. *Emotions & Behavior Monographs, 3*, 347–375.

Kosawa, H. (2009). Two kinds of guilt feelings: The Ajase complex. In S. Akhtar (Ed.), *Freud and the Far East: Psychoanalytic perspectives on the people and culture of China, Japan, and Korea* (pp. 61–70). Lanham, MD: Jason Aronson.

Kraepelin, E. (1904). Vergleichende psychiatrie [Comparative psychiatry]. *Zentralblatt fur Nervenherlikande und Psychiatrie, 15*, 433–437.

Krapf, E. E. (1955). The choice of language in polyglot psychoanalysis. *The Psychoanalytic Quarterly, 24*, 343–357.

Kristeva, J., & Moi, T. (1986). *The Kristeva reader.* New York, NY: Columbia University Press.

Lacan, J. (1981). *The four fundamental concepts of psycho-analysis.* J. Miller (Ed.). (A. Sheridan, Trans.). New York, NY: W. W. Norton.

Lachmann, F. M. (2004). Identity and self. *International Forum of Psychoanalysis, 13*, 246–253. http://dx.doi.org/10.1080/08037060410004700

Lahiri, J. (1999). *Interpreter of maladies.* New York, NY: Mariner Books.

Lam, M. (2011). Diasporic literature: The politics of identity and language. *Journal of Asian Pacific Communication, 21*, 309–318. http://dx.doi.org/10.1075/japc.21.2.08lam

Lane, C. (1998). *The psychoanalysis of race.* New York, NY: Columbia University Press.

La Roche, M. J. (2005). The cultural context and the psychotherapeutic process: Toward a culturally sensitive psychotherapy. *Journal of Psychotherapy Integration, 15*, 169–185. http://dx.doi.org/10.1037/1053-0479.15.2.169

La Roche, M. J. (2013). *Cultural psychotherapy: Theory, methods, and practice.* Los Angeles, CA: Sage Publications.

La Roche, M. J., & Christopher, M. S. (2009). Changing paradigms from empirically supported treatment to evidence-based practice: A cultural perspective. *Professional Psychology: Research and Practice, 40*, 396–402. http://dx.doi.org/10.1037/a0015240

Layton, L. (1995). Trauma, gender identity and sexuality: Discourses of fragmentation. *American Imago, 52*, 107–125.

Layton, L. (2004). A fork in the royal road: On "defining" the unconscious and its stakes for social theory. *Psychoanalysis, Culture & Society, 9*, 33–51. http://dx.doi.org/10.1057/palgrave.pcs.2100001

Layton, L. (2006). Racial identities, racial enactments, and normative unconscious processes. *The Psychoanalytic Quarterly, 75*, 237–269. http://dx.doi.org/10.1002/j.2167-4086.2006.tb00039.x

Lear, J. (2007). Working through the end of civilization. *The International Journal of Psychoanalysis, 88*(Pt. 2), 291–308. http://dx.doi.org/10.1516/1358-2877-55X2-6888

Leary, K. (2000). Racial enactments in dynamic treatment. *Psychoanalytic Dialogues, 10*, 639–653. http://dx.doi.org/10.1080/10481881009348573

Leary, K. (2006). In the eye of the storm. *The Psychoanalytic Quarterly, 75*, 345–363. http://dx.doi.org/10.1002/j.2167-4086.2006.tb00043.x

Leary, K. (2007). Racial insult and repair. *Psychoanalytic Dialogues, 17*, 539–549. http://dx.doi.org/10.1080/10481880701487292

Leary, K. (2012). Race as an adaptive challenge: Working with diversity in the clinical consulting room. *Psychoanalytic Psychology, 29*, 279–291. http://dx.doi.org/10.1037/a0027817

Leavy, S. A. (2010). What happened to psychoanalysis? *American Imago, 67*, 73–87.

Lee, D. L., & Tracey, T. J. G. (2008). General and multicultural case conceptualization skills: A cross-sectional analysis of psychotherapy trainees. *Psychotherapy: Theory, Research, Practice, Training, 45*, 507–522.

Lee, H. H., & Friedlander, M. L. (2014). Predicting depressive symptoms from acculturative family distancing: A study of Taiwanese parachute kids in adulthood. *Cultural Diversity and Ethnic Minority Psychology, 20*, 458–462. http://dx.doi.org/10.1037/a0036524

Leichsenring, F., & Rabung, S. (2008). Effectiveness of long-term psychodynamic psychotherapy: A meta-analysis. *JAMA: Journal of the American Medical Association, 300*, 1551–1565. http://dx.doi.org/10.1001/jama.300.13.1551

Leichsenring, F., & Salzer, S. (2014). A unified protocol for the transdiagnostic psychodynamic treatment of anxiety disorders: An evidence-based approach. *Psychotherapy (Chic), 51*, 224–225. http://dx.doi.org/10.1037/a0033815

Leigh, I. W. (2012). Not just deaf: Multiple intersections. In R. Nettles & R. Balter (Eds.), *Multiple minority identities: Applications for practice, research, and training* (pp. 59–80). New York, NY: Springer.

Lemma, A. (2014). *Minding the body in psychoanalysis and beyond.* Hoboken, NJ: Taylor and Francis.

Leong, F. T. (2007). *Handbook of Asian American psychology.* Thousand Oaks, CA: Sage Publications.

Leuzinger-Bohleber, M. (2008). Biographical truths and their clinical consequences: Understanding "embodied memories" in a third psychoanalysis with a traumatized patient recovered from severe poliomyelitis. *The International*

Journal of Psychoanalysis, 89, 1165–1187. http://dx.doi.org/10.1111/j.1745-8315.2008.00100.x

Lewes, K. (1988). *The psychoanalytic theory of male homosexuality.* New York, NY: Simon and Schuster.

Lewes, K., Young-Bruehl, E., Roughton, R., Magee, M., & Miller, D. C. (2008). Homosexuality and psychoanalysis I: Historical perspectives. *Journal of Gay & Lesbian Mental Health, 12,* 299–323. http://dx.doi.org/10.1080/19359700802196909

Liang, B., Tummala-Narra, P., & West, J. (2011). Revisiting community work from a psychodynamic perspective. *Professional Psychology: Research and Practice, 42,* 398–404. http://dx.doi.org/10.1037/a0024687

Lichtenberg, J. D. (2001). Motivational systems and model scenes with special references to bodily experience. *Psychoanalytic Inquiry, 21,* 430–447. http://dx.doi.org/10.1080/07351692109348945

Lichtenstein, H. (1964). The role of narcissism in the emergence and maintenance of a primary identity. *International Journal of Psychoanalysis, 45,* 49–56.

Lijtmaer, R. M. (1999). Language shift and bilinguals: Transference and countertransference implications. *Journal of the American Academy of Psychoanalysis, 27,* 611–624.

Lijtmaer, R. M. (2001). Splitting and nostalgia in recent immigrants: Psychodynamic considerations. *Journal of the American Academy of Psychoanalysis, 29,* 427–438.

Lijtmaer, R. M. (2009). The patient who believes and the analyst who does not. *Journal of the American Academy of Psychoanalysis & Dynamic Psychiatry, 37,* 99–110. http://dx.doi.org/10.1521/jaap.2009.37.1.99

Lippmann, P. (2006). The canary in the mind: On the fate of dreams in psychoanalysis and in contemporary culture. *The American Journal of Psychoanalysis, 66,* 113–130. http://dx.doi.org/10.1007/s11231-006-9010-x

Little, M. (1960). Counter-transference. *British Journal of Medical Psychology, 33,* 29–31. http://dx.doi.org/10.1111/j.2044-8341.1960.tb01222.x

Liu, W. M. (2002). The social class-related experiences of men: Integrating theory and practice. *Professional Psychology: Research and Practice, 33,* 355–360. http://dx.doi.org/10.1037/0735-7028.33.4.355

Loewenstein, R. M. (1956). Some remarks on the role of speech in psycho-analytic technique. *The International Journal of Psychoanalysis, 37,* 460–468.

Lombardi, R. (2008). The body in the analytic session: Focusing on the body–mind link. *The International Journal of Psychoanalysis, 89,* 89–110. http://dx.doi.org/10.1111/j.1745-8315.2007.00008.x

Lombardi, R. (2013). Object relations and the ineffable bodily dimension. *Contemporary Psychoanalysis, 49,* 82–102. http://dx.doi.org/10.1080/00107530.2013.10746534

Louv, R. (2005). *Last child in the woods: Saving our children from nature-deficit disorder.* Chapel Hill, NC: Algonquin Books of Chapel Hill.

Luborsky, L., & Barrett, M. S. (2006). The history and empirical status of key psycho-analytic concepts. *Annual Review of Clinical Psychology, 2,* 1–19. http://dx.doi.org/10.1146/annurev.clinpsy.2.022305.095328

Lykes, M. B. (2013). Participatory and action research as a transformative praxis: Responding to humanitarian crises from the margins. *American Psychologist, 68,* 774–783. http://dx.doi.org/10.1037/a0034360

Lyons, H. Z., Bieschke, K. J., Dendy, A. K., Worthington, R. L., & Georgemiller, R. (2010). Psychologists' competence to treat lesbian, gay and bisexual clients: State of the field and strategies for improvement. *Professional Psychology: Research and Practice, 41,* 424–434. http://dx.doi.org/10.1037/a0021121

Mahalik, J. R., Good, G. E., Tager, D., Levant, R. F., & Mackowiak, C. (2012). Developing a taxonomy of helpful and harmful practices for clinical work with boys and men. *Journal of Counseling Psychology, 59,* 591–603. http://dx.doi.org/10.1037/a0030130

Mahalingam, R., Balan, S., & Haritatos, J. (2008). Engendering immigrant psychology: An intersectionality perspective. *Sex Roles, 59,* 326–336. http://dx.doi.org/10.1007/s11199-008-9495-2

Mahler, M. S. (1970). On human symbiosis and the vicissitudes of individuation. *Journal of Nervous and Mental Disease, 151,* 71–72. http://dx.doi.org/10.1097/00005053-197007000-00011

Mann, M. A. (2004). Immigrant parents and their emigrant adolescents: The tension of inner and outer worlds. *The American Journal of Psychoanalysis, 64,* 143–153. http://dx.doi.org/10.1023/B:TAJP.0000027269.37516.16

Mann, M. A. (2006). The formation and development of individual and ethnic identity: Insights from psychiatry and psychoanalytic theory. *The American Journal of Psychoanalysis, 66,* 211–224. http://dx.doi.org/10.1007/s11231-006-9018-2

Marks, D. (1999). Dimensions of oppression: Theorising the embodied subject. *Disability & Society, 14,* 611–626. http://dx.doi.org/10.1080/09687599925975

Markus, H. R., & Kitayama, S. (1991). Culture and the self: Implications for cognition, emotion, and motivation. *Psychological Review, 98,* 224–253. http://dx.doi.org/10.1037/0033-295X.98.2.224

Markus, H. R., & Kitayama, S. (2010). Cultures and selves: A cycle of mutual constitution. *Perspectives on Psychological Science, 5,* 420–430. http://dx.doi.org/10.1177/1745691610375557

Marmor, J. (Ed.). (1965). *Sexual inversion: The multiple roots of homosexuality.* New York, NY: Basic Books.

Marsella, A. J., & Yamada, A. M. (2010). Culture and psychopathology: Foundations, issues, directions. *Journal of Pacific Rim Psychology, 4,* 103–115. http://dx.doi.org/10.1375/prp.4.2.103

Martín-Baró, I. (1994). *Writings for a liberation psychology.* Cambridge, MA: Harvard University Press.

McNamara, S. (2013). Gay male desires and sexuality in the twenty-first century: How I listen. Panel report. *Journal of the American Psychoanalytic Association, 61,* 341–362. http://dx.doi.org/10.1177/0003065113478654

McWilliams, N. (1999). *Psychoanalytic case formulation.* New York, NY: Guilford Press.

McWilliams, N. (2003). The educative aspects of psychoanalysis. *Psychoanalytic Psychology, 20,* 245–260. http://dx.doi.org/10.1037/0736-9735.20.2.245

McWilliams, N. (2004). *Psychoanalytic psychotherapy: A practitioner's guide.* New York, NY: Guilford Press.

McWilliams, N. (2005). Preserving our humanity as therapists. *Psychotherapy: Theory, Research, Practice, Training, 42,* 139–151. http://dx.doi.org/10.1037/0033-3204.42.2.139

McWilliams, N. (2012). Beyond traits: Personality as intersubjective themes. *Journal of Personality Assessment, 94,* 563–570. http://dx.doi.org/10.1080/00223891.2012.711790

McWilliams, N. (2013a). The impact of my own psychotherapy on my work as a therapist. *Psychoanalytic Psychology, 30,* 621–626. http://dx.doi.org/10.1037/a0034582

McWilliams, N. (2013b). Psychoanalysis and research: Some reflections and opinions. *Psychoanalytic Review, 100,* 919–945. http://dx.doi.org/10.1521/prev.2013.100.6.919

McWilliams, N. (2014). Psychodynamic therapy. In L. S. Greenberg, N. McWilliams, & A. Wenzel (Eds.), *Exploring three approaches to psychotherapy* (pp. 71–127). Washington, DC: American Psychological Association. http://dx.doi.org/10.1037/14253-003

Mehta, P. (1997). The import and export of psychoanalysis: India. *Journal of the American Academy of Psychoanalysis, 25,* 455–471.

Meissner, W. W. (2002). The problem of self-disclosure in psychoanalysis. *Journal of the American Psychoanalytic Association, 50,* 827–867. http://dx.doi.org/10.1177/00030651020500031501

Menninger, K. (1930). *The human mind.* New York, NY: Alfred A. Knopf.

Meyer, O., Zane, N., & Cho, Y. I. (2011). Understanding the psychological processes of the racial match effect in Asian Americans. *Journal of Counseling Psychology, 58*(3), 335–345. http://dx.doi.org/10.1037/a0023605

Millán, F. (2010). On supervision: Reflections of a Latino psychologist. *Training and Education in Professional Psychology, 4,* 7–10. http://dx.doi.org/10.1037/a0016977

Miovic, M. (2004). An introduction to spiritual psychology: Overview of the literature, east and west. *Harvard Review of Psychiatry, 12,* 105–115. http://dx.doi.org/10.1080/10673220490447209

Mitchell, J. (2000). *Psychoanalysis and feminism: A radical reassessment of Freudian psychoanalysis.* New York, NY: Basic Books.

Mitchell, S. A. (1981). The psychoanalytic treatment of homosexuality: Some technical considerations. *International Review of Psycho-Analysis*, 8, 63–80.

Mitchell, S. A. (1988). *Relational concepts in psychoanalysis: An integration.* Cambridge, MA: Harvard University Press.

Mitchell, S. A. (1997). *Influence and autonomy in psychoanalysis.* New York, NY: Taylor & Francis.

Mitchell, S. A. (1998a). The analyst's knowledge and authority. *The Psychoanalytic Quarterly*, 67(1), 1–31.

Mitchell, S. A. (1998b). Letting the paradox teach us. In J. G. Teicholz, D. H. Kriegman & S. Fairfield (Eds.), *Trauma, repetition, and affect regulation: The work of Paul Russell* (pp. 49–58). New York, NY: The Other Press.

Mitchell, S. A. (2002). The psychoanalytic treatment of homosexuality: Some technical considerations. *Studies in Gender and Sexuality*, 3, 23–59. http://dx.doi.org/10.1080/15240650309349187

Miville, M. L., Gelso, C. J., Pannu, R., Liu, W., Touradji, P., Holloway, P., & Fuertes, J. (1999). Appreciating similarities and valuing differences: The Miville-Guzman Universality-Diversity Scale. *Journal of Counseling Psychology*, 46, 291–307. http://dx.doi.org/10.1037/0022-0167.46.3.291

Mizock, L., Harrison, K., & Russinova, Z. (2014). Lesbian, gay, and transgender individuals with mental illness: Narratives of the acceptance process. *Journal of Gay & Lesbian Mental Health*, 18, 320–341. http://dx.doi.org/10.1080/19359705.2013.828007

Modell, A. H. (2005). Emotional memory, metaphor, and meaning. *Psychoanalytic Inquiry*, 25, 555–568. http://dx.doi.org/10.2513/s07351690pi2504_9

Moglen, S. (2005). On mourning social injury. *Psychoanalysis, Culture & Society*, 10, 151–167. http://dx.doi.org/10.1057/palgrave.pcs.2100032

Moncayo, R. (1998). Cultural diversity and the cultural and epistemological structure of psychoanalysis: Implications for psychotherapy with Latinos and other minorities. *Psychoanalytic Psychology*, 15, 262–286. http://dx.doi.org/10.1037/0736-9735.15.2.262

Morales, E. S. (1989). Ethnic minority families and minority gays and lesbians. *Marriage & Family Review*, 14, 217–239. http://dx.doi.org/10.1300/J002v14n03_11

Morawska, E. (2011). "Diaspora" diasporas' representations of their homelands: Exploring the polymorphs. *Ethnic and Racial Studies*, 34, 1029–1048. http://dx.doi.org/10.1080/01419870.2010.533783

Morris, D. O. (2003). Race in the analytic situation: Reflections of an African American therapist. In A. Roland, B. Ulanov, & C. Barbre (Eds.), *Creative dissent: Psychoanalysis in evolution* (pp. 187–195). Westport, CT: Praeger.

Moskowitz, M. (1995). Ethnicity and the fantasy of ethnicity. *Psychoanalytic Psychology*, 12, 547–555. http://dx.doi.org/10.1037/h0079690

Nadkarni, A., & Santhouse, A. (2012). Diagnostic and statistical manual of mental disorders (DSM): A culture bound syndrome? *Asian Journal of Psychiatry, 5,* 118–119. http://dx.doi.org/10.1016/j.ajp.2012.01.002

Nagata, D. K., & Cheng, W. J. Y. (2003). Intergenerational communication of race-related trauma by Japanese American former internees. *American Journal of Orthopsychiatry, 73,* 266–278. http://dx.doi.org/10.1037/0002-9432.73.3.266

Nagel, J. J. (2013). *Melodies of the mind: Connections between psychoanalysis and music.* New York, NY: Routledge/Taylor & Francis Group.

Napier, W. (Ed.). (2000). *African American literary theory* (pp. 17–23). New York: New York University Press.

National Association of Social Workers. (1999). *Code of ethics of the National Association of Social Workers.* Retrieved from http://www.socialworkers.org/pubs/code/default.asp

National Association of Social Workers. (2007). *Indicators for the achievement of NASW standards for cultural competence in social work practice.* Retrieved from http://www.socialworkers.org/practice/standards/Indicators_for_Cultural_Competence.asp

Newman, C. F. (2010). Competency in conducting cognitive–behavioral therapy: Foundational, functional, and supervisory aspects. *Psychotherapy, 47,* 12–19.

Norcross, J. C., Pfund, R. A., & Prochaska, J. O. (2013). Psychotherapy in 2022: A Delphi poll on its future. *Professional Psychology: Research and Practice, 44,* 363–370. http://dx.doi.org/10.1037/a0034633

Ogden, T. H. (1994). *Subjects of analysis.* London, United Kingdom: Karnac Books.

Ogden, T. H. (2009). *Rediscovering psychoanalysis: Thinking and dreaming, learning and forgetting.* London, United Kingdom: Routledge.

Ogden, T. H., & Gabbard, G. O. (2010). The lure of the symptom in psychoanalytic treatment. *Journal of the American Psychoanalytic Association, 58,* 533–544.

Okinogi, K. (2009). Psychoanalysis in Japan. In S. Akhtar (Ed.), *Freud and the Far East: Psychoanalytic perspectives on the people and culture of China, Japan, and Korea* (pp. 9–25). New York, NY: Jason Aronson.

Olkin, R. (1999). *What psychotherapists should know about disability.* New York, NY: Guilford Press.

Olkin, R. (2002). Could you hold the door for me? Including disability in diversity. *Cultural Diversity and Ethnic Minority Psychology, 8,* 130–137.

Orange, D. M., Atwood, G. E., & Stolorow, R. D. (1997). *Working intersubjectively: Contextualism in psychoanalytic practice.* Mahwah, NJ: Analytic Press.

Orfanos, S. (2006). Mythos and logos. *Psychoanalytic Dialogues, 16,* 481–499.

Ornstein, A. (2009). Do words still matter? Further comments on the interpretive process and the theory of change. *International Journal of Psychoanalytic Self Psychology, 4,* 466–484. http://dx.doi.org/10.1080/15551020903185824

Ornstein, A. (2010). The missing tombstone: Reflections on mourning and creativity. *Journal of the American Psychoanalytic Association, 58,* 631–648.

Ornstein, A. (2012). Mass murder and the individual: Psychoanalytic reflections on perpetrators and their victims. *International Journal of Group Psychotherapy, 62,* 1–20. http://dx.doi.org/10.1521/ijgp.2012.62.1.1

Orzolek-Kronner, C., & DeSimone, J. (2012). Seeing through the eyes of the blind: Psychodynamically informed work with persons with low vision. In J. Berzoff (Ed.), *Falling through the cracks: Psychodynamic practice with vulnerable and oppressed populations* (pp. 261–297). New York, NY: Columbia University Press.

Ozawa-de Silva, C. (2007). Demystifying Japanese therapy: An analysis of Naikan and the Ajase complex through Buddhist thought. *Ethos, 35,* 411–446.

Parent, M. C., DeBlaere, C., & Moradi, B. (2013). Approaches to research on intersectionality: Perspectives on gender, LGBT, and racial/ethnic identities. *Sex Roles, 68,* 639–645. http://dx.doi.org/10.1007/s11199-013-0283-2

Parsons, W. B. (2001). Themes and debates in the psychology-comparativist dialogue. In D. Jonte-Pace & W. B. Parsons (Eds.), *Religion and psychology: Mapping the terrain* (pp. 230–253). New York, NY: Routledge.

Paschal, A. G. (Ed.). (1971). *A W. E. B. DuBois reader.* New York, NY: Collier-Macmillan.

PDM Task Force. (2006). *Psychodynamic diagnostic manual (PDM).* Silver Spring, MD: Alliance of Psychoanalytic Organizations.

Pedersen, P. B. (1991). Multiculturalism as a generic framework. *Journal of Counseling & Development, 70,* 6–12. http://dx.doi.org/10.1002/j.1556-6676.1991.tb01555.x

Peña, E. (2003). Reconfiguring epistemological pacts: Creating a dialogue between psychoanalysis and Chicano/a subjectivity, a cosmopolitan perspective. *Journal for the Psychoanalysis of Culture & Society, 8,* 308–319.

Petrucelli, J. (2014). *Body-states: Interpersonal and relational perspectives on the treatment of eating disorders.* New York, NY: Routledge.

Phinney, J. S. (1996). When we talk about American ethnic groups, what do we mean? *American Psychologist, 51,* 918–927.

Pierce, C. (1970). Offensive mechanisms. In F. Barbour (Ed.), *The Black seventies* (pp. 265–282). Boston, MA: Porter Sargent.

Pope-Davis, D. B., Liu, W. M., Toporek, R. L., & Brittan-Powell, C. S. (2001). What's missing from multicultural competency research: Review, introspection, and recommendations. *Cultural Diversity and Ethnic Minority Psychology, 7,* 121–138. http://dx.doi.org/10.1037/1099-9809.7.2.121

Poteat, V. P., Scheer, J. R., DiGiovanni, C. D., & Mereish, E. H. (2014). Short-term prospective effects of homophobic victimization on the mental health of heterosexual adolescents. *Journal of Youth and Adolescence, 43*(8), 1240–1251.

Powell, D. R. (2012). Psychoanalysis and African Americans: Past, present, and future. In S. Akhtar (Ed.), *The African American experience: Psychoanalytic perspectives* (pp. 59–84). Lanham, MD: Jason Aronson.

Prathikanti, S. (1997). East Indian American families. In E. Lee (Ed.), *Working with Asian Americans: A guide for clinicians* (pp. 79–100). New York, NY: Guilford Press.

Prince, R. (2009). Psychoanalysis traumatized: The legacy of the Holocaust. *The American Journal of Psychoanalysis, 69,* 179–194. http://dx.doi.org/10.1057/ajp.2009.13

Purdie-Vaughns, V., & Eibach, R. P. (2008). Intersectional invisibility: The distinctive advantages and disadvantages of multiple subordinate-group identities. *Sex Roles, 59,* 377–391. http://dx.doi.org/10.1007/s11199-008-9424-4

Pytluk, S. D. (2009). The case of John: A generation gap in the clinical dyad. *Psychoanalysis, Culture & Society, 14,* 350–355. http://dx.doi.org/10.1057/pcs.2009.19

Rabin, H. M. (2003). Love in the countertransference: Controversies and questions. *Psychoanalytic Psychology, 20,* 677–690. http://dx.doi.org/10.1037/0736-9735.20.4.677

Rachman, A. W. (2007). Sándor Ferenczi's contributions to the evolution of psychoanalysis. *Psychoanalytic Psychology, 24,* 74–96. http://dx.doi.org/10.1037/0736-9735.24.1.74

Racker, H. (1957). The meanings and uses of countertransference. *The Psychoanalytic Quarterly, 26,* 303–357.

Rado, S. (1940). A critical examination of the concept of bisexuality. *Psychosomatic Medicine, 2,* 459–467. http://dx.doi.org/10.1097/00006842-194010000-00007

Rastogi, M., & Wieling, E. (Eds.). (2005). *Voices of color: First-person accounts of ethnic minority therapists.* Thousand Oaks, CA: Sage Publications.

Rayburn, C. A., & Comas-Díaz, L. (2008). *WomanSoul: The inner life of women's spirituality.* Westport, CT: Praeger.

Renik, O. (1996). The analyst's self-discovery. *Psychoanalytic Inquiry, 16,* 390–400. http://dx.doi.org/10.1080/07351699609534090

Renik, O. (2006). *Practical psychoanalysis for therapists and patients.* New York, NY: Other Press.

Richards, A. (2013). Freud's free clinics: A tale of two continents. *Psychoanalytic Review, 100,* 819–838. http://dx.doi.org/10.1521/prev.2013.100.6.819

Richards, G. (2012). *"Race," racism, and psychology: Towards a reflexive history.* New York, NY: Routledge.

Ricoeur, P. (1986). The self in psychoanalysis and in phenomenological philosophy. *Psychoanalytic Inquiry, 6,* 437–458. http://dx.doi.org/10.1080/07351698609533644

Riquelme, L. F. (2013). Cultural competence for everyone: A shift in perspectives. *Perspectives on Gerontology, 18*(2), 42–49.

Rizzuto, A. (1996). *The birth of the living God: A psychoanalytic study.* Chicago, IL: University of Chicago Press.

Rizzuto, A. (2004). Roman Catholic background and psychoanalysis. *Psychoanalytic Psychology, 21*, 436–441. http://dx.doi.org/10.1037/0736-9735.21.3.436

Rogers, S. (2014). The moving psychoanalytic frame: Ethical challenges for community practitioners. *International Journal of Applied Psychoanalytic Studies, 11*, 151–162. http://dx.doi.org/10.1002/aps.1403

Roland, A. (1996). *Cultural pluralism and psychoanalysis: The Asian and North American experience*. New York, NY: Routledge.

Roland, A. (2005). Between civilizations: Psychoanalytic therapy with Asian North Americans. *Counselling Psychology Quarterly, 18*, 287–293. http://dx.doi.org/10.1080/09515070500469830

Roland, A. (2006). Across civilizations: Psychoanalytic therapy with Asians and Asian Americans. *Psychotherapy (Chic), 43*, 454–463. http://dx.doi.org/10.1037/0033-3204.43.4.454

Rothbaum, F., Weisz, J., Pott, M., Miyake, K., & Morelli, G. (2001). Deeper into attachment and culture. *American Psychologist, 56*, 827–829. http://dx.doi.org/10.1037/0003-066X.56.10.827

Rubin, J. B. (1999). The illusion of a nonfuture: Reflections on psychoanalysis in the twenty-first century. *Journal of the American Academy of Psychoanalysis, 27*, 61–72.

Rubin, J. B. (2003). A well-lived life: Psychoanalytic and Buddhist contributions. In J. D. Safran (Ed.), *Psychoanalysis and Buddhism: An unfolding dialogue* (pp. 387–425). Boston, MA: Wisdom Publications.

Russell, P. L. (1998). Role of paradox in the repetition compulsion. In J. G. Teicholz, D. H. Kriegman, & S. Fairfield (Eds.), *Trauma, repetition, and affect regulation: The work of Paul Russell* (pp. 1–22). New York, NY: The Other Press.

Ruth, R. (2012). Contemporary psychodynamic perspectives on multiple minority identities. In R. Nettles & R. Balter (Eds.), *Multiple minority identities: Applications for practice, research, and training* (pp. 163–184). New York, NY: Springer.

Sacco, F. C., Campbell, E., & Ledoux, M. (2014). Soul of an agency: Psychodynamic principles in action in the world of community mental health. *International Journal of Applied Psychoanalytic Studies, 11*, 101–113. http://dx.doi.org/10.1002/aps.1401

Safran, J. D. (2003). *Psychoanalysis and Buddhism: An unfolding dialogue*. Boston, MA: Wisdom Publications.

Saketopoulou, A. (2011). Minding the gap: Intersections between gender, race, and class in work with gender variant children. *Psychoanalytic Dialogues, 21*, 192–209. http://dx.doi.org/10.1080/10481885.2011.562845

Saketopoulou, A. (2014). Mourning the body as bedrock: Developmental considerations in treating transsexual patients analytically. *Journal of the American Psychoanalytic Association, 62*, 773–806. http://dx.doi.org/10.1177/0003065114553102

Salamon, G., & Corbett, K. (2011). Speaking the body/mind juncture: An interview with Gayle Salamon "Assuming a body: Transgender and rhetorics of materiality."

Psychoanalytic Dialogues, 21, 221–229. http://dx.doi.org/10.1080/10481885. 2011.562847

Sand, S. (2012). When the patient is gay: Psychodynamic reflections on navigating the medical system. In M. O'Reilly-Landry (Ed.), *A psychodynamic understanding of modern medicine: Placing the person at the center of care* (pp. 204–213). Milton Keynes, United Kingdom: Radcliffe Publishing.

Santiago-Rivera, A. L., & Altarriba, J. (2002). The role of language in therapy with the Spanish-English bilingual client. *Professional Psychology: Research and Practice, 33*, 30–38. http://dx.doi.org/10.1037/0735-7028.33.1.30

Sarnat, J. (2010). Key competencies of the psychodynamic psychotherapist and how to teach them in supervision. *Psychotherapy (Chic), 47*, 20–27. http://dx.doi.org/10.1037/a0018846

Saussure, F. (1966). *Course in general linguistics* (W. Baskin, Trans.). In C. Bally & A. Sechehaye (Eds., with Reidlinger A.). New York, NY: McGraw-Hill Book Company. http://dx.doi.org/10.2307/538001

Schimek, J. G. (1987). Fact and fantasy in the seduction theory: A historical review. *Journal of the American Psychoanalytic Association, 35*, 937–965. http://dx.doi.org/10.1177/000306518703500407

Schore, J. R., & Schore, A. N. (2014). Regulation theory and affect regulation psychotherapy: A clinical primer. *Smith College Studies in Social Work, 84*, 178–195. http://dx.doi.org/10.1080/00377317.2014.923719

Schwartz, S. J., Unger, J. B., Zamboanga, B. L., & Szapocznik, J. (2010). Rethinking the concept of acculturation: Implications for theory and research. *American Psychologist, 65*, 237–251. http://dx.doi.org/10.1037/a0019330

Searles, H. F. (1988). The schizophrenic's vulnerability to the therapist's unconscious processes. In B. Wolstein (Ed.), *Essential papers on countertransference* (pp. 202–224). New York, NY: New York University Press.

Seeley, K. (2005). The listening cure: Listening for culture in intercultural psychological treatments. *Psychoanalytic Review, 92*, 431–452. http://dx.doi.org/10.1521/prev.92.3.431.66539

Seeley, K. M. (2000). *Cultural psychotherapy: Working with culture in the clinical encounter*. Northvale, NJ: Jason Aronson.

Seligman, R., & Kirmayer, L. J. (2008). Dissociative experience and cultural neuroscience: Narrative, metaphor and mechanism. *Culture, Medicine and Psychiatry, 32*, 31–64. http://dx.doi.org/10.1007/s11013-007-9077-8

Sellers, R. M., Copeland-Linder, N., Martin, P. P., & Lewis, R. L. (2006). Racial identity matters: The relationship between racial discrimination and psychological functioning in African American adolescents. *Journal of Research on Adolescence, 16*, 187–216. http://dx.doi.org/10.1111/j.1532-7795.2006.00128.x

Serani, D. (2001). Yours, mine, and ours: Analysis with a deaf patient and a hearing analyst. *Contemporary Psychoanalysis, 37*, 655–672. http://dx.doi.org/10.1080/00107530.2001.10746434

Seshadri-Crooks, K. (2000). *Desiring Whiteness: A Lacanian analysis of race*. New York, NY: Routledge. http://dx.doi.org/10.4324/9780203454787

Settles, I. H. (2006). Use of an intersectional framework to understand Black women's racial and gender identities. *Sex Roles, 54*, 589–601. http://dx.doi.org/10.1007/s11199-006-9029-8

Sharabany, R., & Israeli, E. (2008). The dual process of adolescent immigration and relocation: From country to country and from childhood to adolescence—its reflection in psychodynamic psychotherapy. *The Psychoanalytic Study of the Child, 63*, 137–162.

Sharma, D. (2003). *Childhood, family, and sociocultural change in India: Reinterpreting the inner world*. New Delhi, India: Oxford University Press.

Shedler, J. (2010). The efficacy of psychodynamic psychotherapy. *American Psychologist, 65*, 98–109. http://dx.doi.org/10.1037/a0018378

Sherry, S., & Ornstein, A. (2014). The preservation and transmission of cultural values and ideals: Challenges facing immigrant families. *Psychoanalytic Inquiry, 34*, 452–462. http://dx.doi.org/10.1080/07351690.2013.846034

Shin, H. B., & Kominski, R. (2010). *Language use in the United States, 2007*. Washington, DC: U.S. Department of Commerce, Economics and Statistics Administration, U.S. Census Bureau.

Shweder, R. A. (1991). *Thinking through cultures: Expeditions in cultural psychology*. Cambridge, MA: Harvard University Press.

Shweder, R. A., & LeVine, R. A. (1984). *Culture theory: Essays on mind, self, and emotion*. Cambridge, MA: Cambridge University Press.

Singer, R. R., & Tummala-Narra, P. (2013). White clinicians' perspectives on working with racial minority immigrant clients. *Professional Psychology: Research and Practice, 44*, 290–298.

Sirin, S. R., & Fine, M. (2008). *Muslim American youth: Understanding hyphenated identities through multiple methods*. New York, NY: New York University Press.

Sirin, S. R., Ryce, P., Gupta, T., & Rogers-Sirin, L. (2013). The role of acculturative stress on mental health symptoms for immigrant adolescents: A longitudinal investigation. *Developmental Psychology, 49*, 736–748. http://dx.doi.org/10.1037/a0028398

Sklarew, B., Twemlow, S. W., & Wilkinson, S. M. (2004). *Analysts in the trenches: Streets, schools, war zones*. Hillsdale, NJ: Analytic Press.

Slavin, J. H. (1998). Influence and vulnerability in psychoanalytic supervision and treatment. *Psychoanalytic Psychology, 15*, 230–244. http://dx.doi.org/10.1037/0736-9735.15.2.230

Smith, B. L., & Tang, N. M. (2006). Different differences: Revelation and disclosure of social identity in the psychoanalytic situation. *The Psychoanalytic Quarterly, 75*, 295–321. http://dx.doi.org/10.1002/j.2167-4086.2006.tb00041.x

Smith, J. M. (2003). *A potent spell: Mother love and the power of fear*. Boston, MA: Houghton Mifflin.

Smith, L. (2005). Psychotherapy, classism, and the poor: Conspicuous by their absence. *American Psychologist, 60*, 687–696.

Smith, L. (2013). So close and yet so far away: Social class, social exclusion, and mental health practice. *American Journal of Orthopsychiatry, 83*, 11–16. http://dx.doi.org/10.1111/ajop.12008

Smith, T. B., & Silva, L. (2011). Ethnic identity and personal well-being of people of color: A meta-analysis. *Journal of Counseling Psychology, 58*, 42–60. http://dx.doi.org/10.1037/a0021528

Sodowsky, G. R., Kuo-Jackson, P. Y., Richardson, M. F., & Corey, A. T. (1998). Correlates of self-reported multicultural competencies: Counselor multicultural social desirability, race, social inadequacy, locus of control racial ideology, and multicultural training. *Journal of Counseling Psychology, 45*, 256–264. http://dx.doi.org/10.1037/0022-0167.45.3.256

Sonntag, M. E. (2011). No place to live: The uninhabitable body. *Studies in Gender and Sexuality, 12*, 221–231. http://dx.doi.org/10.1080/15240657.2011.585925

Spanierman, L. B., Poteat, V. P., Wang, Y., & Oh, E. (2008). Psychosocial costs of racism to white counselors: Predicting various dimensions of multicultural counseling competence. *Journal of Counseling Psychology, 55*, 75–88. http://dx.doi.org/10.1037/0022-0167.55.1.75

Spezzano, C., & Gargiulo, G. J. (1997). *Soul on the couch: Spirituality, religion, and morality in contemporary psychoanalysis*. Hillsdale, NJ: Analytic Press.

Stark, M. (1999). *Modes of therapeutic action: Enhancement of knowledge, provision of experience, and engagement in relationship*. Northvale, NJ: Jason Aronson.

Steele, C. M. (1997). A threat in the air. How stereotypes shape intellectual identity and performance. *American Psychologist, 52*, 613–629. http://dx.doi.org/10.1037/0003-066X.52.6.613

Steele, C. M. (2010). *Whistling Vivaldi and other clues to how stereotypes affect us*. New York, NY: W.W. Norton & Company.

Stein, A. (2012). Engendered self-states: Dissociated affect, social discourse, and the forfeiture of agency in battered women. *Psychoanalytic Psychology, 29*, 34–58. http://dx.doi.org/10.1037/a0024880

Stein, G. L., Kiang, L., Supple, A. J., & Gonzalez, L. M. (2014). Ethnic identity as a protective factor in the lives of Asian American adolescents. [Advance online publication.] *Asian American Journal of Psychology, 5*, 206–213. http://dx.doi.org/10.1037/a0034811

Stern, D. B. (1997). *Unformulated experience: From dissociation to imagination in psychoanalysis*. Mahwah, NJ: Analytic Press.

Stern, D. B. (2008). "One Never Knows, Do One?": Commentary on Paper by the Boston Change Process Study Group. *Psychoanalytic Dialogues, 18*, 168–196. http://dx.doi.org/10.1080/10481880801909542

Stern, D. B. (2009). Partners in thought: A clinical process theory of narrative. *The Psychoanalytic Quarterly, 78*, 701–731. http://dx.doi.org/10.1002/j.2167-4086.2009.tb00410.x

Stern, D. B. (2010). Unconscious fantasy versus unconscious relatedness. *Contemporary Psychoanalysis, 46,* 101–111. http://dx.doi.org/10.1080/00107530.2010.10746041

Stern, D. N. (1985). *The interpersonal world of the infant: A view from psychoanalysis and developmental psychology.* New York, NY: Basic Books.

Stern, D. N. (1995). *The interpersonal world of the infant: A view from psychoanalysis and developmental psychology.* London, United Kingdom: Karnac.

Stern, D. N. (2005). The psychic landscape of mothers. In S. F. Brown (Ed.), *What do women want? Developmental perspectives, clinical challenges* (pp. 3–18). New York, NY: Routledge.

Stolorow, R. D. (1988). Intersubjectivity, psychoanalytic knowing, and reality. *Contemporary Psychoanalysis, 24,* 331–338. http://dx.doi.org/10.1080/00107530.1988.10746247

Stolorow, R. D. (2003). Trauma and temporality. *Psychoanalytic Psychology, 20,* 158–161. http://dx.doi.org/10.1037/0736-9735.20.1.158

Stolorow, R. D., Brandchaft, B., & Atwood, G. E. (1987). *Psychoanalytic treatment: An intersubjective approach.* Hillsdale, NJ: Analytic Press.

Straker, G. (2004). Race for cover: Castrated whiteness, perverse consequences. *Psychoanalytic Dialogues, 14,* 405–422. http://dx.doi.org/10.1080/10481881409348795

Suárez-Orozco, C. (2000). Identities under siege: Immigration stress and social mirroring among the children of immigrants. In A. Robben & M. Suárez-Orozco (Eds.), *Cultures under siege: Social violence & trauma* (pp. 194–226). Cambridge, United Kingdom: Cambridge University Press.

Suárez-Orozco, C., & Suárez-Orozco, M. M. (2001). *Children of immigration.* Cambridge, MA: Harvard University Press.

Suárez-Orozco, C., Suárez-Orozco, M. M., & Todorova, I. (2008). *Learning a new land: Immigrant students in American society.* Cambridge, MA: Belknap Press of Harvard University Press.

Suchet, M. (2004). A relational encounter with race. *Psychoanalytic Dialogues, 14,* 423–438. http://dx.doi.org/10.1080/10481881409348796

Suchet, M. (2007). Unraveling Whiteness. *Psychoanalytic Dialogues, 17,* 867–886. http://dx.doi.org/10.1080/10481880701703730

Suchet, M. (2011). Crossing over. *Psychoanalytic Dialogues, 21,* 172–191. http://dx.doi.org/10.1080/10481885.2011.562842

Sue, C. A., & Telles, E. E. (2007). Assimilation and gender in naming. *American Journal of Sociology, 112,* 1383–1415. http://dx.doi.org/10.1086/511801

Sue, D. W. (2001). Multidimensional facets of cultural competence. *The Counseling Psychologist, 29,* 790–821. http://dx.doi.org/10.1177/0011000001296002

Sue, D. W., Bingham, R. P., Porché-Burke, L., & Vasquez, M. (1999). The diversification of psychology: A multicultural revolution. *American Psychologist, 54,* 1061–1069. http://dx.doi.org/10.1037/0003-066X.54.12.1061

Sue, D. W., Capodilupo, C. M., Torino, G. C., Bucceri, J. M., Holder, A. M., Nadal, K. L., & Esquilin, M. (2007). Racial microaggressions in everyday life: Implications for clinical practice. *American Psychologist, 62,* 271–286. http://dx.doi.org/10.1037/0003-066X.62.4.271

Sue, D. W., Gallardo, M. E., & Neville, H. A. (2014). *Case studies in multicultural counseling and therapy.* Hoboken, NJ: John Wiley & Sons.

Sue, S. (1998). In search of cultural competence in psychotherapy and counseling. *American Psychologist, 53,* 440–448. http://dx.doi.org/10.1037/0003-066X.53.4.440

Sue, S. (2003). In defense of cultural competency in psychotherapy and treatment. *American Psychologist, 58,* 964–970. http://dx.doi.org/10.1037/0003-066X.58.11.964

Suh, S. (2013). Stories to be told: Korean doctors between hwa-byung (fire-illness) and depression, 1970–2011. *Culture, Medicine and Psychiatry, 37,* 81–104. http://dx.doi.org/10.1007/s11013-012-9291-x

Sullivan, H. S. (1953). *The interpersonal theory of psychiatry.* New York, NY: W. W. Norton.

Summers, F. (2000). The analyst's vision of the patient and therapeutic action. *Psychoanalytic Psychology, 17,* 547–564. http://dx.doi.org/10.1037/0736-9735.17.3.547

Summers, F. (2009). Violence in American foreign policy: A psychoanalytic approach. *International Journal of Applied Psychoanalytic Studies, 6,* 300–320. http://dx.doi.org/10.1002/aps.202

Summers, F. (2011). Psychoanalysis: Romantic, not wild. *Psychoanalytic Psychology, 28*(1), 13–32. http://dx.doi.org/10.1037/a0022558

Summers, F. (2013). *The psychoanalytic vision: The experiencing subject, transcendence, and the therapeutic process.* New York, NY: Routledge.

Summers, F. (2014). Ethnic invisibility, identity, and the analytic process. *Psychoanalytic Psychology, 31,* 410–425.

Supple, A. J., Ghazarian, S. R., Frabutt, J. M., Plunkett, S. W., & Sands, T. (2006). Contextual influences on Latino adolescent ethnic identity and academic outcomes. *Child Development, 77,* 1427–1433. http://dx.doi.org/10.1111/j.1467-8624.2006.00945.x

Swartz, E. E. (2013). Removing the master script: Benjamin Banneker "remembered." *Journal of Black Studies, 44,* 31–49. http://dx.doi.org/10.1177/0021934712464052

Szasz, T. S. (1960). The myth of mental illness. *American Psychologist, 15,* 113–118. http://dx.doi.org/10.1037/h0046535

Taiana, C. (2006). The emergence of Freud's theories in Argentina: Towards a comparison with the United States. *Canadian Journal of Psychoanalysis, 14,* 269–295.

Tang, N. M., & Gardner, J. (1999). Race, culture, and psychotherapy: Transference to minority therapists. *The Psychoanalytic Quarterly, 68,* 1–20. http://dx.doi.org/10.1002/j.2167-4086.1999.tb00634.x

Taras, V., Sarala, R., Muchinsky, P., Kemmelmeier, M., Singelis, T. M., Avsec, A., . . . Sinclair, H. C. (2014). Opposite ends of the same stick? Multi-method test of the dimensionality of individualism and collectivism. *Journal of Cross-Cultural Psychology, 45,* 213–245. http://dx.doi.org/10.1177/0022022113509132

Teicholz, J. G., Kriegman, D. H., & Fairfield, S. (1998). *Trauma, repetition, and affect regulation: The work of Paul Russell.* New York, NY: The Other Press.

Thomas, A. J., Hacker, J. D., & Hoxha, D. (2011). Gendered racial identity of Black young women. *Sex Roles, 64,* 530–542. http://dx.doi.org/10.1007/s11199-011-9939-y

Thomas, K. R. (2008). Macrononsense in multiculturalism. *American Psychologist, 63,* 274–275. http://dx.doi.org/10.1037/0003-066X.63.4.274

Thompson, C. (1950). *Psychoanalysis, evolution, and development: A review of theory and therapy.* New York, NY: Hermitage House.

Thompson, R. (2006). Bilingual, bicultural, and binomial identities: Personal name investment and the imagination in the lives of Korean Americans. *Journal of Language, Identity, and Education, 5,* 179–208. http://dx.doi.org/10.1207/s15327701jlie0503_1

Tomkins, S. S. (1991). *Affect, imagery, consciousness/anger and fear.* New York, NY: Springer.

Toporek, R. L., Lewis, J. A., & Crethar, H. C. (2009). Promoting systemic change through the ACA Advocacy Competencies. *Journal of Counseling & Development, 87,* 260–268. http://dx.doi.org/10.1002/j.1556-6678.2009.tb00105.x

Trask, H. (1999). *From a native daughter: Colonialism and sovereignty in Hawaii.* Honolulu, HI: University of Hawaii Press.

Triandis, H. C. (2001). Individualism-collectivism and personality. *Journal of Personality, 69,* 907–924. http://dx.doi.org/10.1111/1467-6494.696169

Trimble, J., Trickett, E., Fisher, C., & Goodyear, L. (2012). A conversation on multicultural competence in evaluation. *American Journal of Evaluation, 33,* 112–123. http://dx.doi.org/10.1177/1098214011430377

Tummala-Narra, P. (2004). Dynamics of race and culture in the supervisory encounter. *Psychoanalytic Psychology, 21,* 300–311. http://dx.doi.org/10.1037/0736-9735.21.2.300

Tummala-Narra, P. (2005). Addressing political and racial terror in the therapeutic relationship. *American Journal of Orthopsychiatry, 75,* 19–26. http://dx.doi.org/10.1037/0002-9432.75.1.19

Tummala-Narra, P. (2007). Skin color and the therapeutic relationship. *Psychoanalytic Psychology, 24,* 255–270. http://dx.doi.org/10.1037/0736-9735.24.2.255

Tummala-Narra, P. (2008). Reflections on the relevance of Sigmund Freud's ideas for modern society. In J. P. Merlino, M. S. Jacobs, J. A. Kaplan, & K. L. Moritz (Eds.), *Freud at 150: Twenty-first century essays on a man of genius* (pp. 115–118). New York, NY: Jason Aronson.

Tummala-Narra, P. (2009a). The immigrant's real and imagined return home. *Psychoanalysis, Culture & Society, 14,* 237–252. http://dx.doi.org/10.1057/pcs.2009.9

Tummala-Narra, P. (2009b). The relevance of a psychoanalytic perspective in exploring religious and spiritual identity in psychotherapy. *Psychoanalytic Psychology, 26,* 83–95. http://dx.doi.org/10.1037/a0014673

Tummala-Narra, P. (2009c). Teaching on diversity: The mutual influence of students and instructors. *Psychoanalytic Psychology, 26,* 322–334. http://dx.doi.org/10.1037/a0016444

Tummala-Narra, P. (2011). A psychodynamic perspective on the negotiation of prejudice among immigrant women. *Women & Therapy, 34,* 429–446. http://dx.doi.org/10.1080/02703149.2011.591676

Tummala-Narra, P. (2013a). Psychoanalytic applications in a diverse society. *Psychoanalytic Psychology, 30,* 471–487. http://dx.doi.org/10.1037/a0031375

Tummala-Narra, P. (2013b). Psychotherapy with South Asian women: Dilemmas of the immigrant and first generations. *Women & Therapy, 36,* 176–197. http://dx.doi.org/10.1080/02703149.2013.797853

Tummala-Narra, P. (2014a). Cultural identity in the context of trauma and immigration from a psychoanalytic perspective. *Psychoanalytic Psychology, 31,* 396–409. http://dx.doi.org/10.1037/a0036539

Tummala-Narra, P. (2014b). Race psychology. In T. Teo (Ed.), *Encyclopedia of critical psychology* (pp. 1629–1637). New York, NY: Springer. http://dx.doi.org/10.1007/978-1-4614-5583-7_544

Tummala-Narra, P. (2015). Cultural competence as a core emphasis of psychoanalytic psychotherapy. *Psychoanalytic Psychology, 32,* 275–292. http://dx.doi.org/10.1037/a0034041

Tummala-Narra, P. (2016). Names, name changes, and identity in the context of immigration. In J. Beltsiou (Ed.), *Immigration in psychoanalysis: Locating ourselves.* New York, NY: Routledge.

Tummala-Narra, P., & Claudius, M. (2013). Perceived discrimination and depressive symptoms among immigrant-origin adolescents. *Cultural Diversity and Ethnic Minority Psychology, 19,* 257–269. http://dx.doi.org/10.1037/a0032960

Tummala-Narra, P., Inman, A. G., & Ettigi, S. (2011). Asian Indians' responses to discrimination: A mixed-method examination of identity, coping, and self-esteem. *Asian American Journal of Psychology, 2,* 205–218.

Tummala-Narra, P., & Sathasivam-Rueckert, N. (2013). Perceived support from adults, interactions with police, and adolescents' depressive symptomology: An examination of sex, race, and social class. *Journal of Adolescence, 36,* 209–219.

Tummala-Narra, P., & Sathasivam-Rueckert, N. (in press). The experience of ethnic and racial group membership among immigrant-origin adolescents. *Journal of Adolescent Research.*

Tummala-Narra, P., Singer, R., Li, Z., Esposito, J., & Ash, S. E. (2012). Individual and systemic factors in clinicians' self-perceived cultural competence. *Profes-*

sional Psychology: Research and Practice, 43, 165–174. http://dx.doi.org/10.1037/a0025783

Turken, H. (2007). The ego-ideal, conflict, and the primacy of the self: Women and the cultural restrictions of love object choice. *International Journal of Applied Psychoanalytic Studies, 4,* 52–62. http://dx.doi.org/10.1002/aps.123

Turkle, S. (2004). Whither psychoanalysis in computer culture? *Psychoanalytic Psychology, 21,* 16–30. http://dx.doi.org/10.1037/0736-9735.21.1.16

Twemlow, S. W., Fonagy, P., Sacco, F. C., Vernberg, E., & Malcom, J. M. (2011). Reducing violence and prejudice in a Jamaican all age school using attachment and mentalization theory. *Psychoanalytic Psychology, 28,* 497–511. http://dx.doi.org/10.1037/a0023610

Twemlow, S. W., & Parens, H. (2006). Might Freud's legacy lie beyond the couch? *Psychoanalytic Psychology, 23,* 430–451. http://dx.doi.org/10.1037/0736-9735.23.2.430

Umaña-Taylor, A. J., Diversi, M., & Fine, M. A. (2002). Ethnic identity and self-esteem of Latino adolescents: Distinctions among the Latino population. *Journal of Adolescent Research, 17,* 303–327. http://dx.doi.org/10.1177/0743558402173005

U.S. Census Bureau. (2010). *Place of birth of the foreign born population: 2009.* Retrieved from http://www.census.gov/prod/2010/pubs/acsbr09-15.pdf

U.S. Department of Health and Human Services. (2001). *Mental health: Culture, race, and ethnicity: A supplement to mental health: A report of the Surgeon General.* Rockville, MD: U.S. Department of Health and Human Services, Public Health Service.

Utsey, S. O., & Gernat, C. A. (2002). White racial identity attitudes and the ego defense mechanisms used by White counselor trainees in racially provocative counseling situations. *Journal of Counseling & Development, 80,* 475–483. http://dx.doi.org/10.1002/j.1556-6678.2002.tb00214.x

van Waning, A. (2009). Naikan—A Buddhist self-reflective approach: Psychoanalytic and cultural reflections. In S. Akhtar (Ed.), *Freud and the Far East: Psychoanalytic perspectives on the people and culture of China, Japan, and Korea* (pp. 255–273). Lanham, MD: Jason Aronson.

Vasquez, M. J. (2012). Psychology and social justice: Why we do what we do. *American Psychologist, 67,* 337–346. http://dx.doi.org/10.1037/a0029232

Volkan, V. D. (1993). Immigrants and refugees: A psychodynamic perspective. *Mind and Human Interaction, 4,* 63–69.

Volkan, V. D. (1998). *Bloodlines: From ethnic pride to ethnic terrorism.* Boulder, CO: Westview Press.

Volkan, V. D. (2004). After the violence: The internal world and linking objects of a refugee family. In B. Sklarew, S. W. Twemlow, & S. M. Wilkinson (Eds.), *Analysts in the trenches: Streets, schools, war zones* (pp. 77–102). Hillsdale, NJ: Analytic Press.

Wachtel, P. L. (2002). Psychoanalysis and the disenfranchised: From therapy to justice. *Psychoanalytic Psychology, 19,* 199–215. http://dx.doi.org/10.1037/0736-9735.19.1.199

Wachtel, P. L. (2007). Commentary: Making invisibility visible—Probing the interface between race and gender. In J. C. Muran (Ed.), *Dialogues on difference: Studies of diversity in the therapeutic relationship* (pp. 132–140). Washington, DC: American Psychological Association. http://dx.doi.org/10.1037/11500-014

Wachtel, P. L. (2009). Knowing oneself from the inside out, knowing oneself from the outside in: The "inner" and "outer" worlds and their link through action. *Psychoanalytic Psychology, 26,* 158–170. http://dx.doi.org/10.1037/a0015502

Wachtel, P. L. (2014). *Cyclical psychodynamics and the contextual self: The inner world, the intimate world, and the world of culture and society.* New York, NY: Routledge.

Wake, N. (2007). The military, psychiatry, and "unfit" soldiers, 1939–1942. *Journal of the History of Medicine and Allied Sciences, 62,* 461–494. http://dx.doi.org/10.1093/jhmas/jrm002

Wallerstein, R. S. (2009). What kind of research in psychoanalytic science? *The International Journal of Psychoanalysis, 90,* 109–133. http://dx.doi.org/10.1111/j.1745-8315.2008.00107.x

Wallerstein, R. S., & Fonagy, P. (1999). Psychoanalytic research and the IPA: History, present status and future potential. *The International Journal of Psychoanalysis, 80,* 91–109. http://dx.doi.org/10.1516/0020757991598585

Walls, G. B. (2004). Toward a critical global psychoanalysis. *Psychoanalytic Dialogues, 14,* 605–634. http://dx.doi.org/10.1080/10481880409353129

Wang, C. D., & Mallinckrodt, B. (2006). Acculturation, attachment, and psychosocial adjustment of Chinese/Taiwanese international students. *Journal of Counseling Psychology, 53,* 422–433. http://dx.doi.org/10.1037/0022-0167.53.4.422

Watermeyer, B. (2012). Is it possible to create a politically engaged, contextual psychology of disability? *Disability & Society, 27,* 161–174. http://dx.doi.org/10.1080/09687599.2011.644928

Watkins, C. E. (2012). Race/ethnicity in short-term and long-term psychodynamic psychotherapy treatment research: How "White" are the data? *Psychoanalytic Psychology, 29,* 292–307. http://dx.doi.org/10.1037/a0033616

Watkins, C. E. (2013). Do cultural and sociodemographic variables matter in the study of psychoanalysis? A follow-up comment and simple suggestion. *Psychoanalytic Psychology, 30,* 488–496. http://dx.doi.org/10.1037/a0033616

Weingarten, K. (2010). Intersecting losses: Working with the inevitable vicissitudes in therapist and client lives. *Psychotherapy: Theory, Research, Practice, Training, 47,* 371–384. http://dx.doi.org/10.1037/a0021170

Westen, D., Novotny, C. M., & Thompson-Brenner, H. (2004). The empirical status of empirically supported psychotherapies: Assumptions, findings, and reporting in controlled clinical trials. *Psychological Bulletin, 130*, 631–663. http://dx.doi.org/10.1037/0033-2909.130.4.631

Wexler, L. (2014). Looking across three generations of Alaska Natives to explore how culture fosters indigenous resilience. *Transcultural Psychiatry, 51*, 73–92. http://dx.doi.org/10.1177/1363461513497417

Wheeler, S. (2006). *Difference and diversity in counselling: Contemporary psychodynamic perspectives*. New York, NY: Palgrave Macmillan.

White, C. (2004). Culture, influence, and the "I-ness" of me: Commentary on papers by Susan Bodnar, Gary B. Walls, and Steven Botticelli. *Psychoanalytic Dialogues, 14*, 653–691. http://dx.doi.org/10.1080/10481880409353131

Whitson, G. (1996). Working-class issues. In R. P. Foster, M. Moskowitz, & R. A. Javier (Eds.), *Reaching across boundaries of culture and class: Widening the scope of psychotherapy* (pp. 143–157). Northvale, NJ: Jason Aronson.

Winnicott, D. W. (1947). Hate in the countertransference. In D. W. Winnicott (Ed.), *Collected papers: Through paediatrics to psycho-analysis* (pp. 194–203). New York, NY: Basic Books.

Winnicott, D. W. (1971). *Playing and reality*. New York, NY: Routledge.

Winnicott, D. W. (1986). *Home is where we start from: Essays by a psychoanalyst*. New York, NY: W.W. Norton.

Wyche, S. P. (2012). An African American's becoming a psychoanalyst: Some personal reflections. In S. Akhtar (Ed.), *The African American experience: Psychoanalytic perspectives* (pp. 321–336). Lanham, MD: Jason Aronson.

Yakushko, O., Davidson, M. M., & Williams, E. N. (2009). Identity salience model: A paradigm for integrating multiple identities in clinical practice. *Psychotherapy: Theory, Research, Practice, Training, 46*, 180–192. http://dx.doi.org/10.1037/a0016080

Yassen, J. (1995). Preventing secondary traumatic stress disorder. In C. Figley (Ed.), *Compassion fatigue: Coping with secondary traumatic stress disorder in those who treat the traumatized* (pp. 178–208). Philadelphia, PA: Brunner/Mazel.

Yi, K. (2014a). From no name to birth of integrated identity: Trauma-based cultural dissociation in immigrant women and creative integration. *Psychoanalytic Dialogues, 24*, 37–45. http://dx.doi.org/10.1080/10481885.2014.870830

Yi, K. (2014b). Toward formulation of ethnic identity beyond the binary of the White oppressor and racial other. *Psychoanalytic Psychology, 31*, 426–434. http://dx.doi.org/10.1037/a0036649

Yi, K. Y. (1998). Transference and race: An intersubjective conceptualization. *Psychoanalytic Psychology, 15*, 245–261. http://dx.doi.org/10.1037/0736-9735.15.2.245

Young-Bruehl, E. (1996). *The anatomy of prejudices*. Cambridge, MA: Harvard University Press.

Zane, N., & Ku, H. (2014). Effects of ethnic match, gender match, acculturation, cultural identity, and face concern on self-disclosure in counseling for Asian Americans. *Asian American Journal of Psychology, 5*(1), 66–74. http://dx.doi.org/10.1037/a0036078

Zayas, L. H., & Torres, L. R. (2009). Culture and masculinity: When therapist and patient are Latino men. *Clinical Social Work Journal, 37*, 294–302. http://dx.doi.org/10.1007/s10615-009-0232-2

Ziegler, K. R., & Rasul, N. (2014). Race, ethnicity, and culture. In L. Erickson-Schroth (Ed.), *Trans bodies, trans selves: A resource for the transgender community* (pp. 24–39). New York, NY: Oxford University Press.

INDEX

Complex cultural identities
        case illustration of, 191–196
        conflicting and shifting loyalties
                related to, 180–184, 191–196
        cultural competence with, 64,
                81–83, 154–156, 171–197
        cultural hybridity of, 186–191
        cultural identity and conflict in,
                174–185
        dis/ability status in, 177, 178
        diversity issues reflecting, 57, 61–62
        friendships and adjustments to,
                183–184
        gender in, 179, 186, 187, 189
        immigrant and refugee status in, 177,
                178, 181–184, 191–196
        intersectionality of identities,
                185–191
        overview of, 171–174, 197
        race and ethnicity in, 173, 175–177,
                179, 186, 187, 191–196
        religion and spirituality in, 171–172,
                180–181, 182, 189, 194–195
        sexuality in, 171–172, 178, 179,
                180–181, 187, 191–196
        sexual orientation in, 178, 179,
                180–181, 187, 191–196
        shifting or diverging identifications
                and, 179–181, 191–196
        social oppression experiences related
                to, 154–156, 175–179, 187, 196
        socioeconomic status in, 178–179, 186
        technology and transnational space
                impacting, 184–185
        therapeutic implications of
                intersectionality and hybridity
                for, 188–191
The Concept of Repression (Bose), 15, 94
Cook, Donelda, 148
Corbett, Ken, 56
Crenshaw, Kimberle, 185–186
Cultural competence. See also
        Sociocultural issues
        ADDRESSING framework for, 68, 72
        advocacy role in, 68–69
        central features of psychoanalytic
                psychotherapy and, 70–72
        in cognitive-behavioral therapy, 72
        with complex cultural identities, 64,
                81–83, 154–156, 171–197

culturally informed psychoanalytic
        framework for, 78–84, 85–110,
        111–138, 139–169, 171–197,
        199–230, 231–243
definition and description of, 66–67,
        77–78
with dis/ability status, 125, 128, 151,
        152, 177, 178, 205, 206
with gender issues, 79, 95, 96–97,
        100, 116–117, 125, 128,
        140–141, 144, 153–154, 155,
        179, 186, 187, 189
with immigrant and refugee issues,
        79, 85–87, 101, 111–112,
        118–119, 120–124, 132–137,
        147–148, 149, 151–153, 154,
        157, 163–169, 177, 178,
        181–184, 191–196, 205, 211
implications of, 231–243
with indigenous narrative, 74,
        78–79, 85–110
with language and affect, 80, 92,
        111–138, 167, 178, 211
overlap of multicultural psychology
        and psychoanalytical theory
        in relation to, 73–77
overview of, 63–65, 84
from psychoanalytic perspective,
        77–84
in psychology, 65–70, 73–77
with race and ethnicity, 64, 67–68,
        95–96, 97, 100–101, 104–109,
        121, 122–124, 128, 135–137,
        140–141, 144–145, 146–147,
        148–153, 155–156, 157,
        161–162, 163, 173, 175–177,
        179, 186, 187, 191–196,
        201–203, 206–208, 227–229,
        241–242
with religion and spirituality, 83,
        94, 108, 115–116, 122, 165,
        171–172, 180–181, 182, 189,
        194–195, 227–228
with self-examination, 83, 199–230
with sexuality, 82, 116, 125, 129,
        131–132, 142–143, 152, 154,
        155, 164, 165–168, 171–172,
        178, 179, 180–181, 187,
        191–196, 205, 206, 210
with sexual orientation, 82, 116,
        125, 129, 152, 154, 155, 178,

179, 180–181, 187, 191–196,
205, 206, 210
social justice relationship to, 76,
141–142
with social oppression experiences,
80–81, 122, 128–129, 139–169,
175–179, 187, 196, 206,
209–210
with socioeconomic status, 105–107,
125, 152, 160, 178–179, 186
Cultural dissociation, 155–156
Cultural issues. *See* Sociocultural issues
Culturally informed psychoanalytic
framework
complex cultural identities in,
81–83, 171–197
future directions for, 231–243
implications of, 231–243
indigenous narrative in, 78–79,
85–110
language and affect nuances in, 80,
111–138
overview of, 78–84
self-examination in, 83, 199–230
social oppression experiences in,
80–81, 139–169
Cultural school of psychoanalysis, 24–27
Cushman, Philip, 9, 34, 201

Dalal, Farhad, 43
Darwin, Charles, 19
Davids, M. Fakhry, 151–152
Davies, J. E., 215
Davies, Jody, 36, 37
Davis, J. T., 186
Demos, John, 13
Derrick, Janet, 101
Desai, Bhupen, 16
Devereaux, Georges, 65
Diagnostic practices, 11, 20, 66, 71,
74–75, 87–88, 93–94, 149
Diaspora, 184–185
Dimen, Muriel, 36, 40
Dis/ability status
affect and, 125, 128
complex cultural identities including,
177, 178
cultural competence with, 125, 128,
151, 152, 177, 178, 205, 206
psychoanalytic contributions to
understanding, 60–61

social oppression based on, 128, 151,
152, 177, 178
therapist's self-examination of issues
related to, 205, 206
Discrimination. *See* Social oppression
experiences
Dissociation, 88–89, 125–126, 129–130,
142–143, 205. *See also* Cultural
dissociation
Diversity issues. *See also* Sociocultural
issues
dis/ability status as, 60–61
gender as, 38–43, 55–56
immigration as, 35, 48–53, 54
multiple, overlapping, 57, 61–62
(*see also* Complex cultural
identities)
object relations theory and, 34–35,
36, 50, 58
overview of progress related to,
31–34, 62
psychoanalytic contributions to
understanding, 31–62
race and ethnicity as, 31–32, 43–48,
52–53, 202–203
relational psychoanalysis and, 35–38,
50–51, 55–56, 58
religion and spirituality as, 58–60
self-psychology theory and, 35, 36, 44
sexual orientation as, 55–57
social class/socioeconomic status as,
53–54
therapeutic relationship in context
of, 33, 36–38, 40–41, 47–48,
53–54, 55, 56–57, 58–60,
61–62, 202–204
therapist's self-examination of
investment in, 202–204
Doi, Takeo, 91
Du Bois, W. E. B., 6
Dreams, 102–103, 108–109, 114
Dynamic psychiatry, 10

Ego psychology movement, 21–22, 24,
26, 50
Ehrensaft, Diane, 42
Emotions. *See* Affect
Eng, David, 44, 157, 185
Epstein, Mark, 59
Erikson, Erik, 24, 58, 65, 174

Ethnicity. *See* Race and ethnicity
Ethnocultural allodynia, 148
Eugenics movement, 19
Evenly hovering attention, 190–191
Evenly suspended attention, 119, 131
Evidence-based practice, 73–74, 236
Evolution, theory of, 19

Fabrega, Horatio, 87
Fairbairn, Ronald, 27
Families
    attachment to caregivers in, 26–27,
        34–35, 89–91, 94, 131
    historical changes in views on, 12,
        26–27
    relational psychoanalysis on impact
        of, 35–36
    social oppression experiences
        impacting, 150
Fanon, Frantz, 52–53, 146–147
Farah (social oppression case illustration),
    163–169
Feminist psychology
    on complex cultural identities, 189
    on cultural competence, 65, 73,
        74–75, 76
    on gender issues, 39, 41, 42
    overlap with psychoanalytic theory,
        73, 74–75, 76
    on social oppression, 141–142
Ferenczi, Sándor, 35–36, 76, 215–216,
    217
Fine, Michelle, 102, 182
Foster, Rose Marie Perez, 119, 221
Frankl, Viktor, 58
Freeman, Mark, 92–93
Freud, Anna, 13, 24, 186–187
Freud, Sigmund
    on affect, 127, 130
    Ajase complex introduced to, 16
    Anna O. case of, 112–113
    on dreams and myths, 102, 114
    on evenly suspended attention, 119
    Ferenczi split with, 36
    on homosexuality, 20
    as immigrant and refugee, 9, 13
    Jewish ancestry of influencing, 21
    on language, 114
    on melancholia, 156–157
    on mourning, 156, 158

    psychoanalysis developed by (*see*
        Psychoanalytic perspective)
    on religion and spirituality, 18, 58
    sociocultural issues not in theories
        of, 9, 15, 17–18, 94
    training under, 13, 25
    on transference and countertrans-
        ference, 215
Frie, R., 93
Fromm, Erich, 24–25, 58, 65
The Future of Illusion (Freud), 18

Galdi, Giselle, 205
Gallardo, Miguel, 73, 239
Galton, Francis, 19
Garner, Eric, 175
Garth, Thomas Russell, 19
Gay/lesbian orientation. *See*
    Homosexuality; Sexual orientation
Gender. *See also* Women
    affect and, 125, 128
    complex cultural identities
        including, 179, 186, 187, 189
    cultural competence with, 79, 95,
        96–97, 100, 116–117, 125,
        128, 140–141, 144, 153–154,
        155, 179, 186, 187, 189
    gender identity issues, 42, 55–56, 154
    historical psychoanalytic perspectives
        on, 18, 19, 20–21, 25, 38–43,
        55–56
    indigenous narrative related to, 79,
        95, 96–97, 100
    language related to, 116–117
    massive gender trauma, 42
    psychoanalytic contributions to
        understanding, 38–43
    social constructions of, 40, 55–56
    social oppression based on, 44, 128,
        140–141, 144, 153–154, 155,
        179, 187
    therapeutic relationship impacted
        by, 40–41
    transgender issues, 42, 154, 187
Ghent, Emmanuel, 36
Gill, Merton, 201, 217
Gina (indigenous narrative case
    illustration), 104–109
Good, Byron, 87
Goodley, Dan, 151

Homosexuality, *continued*
    queer theory on, 55–56
    social oppression based on, 129, 152,
        154, 155, 206
    therapist's self-examination of issues
        related to, 205, 206, 210
Hooker, Evelyn, 20
Horney, Karen, 18, 24, 25, 65
Hwa-byung, 93–94

Immigrants and refugees
    binomial identities of, 122–124
    complex cultural identities of, 177,
        178, 181–184, 191–196
    cultural competence with, 79, 85–87,
        101, 111–112, 118–119,
        120–124, 132–137, 147–148,
        149, 151–153, 154, 157,
        163–169, 177, 178, 181–184,
        191–196, 205, 211
    cultural mourning of, 49, 50, 183
    cultural values and ideals impacting,
        51–52
    factors influencing psychological
        experience of, 49
    friendships and adjustments of,
        183–184
    historical psychoanalysis experiences
        of, 9–17, 21–22, 35, 48–53, 54
    indigenous narrative of, 79, 85–87,
        101
    language and affect of, 51, 111–112,
        118–119, 120–124, 132–137,
        167, 178
    names/name changes among, 121,
        122–124
    psychoanalytic contributions to
        understanding, 48–53
    racial and ethnic issues for, 14,
        52–53, 122–124, 135–137,
        147, 151–153, 157, 191–196
    religion and spirituality among, 14,
        15, 16, 21, 122, 165, 182
    shifting loyalties among children
        and, 181–184, 191–196
    social mirroring of, 35
    social oppression experiences of,
        147–148, 149, 151–153, 154,
        157, 163–169, 177
    socioeconomic status of, 54

therapists as, 9, 13, 21–22, 101–102,
    118–119, 121, 166–167,
    168–169, 205, 211
therapist's self-examination of issues
    related to, 205, 211
war, trauma, and exile of, 10–11,
    13–17, 21, 50, 122, 149, 205
India, psychoanalysis and culture in,
    15–16, 94–95
Indigenous narrative
    case illustration of, 104–109
    colonialism and, 94–95, 97
    cultural competence with, 74,
        78–79, 85–110
    culture and theory on, 87–93
    definition and description of, 87
    development norms in relation to,
        90–91
    diagnostic practices in relation to,
        87–88, 93–94
    dominant national identity and
        narrative *vs.*, 96
    dreams in, 102–103, 108–109
    gender issues reflected in, 79, 95,
        96–97, 100
    generational differences in, 97
    immigrant and refugee experiences
        reflected in, 79, 85–87, 101
    individualism and attachment views
        in relation to, 89–92, 94
    listening to, in psychotherapy,
        98–103
    mothers in, 85–87, 89–90, 94,
        96–97, 100
    narrative unconscious, 93
    outliers among, 102, 107
    overview of, 85–87, 109–110
    ownership of, 93–97
    race and ethnicity reflected in,
        95–96, 97, 100–101, 104–109
    religion and spirituality reflected in,
        94, 108
    socioeconomic status reflected in,
        105–107
    therapist's, 86–87, 100–103
    unequal representations of, 95–96
    variations of narratives within
        cultural groups, 96–97
Individualism, 89–92
Internet, 131, 184–185

cultural competence with, 64,
    67–68, 95–96, 97, 100–101,
    104–109, 121, 122–124, 128,
    135–137, 140–141, 144–145,
    146–147, 148–153, 155–156,
    157, 161–162, 163, 173,
    175–177, 179, 186, 187,
    191–196, 201–203, 206–208,
    227–229, 241–242
Eugenics movement on, 19
historical psychoanalytic
    perspectives on, 14, 15–16,
    19–21, 23, 31–32, 43–48,
    52–53
immigrant and refugee issues of, 14,
    52–53, 122–124, 135–137,
    147, 151–153, 157, 191–196
indigenous narrative reflecting,
    95–96, 97, 100–101, 104–109
language reflecting ties to, 121,
    122–124
microaggressions related to, 148,
    150–151, 153, 177
model minority stereotype of, 45,
    147, 157, 176–177, 195
names reflecting, 121, 122–124
"primitive" preoccupation and views
    of, 19–20
psychoanalytic contributions to
    understanding, 43–48
racial and ethnic identity issues, 46,
    67–68, 173
racial enactments in therapeutic
    relationship, 47–48, 135–136,
    162
racial/ethnic matching in therapeutic
    dyad, 201–202
racial melancholia related to, 45, 48,
    157
racism/social oppression based on,
    19–20, 43–48, 52–53, 128,
    140–141, 144–145, 146–147,
    148–153, 155–156, 157,
    161–162, 163, 175–177,
    187, 196
social construction of, 43
socioeconomic status in relation to,
    43–44
therapist's self-examination related
    to, 201–203, 206–208,
    227–229

Racker, Heinrich, 216
Rado, Sandor, 20
Rapaport, David, 14, 22
Rabung, S., 84
Refugees. *See* Immigrants and refugees
Relational psychoanalysis, 35–38,
    50–51, 55–56, 58, 141, 174, 213
Religion and spirituality
    Buddhism as, 16, 25, 59
    Christianity as, 58
    complex cultural identities
        including, 171–172, 180–181,
        182, 189, 194–195
    cultural competence with, 83, 94,
        108, 115–116, 122, 165,
        171–172, 180–181, 182, 189,
        194–195, 227–228
    Freud on, 18, 58
    Hinduism as, 15, 59, 94, 171–172,
        227–228
    historical psychoanalytic
        perspectives related to, 14, 15,
        16, 18, 21, 25, 44, 58–60, 209
    immigrant experiences of, 14, 15, 16,
        21, 122, 165, 182
    indigenous narrative reflecting, 94,
        108
    Islam as, 165, 182
    Judaism as, 14, 21, 25, 44, 58, 83,
        122, 209
    language and myths in, 115–116
    names reflecting ties to, 122
    object relations and relational
        psychoanalysis approaches
        to, 58
    psychoanalytic contributions to
        understanding, 58–60
    racial categorization based on, 14, 21
    social oppression based on, 14, 21,
        44, 122
    therapists' self-examination of, 83,
        227–228
Renik, Owen, 36
Research, psychoanalytic, 235–236
Richards, G., 19
Ricoeur, Paul, 92
Rizzuto, Ana-Maria, 58
Rogers, Carl, 58
Roland, Alan, 52, 59
Rubin, Jeffrey, 59, 223

Runswick-Cole, Katherine, 151
Russell, Paul, 127
Ruth, Richard, 186–187

Safran, Jeremy, 59
Salmon, Thomas W., 10–11
Schizophrenia, 25–26, 216
Seduction theory, 17
Seeley, Karen, 87, 98, 103
Self-examination
    case illustration of, 225–230
    cultural competence with, 83,
        199–230
    of dis/ability status issues, 205, 206
    of immigrant and refugee issues, 205,
        211
    of institutional challenges, 208–213
    of minority status, 206–208
    overview of, 199–202, 230
    of personal investment in diversity
        issues, 202–204
    of potential boundary violations,
        219–220
    of racial and ethnic issues, 201–203,
        206–208, 227–229
    of religious issues, 83, 227–228
    of responsibility to explore
        sociocultural issues, 213–215
    of self-disclosure, 218, 222–225,
        227–229
    of sexual orientation issues, 205, 206,
        210
    of social oppression experiences,
        209–210
    sociocultural context importance in,
        202–215
    of therapist's needs, 218–221
    of transference and
        countertransference, 201–202,
        204–205, 208, 215–225
    of trauma experiences, 204–205
Self-psychology theory, 27, 35, 36, 44
Sexuality
    affect and, 125
    complex cultural identities
        including, 171–172, 178, 179,
        180–181, 187, 191–196
    cultural competence with, 82, 116,
        125, 129, 131–132, 142–143,

152, 154, 155, 164, 165–168,
        171–172, 178, 179, 180–181,
        187, 191–196, 205, 206, 210
    historical psychoanalytic
        perspectives on, 11, 17, 18,
        20, 23, 25–26, 36, 38–39, 41,
        44, 55–57
    seduction theory on, 17
    sexual abuse/violence, 17, 36, 38–39,
        131–132, 142–143, 155, 164,
        165–168
    sexual orientation, 20, 23, 25–26, 44,
        55–57, 82, 116, 125, 129, 152,
        154, 155, 178, 179, 180–181,
        187, 191–196, 205, 206, 210
    stereotypes related to, 152
    therapist's self-examination of issues
        related to, 205, 206, 210
Sexual orientation
    affect and, 125, 129
    complex cultural identities
        including, 178, 179, 180–181,
        187, 191–196
    cultural competence with, 82, 116,
        125, 129, 152, 154, 155, 178,
        179, 180–181, 187, 191–196,
        205, 206, 210
    historical psychoanalytic
        perspectives on, 20, 23,
        25–26, 44, 55–57
    language related to, 116
    psychoanalytic contributions to
        understanding, 55–57
    queer theory on, 55–56
    social constructions of, 55–56
    social oppression based on, 44, 129,
        152, 154, 155, 187, 206
    therapist's self-examination of issues
        related to, 205, 206, 210
Sherry, Susannah, 187
Shorter-Gooden, Kumea, 100
Silence, meaning of, 80, 111–112, 140,
    158, 166
Sinha, Tarun, 16
Singer, R. R, 203
Sirin, S. R., 182
Smith, Janna M., 96–97
Smith, Laura, 175
Social class. See Socioeconomic status

Social justice, 75–76, 141–142
Social media, 131, 184–185
Social mirroring, 35, 99, 107, 143, 176
Social oppression experiences
    case illustration of, 163–169
    complex cultural identities impacted
        by, 154–156, 175–179, 187,
        196
    cultural competence with, 80–81,
        122, 128–129, 139–169,
        175–179, 187, 196, 206,
        209–210
    cultural dissociation and, 155–156
    with dis/ability status, 128, 151, 152,
        177, 178
    effects of, 142–156
    expressions of, in psychotherapy,
        144–146
    with gender, 44, 128, 140–141, 144,
        153–154, 155, 179, 187
    with immigrants and refugees,
        147–148, 149, 151–153, 154,
        157, 163–169, 177
    intrapsychic and relational life
        impacted by, 146–154
    mourning and enactment in
        psychotherapy related to,
        156–163
    multiple marginalization, 154–156
    overview of, 139–142, 169
    "primitive" preoccupation as basis
        for, 19–20
    with race and ethnicity, 19–20,
        43–48, 52–53, 128, 140–141,
        144–145, 146–147, 148–153,
        155–156, 157, 161–162, 163,
        175–177, 187, 196
    with religion and spirituality, 14, 21,
        44, 122
    with sexual orientation, 44, 129,
        152, 154, 155, 187, 206
    socialization impacted by, 153–154
    with socioeconomic status, 152, 160,
        178–179
    stereotypes as, 151–152
    therapist's self-examination related
        to, 209–210
    transference and countertransference
        issues due to, 144–145, 160

witnessing, in psychotherapy,
        159–160, 162, 169, 209–210
Sociocultural issues
    ADDRESSING framework for, 68,
        72
    affect reflecting, 80, 111–113,
        124–138
    cultural competence in addressing
        (see Cultural competence)
    current U.S. setting for, 3–6
    dis/ability status as, 60–61, 125, 128,
        151, 152, 177, 178, 205, 206
    gender as, 18, 19, 20–21, 25, 38–43,
        55–56, 79, 95, 96–97, 100,
        116–117, 125, 128, 140–141,
        144, 153–154, 155, 179, 186,
        187, 189
    historical psychoanalytic approach
        to, 7–29, 31–62, 208–210
    immigrant and refugee issues as,
        9–17, 21–22, 35, 48–53, 54,
        79, 85–87, 101, 111–112,
        118–119, 120–124, 132–137,
        147–148, 149, 151–153, 154,
        157, 163–169, 177, 178,
        181–184, 191–196, 205, 211
    indigenous narrative relating, 74,
        78–79, 85–110
    language as, 51, 80, 92, 111–124,
        132–138, 167, 178, 211
    multiple, overlapping, 57, 61–62, 64,
        154–156 (see also Complex
        cultural identities)
    race and ethnicity as, 14, 15–16,
        19–21, 23, 31–32, 43–48,
        52–53, 64, 67–68, 95–96, 97,
        100–101, 104–109, 121,
        122–124, 128, 135–137,
        140–141, 144–145, 146–147,
        148–153, 155–156, 157,
        161–162, 163, 173, 175–177,
        179, 186, 187, 191–196,
        201–203, 206–208, 227–229,
        241–242
    religion and spirituality as, 14, 15,
        16, 18, 21, 25, 58–60, 83,
        94, 108, 115–116, 122, 165,
        171–172, 180–181, 182, 189,
        194–195, 209, 227–228